Gideon Brough holds a PhD from Cardiff University where, for the past decade, he has taught European History, notably on conflict and diplomacy. His main academic interests are warfare, diplomacy, power relations, geopolitics, insurgencies and identity in western Europe, particularly in France and the nations of the British Isles.

'Wales has too often been relegated to the sidelines of history; this book places the events of Glyn Dŵr's revolt into the centre of the history of Europe in the early fifteenth century.'

Helen Nicholson, Professor of Medieval History, Cardiff University

'In this stimulating, revisionist study of a remarkable soldier and statesman, Gideon Brough explores how and why Owain Glyn Dŵr was able to secure French support for his struggle against England, thereby ensuring that the Welsh rebellion became a distinctive thread within the tangled skein of the Hundred Years' War. From the bloody battle on the slopes of Bryn Glas to the stand-off near Worcester between the Franco-Welsh army and Henry IV's host, the military aspects of the story are compelling. But it is in his exploration of the protagonists' diplomatic manoeuvres, perhaps most notably those of the English envoys who broke the Franco-Welsh alliance, that Brough's book particularly impresses.'

Dr Andrew Ayton, Honorary Senior Research Fellow at the University of Hull and the University of Keele

Figure 1 Soldiers killing villagers or townsfolk.

THE RISE and FALL of OWAIN GLYN DŴR

England, France and the Welsh Rebellion in the Late Middle Ages

GIDEON BROUGH

I.B.TAURIS
LONDON · NEW YORK

Published in 2017 by
I.B.Tauris & Co. Ltd
London • New York
www.ibtauris.com

Every attempt has been made to gain permission for the use of the images in
this book. Any omissions will be rectified in future editions.

References to websites were correct at the time of writing.

The cover design is an interpretation of the image viewed on one side of
Owain's Great Seal. The current debates on the lions' posture and colours are
acknowledged here. However, it is reasonable to assert that their posture was
rampant rather than salient. Also, there has been some discussion whether
their colours were red and gold, or if the black lion of Powys Fadog had also
been blended into the design. Bearing these points in mind, the cover image
seems a reasonable representation of his probable colours.

ISBN: 978 1 78453 593 3
eISBN: 978 1 78672 110 5
ePDF: 978 1 78673 110 4

A full CIP record for this book is available from the British Library
A full CIP record is available from the Library of Congress

Library of Congress Catalog Card Number: available

Typeset by Fakenham Prepress Solutions, Fakenham, Norfolk NR21 8NN
Printed and bound in Great Britain by T. J. International, Padstow, Cornwall

For Mary, my passionate, fiery, enthusiastic mother,

and

Fred, my kind, loving, impressive father,

Halen Daear Cymru.

Figure 2 A French–Scots force in action. This stylised scene shows the
heavy armour types appropriate for the time of the rebellion in Wales.
Imagining Welsh–French flags displayed in this scene affords a vision of how
the storming of Carmarthen in 1405 might have been presented.

Contents

Figure 3 Lightly armoured troops looting a village. Late fourteenth century. From *Royal Ms 20 CVII* in the British Museum.

List of Illustrations

Acknowledgements

There is never sufficient space to adequately thank everyone involved in matters such as research, publications and life in general. So, in whittling this part of the process down to the barest minimum, I first wish to thank Peter Coss and Peter Edbury for their consistently positive feedback throughout my doctoral research. In addition, I owe Peter Edbury my deep personal and professional gratitude for his advice and support when I particularly needed it. With regard to this project, it was he who encouraged me to critically examine the foundations on which our received wisdom stands. The new vision of the beginning and the end of the revolt proposed here, among other elements, is largely the result of the application of this close scrutiny. I also express my appreciation to Andrew Ayton and Helen Nicholson for their valuable advice in numerous matters, as well as for one of the most enjoyable conversations of my life: my viva.

I am also grateful to Cardiff University for the scholarship I was awarded which enabled me to follow my doctoral studies there and notably to Professor Chris Williams and Professor Justin Lewis for their support in accessing Cardiff University funding assisting scholarly publications in the fields of Welsh culture, history and literature. In addition, I am thankful that the publishers, I.B.Tauris, have provided me this opportunity to disavow a work from 2002. Although polemics can serve a purpose by offering a mirror to the excesses of other, accepted perspectives, I am pleased to disassociate myself with that problematic publication for numerous reasons; this work erases and replaces it. I am grateful to Lester Crook, Joanna Godfrey, Sara Magness and others at I.B.Tauris who helped bring this project to fruition.

For a blend of academic and personal reasons, I also wish to give my immeasurable thanks to Dave Wyatt and Richard Marsden. I am grateful to Dave for his support along the way, but particularly for giving me opportunities to become involved in teaching at Cardiff – I hope that my efforts in the classroom have repaid that act of faith. I owe perhaps the greater debt to Rich for his time and for sharing his exceptional knowledge; in the hallowed confines of the pub, I don't think there is any issue, problem or topic for which we could not find temporarily viable solutions. In addition, I thank Rob Jones for his frequent words of wisdom. Similarly, I benefitted from an evening spent in Rees Davies's company in 1999; his encouragement led me further into this field. I am grateful to Huw Edwards of BBC News for his encouragement and for his thoughts at a notably low moment. Also, I never forget my students, who do not realise the contribution they make to their teachers' subjects; I thank them all.

Thanks are also due to a whole cast of people for a range of helpful acts, many of which are not directly related to this subject, but have nevertheless been in support of this project. Although others could be mentioned, I offer special thanks to Valerie Brown, Matthew and Aleida Cullen, Craig and Michelle O'Dare, Jean-Roger David, Stephen David, Big Easy, Neil Ferrissey, Ben Hodges, Suzanne Hathaway, Ollie Hopkins, Dan Jewson, Huw Knight, the Laceys of Cwmaman and elsewhere, Tim and Kelly Lewis, Dave McElhill, Edgar Miranda, Anne M. Pilling, Hervé Potieris of Martinique, Jim Rowlands in Brittany and Rob Toogood. It was Jim who asked why nothing much seemed to happen in 1406 – a question which opened a fresh avenue of research, detailed in this work. Also, to two of my Antipodean friends, Nathan McGrath of Trinity College, South Australia, and Jannine Mullany of Auckland, New Zealand, who gave me my first copy of Rees Davies's epic, *Revolt*.

I recognise that the drive to torture oneself into engaging in such pursuits is always personal and I accept that the errors within are my own; however, I acknowledge the immense influence of my parents in setting out on this road. Of particular note were my mum's passion for all things Welsh, but particularly for the people and their plight, and my dad's enthusiasm, love and care for his family. I miss them both.

Finally, I also dedicate this work to Rebecca, Caitlin and Gethin, in the hope that it will help grow in them an appreciation of our beautiful country and its extraordinary and, to some extent, untold history.

Note on Place Names and People Involved

Throughout this work I have tried to use the most common versions of names occurring within. Where there are people with similar or identical names, then I hope the distinction is clear in context. There are two Henry Percys, for example, whom I distinguish as 'senior' and 'junior', or 'Northumberland' and 'Hotspur'. I have tried to keep the spelling of Welsh, French and other names and places as near to their origins as possible, although some adaptation has been occasionally required, not least of which in the name of the chief protagonist. The name 'Owain Glyn Dŵr' requires brief discussion. In my opinion, there is no difference between 'Glyn Dŵr' and 'Glyndŵr'; both are equally acceptable. However, he never used either version of that surname in his letters, and it appears to have been popularised, perhaps even invented, by writers and syllable-concerned poets, mostly writing after his time. 'Owain (y) Glyn' was another common alternative they used. Owain's 'real' name, according to his time, was *Owain ap Gruffydd Fychan*. Even this was never recorded uniformly; for example, both principal names appear in a variety of spellings in Welsh, English and Latin (*Yweyn, Owen, Owynus* and *Gruffydd* or *Gruffuth*, and so on). The surname most commonly attributed to him in contemporary documents is a variant of his principal seat, Glyndyfrdwy, and often appears as 'Glyndourdy' or a cognate. Nobles commonly described themselves after their main territory or holding, such as Henry of Lancaster, Louis d'Orléans and so on. 'Owain' so signed a letter in Latin to his peer, Henry Don of Kidwelly: *Yweyn ap Gruffuth, Dominum de Glyn Dwfrdwy*. Therefore, he used neither 'Owain' nor 'Glyn Dŵr' nor 'Glyndŵr', but he did put a gap between 'Glyn' and the following word. In modern times, J. E. Lloyd used both surname forms without making distinction between them. Also, Rees Davies used the two-word form, 'Glyn Dŵr', in the most influential publication on the subject, *The Revolt of Owain Glyn Dŵr*. More recently, Gruffydd Aled Williams has written an excellent discussion of the use of Owain's name in poetry.

So, although he did not call himself by that name or spell it 'Owain Glyn Dŵr', this is the modern name for him and this book will continue that tradition, having cautiously noted its inaccuracy. Although both versions of his surname are equally viable, I simply have a personal preference for the two-word form.[1]

Abbreviations

Abbreviation	Full title
ANLP	M. D. Legge, ed., *Anglo–Norman Letters and Petitions* (Oxford: Blackwell, 1941)
BBCS	*Bulletin of the Board of Celtic Studies*
BJRL	*Bulletin of the John Rylands Library*
CAU	C. Given-Wilson, *The Chronicle of Adam Usk, 1377–1421* (Oxford: Oxford University Press, 1997)
CCR	H. E. Maxwell-Lyte and A. E. Stamp, eds, *Calendar of the Close Rolls Preserved in the Public Record Office* (London: HMSO, 27 vols, 1892–1938)
CFR	H. E. Maxwell-Lyte and A. E. Stamp, eds, *Calendar of the Fine Rolls Preserved in the Public Record Office* (London: HMSO, 11 vols, 1913–34)
CPR	H. E. Maxwell-Lyte, ed., *Calender of the Patent Rolls Preserved in the Public Record Office: Edward III* (London: HMSO, 16 vols, 1891–1916), *Richard II* (London: HMSO, 6 vols, 1895–1909), *Henry IV* (London: HMSO, 4 vols, 1903–9), *Henry V* (London: HMSO, 2 vols, 1910–11)
Clarke and Galbraith, 'Deposition'	M. V. Clarke and V. H. Galbraith, eds, 'The Deposition of Richard II: Chronicle of Dieulacres Abbey, 1381–1403', *Bulletin of the John Rylands Library* 14 (1930): 125–81
Courteault, *Le Héraut Berry*	H. Courteault, ed., *Les Chroniques Du Roi Charles VII Par Gilles Le Bouvier, Dit Le Héraut Berry* (Paris: Centre National de la Recherche Scientifique, 1979)
Ellis, *Letters*	H. Ellis, *Original Letters Illustrative of English History* (London: Harding and Lepard, 1827)

Fœdera	T. Rymer, ed., *Fœdera, conventiones, literae, et cujuscunque generis acta publica, inter reges Angliae, et alios quosvis imperatores, reges, pontifices, principes, vel communitates, ab ineunte saecula duodecimo, viz. ab anno 1101, ad nostra usque tempora, habita aut tractata; ex autographis, infra tempora, habita aut tractata; ex autographis, infra secretiores Archivorum regiorum thesaurarias, per multa saecula reconditis, fideliter exscripta.* (London: HMSO, 20 vols, 1704–35)
Given-Wilson, *Chronicles*	C. Given-Wilson, *Chronicles of the Revolution, 1397–1400, the Reign of Richard II* (Manchester: Manchester University Press, 1993)
Glendower	J. E. Lloyd, *Owen Glendower (Owain Glyndŵr)* (Felinfach: Llanerch Press, 1992, orig. 1931)
La France gouvernée	B.-A. Pocquet du Haut-Jussé, *La France gouvernée par Jean Sans Peur, Les Dépenses du Receveur Général du Royaume* (Paris: Presses Universitaires de France, 1959)
La Querelle	J. d'Avout, *La Querelle des Armagnacs et des Bourguignons, Histoire d'une crise d'Autorité* (Paris: Gallimard, 1943)
Marchant, *Chronicles*	A. Marchant, *The Revolt of Owain Glyndŵr in Medieval English Chronicles* (Woodbridge: Boydell & Brewer, 2014)
ODNB	*Oxford Dictionary of National Biography*
OGC	M. Livingston and J. K. Bollard, eds, *Owain Glyndŵr, A Casebook* (Liverpool: Liverpool University Press, 2013)
PIMA	H. Pryce and J. Watts, eds, *Power and Identity in the Middle Ages. Essays in Memory of Rees Davies* (Oxford: Oxford University Press, 2007)
POPCE	H. Nicolas, ed., *Proceedings and Ordinances of the Privy Council of England* (London: Record Commission, 7 vols, 1834–7)
Preest, *Chronica Maiora*	D. Preest, *The Chronica Maiora of Thomas Walsingham* (Woodbridge: Boydell, 2005)

PROME	C. Given-Wilson et al., eds, *The Parliament Rolls of Medieval England, 1275–1504* (London: Boydell, 16 vols, 2005–10)
Revolt	R. R. Davies, *The Revolt of Owain Glyn Dŵr* (Oxford: Oxford University Press, 1997)
RHL Henry IV	F. C. Hingeston, *Royal and Historical Letters during the reign of Henry IV* (London: Longman, 2 vols, 1860–4)
Saint-Denys	L. Bellaguet, ed., *Chronique du Religieux de Saint-Denys, le Regne de Charles VI, de 1380 à 1422* (Paris: Crapelet, 6 vols, 1840)
Thomas, 'Oswestry'	G. C. G. Thomas, 'Oswestry 1400: Glyndwr's Supporters on Trial', *Studia Celtica* 40 (2006): 117–26
Webb, 'Creton'	J. Webb, 'A Translation of a French Metrical History of the deposition of King Richard the Second by Jehan Creton', *Archaelogia* 20 (1823)
Welsh Records	T. Matthews, ed., *Welsh Records in Paris* (Carmarthen: Spurrell, 1910)
WHR	*Welsh History Review*

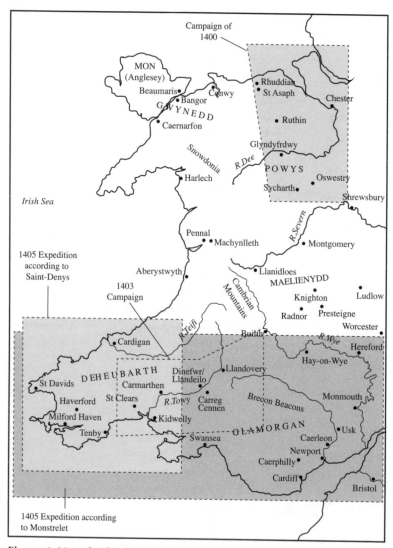

Figure 4 Map of Wales showing places and regions which frequently featured during the course of the revolt. The outlined areas show the regions affected by the campaigns of 1400, 1403 and 1405.

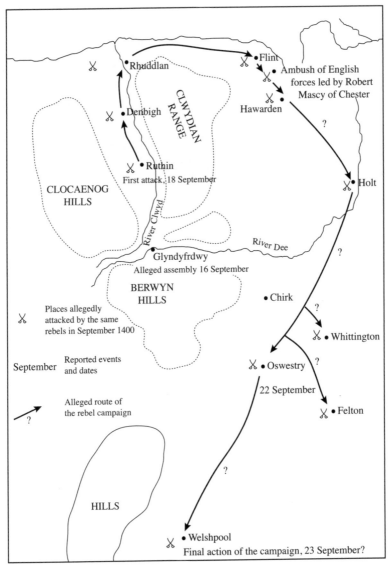

Figure 5 The alleged route of the campaign of September 1400.

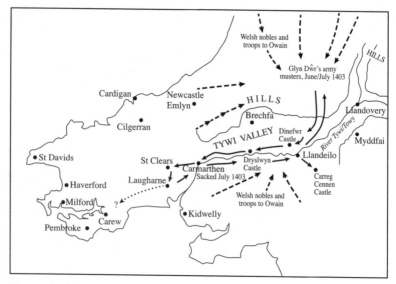

Figure 6 The main elements, actions and places involved in the 1403 campaign against Carmarthen.

Figure 7 The route of the 1405 expedition to Wales according to the Chronicle of Saint-Denys.

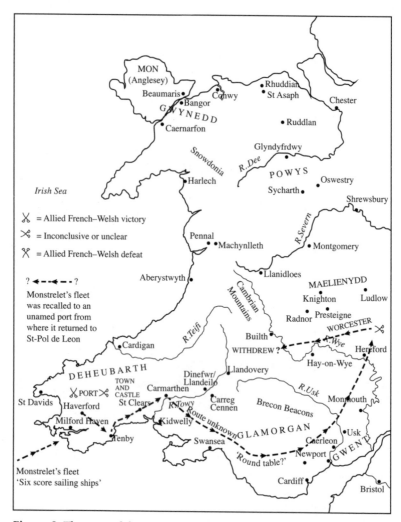

Figure 8 The route of the 1405 expedition to Wales according to Enguerrand de Monstrelet.

Introduction

It is never easy to recreate the history of a revolt. The action is too spontaneous and fast-moving to be captured in the leaden prose of historical narrative. There is rarely a single stage on which the story unfolds neatly; rather are revolts often composed of fragmented and disconnected episodes and it is only with hindsight that patterns and connections can be imposed on them ... Revolts by their very nature lie largely, if by no means entirely, outside the established government's documentary record which constitutes, especially for the later Middle Ages, so much of the material from which the historian must try to reconstruct the past; while the rebels for their own part are normally too busy trying to turn the world upside down to have the time to commit an account of their actions to writing.[1]

This new work on Owain Glyn Dŵr stems from my doctoral research which evaluated the French–Welsh alliances of the medieval period. This publication introduces some of the new evidence and perspectives derived from that research. As the above quote from Rees Davies indicates, studying revolts is a difficult task, primarily because much of the record evidence on which such a reconstruction must stand is skewed, inaccurate or simply missing. I agree with Rhydian Griffiths, who wrote that 'the full military story of the Glyndŵr rising will probably never be told'.[2] In attempting to contribute to this field, it is essential to recognise the difficulties encountered with the available sources. It should be assumed that all of the sources contain inaccuracies which, inevitably, make them problematic. Considering that each piece of evidence is differently wrong to the next only compounds the problems faced. In creating this account of the rebellion, I have tried to use those sources which appear to be more consistently accurate or as close to accurate as can be determined. Conversely, I have tried to set aside, where possible, those which are often notably incorrect or the isolated, unsupported claims which also appear in the revolt narrative. The latter examples are particularly troublesome but have been judiciously considered where incorporated; certain I have included, others I have discarded. For example, I have cautiously retained the often unreliable *Chronicle of Adam Usk*. It is a highly interesting but biased source which makes wild claims, some of which are extremely unrealistic, such as Adam's claim that Owain had a 30,000-strong force behind him and that there were 8,000 casualties at Bryn Glas. However, on balance, other things mentioned by Adam seem reasonable, such as his transcription of Owain's alleged letters to the Scots and the Irish. In making stylistic comparisons with Owain's other letters, these two appear consistent with Glyn Dŵr's hand and so are included in this work as probably genuine. So, although several of Adam's offerings are retained, his chronicle is to be treated with care. Another well-known source, the *Annals of Owen Glyn Dŵr*, although I make reference to it in places to support the arguments presented here, I have discarded entirely as a usable source, whether positive or negative about the revolt. Having done so, the probable course of the revolt seems to have benefitted from the removal of this troublesome source. Although this work makes reference to the *Annals* in the relevant places below for comparative purposes, this study therefore sets aside its account of Owain's alleged signal victory at Hyddgen and the massacre of 1,000 Welshmen including an unnamed son of Owain at an unnamed place by an unknown army under an unknown leader. The rationale behind this is that the earliest extant copy of the *Annals* appears to be Gruffydd Hiraethog's from the mid-sixteenth century; the other two versions date from the second half of the eighteenth century. Even though Hiraethog's work is reportedly based on a fifteenth century text, the accuracy of the original and the fidelity of his reproduction remain unknown. Therefore, irrespective of its notable omissions and problematic claims, as it was written almost 150 later, I believe that the *Annals* is too late to be considered primary material and does not warrant inclusion as such in this work, or any other on the revolt. Therefore, the quality of the sources has been a consideration in preparing this study, as it was for my thesis. However, the inclusion of a range of sources of varying degrees of reliability has been unavoidable.

Throughout, this work makes a case that this Welsh rebellion should be considered as another theatre of the Hundred Years' War, similar to conflicts in Brittany, Scotland or Spain. All of the major powers were involved in some way, and therefore it forms part of that wider, long-running conflict. Another aim of this research is to set the rebellion within its European context; it clearly fits within the events and movements of the time and was not simply a struggle between a king and some malcontents on an isolated fringe of the continent.

This study also challenges a number of aspects of the current understanding of the revolt. Perhaps in the first instance, it attempts to displace Owain's 'perceived centrality', to borrow Alicia Marchant's term.[3] Violence in Wales erupted over a year before Owain rose in insurrection against the authorities; the evidence for that new vision of the outbreak of rebellion in Wales is presented below. In addition, other elements of the standard tale of the revolt are questioned, particularly its ending. The evidence appears to present a picture of a functioning rebel state, the continental support for which was brought down by the actions of England's diplomats in France some time before Henry's armies moved against rebel strongholds in Wales. As such, this constitutes a distinct victory for the English which was brought about by the actions of men deliberately intending to improve England's fortunes and, consequently, bring about the fall of the Welsh rebel state. The contemporary evidence does not support the notion that the revolt withered through war weariness; the opposite seems to be true, that the rebels tenaciously continued as long as they were able. However, the notion of a structured English victory is fully described here.

Also, while Glyn Dŵr's reputation as a warrior seems secure, this study recasts him as more of a leader and thinker than just a soldier. I believe that, in closely reading his letters, Owain's voice appears clear, and he emerges as an angry but highly intelligent man. This work also attempts to flesh his bones with some of the human attributes that are revealed by his words and actions. Moreover, his achievements as the leader of a command group, when put under close scrutiny, seem far more impressive than have previously been revealed. He was, however, one of a number of men who led the rebellion and, between them, these men and their troops brought down the governmental structure of a much larger state that had dominated their land for over a century. They created their own state with its own parliaments and conducted diplomatic ventures in its name. In all probability, they ruled over an economy of sorts too, although the definitive evidence for that is missing. What these men achieved with so few resources is worthy of further study. This research does that in part by applying certain military theories to this conflict. In all, this work proposes new visions of aspects of the rebellion and presents Owain Glyn Dŵr in a new light.

There have been numerous books on Owain, which are discussed in detail elsewhere. However, the leading works in this field are Sir John Lloyd's classic from 1931, *Owen Glendower*, and Sir Rees Davies's landmark publication *The Revolt of Owain Glyn Dŵr*, first published in 1995. The latter remains the most complete volume on the subject. Lloyd's meticulous research was the first to simultaneously present the subject as academically credible and publicly accessible. Davies recognised and praised Lloyd, and then significantly advanced the subject with arguably his best-known publication. That book is rightly viewed as the pre-eminent work on the subject. Studying *Revolt* again in this attempt to contribute to the field increased my appreciation for Davies's ability to condense so much quality research and analysis into individual paragraphs, yet still construct a towering work which retained its subtle, nuanced approach throughout. I had the opportunity to meet Rees Davies in 1999 to discuss *Revolt* and Glyn Dŵr in general. He was welcoming of enthusiasm for the subject and was quite clear about the need for more research into the area. In some part, this work aims to respect his wishes and, to that end, it looks at areas largely untouched by Lloyd and Davies. It most notably does this by considering the rebellion beyond a solely Welsh or British environment, placing it within its European context.[4] A particular focus falls on the role of the French, who are acknowledged in other works, but nowhere else are they discussed in depth as the vital other half of the alliance with the Welsh. Their efforts deserve to be brought into light. In addition, this study adopts a different perspective to most writing on Owain, which adheres to his 'perceived centrality'. Glyn Dŵr was, of course, a key figure in this event, but he was one of many who played important roles. This work attempts to interweave the other people essential to the story into what is otherwise largely presented as something of Owain's doing. In addition, most studies portray Welsh defeat as inexorable because the historical facts deterministically bear out that notion. However, victory appears to have been entirely possible; the factors which brought about defeat were slim ones which nevertheless had grave consequences. At the time, the Welsh certainly appear to have committed themselves fully to the rebellion, while the French also committed their men, money and resources into supporting and advancing the Welsh cause for a number of years. To them, defeat was not inevitable and this study argues that, at one stage, the rebels appeared to have won. This book attempts to balance that aspect of the story against the difficulties posed by that 'besetting sin of the historian', hindsight. Therefore, in the same way that Davies's account varies in places with that of Lloyd, this study also challenges established assumptions by introducing new evidence and by offering alternative visions of otherwise commonly held notions. I believe that debate refreshes and stimulates a subject and so re-evaluating aspects of the story is vital.[5]

A further point, popular with previous writers, concerns Glyn Dŵr's place in modern politics. The best example of this comes from Lloyd who wrote, albeit more subtly when viewed in context, that Owain 'may with propriety be called the father of modern Welsh nationalism'; however, he is not.[6] While he is surely a popular, even inspiring figure in the eyes of modern Welsh nationalists, Owain had no hand in the creation of their movement. He was born in the fourteenth century and had no notion of modern parliamentary democracy arranged along current lines; certain contemporary norms and ideologies would likely seem alien to anyone from that period. He could easily be misinterpreted as being of any modern political colour because he presents so varied a character. He was a monarchist yet a man firmly connected to the lives of common Welsh folk, a man schooled as an English noble but a community figurehead whose beliefs and actions deeply rooted him in Welsh culture, and he was also a soldier who risked his life to further England's power yet he led a furious rebellion against the king of England. Yet, without the extreme provocation he suffered from the hands of Henry IV and his supporters, there is nothing to suggest that Owain would have rebelled. This strongly implies that Owain opposed the hard treatment he received, and was not primarily motivated by an ethnic bias. With so many legitimate contrasts, it is unrealistic to ascribe any modern political colour to him. Therefore, this is an appeal to remove Owain from the contemporary political lexicon. He should be considered as a figure of significant historical stature worthy of further study; several areas of possible future research in this field are discussed below. In addition, for reasons made plain within this work, 16 September should not be considered as a special date used to mark his memory, as it is currently but unofficially. The only firm date we have of any major significance is 22 June, which marks the battle of Bryn Glas.

There are two recent publications on this matter. The first, *Owain Glyndŵr: A Casebook*, edited by Michael Livingston and John K. Bollard, is an anthology of primary sources connected to the revolt. The *OGC*, as some call it, was long overdue and is an extremely helpful reference for this subject and related studies. I have been in contact with Michael Livingston and believe that future editions or related works will be forthcoming in due course, which I believe will be positive for the field. I would like to see the realisation of an internet-based resource, where interested parties can not only access copies of the relevant primary sources and their translations, but which would also be a place where researchers can submit new materials as they arise. I certainly found new evidence during my doctoral research and I believe that there is more waiting to be discovered and incorporated into this story. Anyone interested in creating such a resource should contact me. The *OGC* has been followed by Alicia Marchant's *The Revolt of Owain Glyndŵr in Medieval English Chronicles*, which offers profound insight into the portrayal and significance of Owain, the revolt and the Welsh in the imaginations and chronicles of late medieval and early modern English society.

Since military affairs are core to this rebellion, certain military texts and methods have been used to assist in the synthesis of the rising. Although they have been applied 'judiciously and skeptically', students of warfare should be able to discern the hand, however light, of works such as Sun Tzu, Joseph Nye and counter-insurgency theory, particularly that of David Kilcullen.[7] In addition, this study includes some network analysis and profiling of some of the personalities involved to display their career experience and their interconnectivity in a society where personal connections and familial networks were vital. However, I have attempted to subtly weave these methods into the text without disrupting the narrative stream or to make them overly obvious to any but the initiated.

This book is divided into four parts, the first of which, 'The Winds of War', contains two chapters which examine the outbreak of the revolt and how several rebel groups came to be led by one man. The first chapter, 'The Outbreak of Revolt', challenges several long-standing beliefs about the rebellion. I assert that the revolt was not started by Owain's attack on Ruthin in September 1400; the Welsh had risen over a year earlier. It also proposes a new perspective on the campaign which followed the sacking of Ruthin, and disputes that Owain declared himself 'Prince of Wales' at this early stage. 'Rebels and Risings' details the events of 1401, which saw the government grapple unsuccessfully with a multifaceted insurgency that was beginning to spiral out of control. This chapter also discusses the style apparent in Owain's first overseas diplomatic initiatives.[8]

Part Two, 'Rise', has three chapters which examine the ascent of Glyn Dŵr from being the leader of a nascent insurgency to a point where he was the de facto ruler of Wales, able to project himself to the French as the legitimate prince of Wales. This period showed the rebels' strategy evolve as their power rose and successes enabled them to develop into a more powerful force. 'Owen ... the Rod of God's Anger' describes how they gained sufficient strength to confront an English army in open battle and completely destroy it. The following year, 1403, they mounted a conventional campaign, sweeping through a valley of royal castles and, at its climax, they stormed Carmarthen. This fourth chapter, 'Owain, Prince', highlights these marked evolutions in strategy; all the while the rebels were also conducting a classic guerrilla-style insurgency, stretching crown resources to their limits. By ascertaining what and how the government would defend, the rebels quickly realised what they could effectively attack. During this period, the rebels visibly coalesced into a highly effective military, political and diplomatic force. As 1404 approached, they were very much running their own affairs and appeared unstoppable. By this stage, Owain had become the ruling prince of Wales. Another factor important to the growth in strength of the rebellion was the alliance with France. No other work yet considers the state of the French court to the same degree, so Chapter 5, 'The Ambitions of the French Courtly Factions', gives an insight into the swirling political currents and dangerous landscape of the opposing parties and their power struggles. Into this treacherous world of temporary alliances and intrigue stepped the Welsh ambassadors seeking military support for their new state. While rebel successes made the Welsh attractive to the French and the envoys' negotiating skills brokered an alliance, only certain parties sought conflict with England, while others sought peace and commercial relations. As one faction, bitterly opposed to Henry IV, rose to power, an opportunity for the alliance presented itself; both parties, the Orleanists and the Welsh, enthusiastically engaged. This chapter also considers France's foreign policy initiatives, which clearly sought to project French power across Europe. While the main theatres of interest were likely those concerned with the papacy, an alliance with the Welsh offered the French the opportunity to articulate their power within Britain and harm the English adversary.

Part Three examines 'Glyn Dŵr's Diplomacy' and studies Owain's diplomatic methods, the extant texts and consequences of his efforts.

Chapter 6, 'The Alliance of 1404', looks at the justification behind the treaty and the personalities involved. In addition, this chapter scrutinises the clauses of the treaty and the war fleet gathered with the intention of invading and occupying Wales that year. This failed operation also engaged the military forces of the major protagonists and some of their key allies, Castile and Brittany, elevating the rebellion to being another theatre of the Hundred Years' War. An excerpt from a contemporary Spanish chronicle describing Owain's fight with Henry is included here for the first time in any work connected to the rebellion. The subsequent chapter, 'An Orleanist Coup?', describes the events of the first half of 1405. That year saw the signing of the Tripartite Indenture which planned to divide England between the Mortimers and the Percys, while ceding an enlarged Wales to Owain. While the French were planning their main offensive of that year, an assault on Rome, they were also preparing to insert an army into Wales to honour the promises made to the Welsh during the previous year. This chapter contends that the Orleanists attempted a coup in Britain, in league with the Welsh and English rebels under Henry Percy who rose that summer at York. 'The Two French Invasions of 1405' examines the two main texts describing the French expedition to Wales, those of the monk of Saint-Denys and Enguerrand de Monstrelet. Both chronicles are as inaccurate as they are accurate, and this chapter discusses translations and details of these texts, with the Latin original of the Saint-Denys chronicle appearing in English here for the first time.[9] Consequently, 'Invasion and Truce?' considers the deeds of the 1405 expedition and debates the theory that the allied army, or part of it, confronted King Henry near Worcester. This chapter contends that a truce was agreed between Owain and Henry, and presents evidence to that end. This final chapter in the section analyses the clauses of 'The Pennal Declaration' which pledged Welsh spiritual allegiance to the papal candidate preferred by the French court. In addition, this section makes the case that Owain Glyn Dŵr's voice can be discerned throughout the letters he wrote. It argues that he had a certain style which can be found in his extant letters.

In four chapters, the final part of this book, 'Fall', follows the course of events which led to the eventual demise of the Welsh rebellion. I assert that this was an English victory, won by diplomatic and military actions, rejecting the suggestion that Welsh commitment waned, allowing the authorities to reimpose themselves in Wales. Chapter 11, 'English

Diplomatic Manoeuvring', identifies Henry's ambassadorial team and their actions in France. With remarkable skill they managed to create a breach in the allegiances of the French courtly factions, encouraging the developing civil conflict, though not causing it. Their politicking, particularly in 1406–7, helped bring about a situation revealed in Chapter 12, 'Ailing France, Rising England', in which the English were able to play the main warring factions in France. They did so brilliantly, crippling France and opening the door to future military adventures there. Consequently, with the Bretons and the Burgundians in English amity, and the Orleanists driven south of the Loire, the sea lanes between France and Wales were closed. This window of opportunity, created by Henry's diplomats and armies in France, allowed the crown to suddenly attack Wales, after almost two years of inactivity. The forces sent against the rebel fortresses at Aberystwyth and Harlech laboured to an eventual victory almost two years later. However, the revolt was a long way from finished, even with no urban centres in which to hold official parliaments or to receive foreign dignitaries. Instead it reverted to being a guerrilla force once again. As such, it decreased as areas submitted to English forces, but it flared back into life here and there, and continued to press attacks into England's border counties. Chapter 13, 'Constance – A Last Stand for Wales?', discusses how French diplomats argued for international recognition for Wales. The final chapter, 'Owain's Last Days?', describes the later years of the rebellion, including a gathering insurrection in north Wales under Maredudd ab Owain in 1417, likely connected to French efforts at the Council of Constance. The conclusion section renders an appraisal, using military theories, of the insurgency campaign conducted by the Welsh. Their efforts and achievements were quite remarkable, particularly given their starting point of having virtually no resources and their lands being occupied by a theoretically superior enemy. This section deconstructs the minutiae of their efforts in rising to a peak where they could govern, and it also discusses the factors which led to the rebel defeat.

Although the story of Owain Glyn Dŵr is among one of the most researched subjects in Welsh history, during the course of my doctorate and for this study, it became clear to me that a huge amount of research is still to be done on the subject. To me, this demonstrates that we in Wales have not sufficiently invested in our past and this will be to the detriment of our future unless we remedy this. Contrary to many in academia, I do not necessarily hold with the notion that we should always keep potential research areas secret and I invite others to contribute. I believe that participation by other appropriately qualified people in this field is good for our historical studies; it is unhealthy not to refresh and expand areas of historical debate. In addition, we need to be able to revisit and reanalyse areas touched on by previous historians and, if necessary, to differ in opinion from them. Far from tarnishing their names in disagreeing, rather it would engage with their passions. With that in mind, I include here a non-exhaustive blueprint of research areas in this field. Some of the areas below have been partly covered by the Dyffryn Clwyd Court Rolls project, Helen Watt's investigation into taxation, Adam Chapman's work on garrisons and muster lists, Spencer Smith's archaeological findings, or in *OGC*. However, the following are some of the missing jigsaw pieces as I currently conceive them.

Although some light research has been done on a few members of Owain's council, there has been no collation of that group close to him, and no network analysis describing the circles in which they moved, their connections, what they had done before the rebellion, nor their actions during or after it. A tempting place to begin with would be the careers of the Tudor brothers. Such research into this relatively well-known pair might offer inroads into the other personalities closely involved with the leadership of the revolt. Presenting a piece on the 'Host of Glyn Dŵr' would be highly beneficial in establishing the range of talents which also led the rebellion. A similar exercise could be repeated for all of the courts and personalities connected to this conflict. I also feel that not enough has been done to understand the context of the neighbouring countries. To begin with Scotland, Welsh diplomats were certainly present there during the first two decades of the fifteenth century, as were those of France, England and other parties, such as Henry Percy senior and his envoys. A full examination of all of their interactions with Scotland would certainly create a picture of the external pressures on the Scots. An excellent person to start with might be Gruffydd Yonge. As an ambassador to France and to Scotland, there should be evidence of his actions and dealings with his counterparts in those countries. In addition, work describing the divided politics of the Scots' court would also be useful, as would research establishing which Scots nobles were connected to one another, and which had connections beyond Scotland. In particular, information revealing the actions of the Sinclair earls of Orkney and on shipping in the western seaways during these years would be particularly useful. Any information on Scots' contact with France, the English rebels or the crown, as well as with the Welsh, would undoubtedly contribute to this area. I suspect that there would be records or mention somewhere of the Scots fleet of 1417 which sailed past Wales and went to fight for the French Dauphin instead. The subject of Ireland, particularly the friction between English-held Ireland and the native kingdoms, would be relevant to understanding their roles at this time. Equally, a report on the state and manpower available to the English in Ireland would explain their role in attacking Glyn Dŵr's Wales. Attempting to establish who Owain was seeking to contact there might inform us of those considered potential allies in Ireland. Equally, details of Stephen Scrope's later raid on Anglesey would be instructive. Details of the numbers of troops and ships used, as well as some idea of the treasures and artefacts they took from Wales would assist our understanding of this event. More work into the murky world of French courtly intrigue would also be beneficial to this subject, particularly network analysis on the web of interrelated and opposing members of the nobility. Also, research on the careers of Welshmen in France such as Madoc Howell would also be of note. Research into the French regional records, especially Brittany, Normandy, Picardy, Flanders and Paris, would almost certainly yield previously unseen material on diplomatic interaction, the activities of connected personalities, the recruitment and passage of nobles, troops and ships destined for Wales. In France as in Britain, resources can be searched for at local and national levels, so anyone looking will likely uncover something on any of these matters. Equally, the records of nobles and their households will likely produce some information of relevance, as would manorial records, charters and episcopal records. Similarly, I am unaware of any investigations of sheriff's records, French muster rolls, garrison records or profound research into the Patent Rolls in particular, which might well render useful information, for example, on Henry's hurried construction of an army to resist the French and the Welsh in summer 1405. It seems probable that the papal and other British and continental church records of the years in question would also provide some useful information.

In Wales and the adjacent English border counties, constructing a picture using financial and legal records of the amount of activity seen in the English towns and castles in Wales and the borders would help give a partial account of the undulations in effective governance during the conflict. It should be noted that such a study would only cover a certain aspect of the picture, as medieval transactions were not all cash-based or recorded. So such a study, while extremely valuable, would not be able to account for the invisible part of the economy. Sheriff's, church, legal, manorial and tax records would likely be the prime sources to use in pursuit of such a project. In addition, more work in the field of archaeology would demonstrate its importance in providing an idea of the physical environment of the time; the buildings and the sizes of the communities involved. Other useful conclusions would certainly arise from an expansion of archaeological activity connected to the revolt. Moreover, a series of studies of Welsh, English, French and Breton poetry and other related literature which expresses opinions and emotions would be enormously helpful in attempting to construct a picture of the psychological impact of the conflict. The impact of which was probably more profound and lasting, for the Welsh and the English certainly, than the military and political consequences of the rebellion.

During the course of my doctoral research I unearthed a few gems, such as the chapter discussing Owain in *El Victorial* which had not been translated into English previously, nor had it been used in context with the revolt. It is clear to me that there are numerous relevant texts and manuscripts which require translation. These are primarily in Latin but also it has been brought to my attention that the National Library of Wales houses a corpus of Welsh language poetry from the Hundred Years' War period that remains largely untouched. Translating such works as are still in a usable condition would undoubtedly give more information on the Welsh perspective of the events of the time and would be an extremely useful project demonstrating the utility and beauty of Welsh-language literature. However, there are other documents of value that are known and would be beneficial to translate, including a variety of sources at the Public Record Office and the British Library, such as the text of the submission at Bala in 1414, and various books, such as Benjamin Williams's chronicle of the betrayal and death of King Richard. There are likely other chronicles which have not been consulted in relation to the Welsh rebellion or connected events. The more I investigated the subject, the more research avenues seemed to appear. I welcome and encourage the involvement of others in this field, and hope that this brief description of potential research areas will engage new minds with this rich subject.

A Brief Description of Wales Prior to 1399

Perhaps in the background, but ever-present in 1399, was the fact that following Edward I's second and successful invasion of Gwynedd in 1282, the Welsh had been incorporated into the kingdom of England by legal statute. Although they were initially and theoretically accorded similar rights and recognitions, in reality, particularly after revolts, harsh and restrictive ordinances were enacted against the Welsh which denied them treatment as equal subjects, with the same rights and expectations as all others.[10] From the beginning, the acts and statutes which followed produced a flawed settlement. The repeated rebellions, such as those of Rhys ap Maredudd, 1287–8, Madoc ap Llywelyn, 1294–5, or that of Llywelyn Bren in 1316, demonstrated a people uncomfortable with cohabitation and unwilling to accept their defeated status. Although those energies were redirected into service in the private wars between English magnates during the 1320s, and then recruitment on a grander scale as Edward III sought to press his claim to the French throne, the relationship between the Welsh and the English remained unequal on most levels, and so tension and friction was to be expected. To perhaps simplify the case, the independent Welsh kingdoms were societies in which people could make progress socially through mercantile success or wealth generated by land ownership, careers in the church and, particularly, through martial exploits and prowess. There is a significant corpus of praise poetry from pre-Edwardian times which demonstrates the centrality of the importance of Wales's warrior culture. Post-1282, the Welsh could not lead armies, nor could they own land or trade as merchants on an equal footing to those in England or in the English plantation settlements which appeared in Wales at the end of the thirteenth century. Trade and social progress was possible, but at significant disadvantages due to their ethnicity. Although there were numerous social tensions and friction, which have been identified elsewhere in terms of ethnic and racial discrimination fuelled by legal and economic privileges for non-natives, it seems reasonable to question whether a more balanced and inclusive peace would have resulted in the same tensions. With that in mind, it might be more equitable to identify the primary source of these frictions as legal and economic, rather than advocating a case which so predominantly favours the notion of ethnic bias.[11] The few Welsh noble families which survived Edward's invasions and the subsequent settlement could no longer hold lands in the same manner as they did before Edward imposed the shire system in Wales, and the native territories were carved up between roughly twenty-five marcher families and the crown. Perhaps three Welshmen were knighted during the whole of the fourteenth century, while the first Welsh bishop post-1282 was John Trefor, appointed in 1395. So, for decades, the Welsh had been suppressed by the legal framework imposed on them, largely from 1295 onwards, and these ordinances were reinstituted by Henry IV. These legal, economic, linguistic and ethnic divisions alone seem sufficient to have pushed a people to violent rejection at some point.

Europe as a whole experienced momentous societal changes during the fourteenth century in particular. The immense mortality rates suffered because of the great plagues could only bring significant change. The subsequent changes affected the structure of society to significant degrees and popular revolts erupted against the authorities which sought to conserve a status quo which favoured the privileged few. Nevertheless, change did come, eroding the feudal order and instituting slightly more relaxed social, geographical and economic mobility. The economy, notably in England, experienced significant troughs and occasional peaks, adding to the overall difficulty of life for the many. In addition, the wars between England and France in particular had an impact on numerous aspects of life in those countries and for those within their orbits of influence. This included Wales: England administered it and used it primarily for taxation and troop recruitment, while the French, Scots and Castilians viewed Wales as a territory they could prise from English hands.

During the years 1315–18, trouble again flared in Wales, where an additional, serious threat was posed by the newly independent Scots. They apparently sought to extend their conflict with England onto Welsh soil and the Bruces intrigued with the leading Gwynedd magnate, Gruffudd Llwyd. The danger of external invasion was only alleviated by the failure of the Bruces' Irish expedition in 1318 and the death of its commander, Edward Bruce. Rumours of another Scots plan to invade Wales circulated between 1325–7 and similarly in 1335. Shortly after, the threat of a hostile insertion by combined French–Scots armies was deemed credible enough to warrant the expenditure of crown revenue. In 1338 and 1339, Anglesey and North Wales were fortified against the expected invasion of the region by a combined French–Scots force.[12]

During the 1340s there were violent rejections of foreign rule in Wales; the sheriff of Merioneth was murdered while going about his duties, official records were seized, Rhuddlan came under attack and Henry Shaldeford, England's governor in Wales, was murdered by a band led by a native nobleman. Although the great plagues that swept Europe at that time provided something of a lull in hostilities, fear of the vulnerability of the west to French–Castilian naval penetration was an ongoing feature of the period, and the direct threat of a French invasion of Wales resurfaced in 1346 and 1359.

Such a consistent determination to resist easily played into the hands of external powers eager to throw into disarray the plans of the king of England. While there is evidence of collusion with the Bruces in 1315–17, the later connections to Scots ambitions in Wales during the years 1325–7, 1335 and 1339 demonstrate that the Welsh were clearly viewed by England's enemies as strategically exploitable allies. Other European powers therefore recognised that the Welsh were held by the king of England, but were not necessarily his to command. While 1338–9 brought the threat of a French–Scots invasion, the same spectre, but this time including Castilian support, reappeared in subsequent decades, notably in 1346 and 1359. The treaty of Brétigny, 1360, brought a brief lull in fighting. However, following the recommencement of hostilities in 1369, the government undertook regular reviews of its defences and garrisons in Wales. Invasion fleets allegedly destined for Wales were assembled in France in 1369 and 1372; although both put to sea, neither arrived. A further French–Castilian project to invade Wales withered during 1376–7. Tensions continued to run high, however, and rumours abounded of Castilian spies gathering information on the castles of south-west Wales during 1378. The Scots mounted a short-lived raid on Anglesey in 1381. Wales remained of interest to England's continental adversaries and English reactions, in maintaining an occupying force of garrisons in castles, demonstrate that the threat of native revolt and foreign invasion was sufficient to demand crown expenditure during times of limited finances.[13]

The external struggle for Wales brought it within the sphere of operations of the Hundred Years' War. The revolt which is core to this book engaged the leading protagonists and their allies, and clearly qualifies it as another theatre of that larger conflict. During Owain's lifetime, from 1359 onwards, the pressure resulting from several of the factors mentioned intensified. Similarly to other peoples who lived under the rule of foreigners, the Welsh state of mind was likely a schizophrenic one. On one hand, it is possible to construct a picture of a people who, despite some turbulence, can be portrayed as obedient to the king of England; they served in his armies and paid their taxes. This, however, is grossly simplistic and ignores the fact that the Welsh continued to recall the time of their independent rule, and still lived in their own language, segregated into their own communities and largely under their own legal system. Their most common and vibrant means of expression, poetry, lamented their lost status and way of life, but did not celebrate or welcome the one which had been imposed on them from without. The burden of this duality also contributed to the stresses felt within fourteenth-century Wales.

Elsewhere, the establishment and maintenance of the papacy in Avignon from 1305 onwards provided a root cause of the schism of 1378. Principally, the relocation of the Curia was forced by the threat to the papacy posed by violent instability within the Italian city states, along with intermittent conflicts which saw German armies overrun parts of Italy, as well as further difficulties emanating from the Kingdom of Naples. While in Avignon, the papacy enjoyed physical security for much of the rest of the fourteenth century. This stability enabled it to reform its governmental procedures and construct an efficient administration that transformed papal finances. Also, during the second half of the thirteenth century, the kings of France and the papacy developed increasingly close ties. This resulted in a rise in French influence in the Curia which, perhaps inevitably, led to a succession of Frenchmen ascending the papal throne. While it might be incorrect to claim that France controlled the papacy for three-quarters of the fourteenth century, its preponderant influence over it is undeniable. Naturally, given the papal role as arbiter, its bestowal of official appointments across Europe and its emergence as a growing financial entity, other powers came to resent France's hold on the papacy.

Although several popes based in Avignon attempted to return to Italy during the fourteenth century, endemic political instability and periodic warfare prevented the realisation of those desires. This came to a head in 1378 when Pope Gregory XI died in the process of returning the papacy to Rome, under threat from the Italians, who claimed that they would elect a pope of their own if he did not restore the Holy See to St Peter's. In what might have been a temporary measure to appease the Roman mob, the subsequent conclave elected the archbishop of Bari, Bartolomeo Prignano – not even a cardinal – as Pope Urban VI. Having appeased the mob, the majority of the Cardinalate immediately returned to the safety of Avignon and duly elected Robert of Geneva, connected by blood to the French royal house, as Pope Clement VII. The schism was born, with a Roman and an Avignonese pontiff, and Europe's states aligned themselves into the Urbanist or Clementist factions. Largely, this can be defined as France, her Spanish allies and Scotland falling into Clement's obedience, while England, the Italian states north of Naples and much of the German empire supported Urban. These powers encouraged others to support their candidate, and the issue of papal adherence became a factor cited when seeking allies or denouncing enemies. Many of the geopolitical amities existed prior to 1378, so it would be an overstatement to suggest that these loose, continent-wide alliances began to form because of the schism; nevertheless it became an evident factor in political considerations. While the issue of the papal candidates was overtly relevant to the Pennal Declaration of 1406, it can also be tied to other French expansions, such as into Flanders and Castile in the 1380s, but perhaps more particularly into Italy. The clearest examples of this were Savona in 1394 and Genoa in 1396, where a condition of French support was Genoese allegiance to the French papal candidate. Although this issue appeared to be an ecclesiastical matter, its use in France's efforts to extend its power, into Genoa and Wales for example, demonstrate that the schism was undeniably linked to the politics of the day.

The schism of 1378 provoked a wide range of problems, not the least of which were reactions against the orthodoxy dictated by the two papal factions. In England, John Wyclif's works became increasingly popular and gave rise to the proto-Protestant Lollard movement, and consequently encouraged the rise of the powerful Hussite movement in Bohemia. Many thousands of men, women and children died over issues arising from the schism.

Another factor which affected Wales was the ongoing conflict now known as the Hundred Years' War. During Owain's lifetime the tide seemed to have turned against England's previously dominant position. Welshmen had served in Edward III's armies in France and elsewhere; however, during the 1360s a dashing mercenary commander of Welsh royal descent declared himself for France. That man – Owain Lawgoch, as he became known – was the last legitimate heir of the Welsh noble House of Gwynedd. His short but illustrious career saw him rise to being accepted as a Captain-General of French forces, commanding French troops in battle, assembling fleets purposed to invade Wales in 1369 and 1372, as well as attracting two companies of Welsh mercenaries to his colours. His murder by assassins in England's pay is likely to have caused some form of reaction within Welsh society. The war on the continent appeared to be tipping in France's favour, particularly following the death of Edward, the Black Prince, and the accession of the minor, Richard II. The turbulence of that reign affected all in Richard's influence. The momentous events of the Peasant's Revolt, the Appellant Crisis and the revenge wrought by the king a decade later all had unsettling effects on life in Britain.[14]

Events in England and France helped propel to wider prominence Owain Glyn Dŵr who, prior to 1399, had led a relatively respectable, though largely unremarkable life. His early years can be characterised for the purposes of this study as having been raised in north-east Wales, educated at the Inns of Court in London with other young noblemen, and loyally serving in English armies on at least three occasions, 1384, 1385 and 1387, before retiring from public life by 1388, while probably still in his late twenties.[15] While there is no classic portrait of Owain, there are sufficient mentions of him in contemporary poetry to forge a picture of him as being tall, slender though famously strong, and auburn-haired. He seems to be frequently depicted as fighting with a spear. While the lance was one of the classic weapons of European nobility, it was also the traditional weapon of Gwynedd. Once again, Owain appears to have a foot in two worlds.[16] Although lauded in certain poems in the final decade of the fourteenth century for his lineage, wealth and courage in battle, one appears to criticise him for his lack of leadership in a time the poet Gruffydd Llwyd perceived as a one of dire Welsh need.[17] When revolt in Wales erupted in the summer of 1399 Glyn Dŵr does not appear to have been involved.[18] However, as subsequent events would show, when faced with the unappealing options of a hard and probably short life in hiding, surrendering and most likely being executed, or mounting a seemingly impossible campaign against the crown and government of England, Owain Glyn Dŵr chose the latter, to the eternal benefit of his reputation. His successes proved to be the most surprising and unforeseen element of the first years of fifteenth-century Britain.

PART ONE
The Winds of War

CHAPTER ONE

The Outbreak of Revolt

... and those in parliament said that they cared not for these bare-footed idiots.[1]

The course of events which led to the outbreak of the revolt in Wales seems well-established. The conventional account begins with the invasion of part of Owain Glyn Dŵr's territory by Reginald de Grey, Lord of Ruthin, who also deliberately withheld a royal summons to accompany the new king, Henry IV, on campaign to Scotland in summer 1400. Consequently, when he did not serve the new king on his expedition north, Owain was declared a traitor and his lands were forfeit. Owain's unsuccessful efforts for a mediated solution to the dispute included representation to Henry IV's first parliament by John Trefor, bishop of St Asaph. This appeal, tempered with a warning of a possible Welsh revolt, famously drew the scornful remark that those in parliament did not care for the Welsh, and mocked them as 'bare-footed idiots'. This series of apparent injustices seemingly caused Glyn Dŵr to light the flames of revolt in Wales. The story unfolds further; Owain reportedly gathered his principal supporters and relatives at Glyndyfrdwy on 16 September 1400, where they proclaimed him prince of Wales in defiance of the king. Two days later, Owain led a force, possibly numbering around 300, against Grey's town of Ruthin, thereby beginning a destructive six-day rampage across north-east Wales, encompassing Ruthin, Denbigh, Rhuddlan, Flint, Hawarden, Holt, Oswestry and Welshpool. Suddenly and evocatively, Owain appeared to have single-handedly caused the Welsh to rise, rally to his banner and strike at their oppressors.[2] The accepted account of the revolt, even from its outset at Ruthin in September 1400, unequivocally portrays Owain as the head of a national movement, the leader to whom many Welshmen rallied when summoned and for whose 'cause' this rebellion was fought.[3]

However, the political and military situation in Wales in this period was markedly more complex than has previously been presented. While the actions implicating Owain unquestionably form part of the revolt story, scrutiny of contemporary sources does not fully support the commonly held version of events. In fact, the evidence of the time shows that Owain likely had no involvement in the outbreak of the widespread violence and only a contributory but focal role in the acts of rebellion which flared across Wales in the years 1399 to 1401.

Before Glyn Dŵr took up arms in north-east Wales in September 1400, rebellion erupted in the opposite corner of the country, in Carmarthenshire, in summer 1399. Neither this initial outbreak of violence nor the episodes which immediately followed were instigated by or connected to Owain. The earliest incident of revolt was consequent to Henry Bolingbroke's uprising against Richard II. In 1398, the king had exiled Henry, who went to the French court. Following the death of Henry's powerful father, John of Gaunt, in February 1399, Richard seized Bolingbroke's inheritance. While Richard was campaigning in Ireland, Henry returned from exile and landed in Yorkshire in June. He gathered an army, apparently intending to confront Richard and oblige him to reinstate his inheritance. Richard received news of Bolingbroke's revolt while in Ireland, from where he set sail with his coterie of advisors and his army as soon as weather permitted. Richard appears to have landed in west Wales on 22 or 24 July 1399.[4]

The chronicles of the time clearly described the significant disorder which broke out between the Welsh and the English after Richard's landing in Wales. The Dieulacres Chronicle described how Richard's army dispersed in west Wales while he travelled to Carmarthen. As it did so, violence erupted; 'thus they [the Englishmen in the army] were all scattered, and the Welsh despoiled them to a man, so it was only with difficulty that they got back to their homes'.[5] This was corroborated by Thomas Walsingham who recorded in his *Chronica Maiora*:

> The king's followers – magnates, lords or lesser men, regardless of their status – were harassed by Welshmen ... Of those who had been with or followed the king, scarcely one escaped unless he was prepared to hand over not only his arms but whatever was in his purse as well.[6]

Two of those robbed when they left Milford were the powerful earls of Rutland and Worcester. The former, Edward of Norwich, was Edward III's grandson, who became duke of York in 1402 and later died at Agincourt. Worcester, Sir Thomas Percy, had enjoyed a fine career, principally as a royal ambassador, an admiral and a soldier of long campaigning experience. He had served alongside the notables of his time, such as Richard, earl of Arundel, Hugh Calvely and John of Gaunt, to whom he was related. However, he had also experienced a notable defeat at Soubise in France in 1372, where he and another key English commander, Jean de Grailly, were captured by Owain Lawgoch's men. By the time King Richard reached Flint in north-east Wales, Rutland and Worcester had joined Bolingbroke. The monk of Evesham also noted that '[Bolingbroke] was also joined there by Lord Scales and young Thomas, lord Bardolf, who had come from Ireland and had been robbed while passing through Wales'.[7]

Another period chronicle, the *Chronicque de la Traïson et Mort de Richart Deux roy Dengleterre*, mentioned Welsh–English violence just over the border in England: 'as soon as the Duke [Henry] and his people set out from Chester, the Welsh did him great damage; for, whenever they could entrap the English, they killed and stripped them without mercy'.[8]

Jean Creton, a French knight, was in Richard II's retinue as it returned from Ireland and travelled through Wales. Creton's first-hand account, completed by the end of 1402 or early the next year, regaled a tale of the events surrounding Richard's fall. While his overestimation of the size of the Welsh forces encountered and his claim that they acted out of loyalty to Richard are problematic, his work should be viewed in its contemporary political context.[9] Richard was popular at the French court and had married into their royal family. Richard's father-in-law, King Charles VI, had previously agreed to send troops to support him if required. Creton's work began to percolate the French courts at a time when the Orleanist faction was increasingly advocating hostilities with Henry. Also, news of the burgeoning revolt in Wales had arrived in Paris, so Creton's work likely found a receptive audience there. He wrote that he witnessed much fighting between the Welsh and the English, often involving large numbers of combatants: 'The Welsh, who saw their treason for what it was [Englishmen deserting Richard], attacked them in strength, in groups of one or two thousand ... Thus were the English despoiled by the Welsh.' Creton further related the tale of a horseman who reported to Richard: 'behold how the English were treated by the

Welsh, who had no mercy on them, as they marched like people put to the rout, here ten, here twenty, there forty, there an hundred.'[10]

Additionally, Creton detailed the probably apocryphal account of a Welsh raid on Henry's camp in an apparent attempt to free the captive Richard. The incident reportedly took place near Lichfield, almost seventy miles as the crow flies from Flint where Richard was captured.[11] Although he described it vividly, this incident seems highly unrealistic. It is more likely an effort to present the Welsh to his French courtly audience as faithful supporters of Richard, as were the French, as well as being committed enemies of Henry, as were many of the French but particularly the rising Orleanist faction. Inevitably, Creton's work was connected to movements in the French political sphere, and must be considered in that context.[12]

Despite the confusion caused by Bolingbroke's revolution, these English and French sources consistently and independently demonstrate that, by August 1399 at the latest, considerable numbers of Welshmen had risen in revolt against the incumbent king of England and the man who subsequently ascended the throne. None of these actions were connected to Owain Glyn Dŵr. Moreover, it is possible that Owain acknowledged the Carmarthenshire-born revolt as the beginning of a wider Welsh rebellion. In November 1401, barely a year after he took up arms, Owain wrote a letter seeking support from the lords of Ireland, characterising the conflict in Wales as one which 'we have manfully waged [war] for nearly two years past'.[13]

In 1400, months before Owain appears in the contemporary narrative of the revolt, other incidences of rebellion erupted. First came the Epiphany or Earls' Revolt, during which English nobles sought to kill Henry IV at a tournament, then restore Richard II. Although it was hatched in December 1399, it briefly came to life in southern England in early January 1400, before being crushed in the same month. At its conclusion, Henry IV had executed the earls of Salisbury, Huntingdon and Kent along with two knights, while the barons Despenser and Lumley were killed by mobs of townsfolk. Edward of Norwich was also implicated, but he is suspected to have reported the plot to Henry, leading to his accomplices' certain deaths. It seems likely that the Epiphany revolt caused Henry to recognise that Richard, while alive, would remain a focus for opposition. Shortly after, Richard died in unrecorded circumstances in captivity in Pontefract castle.

Days after the demise of that uprising, another rebellion briefly flourished in Cheshire. Although it was quickly smothered, with judicial

sessions beginning in March 1400, the leaders were not fully brought
to peace through pardons until mid-1401. Due to the fact that Henry
Percy junior raised his rebel army in the area in 1403, it is reasonable
to suggest that the county was not entirely pacified in 1400 and that it
maintained Ricardian sympathies.[14] These two English uprisings demonstrate that some in England were also willing to fight against the new
king. Within this broader landscape of dissatisfaction over the change of
monarch, particularly the manner in which it occurred, other acts of
rebellion arose in Wales and merit incorporation into the history of the
revolt.

Modern and contemporary sources refer to a revolt by the Tudors in
north-west Wales and Anglesey prior or, perhaps, in a similar period to
Owain's attack on Ruthin. Some accounts, probably inaccurately, describe
the Tudors in combat against King Henry. While certain recent authors
connect this poorly evidenced act of Tudor rebellion to Owain's attack on
Ruthin, nothing from the time explicitly does so.[15] It is compelling that
in October 1400, Henry's expeditionary force marched to Bangor and
then Caernarfon, in the Tudor heartland. Although Henry's army briefly
passed though Ruthin, it did not stop at Glyndyfrdwy, nor destroy it, nor
did Henry or his agents seek Owain at that time. Therefore, it seems clear
that at that moment, while in north Wales, the king acted as though the
Tudor rising posed the more serious threat.

Also, before September 1400, north Wales experienced other acts
of violence consistent with revolts, yet nothing contemporary connects
these events to Owain either. Lord Grey reported widespread disorder in
north Wales to Henry, Prince of Wales.[16] A later legal proceeding against
a Denbighshire man, Dafydd ap Cadwaladr Ddu, retrospectively dated
the start of his rebellious activities, in league with others, to 17 August
1400. Owain was yet to enter the fray, but rebellion had already erupted
in south-west, north-west and north-east Wales.[17]

* * * * *

It is at this point that Owain Glyn Dŵr began to appear on documents
recording the Welsh rebellions. At some unknown date, the well-known
events took place which brought into collision the original protagonists.
First, Lord Grey invaded Croesau, part of Owain's land, seizing it for
himself. Then, parliament refused to support the Welshman's consequent
petition for justice, ignoring advice from the bishop of St Asaph that the

Welsh might revolt if justice were not seen to be done. Certain of those in parliament scoffed that the Welsh were a rabble of 'bare-footed idiots' belonging to 'a nation of little reputation'.[18]

The parliamentary session in question was Henry IV's first parliament, which sat between 6 October and 19 November 1399. The bishop of St Asaph and Lord Grey of Ruthin attended; it was during this sitting that Henry IV announced his plan to attack Scotland. No such Welsh affairs appear in Richard II's last parliament in September 1397, while Henry's second parliament sat in 1401 and debated the violence which had already occurred in Wales. This dates Grey's attack on Owain's land as prior to October 1399. This suggests that Glyn Dŵr waited a year for redress, while following the appropriate appeal processes. Such a man appears a reluctant rebel, particularly when significant numbers of Welshmen had already taken up arms.[19]

When Owain failed to join the new king on the expedition to Scotland in summer 1400, Henry declared him a traitor and his lands forfeit. On the same charge, Henry inflicted similar sanctions on English nobles also. Lord Grey had reputedly withheld a royal summons destined for Glyn Dŵr and was thus responsible for Owain's disinheritance.[20] In riposte, Owain and his supporters supposedly gathered at Glyndyfrdwy on 16 September 1400, where they allegedly proclaimed him prince of Wales. Contemporary records named Owain among the many who sacked Ruthin on 18 September 1400 and then conducted a six-day campaign against English towns in north-east Wales.[21]

However, there are a number of significant problems with the traditional story of the beginning of Owain's revolt. First, Henry IV issued orders on 19 September from Northampton, where he had stopped on his march south: he was not marching towards Wales. He wrote two orders; one called for troops and fencible men from several counties to muster in order to accompany him and suppress unspecified hostilities in Wales, the other demanded the mobilisation of troops for the defence of castles in Cheshire against the Welsh.[22] In neither order did he mention Owain because the news from Wales delivered to Henry could not have concerned the attack on Ruthin. There was no standing messenger network during this period and, at well over 100 miles away, Henry was too far away for a message to reach him in that time, had the messengers even known the marching king's whereabouts. Henry's orders of 19 September almost certainly referred to widespread disturbances in north Wales, and probably concerned the Tudor rising, which would explain Henry's focus on Bangor and Caernarfon. It seems probable that news of the attack on Ruthin first went to Chester, the largest regional town. The constable of Chester, Robert Mascy, led a force against the rebels from there, suffering ambush near Flint, roughly ten miles from Chester, on 20 or 21 September 1400. For a force to muster and advance so slowly out of nearby Chester, barely twenty miles from Ruthin, makes it improbable that news of the attack on Ruthin moved swiftly to the king. In addition, Mascy's actions also offer a clue to the question of message speed. While one set of the king's orders was dispersed to numerous counties to raise forces to muster, march and accompany him against the Welsh, the other directive was for local forces to strengthen Cheshire garrisons in anticipation of rebel pressure. Since Flint is not in Cheshire and there are no known orders for commanders to act independently, had Henry's orders arrived beforehand, then Mascy appears to have taken the unlikely step of countermanding the king's command.[23]

The traditional story also contends that Owain's supporters declared him prince of Wales, in opposition to Prince Henry, and that they subsequently attacked a number English towns in Wales, starting with Ruthin and culminating at Welshpool six days later. However, both claims are problematic, even improbable.

The idea that Owain was proclaimed prince of Wales at this stage of the revolt is difficult to support. First, Owain, in his correspondence with Welsh, Scots and Irish interlocutors, did not mention his princely claim at the time when it would have been in his interests to do so. Although Adam Usk referred to Owain's putative title, he and others were likely made aware of the court proceedings against Owain in which the allegation of his seizure of the title was made. However, there is a striking lack of any other references to this significant claim in other contemporary literature. Some time before October 1403, Owain wrote to Henry Don, a Welsh leader from Kidwelly in south Wales, at which time he was still simply styling himself as 'Lord of Glyn Dyfrdwy'. In fact, Owain did not openly refer to himself as prince prior to the alliance with the French in summer 1404, almost four years after the rampage of September 1400 when he was alleged to have first claimed the title. Calling himself prince of Wales in opposition to the English claimant spoke directly to those entangled in the Anglo–French rivalry of the time. Therefore, projecting an image of a noble ruler worthy of French support was shrewd, but also necessary. As a prince, no less, he could legitimately write directly to royal courts, who could more easily reciprocate. As a mere, dispossessed and unknighted squire, he lacked the status of a prince and would most likely have to depend on less direct channels of communication. As a prince, Owain could directly ask for military support at the French court; as a squire, he could not. It is noteworthy that in all of his own letters prior to 1404 and in seemingly all but a few biased contemporary sources of debatable reliability, the title of prince is glaringly absent.[24]

The main contemporary sources which make the princely accusation are two English legal proceedings, but their impartiality has never been questioned. However, both proceedings are almost identical, suggesting a common origin. Notably, they claim that Owain's supporters 'elevated [him] as their Prince of Wales at Glyndyfrdwy'. However, the same sources make other wild claims against Owain, saying that he plotted the death of King Henry, 'the extinction for ever of the crown and regality of ... all his successors, the kings of England, and the death of Henry, prince of Wales', as well as 'all the magnates and nobles of England, and also the death, destruction and everlasting obliteration of the whole English language'.[25] Although all appear together in the source, these accusations have largely been ignored in favour of focusing on the princely claim.

Each of these claims is damning, but also fantastical. It is reasonable to assert that these charges were not founded on fact but were intended to denounce Glyn Dŵr and any who might support him. There is no evidence revealing how the authorities learned of Owain's alleged claims. When taken as a whole, the charges, that Owain sought to murder King Henry IV and all of his successors, including Prince Henry by name, as well as all of the magnates and nobles of England, as well as destroying the entire English language, appear utterly hysterical. Realistically, these claims could never be achieved and nothing suggests that they were even desired. In negotiations with the Percys, Owain showed that he was aware of events in England and the accusations against him, which he denied and still appeared tractable to a peaceful settlement. To underline the improbability of the accusations against him, Owain's wife, his father-in-law who seems to have been a mentor of sorts to him, and several brothers-in-law who would bear arms for him were English nobles. During his military service, Owain fought alongside Englishmen, from squires to earls, in the companies of some of England's great commanders such as Richard, earl of Arundel in 1387. He also fought for England's cause under Richard II and John of Gaunt in Scotland in 1385, and possibly for Henry Bolingbroke at Radcot Bridge in 1387. Although untrue, the accusations appear effective as a means of damning Owain and any who might align themselves with him. Owain's conduct during his life before and during the revolt contrasted significantly with the wild charges levelled against him. It seems safe to conclude that there was no plan to commit large-scale massacres of England's nobility.[26]

Such far-fetched claims that enemies intended to destroy the English king, his people, the country and the language were not unique to this case. In 1344, accusations were made that Philippe of France had a 'firm purpose to destroy the English language and to seize the territories of England'. In 1377, at the beginning of Richard II's reign, parliament was warned that Charles V, with the aid of the Spanish and the Scots, 'intended to destroy the king and the realm of England, and wholly extirpate the English language'. Again, in 1386, announcements were made that the next French king, Charles VI, had 'resolved to invade England with the intention of destroying the realm'. In May 1401, the new king, Henry IV, declared that the Welsh rebels planned to enter the realm, destroy the king, all of his lieges and *nostre langue angloys*. This ploy was also used by Henry V; rumours that the French and the Welsh were coming to England to destroy the realm began circulating in July 1413, just four months after his coronation. In reality, it is improbable that these were genuine proclamations made in wild panic, but were likely gestures designed to galvanise support for the crown at certain moments, while also seeking to dissuade English opposition factions from uniting with foreign powers. Shortly after taking the crown, Henry IV and his council built a case for war against Scotland, in which he accused the Scots of threatening to invade and destroy the realm, the king, the people and the English church. Therefore, it appears formulaic that enemies were so accused. In this light, once Owain had been identified as an enemy of the king, such a claim appears perhaps predictable.[27]

The best-known of the two legal proceedings which make the accusation that Owain was proclaimed prince only mentions Glyn Dŵr in passing. Instead, it focuses on the trial of a certain Englishman, John Kynaston the elder. The extant copy dates from October 1402 and it cannot be verified whether it is wholly faithful to the original 'presentment' of 25 October 1400. Kynaston and his associates were accused of robbery, horse theft and cattle-related crimes. In addition, they were alleged to have been in Owain's company during his brief but destructive September campaign. Kynaston was eventually found innocent, largely on the grounds that the alleged crimes took place outside Shropshire where the charges were levelled. Although the case outlines the irregular mosaic of legal jurisdictions of the time, it is also indicative that loyalties of the time and the area were not strictly understood along ethnic lines.[28]

The more relevant document records the inquisition held in Oswestry on 6 October 1400, which sought to identify those involved with Owain's September campaign.[29] First, it appears to solve one mystery; Owain and his men mounted a *chevauchée* or cavalry operation. Given the movement rates of the time, the campaign appears impossible to achieve as infantry.[30] The campaign began on 18 September by sacking Ruthin. Over the next three days, the towns of Denbigh, Rhuddlan, Flint – where the rebels also fought a relieving force from Chester under Robert Mascy – Hawarden and Holt were attacked. This encompasses an arc of towns and castles, from Ruthin to Holt, most of which lie around the Clwydian range of hills, within striking distance of Glyn Dŵr's home territory, to which his troops could withdraw if needed. By nightfall on 21 September, however, including the advance from Glyndyfrdwy to Ruthin on 17 September, this force had moved over sixty miles in four days and engaged in seven combats, six of which were castle assaults. If this demanding campaign was undertaken by just one fighting party, as the legal proceedings claim, it seems likely that it would have been spent as a fighting force at that point, 21 September, while also laden with booty, and perhaps encumbered by casualties or prisoners.

Notwithstanding, the proceedings state that Owain's force continued, presumably still intact as a unit and carrying their spoils, and wrought significant damage at Oswestry and the surrounding area on Wednesday 22 September. Here, the story becomes particularly problematic. The castle at Oswestry is around twenty miles south-west of their last stated position and heading away from the security of their home territory. To strike at it, the rebels, if the same group, curiously ignored the castle at Chirk, just four miles north of Oswestry. They are also reported to have damaged Whittington and Felton, the latter almost five miles south-east of Oswestry castle. The next day, 23 September 1400, Owain's forces are said to have attacked Welshpool, the final site on their *chevauchée*. Its town and castle are roughly twenty miles south-west of Oswestry where, as with the previous day, they are supposed to have moved and fought on the same day. There, they were reportedly seen off by English forces under Hugh Burnell, who sat on the panel composing the legal proceedings.[31]

The direction and distances involved are troubling. Certainly, to conduct the final two legs of the campaign at least, the rebel force of perhaps 300 men needed to be on horseback. The Oswestry proceeding stated that Owain's was a cavalry force, which paints an evocative picture of the whole affair. The circuit from Ruthin to Flint, around the probable nightly repair of the Clwydian range, seems reasonable for a force starting from Glyndyfrdwy. The additional sites at Hawarden and Holt put a distance between the attackers and safety, perhaps raising questions over the accuracy of the reported version of events. However, Oswestry and Welshpool are, in contemporary campaigning terms, some distance to the south. It is difficult to associate the compact route around the Clwydian range, where all sites are a short distance from each other and from relative safety, with the alleged last two days of the campaign, where the rebels appear to be stretching away beyond the support afforded by their home area. Also, it seems difficult to determine this force's ultimate intended destination. Considering the number of other localised revolts during this period, the mileage covered and the number of targets assaulted in such a short space of time, it is reasonable to assert that that there was more than one rebel force active in the area and that Owain has served as a convenient local scapegoat.

The government's response to the violence in north Wales was significant. It comprised a military expedition led by King Henry himself, executions, fines and pardons. Henry's army was returning from Scotland before diverting towards Wales. North of the border, Henry fielded a fighting force of more than 13,000 soldiers. This totalled between 15,000 and 20,000 men when support elements are included.[32] Similarly to his march against the Scots, Henry's insertion into Wales was largely unremarkable and his army met no significant opposition. Documents produced during the expedition supply further information on the most notable rebels. Owain and others were condemned in a hearing made at Bangor, in lands traditionally considered Tudor territory, on 7 October. On 18 October, when Henry and the army re-entered England, orders were issued 'to David Gamme and John Hauard to arrest Rees Kiffyn, esquire, and bring him before the king in person'. However, there were no orders to arrest Owain, suggesting that 'Rees Kiffyn', or Rhys Gethin, was initially the single most sought-after rebel. This implies that at that point, there was no clear rebel leader, no unified rebel movement, nor one lone government scapegoat. Henry's failure to pursue Glyn Dŵr or destroy his property while he had the opportunity clearly gives weight to this assertion.[33]

After Wales had seemingly been pacified, the government sought to secure the peace with political action. On 8 November 1400, Owain was declared dispossessed of his territories and possessions in north and south Wales. They were given to John Beaufort, earl of Somerset, Henry IV's half-brother.[34] Richard II had legitimised the Beauforts and thus they also held a potential claim to the crown. By bringing them into his patronage, Henry shrewdly nullified the potential threat posed by his father's other family. As the dispenser of gifts and land, Henry asserted himself as the senior noble in their relationship. When the news of the forfeiture and gift of his estates reached Glyn Dŵr, he likely realised that his full restoration was impossible in his or Beaufort's lifetime; the king would not dispossess an English earl in favour of a Welsh squire attainted for treason. Owain's lands were lost to him, seemingly unjustly, and he most likely reflected on that with some bitterness over the winter months.

Also, a general pardon was issued on 30 November, with the caveat that it would be valid until the next parliament. Meeting between 20 January and 10 March 1401, parliament reaffirmed the general pardon covering the year from 'Saint Hilary, 1 Henry IV, to Epiphany last' (14 January 1400 to 6 January 1401). The pardon was extended to all who submitted except three men, named as 'Owynni de Glendourdy', 'Reez ap Tudour' and 'Willielmum ap Tudour'. While this long period encompassed by the pardon of 10 March 1401 does not cover the acts of 1399 or the Epiphany Rising, it plainly starts too early to solely refer to the attack on Ruthin.[35]

Owain's heir, Gruffydd ab Owain, and his brother, Tudur ap Gruffydd, took advantage of the pardon offered and submitted to the crown. It was not uncommon for one element of the family to submit or side with the authorities while kinsmen stood in opposition. Such an action should ensure continuation of the family claim, but did not necessarily equate to loyalty to the king. This was certainly not the case for Gruffydd, who would die a prisoner of the crown in London, or Tudur, who would die in battle as a rebel. It was probably not a coincidence that Owain and the Tudor brothers, three of the wealthiest native Welsh landowners, were not pardoned by a new king in need of gifts with which to reward his supporters. The awarding of Owain's lands to Somerset shows that Henry believed that, at that point, it was politically convenient to disinherit and ignore these seemingly powerless and irrelevant Welsh squires.

CHAPTER TWO

Rebels and Risings

All this summer, Owain Glendower and several of the Welsh chieftains, whom the king regarded as traitors and outlaws from his kingdom, severely devastated West Wales and North Wales, taking refuge in the mountains and woodlands before emerging either to pillage or to slaughter those who tried to attack or ambush them.[1]

During the Middle Ages, winter was usually the season of peace and recuperation, so a lack of military activity in this period was common. Before midsummer 1401, a number of conflicts had broken out across Wales. Although several sources describe a new revolt erupting early in 1401 and throughout the middle of the year; Owain Glyn Dŵr can only be connected with certain of these events.[2]

On 21 February 1401, at Henry IV's second parliament, it was recorded that Welsh scholars at Oxford and Cambridge universities had left for Wales, and that Welsh labourers in England had done the same. They were said to have 'strongly equipped themselves with arms, bows, arrows and swords and other weapons of war' and returned to Wales, with the intent of starting 'another, new rebellion'. The Commons asked that the king provide a remedy for this crisis; in their eyes, Wales risked sliding into revolt again. Parliament duly passed a number of strict ordinances against the Welsh. These were measures aimed at tightly controlling the movements and activities of the Welsh, probably with the intention of smothering the revolt. However, they also appeared designed to blame and punish the Welsh, and demarcate further their subordinate legal and economic status compared to English subjects.

The ordinances were a series of harsh pronouncements which were introduced over successive sessions of Henry's parliaments. They were the confirmation of statutes introduced in 1295 which had been allowed to periodically lapse before being revived during the fourteenth century. They were created to build a wall between the Welsh and English and to unequivocally establish the political, social, military and economic superiority of the English over the Welsh. This was not treatment solely reserved for the Welsh; English governance in Ireland in this period was similar, as the Statutes of Kilkenny demonstrated. This method of excessive suppression and rigid separation of populations formed a central part of the English policy towards lands under its control. A number of Edward I's ordinances came into force again in 1401, others would follow in subsequent parliamentary sessions. 'Full-blooded Welshmen' were banned from buying land or tenements in any of the regions adjoining Wales, any Marcher lordship or any English town in Wales. They were also barred from serving in any of the key urban military or civilian posts, and forbidden from carrying arms in these areas. In addition, they could not become burgesses in any English town, whether in England or Wales, nor were they permitted to have 'any other liberty' within the kingdom or its towns.

Henry also ordered the Marcher lords to return to their estates in Wales to take on the rebels locally. They were to kill the rebels 'without allowing them any fine, redemption or other favour' to dissuade others from rebelling. In addition, it was permitted to pursue Welshmen across jurisdictional boundaries into Wales to execute any sentence passed on them. In all probability, this amounted to granting the authority to kill named Welsh rebels wherever they could be found, without needing to resort to further legal process. It seems probable that these measures resulted in Welsh deaths. Another ordinance stated that Welsh rebels could not otherwise attain a pardon without making amends for any damages caused, while another obliged anyone retaining Welsh tenants in England to provide a surety for their behaviour and to pay for any damages attributed to the tenant. Also, no full-blooded Englishman could be convicted of any suit or charge brought by a Welshman, unless convicted by an English justice or by a panel of English burgesses.[3]

Rather than restraining the rebels, this blanket discrimination was more likely to affect those Welshmen who had integrated into English society to some degree, and who possibly supported the authorities. Despite these measures, some Welshmen undoubtedly remained uncommitted. However, many who were not yet rebels appeared effectively charged as such by virtue of their ethnicity. The literature of the revolt often uses 'Welshmen' and 'rebels' interchangeably, and the term was understood as synonymous with treason and behaviour against what was perceived and presented as the natural order. The laws passed by parliament formed part of the political narrative against the Welsh, and their influence can be read in numerous chronicles of the time.[4] Tensions and conflicts in such societies are frequently deepened and prolonged by such emotive invective; this would prove to be the case with this rebellion too.

Many of these ordinances were to prove impractical and, in reality, were partly unenforceable and undesirable for the English in Wales. For years, the English towns and garrisons in Wales had employed native Welshmen in a variety of roles, from scouts and soldiers, to more mundane tasks, such as caring for horses or transporting food and goods. In addition, the English burgesses and garrisons, due to necessity and economic advantage, developed low-level commercial relations with the native Welsh. Immediately severing connections with them would be detrimental not only to life in each of the English towns in Wales, but to the commercial, military and administrative connectivity between those towns and garrisons. In short, the English presence in Wales required Welsh help. Throughout the revolt, small numbers of Welshmen continued to live among English burgesses, alongside whom they fought against the rebels. So, in places and in part, the ordinances were ignored where they were not locally convenient. This was also a statement on the *realpolitik* of the time; ideals held dear in London simply did not match the reality of life on the front line. However, these ordinances are highly likely to have turned some Welshmen towards rebellion and, therefore, Henry's laws augmented the power of the rebels. The effect of the ordinances was temporarily mediated by the issue of the general pardon of 10 March 1401, which was extended to all Welshmen willing to submit, with the exception of Owain Glyn Dŵr and the Tudor brothers, Rhys and Gwilym. The success of the general pardon is difficult to assess; a number did not submit while many others did so. However, many of those pardoned, such as Owain's son and brother, continued as rebels thereafter.[5]

As 1401 wore on, alerts of rebel activity were sent from Wales. The earliest and best-known of these actions was the Tudor capture of Conwy and the subsequent siege by crown forces. There is some speculation over which of the Tudors led the storming of Conwy; some modern historians place Rhys and Gwilym there, but contemporary sources claim that Rhys was absent. On Good Friday, 1 April 1401, one or more members of the Tudor force gained access to the castle by pretending to be arriving for work duties. Having killed the gatehouse guards, the small force entered and seized the castle while the garrison was at prayer.[6] Although a government force of around 500 troops laid siege to Conwy, the affair was quickly concluded through mediation. The considerable gamble of seizing a royal castle in order to conduct negotiations paid off for the Tudors. Despite some resistance in London, they won pardons for themselves and thirty-four men, initially issued on 20 April but finally confirmed on 8 July 1401.

> Pardon, at their supplication, William ap Tudur and Rees ap Tudur his brother of North Wales and their accomplices, who lately rose in insurrection and took the castle of Coneweye in North Wales and burned the town of Coneweye and despoiled the burgesses.[7]

The castle was returned to crown possession around 24 July 1401 and those who stormed the castle went free. The fact that they were all pardoned, leaders and accomplices, likely disproves the claims by Adam Usk and the Dieulacres Chronicle that the Tudors handed over some of their own men for execution when leaving Conwy. The Tudors maintained their power and influence, which they could not reasonably hope to do if they gave up those loyal to them for execution by the enemy.

The significance of the Tudor capture of Conwy has caused disagreement among modern historians. While some see it as intertwined with Owain's cause and part of the same revolt, a few others view the Tudor action as separate and solely self-motivated. The contemporary evidence supports the latter opinion: the siege negotiations did not mention Owain, either in terms of his rising or his supposed claim to the title of prince. In particular, there is no known effort to include him in the pardon being negotiated. The records show that Rhys ap Tudur was not present at Conwy, yet he was pardoned. Therefore, Owain could also have been included in the pardon, had that been a goal of the Tudor negotiations. This strongly suggests that, although their rebellious acts were contemporaneous, these two groups were not working in concert; no solid evidence connects them at that point.[8]

Another notable insurrection began in April 1401 and it too had no tangible connection to Owain. Welshmen rose in the settled, controlled,

even partly anglicised region around Abergavenny, south-east Wales. On
29 April, Sir William Lucy, sheriff of Herefordshire, was commissioned
to 'arrest John Filz Pieres and Maurice ap Meweryk and bring them
before the king and council'. John Filz Pieres had been held on charges
of adultery until his comrades stealthily broke him out of Usk jail. Little
further is known of Maurice ap Meweryk. Those appointed to serve
with Lucy were 'Walter Devereux, Thomas Clanvowe, John ap Herry and
Thomas del Hay'. Perhaps the most evocative action of the Gwent rebels
was recorded:

> On the feast of the Lord's ascension [12 May, 1401] this year, the tenants
> of Abergavenny rose up against their lord, Lord William Beauchamp,
> freeing three men from the gallows and killing with their arrows Sir
> William Lucy, knight, who had been given the task of executing them;
> these three had been condemned to death for theft, and were, by order
> of that second Jezebel, the lady of the lordship, going to be hanged that
> very day, heedless of the festival being celebrated at the time.[9]

The chronicler's anger at executions being held on the Feast of the
Ascension is lost on a modern, largely secular readership. That people
should face execution at such a solemn time, when the populace should
have been reflecting on Christ's death and ascent to Heaven, was highly
offensive to the faithful. Nevertheless, this was not an isolated, coura-
geous rescue mission by local desperadoes; evidence tells of an organised
rebellion in the area which besieged Abergavenny castle. On 16 May
1401, the local gentry of Herefordshire were commissioned to raise the
county posse and resist the 'divers evildoers [that] have assembled in the
parts of South Wales in the Lordship of Bergavenny and there committed
divers homicides and other evils'. The roll call of loyalists, all accorded
the rank of *chivaler*, summoned to suppress the rebels is noteworthy:
'John Chaundos, Walter Devereux, Kinard de la Bere, John Pauncefot,
John Oldcastel, John Greyndore, John ap Henry and John Skydemore.'
The latter eventually married one of Owain's daughters; Greyndore and
Oldcastle remained stalwarts of the crown in south Wales throughout the
rebellion, although Oldcastle later suffered brutal execution as a Lollard
heretic in 1417, as the rebellion waned. Walter Devereux and Kinard de
la Bere met violent deaths at the battle of Bryn Glas in 1402. There are
two Welshmen in the list; Thomas Clanvowe was taken alive at Bryn Glas,

while John ap Henry faithfully served Bolingbroke, eventually becoming MP for Herefordshire. These commanders formed the backbone of the crown's forces in the area, and it was on such men, the gentry, that the authorities would repeatedly call during the rebellion. On 18 May 1401, it was recorded that the situation at Abergavenny was more perilous than it first appeared. Additional orders were despatched to immediately raise and send the Gloucestershire militia to support local troops and those from Herefordshire.[10]

This Gwent rising was clearly considered significant by the authorities of the day, and should not be overlooked as an isolated incident to release three men from the gallows. There is no suggestion anywhere that Owain had influence in south-east Wales, or any connection to this rising. It seems clear that the security situation in Wales had deteriorated significantly even by this stage. In addition, the eruption of a number of widespread but localised revolts, with different immediate aims but probably with similar underlying causes, along with the confusing emergence of a number of possible leaders, characterises this stage of the conflict as the multi-headed hydra of an insurgency. The disjointed, weak and inadequate measures taken by a distant government, distracted by the struggle to establish itself, also assisted the rise of the rebels.

On 26 May, the king recorded that he had received intelligence that the insurgents were poised to overrun Carmarthenshire, southwest Wales. Royal letters, dated 28 May 1401, summoned troops from fourteen English counties and cities to comprise the army he intended to take to Wales to oppose 'Owen Glendourdy and other rebels'. A few days later, word reached Prince Henry from John Charlton, lord of Powys, claiming that some of Charlton's soldiers had attacked Owain and his men. Charlton's letter described how his men had advanced against Owain and his followers who were on high ground. He gave no description of any fight, writing that Owain and his men had fled and had been pursued until nightfall. Certain items were captured, such as weapons, armour and horses, and Charlton's letter included the curious mention of 'a drape of cloth painted with maidens with red hands', which was also seized. Within a few days of Charlton's letter being sent, Henry Percy junior also reported on the state of the rebellion in north Wales. He noted that he had witnessed 'much pillaging and mischief' there, and held that 'all the country is without doubt in great peril of being destroyed by the rebels if I should leave before the arrival of my successor'. Percy urged the king to swiftly send land and naval forces to suppress the rebels, and repeatedly made plain the fact that he was paying for the troops engaged in combating the rebellion, including soldiers in the service of the earl of Arundel. He acknowledged that the news of Charlton's skirmish with Owain had reached him, adding that several of Owain's men had been wounded, but none apparently killed. He confirmed that Charlton was due to meet with him and Thomas Percy, earl of Worcester. Henry Percy also included the intriguing news that his ships had been involved in action at Bardsey Island, 'which was taken from the English by the Scots' and that they had captured a Scots vessel. Although it might simply have been a place used by the Scots as a refuge, the notion that the Scots had taken Bardsey for a time allows the possibility of communications between them and the Welsh rebels.[11] Owain appears to have written an undated letter to Robert III, king of Scotland, assumed to issue from around this time:

Most excellent, powerful and esteemed lord and cousin, I commend myself to your most excellent royal majesty with fitting humility, and with honour and respect in all matters. Most esteemed lord and royal cousin, may it please you and your royal excellence to know that Brutus, your most noble ancestor and mine, was originally the first crowned king to live in this kingdom of England, which used to be known as Great Britain. Brutus fathered three sons, namely Albanactus and Locrinus and Kamber; you are descended from the direct line of this Albanactus, while the descendants of this Kamber ruled as kings until the time of Cadwaladr, who was the last crowned king of my people, and from whose direct line I, your humble cousin, am descended. Since his death, however, my forebears and all my people have been, as we still are, subjected and held in bondage by my and your mortal enemies the Saxons – a fact which you, most esteemed lord and royal cousin, know full well. The prophecy states that, with the help and support of your royal majesty, I shall be delivered from this subjection and bondage. And yet, most esteemed lord and royal cousin, it pains me greatly to inform your royal majesty that I am very short of men-at-arms; it is for this reason, most esteemed lord and royal cousin, that I beg you, humbly and with bended knee, your royal majesty, please to send me a number of men-at-arms who, with the help of God, can help me to resist my and your enemies, most esteemed lord and royal cousin, and to punish them for their evils and injuries which I and my aforesaid forebears of Wales have suffered, and for the many other things inflicted upon us by these mortal enemies of mine and yours. Do not doubt, most esteemed lord and royal cousin, that I shall in consequence consider myself bound to serve and obey your royal majesty for the rest of my days. I cannot send you all my news in writing, but these messengers whom I have sent to you are fully informed of all my affairs, and I beg you therefore to place your trust and confidence in what they tell you by word of mouth on my behalf. Most esteemed lord and royal cousin, may the Lord almighty keep you safe.[12]

The form of many diplomatic letters from the medieval period can be simplified here into two types: introductory letters and replies. Approach letters usually had three distinct parts, replies commonly had four elements. Both types of letter tended to begin by politely addressing the recipient, often recalling their titles and virtues, and they often ended with a similar flourish, presenting the author in a humble or respectable manner. The central and usually the longest section of an introductory letter covered the reason for contact. Replies tended to include, in a form of reported speech that repeated, often verbatim, much of the originator's letter. At the end of this repetition of the message came the recipient's reply. This is one crucial way of distinguishing who initiated contact. This letter to the king of Scotland was clearly an approach by Owain.

This letter, originally written in French, offers a glimpse at the mind behind its creation. Several of Owain's letters have survived and contain a sufficient number of similar elements to be identified as a style. First, he emerges as appropriately polite, engaging and bright. His intelligence is particularly evident in later letters, where he was more able to use linguistic ploys to engage with the interlocutor. In addition, Owain deployed colourful, emotive, often angry phraseology and repetition to emphasise the message he wished to convey. This is also evident throughout Owain's surviving letters.

In this letter to Robert III, his salutation was appropriately respectful, and he also inserted the term *consanguineus*, often translated as 'cousin' but literally inferring that they were 'of the same blood'. They were not closely related, however Owain described the alleged connection between them dating back to the Brutus legend. It was a commonly known story that Brutus escaped the famed siege of Troy and made his way to Britain where he established a noble line of kings, beginning with his three sons, among whom he divided the land. Establishing himself in this way implied Owain's nobility and blood connection to Robert; assisting a noble relative was a legitimate, even honourable, course of action. So, in the language of their time, Owain made a case allowing Robert to help him. By mentioning him first, Owain placed Albanactus, supposed progenitor of the Scots, as the eldest brother and therefore the most senior. Most other readings of the legend describe Locrinus, mythical founder of England's royal lineage, as the eldest. Owain could not have known that Henry IV had already used the Brutus myth and Locrinus's imagined seniority in messages to the Scots designed to make them submit. This caused the Scots to research whether they were descended instead from a different mythical figure called Scota, the daughter of a pharaoh. Trojan ancestor myths were not restricted to late medieval Britain. In a letter to the Roman pope, the Turks cited Roman connections, through famed Trojans Antenor and Aeneas, to a common ancestor they shared with the Turks, Priam. They did this in an attempt to divide support for Venetian calls for a crusade against them. The Turks were locked in conflict with Venetian possessions in the eastern Mediterranean, and sought to stop Christians from mustering behind Venice by citing this mythical, but well-known connection, and by reminding the pope that the Muslims had not killed Christ and also considered him a true prophet. Therefore, although Owain's use of mythology was appropriate for the age, it was unfortunately timed.[13]

Superficially, Owain's use of the word *Sacsouns* to describe the English appears connected to the Welsh term, *Saesson*. In fact, he deliberately chose that word, when he could so easily have used *Anglais*. The use of the term 'Saxons' ties into other European thought and literature of their time. A similar term to describe the English as *Sesnes* appears in contemporary French treatises, such as *A Toute La Chevalerie* which was connected to the longer, multipart *Traité Contre Les Anglais*. This work also included friendly reference to the Welsh and lauded Owain Lawgoch for leading a French army and killing more than 500 *Angloiz* in one fight. This connected the English to a contemporary perception which held that the historical Saxons were non-Christian barbarians. The theme and revulsion of barbarism was current and one to which Owain would return in later letters. Characterising the English as Saxons and, by inference, pagan barbarians not only legitimised attacking them but also resonated with other European writings. Italian writers of the period referred to the German armies which descended on Italy in the same manner. Also, the Scottish chronicler, Walter Bower, described the English as Saxons in specific reference to this conflict with the Welsh, despite calling them English elsewhere.[14]

Owain also referred to a prophecy which suggested that the Scots should join with him in order to defeat their English enemies. While there were numerous prophecies in the air through the medieval period, Owain was probably referring to Merlin's prophecy or the tenth-century Welsh work, *Armes Prydain* (The Prophecy of Britain). Both described the English as Saxons and both claimed that the Welsh, Scots and others would unite and reconquer Britain. Merlin's prophecy had been popularised by the writing of Geoffrey of Monmouth and had been reworked for a new audience during the fourteenth century. Evoking prophecy in 1401 was not the act of a deluded dreamer, as Owain was portrayed by later writers. Other rulers, such as Henry IV, also used prophecy to legitimise their positions and politics. Prophecies were not simply popular culture, but were a medium of communicating the aspirations and legitimacy of leaders and their people; they were a contemporary tool of power.[15]

Owain was clearly looking for allies and asked Robert for troops, explaining that he had too few. It was in Scotland's interest to have others also fight their mutual 'mortal enemies'. As an incentive, Owain also offered his allegiance to Robert 'for the rest of [his] days'. The acquisition of more noble supporters and expanding territory was highly desirable to the prestige and wealth of medieval rulers. However, Robert III was politically weak and physically ailing. Scotland's court was divided and unlikely to act on Owain's request without further incentive, such as English attack or French inducement. Had the Scots responded and Owain's campaign been successful, this poses the intriguing thought that Owain's Wales would have become Scotland's vassal.

One of Owain's literary traits is his use of repetition to make his points. On seven occasions he used the phrase 'most esteemed lord and royal cousin' to impress upon Robert the respect Owain had for him, and to infer that they were related. He also repeated the unpleasant notions of subjection and bondage at the hands of their thrice-mentioned enemies. Evidently, he was describing the poor condition of the Welsh under, as he characterised it, Saxon rule. As they had common enemies, this was a reasonable approach to make, and Owain presented his case using the appropriate terms for the period and for his social class.

Owain's intelligence emerges well in this short letter. First, due to his education and social class, he seems perhaps the most likely person in his entourage in 1401 to have such a comfortable command of French. His reference to Saxons and prophecy demonstrated that he was well versed in the political themes and arguments circulating European courts. This shows that he also had expectations of his interlocutor's education, assuming they too were aware of such subjects, as they evidently were. Owain's education was evidently sufficient to enable him to converse with the highest strata of his society. It is also noteworthy that, despite there being no suggestion anywhere that Owain had served as a diplomat, he was able to craft a letter to a king, using the appropriate language and style. His appeal to Robert was phrased in a manner betraying the linguistic skills and passion of the author: he was pained to humbly beg on bended knee for aid, in order to resist their mutual enemies and punish them for their evils.

This letter brought no immediate aid from Scotland; Adam Usk claimed that Owain's messengers carrying letters to the king of Scotland and the lords of Ireland were captured and beheaded in Ireland. However, Usk also wrote that a Welsh crusader, Dafydd ap Ieuan Goz, was also captured at sea during 1401, having been sent to Scotland by the king of France on Owain's behalf. This demonstrates that the Welsh rebels had also made unrecorded contact with elements within the French court and had already won at least partial support.[16]

* * * * *

During early summer 1401, the supposition is that Owain led his scant forces towards south-west Wales, and that they were harried along the way by John Charlton and others.[17] In reality, several contemporary sources only offer initials of the place names involved, which are too vague to identify with sufficient certainty. If the fight known as the battle of Hyddgen occurred, then it probably happened in late May or early June. However, the evidence upon which this possible event is most commonly cited dates from 1564 and, although it is said to derive from a fifteenth-century document, it must be treated with considerable caution. In reality, it seems unlikely that a force of '120 reckless men, riding in a warlike fashion' defeated a force more than ten times its size in open terrain.[18] The lack of incidental corroborative evidence, such as orders, muster lists, payments, chronicle accounts or any other documentary evidence, casts doubt on this battle taking place. However, other evidence suggests that the security situation in west Wales deteriorated swiftly and widely, in a manner more easily associated with an insurgency but unlike the trail of damage associated with a campaigning army. Adam Usk did not mention any pitched battle at Hyddgen, writing:

> All this summer, Owain Glendower and several of the Welsh chieftains, whom the king regarded as traitors and outlaws from his kingdom, severely devastated West Wales and North Wales, taking refuge in the mountains and woodlands before emerging either to pillage or to slaughter those who tried to attack or ambush them.[19]

Also during summer 1401, fighting broke out around Welshpool on the central Welsh–English border. In August, Owain reputedly stormed the castle at New Radnor, some forty miles south of Welshpool, allegedly ritually decapitating the garrison survivors for offering such stiff resistance. Simultaneously, Harlech, on the north-west coast, was under siege by rebels evidently not commanded by Owain. This siege lasted several months but no evidence places Glyn Dŵr there. As summer turned to autumn, Prince Henry also wrote of the ongoing insurrection in south Wales, noting that crown tenants and subjects were refusing to pay dues owed to the crown. The king wrote to Prince Henry on the matter of the siege of Harlech, advising him that it was easier to hold such castles than to retake them. In response, a relief force of 500 men was despatched in November. John Charlton, lord of Powys, died in unrecorded circumstances in October, and was succeeded by his capable brother, Edward.[20]

Henry IV's campaign to south Wales in October 1401 was as short and unsuccessful as his expedition to north Wales the previous autumn. Nevertheless, his personal, large-scale response to the rebel threat in south-west Wales reveals the perceived seriousness of the southern rising in summer 1401. Henry's army lumbered fruitlessly from Worcester to Brecon, then along the Tywi valley to Carmarthen, before making for the monastery at Strata Florida in Cardiganshire. Glyn Dŵr, if present at all, was not drawn to battle. It was certainly not in Owain's interests to face a much larger, better-equipped force on their terms, particularly when they could be made to chase ghosts around the countryside to no avail, exhausting themselves and the king's coffers. The expedition of

1401 offers subtle clues about the power relationship between Owain and Henry at that stage. Superficially, Henry looked imposingly powerful, yet his behaviour and movements were being framed by Owain and his actions. Owain had the initiative and, as the year went on, he appeared to be increasingly successful with it. Moreover, Henry's repeated lack of campaign success against the Welsh was humiliating for him; having personally derided the Welsh as being of meagre reputation, he had again failed to defeat them.

The royal expedition to west Wales in 1401 is best remembered for its destructive brutality. At Llandovery, Henry ordered the execution of a local nobleman, Llywelyn ap Gruffydd Fychan, and his son who was alleged to be a rebel. Llywelyn gained honour in the way he met his death, which was recorded in the *Historia Vitae* as well as by Adam Usk. When given the choice of revealing intelligence on Owain or facing death, he reportedly knelt and stretched his own neck before the executioner. This was an early sign that some were willing to die for Owain, despite there being no obvious connection between him and Llywelyn. On this expedition, Henry's army not only killed monks and at least one local noble, but they 'invaded the area, ravaging and utterly destroying it with fire, sword and famine, sparing neither churches nor children'. It also reportedly sacked the monastery at Strata Florida, stealing the silverware and using it as a stable. Strata Florida was founded by the revered twelfth-century ruler Rhys ap Gruffydd, the Lord Rhys, and was the burial place of many of Wales's leading nobles. By damaging the monastery, stealing from it and allowing his horses to defecate in it, Henry was making a clear cultural gesture as well as committing a sacrilege. Adam Usk added that Henry's army gathered up 1,000 Welsh children and led them to England to be put into service. If accurate, the king's actions were certain to push more natives to rebel.[21]

According to Adam Usk, in early November, Owain led an unsuccessful attack on Caernarfon, apparently losing 300 men in the event. However, beforehand, Adam recorded that Owain raised the standard of Uther Pendragon, 'a golden dragon on a white field'. If accurate, Owain had evoked an emblem recalling a myth from Wales's past, the importance of which his contemporaries would have recognised. It seems reasonable to assert that this was a significant symbolic act and, in so doing, he claimed leadership of Gwynedd, where he raised Uther's banner. Considering Gwynedd's historical dominance of Wales, with this act he also asserted himself as leader over the rest of the Welsh. If Adam Usk was correct, Owain had also either challenged or invited the Tudors and the men of the region, while attacking a strong symbol of Edward I's legacy in the heart of Gwynedd. If true, Owain was, perhaps, claiming leadership of the Welsh.[22]

Towards the end of the year there were signs that the situation was tipping in the rebels' favour. Tenants on crown lordships in usually calm areas of south Wales were still refusing to pay rents unless the king proved he could suppress the rebels. Negotiating along those lines suggests that the native Welsh were willing to recognise the local power only, rather than a standing agreement with a distant authority. This level of defiance on the part of the Welsh was reflected in the actions of some of Henry's commanders in Wales. While Charlton's troops had pursued Owain in open country in May, by November, certain English commanders were unwilling to venture out against the rebels. The assumption of a defensive posture based on the security of their fortifications indicated that, in some parts of Wales, they had already lost control.[23]

Owain wrote a letter in Latin to the lords of Ireland, dated 29 November, requesting their help in the fight against Henry.

> Greetings and much love, most esteemed lord and trusted kinsman. As you will know, a great struggle, not to say a war, has broken out between us and our, and your mortal enemies, the Saxons, a war which we have maintained vigorously for nearly two years now, and which, by the grace of God our saviour, and with your help and support, we hope and plan to go on maintaining until it can be brought to an effective and favourable conclusion. It is commonly said in the prophecy, however, that, before we can gain the upper hand in this contest, you and your noble kinsmen in Ireland shall come to our aid in this matter; considering our plight, therefore, we warmly and earnestly request you, esteemed lord and trusted kinsman, to send over to us, as soon as you possibly can – saving your honourable estate in all things – as many mounted and unmounted men-at-arms as you can properly and honestly afford, in order to help us and our people, who have for so long been oppressed by these aforesaid enemies of ours and yours, to defeat the perfidious and deceitful purpose of these same enemies of ours. We beg you, moreover, for the love that we bear you and the great trust that we place in you, and despite the fact that we are unknown to your esteemed person, not to delay in doing this; understand, too – as you doubtless do,

most esteemed lord and kinsman – that for as long as we are able to go on maintaining this warlike struggle in our land, you and all the other lords in your land of Ireland will in the meantime be able to enjoy the sort of peace and quiet which you desire. Moreover, lord and kinsman, since the bearers of these letters shall keep you fully informed by word of mouth, may it please you to put your trust in whatever they say on our behalf, and if there is anything which you would like to see done by us, your humble kinsman, you may with confidence commit it to them. May the Almighty preserve your reverence and lordship in prosperity for many days to come, esteemed lord and kinsman. Written in North Wales, 29 November.[24]

Similarly to the letter to Robert III, Owain used the Latin word '*Saxones*' for the English. His consistency in so doing demonstrates that he was making a point, when he could easily have used *Anglie* or the appropriate cognate. On five occasions Owain mentioned the notion of their kinship and emphasised his esteem for the recipient. The theme is the same as his letter to Robert III, that he needed troops to help in his fight against their mutual enemies. Although the letter to the Irish lords was speculative, Owain admitted that they did not know one another, the message of mutually beneficial co-operation made political sense. The anger and passion of the author comes through in this message also, which spoke of being oppressed by mutual enemies and his desire to defeat their 'perfidious and deceitful purpose'. As he begged for aid, Owain wrote of the love he had for his unnamed interlocutors. He vowed that the Welsh would continue their 'warlike struggle' which, in turn, would bring peace to Ireland. Owain invited the Irish lords to respond and by offering to perform tasks they might name. There is no known Irish response to Owain's letter, Adam Usk believed that the messengers had been captured and beheaded. With the hindrance of hindsight, it seems clear that these unknown lords would not send aid. They seem to have been divided among themselves and a significant English presence in Ireland separated them from the Welsh.

However, this letter not only contributes to knowledge of Owain's form and style, it also reveals that by the end of 1401, he had developed a multifaceted strategy and was attempting to implement it. Through the year, Owain held negotiations with Henry Percy junior and his uncle, Thomas Percy, earl of Worcester, during which he allegedly refuted the charges against him, sought a pardon and some sort of inheritance. Henry Percy junior, in correspondence with Prince Henry, conceded that Glyn Dŵr had made a number of other salient points too. Percy clashed with courtier knights at parliament who believed that he should have attempted to seize or kill Owain at parley. Not only would that have been a highly dishonourable act, but it should be recalled that Owain was known to be an extremely capable opponent.[25] Nevertheless, Owain continued to appear tractable to mediating a peaceful settlement with the king and a return to a quiet life on his estates.

It is also evident that he was no longer solely relying on justice to be done; his other activities demonstrated that Owain was also preparing to fight. Clearly, his letters to Scotland, Ireland and probably to France and Brittany as well, show that he looking for allies and their troops to counter superior English numbers. Therefore, there was an international aspect to his plan. In Wales, his activities and growing support show that others were willing to follow, support, fight and die for him. In part, it is likely that these people were motivated by the circumstances of the moment, including the behaviour of the authorities, as well as somehow deciding to invest their loyalty in Owain. However, by the end of 1401, Carmarthenshire, Gwent, Gwynedd, Merioneth and Powys had been touched by revolt. Although Owain is usually connected to these events, he was evidently not responsible for all of which he was accused. Other, significant episodes of violence had flared across Wales and all of these form part of the fabric of the revolt. However, it is clear that 1401 witnessed a surge in violence across Wales. It is plausible that Owain travelled to a number of places in Wales during the year and this might indicate that he was attempting to assume leadership of the Welsh rebels; however, there were plainly many willing to rebel for their own reasons. Each branch of his emerging strategies would require Owain to display previously unknown diplomatic talent, whether in gathering support in Wales, approaching and enticing foreign powers, or seeking resolution with the Crown. The success of his diplomacy would, to some extent, determine the longevity and success of the rebellion.

PART TWO

Rise

CHAPTER THREE

'Owen ... the Rod of God's Anger'

My heart trembles when I think of this dire blow against English rule inflicted by Owen ... What more can I say? Like another Assyrian, the rod of God's anger, he vented his fury with fire and sword in unprecedented tyrannies.[1]

Although numerous chronicles of the age described the flight of Halley's Comet across Europe's skies in 1402 as the herald of grave portents, in reality, subsequent events had more mundane, human causes. By the end of 1401, Henry IV's military and political methods of controlling the rebellion in Wales were proving unsuccessful; in fact, they helped to strengthen the revolt. The decline in governmental authority in Wales would also develop into a partial collapse in tax collection.[2] This would, in turn, have small but notable economic consequences. The rulers of medieval England presided over a relatively limited treasury. Diminishing the royal budget, even by small degrees, weakened the king's ability to fully execute the demands of governance. Unless he prioritised the rebels or found new streams of income, the decline in revenue from Wales would also limit Henry's scope to reinforce his positions or act against his enemies there. This would also strengthen the rebel cause, materially and psychologically. As 1402 dawned, the government needed to act swiftly and appropriately in order to stanch the surge in rebel activity.

However, Owain moved first, devastating Grey lands around Ruthin in January and February, pressing further attacks in the vale of Clwyd in February and March 1402. Glyn Dŵr appeared to be conducting a vendetta with these highly specific attacks and, from this perspective, his actions appear to have a personal, rather than a national dimension. This aspect of the revolt reached a high point in early April when Owain captured Reginald, Lord Grey, by luring him into an ambush in which many of Grey's men reportedly died. Contemporary sources attributed this notable success to treachery on the part of Welshmen in Grey's household.[3] Although this possibly reflects the biases of the chroniclers, designed to tarnish Welshmen as treacherous rebels, if true, it would demonstrate that even those employed in key posts in the English administration in Wales were vulnerable to rebel seduction. It would also show that even crown stalwarts such as Grey were willing to ignore certain of the harsh laws passed against the Welsh, if it suited them. Grey was held until November 1402 when a significant portion of his 10,000 mark ransom was paid, and his heir was handed over as an indemnity for the remaining sum.[4] Although the precise terms of his release are unrecorded, despite occupying a front-line position in Ruthin castle, Grey does not appear to have actively campaigned against Owain again, implying that he had agreed not to bear arms again against his captor. Such agreements were not uncommon in this period; a nobleman's reputation depended significantly on his honour and reliability. Keeping his word to the man who had vanquished him was expected in most circumstances. As the fighting season of 1402 began, Owain had already struck the first notable blow which exemplified how the government's ineffectiveness contrasted with that of the flourishing rebels.

The capture and ransom of Grey were significant events. In the first instance, if Owain planned to massacre England's nobles, as claimed in the legal proceedings of October 1400, it seems highly likely that he would have readily started by killing his helpless enemy, Grey. There is no evidence that Owain killed any of his prisoners and nothing suggests that he treated them contrary to the expected norms of the time. In word and deed, Owain demonstrated that the accusations levelled against him were incorrect. While it is not known how Owain spent the ransom money, such a sum would have enabled him to act beyond his usual means, thereby augmenting his power and influence.

The government began its preparations to counter the rebels early in 1402 by appointing the earl of Stafford and John Trefor, bishop of St Asaph, to attempt to restore orderly governance in north Wales. In March, Henry IV appointed Hotspur and Thomas Percy, earl of Worcester, as lieutenants in north and south Wales respectively. They swiftly set about castle rebuilding work around the border and coastal fringes of Wales. The Percys also maintained and strengthened castle garrisons, sent a naval patrol from Chester to relieve northern castles and they hurried troops to flare points, such as Denbigh in early June. Although a balanced strategy, this represents a defensive, reactive posture which allowed rebel forces freedom of movement and handed them the initiative.

Clerical records portray the declining state of government authority even in areas adjacent to the border. Consequently, Henry IV resolved to counter rebel forces who, by early summer, had pushed south-east into the central March and were expanding the territory under their sway. Along the way, the Welsh laid waste to territories which were nominally Mortimer lands but were held by the king during the minority of the next earl of March, nine-year-old Edmund. The boy's uncle, also Edmund, the acting earl of March, was tasked with raising a force to stop the insurgents. As the rebels advanced, districts defected to them, swelling insurgent ranks as well as assuring that their lands were not destroyed. Numerous clergy within these areas were identified as being 'enemies and rebels of the king'.[5] Edmund Mortimer, the twenty-six-year-old brother of the former earl, raised a substantial militia force in Herefordshire to serve as the mainstay of his army. He augmented it with troops raised from his estates, including archers from Maelienydd, and members of the border gentry and their retainers. The leaders of Edmund's army were notable for their military experience and their close courtly connections. In addition, all had served as justices of the peace, sheriffs and Members of Parliament for Herefordshire. These men and their families formed a significant part of the structure of continuous governance of the border. The eldest of them, Sir Robert Whitney, was probably in his late fifties and had long served Richard II. As MP for Herefordshire, he had petitioned parliament for aid against Welsh raids into the county in 1378. His military career earned him the title of 'king's knight' and took him on campaign to Scotland in 1385 and Ireland in the 1390s. He also conducted elements of the logistical preparations for Richard's expeditions to Ireland, including the acquisition and storage of provisions, as well as a survey of Irish ports. Whitney also served as an ambassador to Aragon and Foix during the 1390s and was possibly serving as Henry IV's knight marshal at the time he joined Mortimer. In all, his long years of strategic and logistical planning, as well as his diplomatic experience, would be highly valuable for a campaign in Wales.

Sir Kinard de la Bere's family had close ties with the royal family; his father served in the Black Prince's retinue, militarily and as his chamberlain. Kinard fought in Richard II's armies in Scotland and Ireland at the same time as Robert Whitney, also becoming a 'king's knight'. He was a supporter of the Appellant cause in 1387, which also connected him to Henry Bolingbroke. During Richard's Irish campaigns, Kinard served in the retinue of the well-respected Roger Mortimer, earl of March, and was an executor of the earl's estates following his death in 1398. A fellow executor was William Beauchamp, lord of Abergavenny, whom Kinard was commissioned to rescue during the siege of 1401.

A third notable commander of Edmund's army of the March was Sir Walter Devereux, who also assisted in the relief of Abergavenny. The Devereux family also had close ties to the councils of the Black Prince and Richard II. Similarly, Walter had served in Scotland and Ireland with his co-commanders under Richard, initially as a 'king's esquire' before being knighted in 1391. He also supported the Appellants but returned to serve Richard. It was perhaps as constable of Builth castle that he first came into contact with Rhys Gethin (Rhys the Fierce) of Builth, who opposed him at Bryn Glas. Walter and Kinard appear to have been a similar age to Owain.[6]

Probably the youngest of Edmund's leaders was Sir Thomas Clanvowe, who was also Robert Whitney's son-in-law. Although his family was of Welsh descent, they had served the royal court for several generations and never wavered in their support. Thomas had served in Ireland with Richard, also beginning as a 'king's esquire' before being knighted. He also served Henry IV as a 'king's knight' and was one of the party which returned Richard's queen, Isabella, to France in June 1401. Closely connected to the Whitneys, the Clanvowes were also linked to other major Marcher families, such as the Skidmores and the infamous Lollards, the Oldcastles.[7] The ties between these men exemplify the degree of interconnectivity of local power relations and individual loyalties typical of the period. Although Edmund Mortimer lacked his brother's military credentials, his commanders were all campaign-hardened. He led these amalgamated forces into Wales intending to confront the rebels. The Welsh, who appear to have been led by Owain Glyn Dŵr and Rhys Gethin, gave battle to the army of the March at Bryn Glas on 22 June 1402. It seems more likely that Owain was with Rhys Gethin of Builth, rather than his namesake from Nant Conwy. Although the composition of Welsh forces is unknown, it is clear that, similarly to their English opponents, many were veterans of recent conflicts in France, Scotland and Ireland. The result was a crushing victory for the Welsh.

There are no known eye-witness accounts of the battle and contemporary sources are confused, inconsistent and speculatory. Evidence detailing force sizes or casualties sustained provides a range of figures. The highest numbers come from the fascinating but often hysterical Adam Usk, who attributed to Owain the impossibly high figure of 30,000 soldiers and proclaimed an equally inaccurate battlefield death toll of 8,000. The lowest figures emerging from period documents ascribe casualties in the hundreds. Some of the more consistently reliable chronicles of the time declared the number of English dead to be between 1,000 and 1,500 men; Welsh losses are unknown but were undoubtedly fewer. Edmund Mortimer and Thomas Clanvowe were taken prisoner, but Robert Whitney, Kinard de la Bere and Walter Devereux were killed, the latter possibly succumbing to his wounds three days later.

The tactics employed that day are also obscure; the only certainties seem to be that the Welsh initially stood on top of the hill, Bryn Glas, and descended to meet the English as they advanced up its steep face. There are two points of contention concerning the battle's denouement: that Mortimer's Welsh archers changed sides during the battle, and that Welsh women took to the field afterwards and mutilated the dead and wounded English.[8]

If the Maelienydd archers did fight against Mortimer, then this would demonstrate a supreme tactical coup by the insurgents. Such a ploy would logically need to be prearranged to have any chance of success. Without prior agreement, it seems implausible that loyal troops would commit a total volte-face during the tumult of battle. While they could react to a prearranged signal and effect a surprise attack, it seems unrealistic to think that, amid the noise, fear and distractions of the fighting, they could credibly receive inducement from the rebels on the field. There was little real possibility of secret messaging once both armies had reached the point of conflict. If the English, who appear to have outnumbered the Maelienydd archers, caught wind that treachery might be afoot, they would no doubt have set upon them. Also, if this were not prearranged, the archers would have to discuss the offer as a group because troops rarely, if ever, willingly shoot their comrades without significant inducement. Initiating a conversation with so many men when fighting or advancing against the enemy seems perhaps implausible, to agree to turn when on the field and to do so united and secretly appears impossible. When faced with such a spontaneous quandary, it is probable that some would stay loyal, some would flee and some might rebel – reducing the utility of these troops to Owain and Rhys. Without prior agreement, the archers had no guarantee that the rebels, if victorious, would not treat them as enemies if the battle swung in their favour. In reality, the uncertainty and risks to the rebels and the archers of trying to negotiate their defection while the battle was ongoing strongly favours the notion that they were sent by the Welsh commanders to Mortimer's army. The successful insertion of men loyal to him into the enemy force is a sure sign of Owain's capabilities as a commander.

The issue of the mutilations allegedly committed by the Welsh women seems less clear; certain evidence blamed Rhys Gethin for the event. While it remains possible that the event is a fiction designed to denigrate the Welsh reputation, this sort of act was not unheard of during the medieval period, and similar events have occurred in wars from ancient to modern times. If Adam Usk were even partially correct about Henry's troops enslaving and removing 1,000 Welsh children in late 1401, then Welsh forces and the women camp followers might have been motivated to exact such a gruesome revenge. Some evidence suggests that Sir Walter Devereux died of his wounds three days later which, if accurate, might count against the mutilation idea. Such a high-value person would have attracted attention from post-battle looters and, doubtless, the women castrators. Nevertheless, while apparently unsolvable, the incident remains an intriguing detail of the conflict.[9]

The battle of Bryn Glas had a significant impact on contemporary society in material, military, psychological and political terms. The English appear to have lost a notable number of men, and no doubt their equipment was used to strengthen Welsh military resources. The network of families which guaranteed the stable governance of the central March had lost many of its key figures. The revolt subsequently grew in strength and began to overbear the English military and civilian administration in Wales.

There was a pulse of activity in the days and weeks immediately following the battle. On 25 June, such was the panic provoked by the defeat at Bryn Glas that King Henry sent letters to the clergy and sheriffs of twelve midland counties, ordering the lords, knights and squires of those areas to report to him shortly afterwards, armed and mounted. Simultaneously, he ordered the men of the five northern counties to report to his commanders in the Scottish Marches. His orders were also sent to the sheriffs of eleven southern counties to prepare to defend the coasts from foreign invasion. That summer, with so much of England's military power mobilised and deployed, it might have seemed as if England itself were besieged and Henry's men were manning its border ramparts. If this were deliberate, then it showed shrewdness on the part of Henry's government: defining an immediate foreign, yet nearby threat often aids social cohesion and loyalty to the leader. On England's frontier with Wales, border towns strengthened their defences, and repaired their walls and ditches. Troops and supplies were sent to a number of castles, including a force for Harlech and Caernarfon under Prince Henry. Edward Charlton, lord of Powys, was sent to Welshpool, effectively, on the front line. Similarly, Richard, baron Grey of Codnor, was put in Brecon and reinforced with 750 troops funded by the government. Before the end of July, Henry had created two new border commands, to which he appointed senior commanders. He commissioned the formidable earl of Arundel, Thomas Fitzalan, to the northern command. Glyn Dŵr had served under Thomas's father's banner in Flanders in 1387. Shortly after his father's execution by Richard II in 1397, Thomas had been in exile with Henry Bolingbroke and returned with him to challenge Richard in 1399. He would prove to be a key military figure during Henry IV's reign. Before the arrival of autumn, Arundel had launched an expedition into north Wales. The southern sector was given to Edmund, earl of Stafford, who married Henry IV's cousin, Anne of Gloucester. The appointment of such trusted leaders and kinsmen constituted a determined effort by the king to wrest control back from the Welsh. In addition, it replicates the personal networks shown among the border gentry, demonstrating the importance of personal ties, even in government and warfare. In early September, Henry gathered his forces and pushed into north Wales. His expedition was as shambolic as his previous efforts, succeeding only in burning Llanrwst. While on campaign, Henry narrowly avoided being killed by a tree falling on his tent while he slept in his armour. Part of the mythology surrounding Owain stemmed from his supposed ability to control weather by magic. The flash floods which swept away part of Henry's camp on the banks of the Dee were celebrated in verse. Henry's bedraggled army returned to England unsuccessful, for a third time in as many years.[10]

The Welsh victory at Bryn Glas was a watershed moment. In contrast to 1401, where the fog of the conflict left an indistinct picture, after this battle it was clear that the rebels had the upper hand. Although the English administration in Wales did not come crashing to the ground in its immediate aftermath, civilian and military governance began to slide out of control. The last relatively complete records of an English-administered Wales date to the end of September 1402. Even then, many of the records cited to prove effective governance, such as legal records and revenue collection, can give a skewed picture. Judicial sessions held within the confines of an English town in Wales only show that, in reality, the crown's authority extended only over those contained within that urban, fortified area. Revenue collection can also be misleading: in cases where Welsh districts did not pay their taxes, neighbouring English areas such as Herefordshire were expected to meet the revenue shortfall. Even where some revenue was garnered, the lion's share was paid by the English tenants in Wales.[11] Therefore, revenue levels registered in official ledgers appeared healthier than they were. In reality, due to the lack of sustained government support, rebel actions had, in just a few years, rapidly dragged the English administration in Wales towards the point of collapse. Although it would suffer a drawn-out death brought about by many small wounds, the most notable single event which sent a shock wave from the battlefield to the king, passing through society's various strata as it did so, was the battle of Bryn Glas. Adam Usk had left for the continent months before the battle, nevertheless, his colourful commentary continued from afar:

> My heart trembles when I think of this dire blow against English rule inflicted by Owen ... Like another Assyrian, the rod of God's anger, he vented his fury with fire and sword in unprecedented tyrannies.[12]

Likening Owain to the Assyrian, one of whose biblical roles was to punish God's chosen people when they strayed from the righteous path, demonstrates that although traces remain of a time when Adam appeared to favour the rebels, the surviving version of his chronicle put him unequivocally in Henry's camp. The rebels' post-battle campaigning appears modest. Although there is some suggestion that there were attacks on Usk, Caerleon and Newport, far to the south, the firmest evidence, based on clerical taxation figures, suggested a more localised campaign which laid waste to Elfael, the upper Wye valley, the Irfon valley around Builth and possibly encompassed the destruction of Whitney-on-Wye.[13] It seems that having annihilated the army that opposed them, they then destroyed the nearby estates of its leaders. Attacking such a restricted area would demonstrate that the rebels were a well-organised force which operated in short bounds in areas they were able to control, even if only temporarily. In contrast, if Adam Usk were correct and they instead conducted a risky sweep into regions beyond their influence, this might imply that rebel forces were wild and poorly led.

Any notion that Mortimer colluded with Glyn Dŵr prior to the battle appears incorrect, and even its basic premise seems illogical. There is no evidence of pre-campaign contact, and had they been planning to combine forces before his capture, then there was nothing to stop Mortimer from simply joining Owain at any point. The force destroyed by Owain and Rhys Gethin contained many of Edmund's friends, kinsmen and retainers; men he would count on to form an army. Had an alliance between them been in the air before the battle, then killing these potential allies was entirely and painfully counterproductive. Owain's letters plainly sought alliances with other powers and betrayed his need for troops. In the face of Henry IV's striking unwillingness to pay his cousin's ransom, in contrast to that of Lord Grey, it is unsurprising that Mortimer eventually joined forces with Glyn Dŵr. Henry was aware of the arguably superior Mortimer claim to England's throne, having a potential rival removed by his enemy was likely desirable as well as convenient. By marrying Owain's daughter, Catrin, on 30 November, 1402, Edmund Mortimer performed a common cultural act which signified the sealing of an alliance.

It is convenient to use Bryn Glas as a milestone, even though other factors contributed to the results apparently revealed by its outcome. Remarkably, after this point, Welsh forces were able to increase and sustain their campaign efforts beyond the traditional summer fighting season. For perhaps three years after, they campaigned at an increased tempo throughout the year, including the winter, which was unusual for the period. While this might attract accolades concerning their campaigning fortitude and determination, more importantly, this shows that they were organised, competently led, prepared, supplied and they were implementing a strategy. While their actions were still closer to guerrilla warfare tactics of unseen manoeuvre, sudden attack and withdrawal, rather than the more conventional methods of the time, such as presenting their forces in distinguishable units on a battlefield, analysis of their methods reveals that the Welsh were operating according to a plan. Although the conflict shape continued to resemble that of an insurgency, it had clearly evolved from the previous years of localised, uncoordinated attacks by disparate groups. By this stage, the insurgents' campaign aims seemed clearer and increasingly cohesive; they appeared intent on defeating English rule in Wales and governing areas themselves. Although the term 'nation' is tainted by modern political overtones, from this period, the rebels began to exert a dominant, though not entirely decisive, influence over all Welsh-speaking areas and most of the Englishries too. In effect, the insurgents were establishing a territory. Despite examples of a miniscule number of individuals and their relatives who sided with their traditional employers, such as those Welshmen who served in garrisons, there was no significant native opposition to the revolt. For these reasons, the revolt could be described as a national movement, although this should be understood through its military and economic ramifications, rather than through a modern political lens. Bryn Glas offers a measurable point from which it can be seen that the majority of the Welsh were at least tacit supporters of the rebellion, with a smaller but significant number willing to bear arms. Once again, widespread support among the populace combined with an element willing to fight are features common to insurgency warfare.

The year 1402 proved to be a difficult one for Henry IV. In Wales, his authority was crumbling and the rebels held some of his commanders hostage. The fact that he readily raised ransoms for Grey and Clanvowe, but bluntly refused to effect the release of his higher-ranked cousin, Mortimer, likely caused murmurings among England's nobles. Personality politics are a key feature of relationships of power, they heighten the stresses on loyalty, particularly on those to the king. With Mortimer, Henry's behaviour displayed his concept of the value of his nobles. In so doing, Henry created boundaries which were likely to provoke loyalty issues and make enemies, as well as causing many to clamour for the king's goodwill. While his abandonment of Mortimer helped to depower that generation of the dynasty, it also contributed to the provocation of others, such as the Percys, to turn against the king. In addition to his forces meeting repeated defeats and failures in Wales, the rebels had, by this early stage, already caused significant destruction in the English border counties, with Herefordshire and Shropshire bearing the brunt of the pressure. The king was losing face in Wales and in England; a situation which would strengthen his enemies.

During the summer, a large force of Scots launched a plundering attack into north-eastern England. In mid-September, English forces under both Henry Percys confronted them as they returned towards the border. The battle of Homildon remains one of Scotland's heaviest defeats, with its army annihilated and a significant proportion of the force's nobility captured. The Percy victory was assisted by the collusion of the Scottish earl of March, George Dunbar, then living in exile under Henry IV's protection. Dunbar had also led English troops to victory in a skirmish with the Scots at Nesbit Moor in June that year and the major defeat sustained at Homildon further undermined Scots' power. They were already weak under the ailing king, Robert III, and divided by the aggressive politicking of his brother and occasional regent, Robert Stewart, duke of Albany. Superficially, the reduction of the Scots might seem positive for Henry IV; however, the strengthening of the Percys, in terms of prowess and fortune, at the expense of an ailing adversary who posed no existential threat to Henry's crown, appeared problematic. Henry signalled his intended method of enforcing his authority over the Percys by removing the Scottish hostages from them without recompense, when they could have reasonably expected rich reward for their victory.[14] Over the course of the year, Henry also deepened the rift with significant elements of the French court. The previous summer he had finally returned Richard's juvenile queen, Isabella, to her father, King Charles VI. Many at the French court were outraged at Henry's treatment of a French princess and considered Henry's retention of her substantial dowry as highly dishonourable, even tantamount to theft. Her uncle, Louis, duke of Orleans, complained to Henry by letter, demanding satisfaction by duel. Henry's responses appear haughty, insulting and, ultimately, dismissive. He declined battle, principally on the grounds that as a king he didn't even have to speak to a duke, let alone fight him. Although derided by a French chronicler, the exchange of letters was far more than an insignificant spat with a French royal.[15] Henry and Louis had been close enough to form an alliance during his exile at the French court in 1398. Louis, King Charles's brother, was the head of a powerful courtly faction and, by 1402, he was becoming ascendant in his power struggle against the House of Burgundy for control of the government. Henry's abrasive methods would help reignite the long-running conflict with France, with Louis as the catalyst on the French side.

Events arising before the end of the year brought no relief from domestic pressure. With the king's permission, Henry Percy, earl of Northumberland, conducted negotiations with Edmund Mortimer while he was held by Owain. Percy's communiqué on the matter revealed a shrewd Glyn Dŵr, who was fully aware of English political events, but who was also tractable towards peace. Owain was clearly open to negotiations with Northumberland and other nobles under the protection of treaty, but he was unwilling to speak with those who had claimed he intended to destroy the English language. Mentioning that accusation demonstrated that Owain knew of the parliamentary session and other occasions where he was so accused. He also denied the damage and thefts attributed to him, and set his price for peace: restoration to that which was considered justly his. By failing to act on Owain's appeal, Henry squandered that opportunity to end the Welsh rebellion, or at least, Glyn Dŵr's role in it, in late 1402.[16]

In the face of abandonment by his king, Edmund Mortimer had to seek terms with his captor. It is easy to understand why he joined Owain; his life depended on it. Edmund married Catrin, Owain's daughter, and wrote a letter to his friends among the border gentry, explaining his actions and attempting to subvert their loyalties. Mortimer's letter said that Owain had persuaded him to take up his cause which focused on three key issues, namely, the restoration of King Richard if he were still alive, the installation of Edmund's nephew as king if Richard were dead, and to give Owain 'his right' in Wales. He listed a swathe of border estates which had fallen to the rebels and asked the readers not to invade these areas but to supply them at the prices they would charge Mortimer; clearly, he had declared his estates as rebel. He asked for a reply and dated the letter 13 December, stating that it was written in Maelienydd. Couching his appeal for support in pro-Ricardian terms was likely to find support among those who still held sympathies for the late king. There were numerous rumours that Richard was still alive during the early years of Henry IV's reign, these proved durable enough to prompt Henry V to exhume Richard in 1413. This solemn, public honouring and reburial in Westminster Abbey demonstrated that Richard was dead.[17] Mortimer's letter stated that his nephew should replace Henry as king, presumably appealing to Mortimer loyalists, as well as any who disapproved of Henry's regicide. This was a point of debate because the Mortimers were, in the eyes of many, the heirs to Richard's throne by right of descent; their immediate royal ancestor, Lionel of Antwerp, was closer to the throne than Henry's connection through John of Gaunt's line. In riposte, Henry's supporters advocated that the Mortimer claim was void because their ultimate connection to royal blood came through a female line, whereas Henry's was through direct male descent. However, since the Plantagenet claim to the throne of France depended on a claim through a female line, this was a difficult argument to sustain. Therefore, Henry was proclaimed as king through right of conquest, which his adversaries could only challenge through conflict. Mortimer's letter made a conveniently vague point about Owain having 'his right' in Wales. While this likely only referred to the restoration of his estates and inheritance, it could retrospectively be applied to all of Wales. During prior negotiations with Northumberland's envoys, Owain only asked for restoration to that which was his by right. It seems reasonable to contend that this was the limit of his territorial ambition at that stage; no mention was made of any claim to be prince of Wales in any of these exchanges. The Glyn Dŵr–Mortimer alliance offered Owain avenues into the circles of the English nobility which subsequent events would suggest that he sought to exploit.[18]

The issue of the hostages and their ransoms is significant in assessing the behaviour of King Henry and Owain. By selecting who Henry would rescue and who he would not, Henry was clearly dividing his nobles. While this might lead many to seek his grace and favour, it would also, inevitably, alienate others. How Henry dealt with those elements of society would help define the course of his reign. It seems reasonable to assert that this led many to question their loyalties and position in England's social order, and indeed, where the king was leading the country. In the case of Mortimer, by refusing to pay his ransom, Henry alienated those of his supporters who chose not to abandon him. The fact that Hotspur was married to Mortimer's sister would further aggravate tensions with the Percys; denuding them of their Scottish hostages and a number of their lucrative titles and commands would steer that relationship towards its calamitous ending on the battlefield. It is difficult to know whether Henry engineered the rift with the Percys; to credit him with such a political ploy might be too much. However, as winter turned to spring 1403, the Percys and the crown were on a collision course.

CHAPTER FOUR

Owain, Prince

Greetings and love. We inform you that we hope to be able, by God's help and yours, to deliver the Welsh race from the captivity of our English enemies, who, for a long time now elapsed, have oppressed us and our ancestors. And you may know from your own perception that, now, their time draws to a close and [as] to the ordinance of God from the beginning, success turns towards us, no one need doubt a good issue will result, unless it be lost through sloth or strife.[1]

Reports of insurgent pressure on English border areas continued throughout 1403. Places which were relatively unscathed beforehand suddenly became conflict flashpoints. The town of Hope near the Cheshire border was burned on 22 February 1403; further south, English border communities in Shropshire came under rebel pressure. The government sought to implement a two-faceted strategy of defence and attack, but with the weight of its efforts focusing on the former. The authorities strove to hold the periphery: the border and coastal castles. As a countermeasure to rebel pressure on the frontier, garrisons in key frontline castles such as Montgomery and Flint were significantly reinforced. The government's focus on defence was doubtless because it had no intention of relinquishing the lands it formerly controlled, but found that it was unable to hold more at that point. Although the interior seems to have been largely lost to the rebels even by this point, the remaining castles afforded the crown a continued presence, a measure of credibility over the English population in Wales and, perhaps, the castles would offer potential future points of entry. Constables of the key fortresses in the north and west, Caernarfon, Beaumaris, Harlech and Aberystwyth, wrote of their plight as these pillars of crown authority came under rebel pressure. Harlech had to be rescued by a 1,300-strong army in early June and news came that Aberystwyth was also under siege.[2] The crown's offensive plans for Wales saw the sixteen-year-old Prince Henry given an army of around 3,000 soldiers in April, along with a key command position which would allow him to range throughout Wales. In May, his forces crossed the border and burned Glyn Dŵr's houses at Sycharth and Glyndyfrdwy, and then replenished garrisons in north Wales. Some evidence suggests that the king had proclaimed havoc throughout Wales – a command approving the plundering and destruction of the land in an indiscriminate fashion. These destructive, scouring attacks on Wales likely provoked more to side with the rebels, but also signified that the land was lost to the crown, for they would not destroy their own estates.

Before the end of June, reports described a muster of substantial rebel forces at the head of the Tywi valley in mid-west Wales. Radnor garrison was reinforced to protect the border should the rebels cross into England. Instead, they struck south-west, with Owain at the head of an army reportedly 8,240-strong. Southern castle constables detailed the oncoming army, its successes and its leaders. Many of the leading nobles of south Wales joined Owain for this campaign. The foremost of those named in Owain's company were Rhys Gethin, Henry Don, who came with his son, and one of several men named Rhys Ddu (Rhys the Black) who followed Owain, one of whom had served as the sheriff of Cardiganshire and, in line with his duties as such, would have been experienced in mustering and marshalling the county's armed forces. In addition, several other prominent Welsh landowners were also named in Owain's entourage. He also counted among his captains Rhys ap Gruffydd (ap Llywelyn Foethus) and Siancyn ap Llywelyn who had been appointed constables of Dryslwyn and Newcastle Emlyn respectively before joining the rebels. Castle commanders also wrote that all of the commons of the region flocked to Owain.[3] The remarkable fact is that Welsh leaders from south Wales, in this case, came to Owain, even those who had taken an oath to the king. While some joined willingly, some were summoned. As well as writing to foreign leaders, Owain also wrote to his Welsh peers. Although it seems likely that he wrote other letters, now lost, an example of such correspondence has survived. Although undated, the contents of this letter to Henry Don of Kidwelly suggest that it was a call to join Owain on the march to Carmarthen.

Greetings and love. We inform you that we hope to be able, by God's help and yours, to deliver the Welsh race from the captivity of our English enemies, who, for a long time now elapsed, have oppressed us and our ancestors. And you may know from your own perception that, now, their time draws to a close and [as] to the ordinance of God from the beginning, success turns towards us, no one need doubt a good issue will result, unless it be lost through sloth or strife. And because all the Welsh race is in doubt and dread as to the subjection, which we have heard is within the intention of your enemies aforesaid against them, we command, require and entreat, that you will be sufficiently prepared to come to us with the greatest force possible, to the place that you hear that we are, burning our enemies, by destroying them during the march, and this, by divine aid, shall take place shortly. And do not forget this, as you would wish to have your freedom and honour in the future. And be not surprised that you have not had warning of the first rising, because from great apprehension and danger, it suited us to rise without fore-warnings.

By Yweyn ap Gruffuth, Lord of Glyn Dyfrdwy.[4]

Although the external address to Henry Don was in French, the body of the letter was written in Latin. This is a remarkable letter for numerous reasons. First, this resembles an array summons issued by a king, calling to arms his nobles and their retainers. At this point, Owain evidently felt strong enough to command the loyalty of Welsh nobles. This was plainly a challenge to royal authority and the fact that numerous Welsh leaders served Owain indicates that they recognised that Owain's power eclipsed that of Henry in that time and place.

The letter contains elements found in Owain's other letters. God was invoked on three occasions and 'the Welsh race' twice. The latter is noteworthy, for Owain was obviously addressing another Welshman and emphasising that connection. This is clear evidence that a communal bond, if not a sense of nationhood, existed among the Welsh in this age. There are strongly emotive aspects in this letter, typical of Owain's style, which touch on the theme of the Welsh. Owain wrote of delivering the Welsh from captivity and oppression, adding that their people were in dread of being subjected again by their enemies. This suggests a common perception that they believed themselves already freed. His references to saving the people are also noteworthy, because this implies that these were men who cared for those they led. The powerful combination of God and the fate of their people makes a compelling appeal. However, this was not a wistful appeal to prophecy or nostalgia, it was seated in their present. Owain referred to his previous successes and declining English power in Wales: 'you may know from your own perception ... their time draws to a close ... success turns towards us.' It also calls Henry Don to join Owain on the march that was about to happen; the most obvious corresponding event was the campaign along the Tywi valley. Owain also explained that his previous attacks had been conducted without warning out of fear; however, by his time, he was able to announce the campaign beforehand. Although secret movements and surprise attacks are standard fare for guerrilla conflicts, this is another indication that his power had increased. As with Owain's other letters, the aggression is unmistakeable. The imagery of oppression and captivity is perhaps understandable, but his drive to succeed is clear, as was the belief that they would win unless their position was lost 'through sloth or strife'. So, this was a call for unity as well as a call to arms, he was clearly attempting to build something tangible that required obedience and collective action; this could be interpreted as a movement, a war or a state. He also wrote of 'burning' and 'destroying' their enemies in conflict. However, the final section was undoubtedly a thinly veiled threat to Henry: 'do not forget this, as you would wish to have your freedom and honour in the future.' This letter bears the classic hallmarks of Glyn Dŵr's style; intelligently reasoned, evoking the divine, using emotive imagery, repetition and aggression to deliver a decisively clear message. Henry Don's presence on campaign implies that he understood the message, and obeyed.

Owain's army marched down the Tywi valley, besieging the castles of the region, taking some by force, others by less conventional means, such as bribery. They made for the town and castle of Carmarthen, the English administrative capital of south Wales, and by far the largest English borough in Wales, and took it by storm, with notable losses reported among the defenders. They plundered the town and then burned it, before continuing with other sieges and pillaging the region. Owain was said to have lodged in St Clears and then Laugharne, before destroying both areas. Although it is possible that he parleyed with Lord Carew, or his representatives, the idea that Carew engaged the of them in battle and killed 700 rebels appears implausible. There is no corroborating evidence, either in folklore or official records, nor any known or rumoured mass grave, as at Bryn Glas. Owain's reportedly huge forces did not seek vengeance, either at the time or in 1405 when he returned to the area with a joint Welsh–French expeditionary army. If true, Carew's victory would have been welcomed, lauded even, yet no accolades or rewards came to him as a result. While he might have caused a local soothsayer to influence Owain against advancing into Pembrokeshire, in reality, Carmarthen was the probable campaign goal. English evidence describes Welsh forces returning to lay siege to the castles in the Tywi valley after they had sacked Carmarthen. Therefore, it seems safer to conclude that the rebels gathered at a given place and advanced, attacking or surrounding castles in their path. Once they had taken Carmarthen, they returned along their proven route and further prosecuted sieges there before dispersing near where they mustered.[5]

The summer campaign of 1403 marked two impressive articulations of Owain's power. First, he exerted himself over the nobles of south Wales, summoning them to join him on campaign. While some certainly joined him willingly, the letter to Henry Don demonstrated that Owain would reason with and, if necessary, threaten his nobles to ensure obedience, mirroring other rulers of the day. However, they were his nobles to command. While this was not accurate for all Welsh nobles, it was true for a number sufficient for Owain to raise and command significant armies, capable of mounting conventional operations such as that of 1403. Secondly, this campaign demonstrated to all that Owain was able to muster considerable power and bring down his mailed fist onto the centre of English governance in a region not previously considered to be under his influence. Carmarthen had the largest English population in Wales, yet Owain had conquered it and laid waste to the surrounding region: all could see who held power in Wales. Victory in open battle at Bryn Glas and this campaign, where a region's castles and its capital were besieged and taken, demonstrated that Owain was expanding the bounds of his influence and that he was evolving strategically. The impact of Owain's rise was felt far afield, with one monk in St Albans writing: 'Christ, Splendour of God, I beseech you, destroy Glyndŵr.'[6]

A week after Glyn Dŵr's men sacked Carmarthen, but while they were still campaigning in the region, Henry Percy junior rebelled against Henry IV. While Hotspur appears to have treated Owain with due respect during negotiations, there is no proven alliance between Owain and the Percys at this stage of the conflict. One chronicle believed that Owain distrusted the Percys while others suspected collusion. It seems probable that Hotspur knew something of Owain's movements and would have known that his presence in the Percy camp was extremely unlikely, even if some unknown agreement existed between them. Although some Welshmen appear to have joined Hotspur's troops, to assume that Owain had sent them would be to side with the narrative that all Welshmen were Owain's to command and that all Welshmen were rebels and traitors.[7] They probably came from areas under Percy control or were rebels from adjacent areas who had not joined Owain that summer, as such, they might have been 'Owain's men' from previous seasons. In reality, the Percy rising was another example of English noble disaffection with the new king. Henry IV moved against the Percy revolt immediately and battle was joined on 21 July 1403, just outside Shrewsbury. Although both sides sustained casualties in the low thousands, the royalists eventually won the day and engaged in a bloody pursuit of fleeing Percy forces. Hotspur was killed on the field. His uncle, Thomas Percy, defected to the rebels on the day of the battle, but was captured in the defeat. On seeing his nephew's corpse, burst into tears declaring that he no longer cared what fate awaited him. He suffered a traitor's death two days later, being publicly hanged, drawn and quartered, and his head was set on London Bridge. Hotspur's corpse was also quartered and sent to Bristol, London, Newcastle and Chester. His head was placed on a spike on York's north gate where his supporters and kinsmen would see it. The king's actions denoted a personal, vengeful aspect to his style; the Percys had been among Henry's closest supporters in exile and during his revolt against Richard. Professionally, Thomas Percy had served as Seneschal, the king's Lieutenant in south Wales and Admiral of the North. He was also intimately connected with Henry as king; he had not only been Prince Henry's tutor, but he had also escorted Queen Isabella back to France in 1401 and brought Henry IV's new wife, Joanna, from Brittany to England in early 1403. While clearly intelligent and politically adept, Henry IV evidently inspired disloyalty in some and proved willing to kill any of his subjects, even those close to him. Loyalist losses were also heavy at Shrewsbury, with perhaps more than 3,000 killed. Among the notables killed were the earl of Stafford and Sir Walter Blount, the royal standard bearer. Of more concern for the king, Prince Henry, the future Henry V, sustained a significant wound after being shot in the face with an arrow. Prince Henry's wound was sufficient to remove him from the Welsh theatre for over a year and must have left a notable scar.[8]

While the king consolidated his hold on power in England in the wake of his crushing victory over the Percys, the insurgency in Wales continued unabated. At the beginning of August, after months spreading seditious rumours, insurgent infiltrators and spies caused anglicised and settled Flintshire to declare itself for the rebels. The area's inhabitants rose, laying siege to Flint, Hawarden and Rhuddlan. The insurgents burned the English towns in Flintshire and also struck across the border into Shropshire. Here, and elsewhere in the English border counties, the inhabitants made truces with the Welsh. Richard Kingston, a confidant and advisor to King Henry, wrote from Hereford describing one such cross-border raid and how the Welsh had attacked despite there being a truce in force. He and numerous others pleaded with Henry for troops to protect them and feared that the land, Herefordshire, was lost to the rebels. In mid-August, the Welsh of Kidwelly fired the district and unsuccessfully assaulted the castle, causing notable casualties among its defenders. King Henry finally responded to the pleas of his constables and burgesses by embarking on his fourth expedition to Wales in as many years. As with his previous tours, this one also became little more of a procession of the flag. On this occasion, the destination was Carmarthen, where Henry needed to restore his authority after the town had fallen to the Welsh during the summer. He bolstered the garrison, leaving a substantial force of over 500 cavalry there in order to subdue and stabilise the area. After this brief, fruitless incursion into Wales, Henry again returned without a battle, capture or victory to tout. Since he led the army himself, this was a further personal failure; his record against the Welsh was humiliating. As Henry's forces were dispersing to their home counties, the rebels surged back into action, conducting widespread localised attacks across Wales. Moreover, they mounted frequent, sustained raids across the English border, with Prince Henry reporting that the Welsh carried sufficient provisions for a two-week cross-border operation, assuming that they did not resupply themselves in that time. This denotes a well-developed scheme of operations; the Welsh had evidently devised, prepared and executed a campaign plan, and had suitably efficient logistics to adequately equip them.

In response, Henry restructured his command group for Wales. Edward, duke of York, was given lieutenancy over south Wales, while the earl of Warwick and Lord Audley were stationed in strategically important Brecon. Although replacing commanders and reorganising his forces were understandable actions, Henry was simply repeating the same, previously ineffective strategy. Rebel forces adhering to the insurgents' maxim that persistence outlasts resistance would likely welcome such a comparatively inert, defensive opponent; at some point the defenders would likely break. One element of Henry's strategy sensibly aimed at cutting the enemy's supply lines. Legal restrictions were placed on English merchants preventing them from providing the Welsh with the basics required for sustenance and warfare, from grain to armour. The Welsh responded in a different fashion, but one which similarly affected English supplies and provisions. They took food and burned the crops and villages on the English side of the border, devastating the countryside, lessening its utility in food production and potential for tax revenue. A further aspect of the king's plan for Wales focused on maintaining garrisons there by supporting them from neighbouring English counties. South Wales's coastal castles were resupplied from Bristol, Somerset and Devon, Brecon and Hay were supported by Hereford and Worcester, the northern castles received relief from Chester, and the English in Ireland also played a role, notably on Anglesey. This aspect of warfare, the denial of food to the enemy, was not solely prosecuted between the Welsh and the English. This year, the French refused to sell wheat to Henry's envoy, the earl of Pembroke, noticing that England's harvests had been weak, causing famine.[9]

The rebels again laid siege to a number of the key castles in Wales, obliging the crown to relieve Beaumaris and Cardiff by sea in autumn 1403. This denotes intelligent strategising by the rebels. Applying pressure, however light, on multiple sites, achieved a number of aims. First, each attack provoked a reaction from the defenders who reported it and often simultaneously called for help from the government. This put additional pressure on the crown to respond or to risk, at best, falling morale and a dent in its reputation if it failed to react swiftly, at worst, inaction risked the loss of a town or castle. However, the government could not respond quickly to all requests for help; summoning, arraying and moving forces was a slow business and the rebels knew that. In addition, armies were expensive to keep in the field therefore, due to the tight budgets of the period, the government had to prioritise where it sent its forces. Since they likely lacked the manpower to take and hold all of the sites they were attacking, the rebels appeared to be testing the government's response. When stretched financially and militarily for a long period, exploitable gaps appeared in the government's defensive plan for Wales, as subsequent Welsh victories would reveal. Rebel successes demonstrated that they had an effective strategy which was being implemented by capable commanders. Most of the Welsh captains had served in English armies for years and were doubtless aware of the crown's likely responses. As well as being experienced in the conventional warfare of garrisons, sieges, troop movement and supply, they evidently understood the version of insurgency warfare that existed in their age: their successes prove their efficiency in this area. Before the end of 1403, cracks began to appear in the morale of some of the larger forces posted to Wales. From Carmarthen, the earl of Somerset reported that his men would not stay in Wales 'for anything in the world' for even one day longer than their agreed contract. Similarly, the duke of York begged for enough money to keep his troops in place. Orders were issued to Henry's principal commanders along the border to organise the defence of the March and its towns against an invasion by the Welsh. The government's forces were failing to overcome the rebels and their morale was evaporating, there was no doubt, the rebels were winning.[10]

In early October, the Welsh, led by Henry Don, again attacked Kidwelly; significantly, this time he did so in concert with French and Breton troops. This demonstrates that, unseen, Glyn Dŵr had opened a diplomatic channel to France and Brittany and it had clearly borne fruit. Although the attack failed, the insertion of French and Breton troops into south-west Wales was a small but significant coup for the rebels, as well as for the Orleanists at the French court who increasingly advocated war against Henry. The engagement of continental powers and their troops elevated this conflict to becoming another theatre of the Hundred Years' War. The modest foreign forces which joined Henry Don's attack on Kidwelly provided the French with first-hand intelligence on the condition of the rebellion and demonstrated the logistical realities of investing a force into Wales. It also marked an expansion in the use of the sea as a diplomatic and a battle space. French troops had never before landed in Wales and, while that door had been opened by Glyn Dŵr, this event was realised by the hawks who were gaining power in the French court. This small-scale landing near Kidwelly might seem inconsequential to the casual observer; however, it was a significant step which would result in a formal treaty and the arrival of a substantial French expeditionary army in subsequent years.[11] On 3 October 1403, the constable of Kidwelly wrote a letter which arrived in London via Bristol. It revealed that:

Henry Don and all the rebels of south Wales, aided by the men of France and Brittany, are advancing on the castle with all their power. They have destroyed all the corn of your subjects in the countryside all around the castle. Many of the townsmen of Kidwelly have fled to England with their wives and children; the rest have retreated into the castle and are in great fear of their lives.[12]

If proof were needed of the harmful effects of the punitive anti-Welsh laws enacted in 1401, then this siege offered but one example. Kidwelly's steward and receiver, William Gwyn ap Rhys Lloyd and Gwilym ap Philip respectively, were ejected from their posts following the legislation and, in 1403, were part of the joint force which overran the town's defences. Numerous burgesses were killed in the assault, others fled to England by boat, while many raced to the castle for refuge and no doubt bolstered the garrison. The walled town was lost up to the castle gates and the scenario must have impacted on both sides: the rebels stood before the imposing and resolutely defended castle, while those within looked out upon their town in flames, their possessions ransacked, their houses destroyed and several of their number killed by forces containing men they knew. Kidwelly's law court, the Shirehall, was destroyed by fire. While this was practical for the rebels, since all of its legal and other records were consumed by the flames, it was also a symbolic refutation of English law. While the constable's letter showed that the French and the Bretons were present, it also revealed that they and the rebels had targeted and destroyed the region's food stores. The fear palpable in the letter also gives a feel for the psychological effects of war, often difficult to gauge over the distance of the centuries.

The siege was raised as winter set in, with the French and Bretons probably keen to make the crossing before the worst of the winter storms arrived. Although an unsuccessful attack, the extant records offer a snapshot of the situation in this one part of Wales, where the action was certainly less intense than elsewhere. In due course, the defenders received relief, reinforcements and cannon sent by London, although their lives in Kidwelly likely became increasingly miserable. Their salvation came across the water from Bristol because the surrounding countryside was hostile and lost to Owain, who took oaths from the men of the area. This is precisely the sort of behaviour expected of a ruler, and Owain can be seen throughout 1403 as conducting himself as the major power in the land – summoning nobles to serve him on campaign and taking oaths of allegiance from the people. The fact that they attended his summons, swore oaths to him and fought for him shows that for many of the Welsh, Owain was the power they obeyed: he was their prince.[13]

If his actions in Wales implied that a project to govern was being enacted then he would need to communicate with foreign powers, as would any other prince. November 1403 provided a further example of unseen diplomatic connections, before a far greater diplomatic statement came the following year. Although the pope had granted him the right to appoint a confessor in the hour of death in 1397, in November 1403 this was increased to the ability to have full remission of his sins as often as he pleased.[14] While this is far from unique to Owain, this augmenting of his spiritual allowances while in revolt against a major power faithful to Rome shows a mild form of recognition and implied approval, rather than condemnation. It is almost certain that Owain's ambassadors asked for more than they overtly received, but the details of their mission and the discussions they held remain unknown.

The closing months of 1403, November and December, saw Cardiff, Aberystwyth and Harlech under siege again. The insurgents continued the varied rhythm of applying pressure on the crown's static presences, the towns and castles, as well as launching surprise attacks around Wales and, notably, across the border. This was sustained through the early months of 1404 and denotes the rebel ability to continue through the depths of winter, which was atypical for the period. The authorities responded in their usual fashion by bolstering the garrisons of the key border castles, such as Radnor, Welshpool and Bishopscastle, and sending relief columns when propitious. However, for the rebels, 1404 would prove to be even more momentous than previous, increasingly successful years. During the year, key ecclesiastical defections bolstered Owain's council and entourage. The rebels were joined by John Trefor, the bishop of St Asaph who had put Glyn Dŵr's case before a scornful parliament in 1400, and Lewis Byford, the Roman bishop nominate of Bangor. In addition, Gruffydd Yonge, the gifted academic, along with significant numbers of grassroots clergy aligned themselves with the rebels. Yonge was appointed as Owain's Chancellor and bishop of Bangor and, such was his diplomatic prowess, his career continued in the service of France after the Welsh rebellion ended. Later evidence would show that the ecclesiastic and chronicler, Adam Usk, also sided with Owain at this point, but sought reintegration into Henry's favour as the revolt waned.

He wrote the bulk of his chronicle many years later and the extant version reflects his Henrician allegiance. However, before the end of the year, Glyn Dŵr had a significant corpus of clergymen at his disposal. Not only were priests engaged at all levels of society in administering holy service and other church functions, including the influencing of their congregations, they were also literate and able to form the sort of embryonic civil service needed to construct and administer a state.[15]

Militarily, Welsh forces appeared to conduct at least three campaigns during the year. At some point during 1404, the rebels took and garrisoned the fortresses of Aberystwyth and Harlech, and therein established the urban centres critical for this rebellion to transform itself from a rural revolt into a new state. In the south, the region around Haverford in the far south-west fell to the rebels. In the south-east, Cardiff was taken, sacked and burnt, and Coity was besieged. The contest for the rich southern coastal strip was going the way of the rebels, although the crown would not abandon the region entirely. The third campaign had perhaps the greatest psychological impact on the enemy. Rebel forces crossed into the three English border counties, with little to stop them, as well as laying siege to key border castles, such as Montgomery. Records from all three, Cheshire, Shropshire and Herefordshire, demonstrate significant destruction was wrought by Welsh forces pillaging throughout the region. The fact that Welsh forces were prepared and able to conduct forays into England was nothing new; they had done so with increasing frequency since the outbreak of the rebellion. However, the fact that the government was powerless to avert Welsh incursions, or subsequently prevent border communities asking the Welsh for truces and paying them to avoid further ravaging, demonstrated that it was the rebels who exerted most power in the borders at that time. Owain did not lead all of these sieges and attacks, therefore, he must have had a number of capable leaders under his command.[16]

Within a similar timeframe, throughout 1403 and early 1404, French, Breton and Castilian forces were particularly aggressive in the Channel region. During these ventures Dartmouth was taken and burned by the Bretons in early 1404, where one of their most renowned leaders, Guillaume du Châtel, fell in battle on English soil. French troops landed at a number of places along England's Channel coast during the fighting season. In riposte, English fleets took reprisals on Brittany's coastal villages. To all intents, the Bretons were at war with the English, and French forces were increasingly visible in these contests. Significantly, sources recorded

Welshmen among the captured French and Breton forces.[17] Concurrently, a France-based sea captain named Jean d'Espagne attacked Caernarfon and Harlech from the sea in late 1403 and early 1404, landing French troops to assist the Welsh who were laying sieges there.[18] As with the attack on Kidwelly, such co-operation cannot have happened without prior agreement and most probably with guidance from men familiar with those waters and lands. This second landing of French troops in Wales, this time in the north, reveals that the French were increasingly interested in Wales.

As a truce was technically still in place between England and France, the French attacks bore no official endorsement. However, it seems highly unlikely that they sailed without covert sanction. Given the strength of the French and the Bretons, it would obviously be beneficial for Glyn Dŵr to win their friendship. Breton ducal financial accounts for this period teasingly reveal names such as 'frère Jehan Davise' and 'Madoc Houel', any of whom could have assisted the forging of links between Wales, Brittany and France. Certainly, Madoc Howell was to reappear in French records in the years to come as an Orleanist loyalist.[19]

Jean d'Espagne's voyages would certainly have imparted to the French important logistical information on the scale of the tasks faced in Wales. They would also have been aware of the distances and hazards between their home ports and possible target areas. In addition, they had experienced the speed and size of the English naval response to threats in the west. It is notable that ships from Bristol had unsuccessfully hounded Jean d'Espagne, for his flotilla appears to have remained in the waters around north Wales for months after, possibly into 1405. It was probably these allied Welsh and French troops who cleared Anglesey of English forces in perhaps one bloody encounter.[20] The substantial intelligence gained from these two early landings would have been of notable value for French fleet preparations in subsequent years.

Prior to the revolt, the prince of Wales's lands yielded a significant amount of money, making Prince Henry, in this case, one of the richest men in England. However, records show that the revenue collected from the prince's lands in Flintshire, north Wales and south Wales had fallen to zero by 1403–4. This was mirrored elsewhere in Wales.[21] Taxation is only one means of measurement, however; other key factors such as obedience and security were equally absent. Although some elements of the English administration in Wales showed flickers of life in the lee of the castle walls, effectively, across the rest of the country, it was dead. The significance of the fact that, for the first time in over a century, most of this revived Wales was once again led by a native Welshman should not be underestimated.

As the crown's ability to govern gradually collapsed, Owain appeared to increasingly fill the void. Initially, this appeared to be informal, as the letter to Henry Don showed; Owain summoned nobles to him on a seemingly ad hoc basis. By mid-1404, that would become a more formal governmental arrangement. It should be noted though, that the English presence in Wales was still significant, even if it had been substantially reduced. The English-held castles and towns along the border and the northern and southern coastlines guaranteed an ongoing presence, but their role had largely been reduced to one of observation and static defence. This marks a historically significant moment, for a people had overcome the technology designed to constrain them. The castle system in Wales had been constructed to hold down the natives, but this revolt had defeated their purpose, long before the development and prolif-eration of effective gunpowder weaponry rendered them finally useless militarily. It is impossible to know when Owain and his commanders conceived the notion, but by this stage, it had probably dawned on them that an overall military victory over the English was a realistic prospect. The programme of state-building that they undertook shortly afterwards certainly supports that. Most regions of Wales were under largely uncon-tested rebel control. The interior seemed secure, so the rebels applied pressure to significant areas on their effective frontier: the Welsh–English border, parts of Pembrokeshire, the south-eastern coast and the isolated garrisons of the north. This is proof of a strategy being directed.

Despite these convincing military successes, it was in the diplomatic domain that Owain scored his greatest victory yet. Within this rebel-held region, Owain convened the first native parliament for centuries at Machynlleth during the summer.[22] Owain held at least two more parlia-ments over successive years: each is a highly significant milestone on Wales's historical timeline. In doing so, Owain was demonstrating to all that he was the main power in the land. Owain held his parliaments at Machynlleth and Harlech, which denotes these places as significant, but not necessarily as capitals; medieval parliaments were held wherever the ruler summoned his nobles. Owain was also able to prepare a document intended to broker an alliance with the French, probably with the assis-tance of his senior ecclesiastical supporters. While this strategy was almost certainly discussed and agreed at the 1404 parliament, it was likely preceded by discussions with French advisors too. To formalise the relationship, Owain sent an ambassadorial mission to France in the early summer of 1404. This was a striking attempt to gain such a powerful ally, and success would seem likely to greatly enhance Owain's prospects. There is no doubt that the reception of Owain's ambassadors was tempered by the rising power of the Orleanist faction, which advocated a more hostile line against Henry IV. Their rise was in part due to successful politicking on the part of their leader, Louis, duke of Orleans, but also aided by the decline and natural death of their main rival at court, the elderly duke of Burgundy, Philippe *le Hardi*, 'the Bold', in April 1404.

Owain, in keeping with his contemporaries, maintained a council.[23] Such a council need not contain a large number of advisors; studies of contemporary Burgundy provide a comparison on the size and functions of such an organisation. During the period in question, the duchy of Burgundy rose to become a significant European state. It has been characterised as powerful beyond its size and having a well-structured government.[24] Although Burgundy was far wealthier than Wales and was composed of a number of different administrative bodies, the number of members sitting at the ducal council and parliaments summoned was small. The duke's 'grand conseil' was made up of just ten members in 1426. The council of Charles the Bold in 1469, when Burgundy was approaching its zenith in terms of its wealth, size and power, only contained a bishop as chancellor, another suitable to stand in his absence, four leading knights, eight 'maîtres des requêtes' and fifteen secretaries and other aides – effectively the duke, fourteen council members and their administrative staff. The 'maîtres des requêtes' were legal specialists empowered to deputise for the chancellor, determine the ruler's rights and powers on issues, as well as to clarify and execute legal matters. Such highly skilled administrators were essential to the legal and governmental machinery of any medieval parliament. Charles's 1473 parliament at Malines, founded on the French parliamentary model, was attended by a total of forty-five people, among whom were two presidents, four knights of the grand council, six 'maîtres des requêtes' and twenty other councillors.[25] There was no connection between Glyn Dŵr and Burgundy, however small states did not require the relatively heavily populated parliaments of England or France. Glyn Dŵr's diplomatic efforts strongly imply the existence of such a government council, and Owain even wrote of such an institution's existence.[26] While the names of some of Glyn Dŵr's counsellors are known, the other members could only be tentatively suggested. Certainly, his first ambassadors to France, Griffith Yonge and John Hanmer, as chancellor and blood relation, can be safely included as part of Owain's equivalent to Burgundy's grand council. Other known ecclesiastical adherents were the two bishops, John Trefor and Lewis Byford, also Hywel Kyffin, dean of St Asaph, Hugh Eddouyer of the Order of Predicants, as well as his court bard or 'prophet', Crach Ffinant.[27] The identities of the lower orders of serving administrative staff remain elusive, although the names of the legally trained clerk, Benedict Comme, and Glyn Dŵr's secretary, Owain ap Gruffydd ap Rhisiart, are known.[28] There are also several prominent candidates to stand as military representatives within Glyn Dŵr's council. Rhys ap Tudor, Henry Don, Rhys Gethin, Hywel Coetmor and Rhys ap Gruffudd were the most prominent soldiers to consistently appear; however, other names also figure throughout the revolt and could equally have been included. Not only did these men and their peers have long years of military experience, but several had been employed as sheriffs, escheators, stewards, receivers, bailiffs and similar roles. This not only meant that they knew the mechanics of raising, mustering and moving troops, but also how to manage estates, from food-related affairs to practical maintenance issues of buildings and the tools and personnel required. They also had practical experience in the running financial and administrative affairs of areas, the enforcement

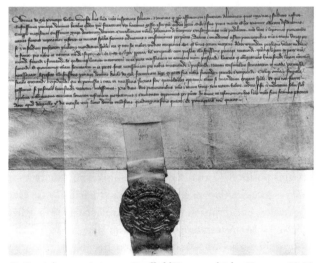

Figure 9 Owain's commission to Gruffydd Yonge and John Hanmer, 10 May 1404. J392. 27.

of laws, including apprehending the wanted, and so on. The stewards and officers of Owain's estates, such as Ednyfed ap Gruffudd and Llywelyn ap Maredudd, also likely played a role in organising and running affairs.[29] Since the promotion of blood connections and nepotism were the normal order of the day, it seems likely that Owain's sons, Gruffydd and Maredudd, his brother, Tudor, as well as members of the Hanmer and the Pulesdon families also had roles, not forgetting Owain's son-in-law, Edmund Mortimer, acting earl of March.[30] A number of these men had attended the English parliament and knew of its composition and functions. Adapting that knowledge to the Welsh context appears a simple task. In addition, the evidence provided by David Whitmore's deception at the Harlech Parliament in 1405 showed that an unknown number of local leaders from across Wales were also invited to attend these parliaments. While this renders impossible a complete presentation of the complement of Glyn Dŵr's council or parliament, this shows that Owain acted entirely in keeping with the norms of his day by summoning representatives of the three estates: the clergy, the nobles and the commons. This was not simply a House of Lords or a gathering of the powerful alone, but a parliament that represented the appropriate sections of its society. Owain consistently appears to conduct his affairs in the appropriate manner for his time and in keeping with other contemporary leaders.[31]

By midsummer 1404, the conflict appeared to some to have been largely won by the Welsh. A Scots chronicler, Walter Bower, commented that God had sided with the Welsh and, with his favour, within three years they had 'expelled all their enemies from Wales' and pushed back their boundaries to those established during the time of Brutus. In August, the communities of Shropshire made a truce with 'the land of Wales', and England's royal council did not oppose the agreement. Wales was a recognisable entity again, and much of it was governed by a native ruler. A number of the castles had been taken or, as the campaigns and sieges of 1403 and 1404 showed, they could be taken, and the remainder were isolated and weak. To secure this position, Owain would need diplomatic victories to match his military successes. He would need allies to help force Henry into conceding Wales, and France was the only regional power which could match England. Owain's attempts to secure an alliance with France would depend not only on his ambassadors' diplomatic talents, but on political currents in France. It was into these turbulent waters that Owain's ambassadorial party sailed, led by Gruffydd Yonge and John Hanmer.[32]

CHAPTER FIVE

The Ambitions of the French Courtly Factions

The diplomatic history of this period is as well-known as it is confusing.[1]

As Glyn Dŵr established himself in Wales following his military successes and his expanding political programme of parliaments and diplomatic efforts, he developed relations with France. The state of contemporary France forms an essential part of the story of the Welsh revolt and the context of these French–Welsh relations were influenced by a number of wider influences. The three most important were the ongoing conflicts between the crowns of England, France and those within their influence or amity, the ecclesiastical schism that began in 1378, and the factional struggles within the French court during the periodically debilitating illness of Charles VI.[2] In addition to the military and ecclesiastical dimensions, there was a strongly political element to this new French–Welsh alliance. The mental infirmity of Charles VI created opportunities for nobles seeking to promote their own positions.[3] The government of France had, by the close of the fourteenth century, become a tug-of-war between factions led by the dukes of court, particularly those of Burgundy and Orleans.[4] Their vying was critical to the events that generated and sustained this Welsh alliance, and ultimately sought to revive it several years after its supposed demise.

French government policy in this period was mediated by the chiaroscuro within the factional struggles of the French court; these have been simplistically portrayed globally as the dispute between Burgundy and Orleans.[5] The latter party became better known as the Armagnacs during the ensuing civil war. The environment in which their well-known dispute grew was far more complex and replete with the subtle consideration and

Figure 10 A royal French golden parade helmet from the reign of Charles VI
shows the level of skill and detail of French helmets similar to the one gifted
to Glyn Dŵr.

balancing of myriad concerns than a simple duel between the heads of two
leading factions. The dominant movement of the time is characterised
as the conflict between the dukes of Orleans and Burgundy. In fact, they
were simply the most overt protagonists. The struggle was for power,
and therefore all elements of the court and government were engaged.
In the first place, while present and alert, the king, Charles VI, was the
undisputed head of state from 1388. His position went unchallenged and
his pronouncements were enacted. However, he was accessible to the
influence and advice of those closest to him; the dukes of court. To define
that close group; his uncles, the dukes of Anjou, Berry and Burgundy, his
maternal uncle, the duke of Bourbon, and his younger brother whom he
made duke of Orleans in 1392 at the age of twenty-one. Within these
groups there was a generally accepted, though little exposed, hierarchy.
For example, Bourbon looked to Anjou as their suzerain below the king.
The other great magnates; the dukes of Brittany, Lorraine and Bar, the

king of Navarre or the southern counts, such as Armagnac and Foix, along with other notable families, were less powerful or engaged in this struggle than the royal dukes. Although all were interconnected in a variety of ways, the lesser families escape further elaboration here.[6]

The governing dukes inevitably sought to secure the king's commands in their favour, which naturally caused competition between them. However, the nature of Charles's illness caused intermittent, unpredictable periods where the king slipped in and out of lucidity, each time for indeterminate periods. This created the innately unstable ground on which the rest of these issues played out. During periods of the king's illness, euphemistically referred to as his 'absences', the dukes directed affairs. Since none had a dominant claim to rule, they competed. Initially, the dukes of Burgundy and Berry ran affairs as they had done in the decade of Charles's minority, with Louis, duke of Bourbon, also playing a role in government. Of these, Philippe the Bold, duke of Burgundy, was dominant despite being younger than Jean, duke of Berry. Although this was perhaps primarily due to his force of character, it was certainly aided by the influence granted by the immense wealth earned from his territorial possessions in Flanders and Burgundy. In theory, Philippe also governed Brittany for a period during the minority of Duke Jean V, which ended on 24 December 1403.[7]

The elevation of the king's brother, Louis, from duke of Touraine to that of Orleans in 1392, and regent designate from 1393, posed a challenge to the contemporary order established by the older dukes. Apart from the county of Soissons, Louis's principal powerbases were west and south of Paris, being also count of Blois, Angoulême and Périgord. This royally proclaimed 'right' to rule, as well as Louis's ambitious personality, made inevitable a conflict for power with those who governed in the king's stead.[8] Later, when the government came under Louis's direction as regent, it undertook other external diplomatic and military activities before and during the years critical to the Welsh alliance. Study of Louis's *modus operandi* before the key years of 1404–5 reveal that he had undertaken other similar strategic endeavours involving the construction of alliances prior to military action and territorial acquisition. Throughout his political career, Louis was a propagator of alliances with noteworthy noble leaders of all ranks. Early in his quest for territory, he cast his eye southwards, to Italy, perhaps to emulate the deeds of his uncle, Louis of Anjou. He acquired a Milanese alliance when he married Valentina Visconti in 1389. With that came the formation of an axis of power between Louis and the duke of

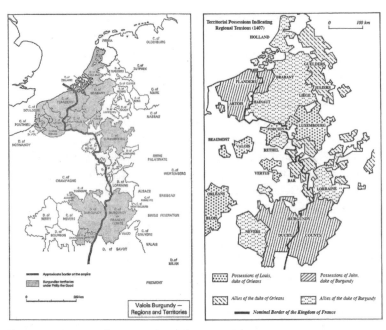

Figure 11 Territorial interests in north-eastern France, circa 1407.

Milan which, after his ascension in 1394, also included Pope Benedict XIII in Avignon. While Louis was not averse to coercing obedience, as witnessed at the submission of Savona in 1394, he evidently enjoyed diplomacy and intrigue. Louis and Valentina drew praise from Christine de Pizan for their wisdom, virtue, their appreciation of learning and science, and for insisting on educating their children. Also, while Henry Bolingbroke was in exile at the French court from 1398–9, Louis and he concluded a secret alliance, extending Louis's interests into England's politics.[9]

For the best part of two decades, Duke Philippe had been the major force in France's government since 1380. He was able to overcome the 'Marmousets', the government of Charles V's royal councillors summoned to rule by Charles VI in 1388, and for much of the next decade he was able to counter and contain the rising influence of the duke of Orleans.[10] By 1398 perhaps, Louis had become a match for his aged uncle, and his attempts to wrest power from Philippe form the basis of the power struggle which, at a certain point, saw the reach of French influence extend to Glyn Dŵr's Wales.

However, the landscape was not simply made up of two power blocks, exemplified by the jigsaw of territories held in eastern and northern France by the dukes of Orleans and Burgundy by 1407. The unmarked lands on the maps of north-eastern France were held by the French crown and other nobles, all of whom had their own interests and ambitions, and were not simply pawns of the two warring houses. The wider-focus map of the region reveals the proximity, even interconnectivity, of the lands of Berry, Bourbon, the German empire, Normandy and Milan, to the areas of focal interest to Burgundy and Orleans. The adherence of territories and nobles was fluid, even those thought to belong to one faction or another. Certain of these acquisitions were either new, such as Louis's purchase of Luxemburg in 1402, or were frequently rebellious and required military suppression, such as Burgundian Flanders.[11] Such territories were at risk of being lost to native elements or prised away by an enemy in a conflict. Equally, since they had their own interests to preserve, allies could not always be counted on. With their own priorities and survival as paramount concerns, they were potentially susceptible to reducing the vigour of their factional support, becoming neutral or perhaps changing allegiance, when faced with seduction or destruction by a powerful faction. The maps of north-eastern France therefore show a snapshot of alliances and power relations at a given time, in a given region, and little more stable can be presumed.

This mosaic of territorial adherences and unstable amities could be redrawn across the whole of France, illuminating the difficulties faced by the protagonists and those who have later sought to describe these events. These shifting allegiances can be characterised by the actions of the other great ducal factions. To take the example of Bourbon and Berry, they can be seen to withdraw amity from the Burgundians for a time after 1407, but then as Philippe's heir, Jean *Sans Peur*, 'the Fearless', seized and controlled the government, and normal governmental processes resumed, for a short period thereafter they engaged with the crown policies he guided.[12] In addition, there were positive military connections between these princes of the blood. Jacques de Bourbon had accompanied Jean, who was count of Nevers at the time, before becoming duke of Burgundy, on the failed crusade that was crushed at Nicopolis in 1396, and Jacques remained within his amity afterwards. In the domestic crisis of late summer 1405, to some degree, the forces of Bourbon and Berry interposed their own troops between those of Orleans and Burgundy to prevent further internecine bloodshed. In so doing, they held the gates of Paris against a feared attack by Orleanist armies, by consequence protecting the Burgundians inside. After Louis's murder by Burgundian agents in 1407, most French nobles sided with the Orleanist faction.[13] However, during the later government of Jean of Burgundy, 1418–19, elements of both ducal branches benefitted from his patronage, and both parties were also 'rebels' against his rule, as Burgundian records described them. Such are the subtle complexities of this subject. Later, when the civil war erupted anew with the murder of Jean, and his successor, Charles, allied himself with England, the dukes became unequivocally opposed to Burgundian policy and evidently took the side of the loyalist forces led by the Armagnacs.[14] Therefore, identifying Berry and Bourbon as necessarily adhering to one faction or the other is simplistic. These families controlled small states of their own within France; they held their own ducal courts, run by their own administrations.[15] Their priorities were, first, to act in their own interests and in those which they perceived most benefitted the government of France. Where their interests conformed to those of the protagonists apparently intent on warring with one another, they are viewed as aligned with that faction. As the conflict played out, the larger part of both families can be identified within the Armagnac camp. However individual figures still made choices; Jacques de Bourbon remained close to Burgundy.[16] To blur the boundaries yet further, military commanders and clerics easily identifiable as adhering to one of the two main factions also worked together on government projects. A good example of this takes the form of the diplomatic agreements and subsequent military co-operation with Owain Glyn Dŵr. Therefore, the opposing factions still functioned together during this period although the dramatic rupture in their relations in November 1407 held serious consequences for the Welsh as well as for the governance of France.[17]

The interests of the other estates can also be seen within this spectrum of nobles vying for dominance. The French church and universities actively debated a remedy to the ecclesiastical trauma of the time, the Great Schism of the Western church, and advanced its preferred solutions. Consensus proved difficult to achieve and maintain, and so that preferred resolution changed throughout the period as church factions also sought supremacy within the ecclesiastical sphere. At times, the opinions of the leading church personalities concurred with those of the temporal princes, which has led to them being labelled as being of one faction or another. To a degree, this is accurate, but as with the dukes of

Bourbon and Berry, the church and the universities can also be seen to act in the interests of the French church and government, as they perceived them at a given moment. Those who held administrative posts within the ducal governments can more safely be issued a firm factional adherence, but most clergymen arguably put the church and the king before their other, lesser, temporal patrons. The ebb and flow of the ecclesiastical arguments at this time gave rise to Gallicanism, an ideology which privileged the needs of the French church and state above papal demands. The merchant classes, particularly in Paris, also made their desires and feelings known, whether through parliamentary protest or violent urban revolt.[18]

Other political currents also affected contemporary government, notably the 'Marmousets' so despised by nobles such as Philippe of Burgundy. The aegis of government by often low-born councillors was anathema to Duke Philippe. Nevertheless, this regime of rational men directing affairs for the benefit of the state, especially its finances, won popularity in some quarters and represented a seismic event in the gradual evolution from whimsical, corrupt governance by the nobility toward the impersonal rule of a modern state run by professional administrators.[19]

In addition, there were two extra-national elements to the factional interplay of the dukes of court. The first involved those matters which the French actively sought and could clearly influence; the second was the movements of the time touching many nations.

French activities beyond their borders during the period 1382–96 reveals the wide extent of their territorial ambitions, which encompassed Flanders, Italy and Scotland, among others. This brought the French into conflict with temporal as well as spiritual powers.

French ducal families married into the equivalent lines of neighbouring countries and so adopted the issues and alignments of their spouses. In some cases these issues were imported right to the heart of French government. Charles VI's bride, Isabeau of Bavaria, was grateful to Philippe of Burgundy for arranging their marriage. This is forwarded elsewhere as the reason for their sharing certain political aims. Isabeau's Bavarian family, the Wittelsbach, were also directly related to Bernabò Visconti, her grandfather, who had been ruler of Milan. Bernabò's nephew, Giangaleazzo Visconti, tricked, seized and deposed Bernabò in a coup d'état in 1385. The new count of Milan, who was eventually made duke, had Bernabò imprisoned where he died shortly after; many of his supporters and sons soon followed him to the grave. In 1389, Louis of

Orleans married Giangaleazzo's daughter, Valentina, thereby creating a conflict at the highest level of French society, even though none of the French had been directly involved in the affair's unravelling.[20]

Flanders was ambiguously connected to both France and England through trade and marriage. Flemish ambassadors had recognised Richard II as their overlord, evidently with their economic and physical security in mind, but France occupied it under the pretext of suppressing a rebellion there in 1382. Urban VI, the Roman pope, issued a papal bull in 1383 legitimising the bishop of Norwich's vain Flanders crusade against the Clementists. Perhaps in riposte, the Avignon pope, Clement VII, proclaimed Duke Louis of Anjou as king of Naples and, in a counterstroke relevant to Glyn Dŵr's later Pennal Declaration, Urban VI declared the new French king in Italy a schismatic and a heretic and proclaimed a crusade against him in January 1384.[21] These actions were the articulation of the regional struggle between France and England, expressed through the pretext of papal legitimacy.

Simultaneously, and for the rest of the 1380s, France pressed its interests in Naples through Louis of Anjou, and then his namesake son, with the support of Clement VII and the Savoyards. This resulted in political manoeuvring and open warfare against the rival claimants, Charles of Durazzo and then his son, Ladislas, who were supported for a time by Urban VI's forces and allies. The central and southern Italian states were consumed with this conflict for the rest of the decade and for some time into the next, although ultimately French ambitions in the south went unsatisfied.[22] This conflict provides a good example of the geopolitical struggles of the time between the stronger temporal powers and their candidates for the papacy, forging alliances with smaller powers in order to achieve political and military victories. These methods and strategies would later embrace Glyn Dŵr and the Welsh rebels.

As well as these areas of historic French involvement, they also developed ambitions in northern Italy following the schism of 1378. The impetus behind this new direction can, to some degree, be attributed to Louis, duke of Orleans.[23] He was a proponent of the *via facti*, seeking a forceful, military solution to the schism. He was also the driving force behind France's entente with Glyn Dŵr; the diplomatic and military contacts took place while his party was ascendant in government, and fit with his aims and methods. Louis's Italian ambitions stemmed from ongoing French interests in Sicily, Naples and Provence. These had been further advanced by his marriage to Valentina Visconti, daughter of the powerful duke of Milan.[24] The French effort to gain territories in Italy during these years was also an extension of the factional struggle between Orleans and Burgundy, with Louis acting in support of the better-established claims in the peninsula of the House of Anjou. The see-sawing of France's inconsistent Italian policy mirrors the frequency with which power changed hands in Paris. The duke of Milan courted French support and involvement in the region in 1392; this resulted in Genoa being designated to the duke's son-in-law, Louis of Orleans, in November 1394. This move deprived Genoa to the Roman pope, who had sought refuge there a few years previously. Louis also made an alliance with neighbouring Montferrat that year, forming a useful regional power bloc. Giangaleazzo, too, appeared content to see his son-in-law settle in Genoa or possibly carve out another kingdom for himself within northern Italy. He was disappointed when Louis sold his rights to the territory early the following year. Genoa was then held by the French government, over which the queen was beginning to exert an increasing influence. Louis had no option but to obey the king's command to sell Genoa.[25]

As the queen and Burgundy exercised their power over the direction of the government, a French alliance was formed with Milan's enemies and a number of indecisive conflicts broke out with Florence, Mantua and other states nominally supported by the French from 1395 onwards. Burgundy was frequently politically connected to Isabeau of Bavaria, Charles VI's queen, whose family bore an enmity towards Valentina's branch of the Visconti. The queen therefore had contrasting transalpine interests to Louis of Orleans, despite the rumours of amorous liaisons between them. Before the end of 1396, the queen had Valentina banished from court on false charges and continued to assist Florence against its enemy, Milan.[26]

The coup by Philippe of Burgundy and Queen Isabeau which thwarted Louis's Genoese ambitions forced him to look elsewhere for possessions. He focused his attention northwards, taking action against those who had revealed their hands in the south. There, between 1398 and 1407, Louis invested his energies and fortune in forging alliances among the lords of north-eastern France and the adjacent regions of the German empire. Strikingly, in 1398, he held a number of closed meetings with the emperor, Wenceslas, and agreed an alliance with him. During this period he also attained the homage of the princes of the region, notably Baden, Cleves, Guelders, Hainault, Lorraine, Nassau, Pont-à-Moussons, Saar,

Saarwerden, Salm, as well as buying Luxemburg and the great lordship of Coucy, from which he also attained homage. Louis showed he had an appreciation for his adversaries' weaknesses, splitting and encompassing Philippe of Burgundy's estates in northern and eastern France. He also remained faithful to Wenceslas in Bohemia and his wife's family in Milan, encompassing in three directions the new emperor, Rupert, who had ousted Wenceslas and who was allied to Philippe and Isabeau. Effectively, this second, eastern, axis of power offered Louis the possibility of moving against his adversaries in the German empire and gave him a stake in imperial affairs; there is evidence to suggest he harboured ambitions towards the imperial crown. These coalitions were no paper tigers. Louis and his partners acted in military concert during 1402–5 and thereafter, pressing their joint interests with diplomatic pressure and military action from Italy to Luxemburg.[27] Within this period, Louis also connected with the Scots and the Welsh, as well as possibly forging links with pro-Ricardian English rebels.[28] Considering his well-practised methods on the continent, his development of friendly contacts with appropriate, willing nobles in Britain resembles an effort to build another league of friendly powers. If Louis were following such a strategic method in Britain as he had used elsewhere, an alliance would be followed by an attack shortly afterwards.

Although the Marmouset-controlled government sponsored a crusade to North Africa under the Bourbons in 1390, by the middle of the decade another such mission was undertaken, but driven by the House of Burgundy. In 1396, it demonstrated its power and religious zeal by raising, sponsoring and, notably, with the blessing of the Roman pope, sending the crusade that ended in disaster at Nicopolis in 1396. At that point no other noble faction could execute such a bold initiative. It is little wonder therefore that Duke Philippe dominated the government and that the solutions favoured by those clerics he patronised, such as Jean Gerson, came to prominence during these years.[29] Nevertheless, in the aftermath of the traumatic defeat at Nicopolis, the French sought Giangaleazzo's aid in securing the return of the French hostages held by the Turks. In the remaining years of the century, a vista of squabbling at the French court can be presented; with the anti-Milanese schemes of Burgundy and the queen being countered by Louis and his allies. Nevertheless, the appointment of Marshal Boucicaut as governor of Genoa in 1401 can be viewed as a coup for Burgundy over Orleans, since the marshal's allegiance was firmly tied to Jean of Burgundy, who as count of Nevers, had saved him from execution after Nicopolis.

This act demonstrates that Philippe, duke of Burgundy, headed the French government at that time.[30] The peace with England and the acquisition of Genoa demonstrated the success of the court's diplomatic talents. It is demonstrative of French power that Genoa was drawn into the orbit of their influence without threat or war. Doubtless, pragmatic security considerations underpinned Genoa's decision; nevertheless France was their prime choice over any other regional or continental power, spiritual or temporal.

It is also significant that while this courtly struggle was ongoing, the French were also able to invest a sizeable expeditionary force into Scotland during 1384–5, as well as assembling a vast fleet in preparation to invade England the following year. The army of 1384–5, led by the admiral, Jean de Vienne, proved to be a disaster, with the Scots and French falling out over the mission and its costs. By 1400, it had not fully recovered to being an operational military alliance in the manner it had been prior to Vienne's mission. In an attempt to rectify this, French troops campaigned with the Scots at sea in 1401–2 and on land in 1402. Louis of Orleans was also connected to these initiatives with the Scots.[31] In September 1402, the Scots were crushed by the English at the battle of Homildon Hill, where many Scottish nobles and some French knights were captured or killed. The enormity of this English victory, masterminded and prosecuted by the Percys, effectively removed the Scots as a land-fighting force for approximately a decade. King Robert III was declining physically and his rule was weak. Also, he appears to have been pursuing peace with England in this period. A definitive end to any prospect of Scots involvement with this French–Welsh alliance came with the capture at sea of Robert III's heir, James, in 1406. He remained a captive of the English crown until 1424.[32] Although considerably weakened by the Homildon defeat and the loss of men of the calibre of those captured there, the Scots were still able to mount occasional harassing attacks around the border area, as well as establishing a visible presence on the sea. Some nobles, such as the Sinclairs of Orkney, were able to conduct individual enterprises against the English during the period of governmental weakness in Scotland.[33] However, due to Scotland's impotence, there was no hope of forming an axis of power involving France, Wales and Scotland at the moment of the inception of the French–Welsh alliance. In light of the temporary fading of Scotland's star, the Welsh rebels no doubt appeared more attractive to France.

Further factors comprising a highly complex web of alliances, friendships and mutual interests also affected all of the Houses and figures involved. Perhaps the simplest examples to advance involve Burgundy. As the ruler of Flanders since 1384, the duke of Burgundy's financial interests were inextricably linked to the region's wool trade with England.[34] Therefore, war between France and England was likely to be financially detrimental to the Burgundians. By 1402, Louis of Orleans acquired Luxemburg and forged alliances with Guelders and Juliers, effectively imposing a territorial block between Burgundian estates in Flanders and Brabant to the north, and Burgundy and Lorraine to the south. The Burgundians probably perceived this as aggressive and connected to their adversarial relationship within France. However, Louis's advances in the region also gave both factions a stake in the affairs of the German empire. Each supported opposing Imperial candidates, Wenceslas or Rupert, during the early years of the fifteenth century. Their choice of allies can, in turn, be seen to be mirrored in this struggle, where each faction created alliances with the higher nobility across Europe to their own benefit.[35] These widespread alliances were also relevant to relations between Charles's government under Louis's influence, and Wales under Glyn Dŵr.

The great issues and events of their period also played a role. Power relations between nations and neighbours were naturally part of the ongoing challenges of the time. The usual issues of the security, alliances, strategic marriages, internal and foreign economic strategies of their own, their allies and their adversaries all shaped the political decisions of the moment. As powerful magnates in their own right, with lands, allies and interests across Europe, as well as being involved in the direction of the French government, the dukes of court were touched by all of these affairs. While devastating plagues ravaged Europe during the fourteenth century in particular, the issue of religion, especially the drawn-out crisis of the schism, further strained relations across Europe. Its role in the French–Welsh alliance is obvious in Glyn Dŵr's Pennal Declaration of 1406.

Therefore, to represent the conflict at the heart of the French court as one between Orleans and Burgundy is grossly simplistic, but nevertheless convenient. While those dukes headed the most aggressively engaged factions, they appear to have held sway when able to sufficiently influence the other parties mentioned. It is the shifting pattern of dominance in the struggle between the leading French dukes, supported by a range of political, economic, ecclesiastical and continental concerns, that formed French government policy during the years in question. Inevitably, these considerations form a vital part of the rise and fall of this French–Welsh alliance.

PART THREE
Glyn Dŵr's Diplomacy

CHAPTER SIX

The Alliance of 1404

In the first place, that the said lords the king and the prince shall be mutually joined, confederated, united, and leagued by the bond of a true covenant and real friendship, and of a sure, good, and most powerful union against Henry of Lancaster, adversary and enemy of both parties, and his adherents and supporters.[1]

The motivations behind French interest in the 1404 treaty between Charles VI, although nominally, and Owain Glyn Dŵr are to be found in the currents within French elites; the church, university and courtly factions. Although their historic manoeuvrings are interconnected with events that shaped their affairs over decades, this episode of France's complex courtly struggle was entwined with the schism of 1378 and the adversarial relations between several royal factions, principally the houses of Orleans and Burgundy.

It was the personalities within the French courtly factions, their conflicts, drives and machinations which were of primary importance in the evolution of this Welsh alliance. Although the proclamations and debates within university and church circles supported or undercut the struggles of the noble factions, as well as influencing the crown's position on the schism, the leading role in this Welsh alliance appears to fall to the temporal princes. Their actions clearly comprised an expansionist military and diplomatic foreign policy. This drive saw French influence spread into Flanders, Scotland and throughout Italy. It also engaged the forces of nations supporting rival popes and saw conflict brought to the heart of the French court, caused by the marriages of Charles VI and Louis of Orleans whose spouses brought their families' rivalries to Paris. The French–Welsh alliance was a further detail in the efforts of these factions to augment and project their power within and beyond France's borders. As such, the French–Welsh alliance forms another theatre within the Hundred Years' War.[2]

The divisions between the French hierarchy ran deep on foreign policy matters and even on the issue of the church. The Orleanists favoured the *via facti*, which aimed to resolve the schism by violent means until one side had finally triumphed. The Burgundians advocated the *via cessionis,* which desired to see both candidates resign their crowns in order to allow normal order to be restored. The French church and the influential University of Paris tended towards the *via cessionis* as a first step towards the *via concilii*, which sought resolution through conciliar debate between all of the ecclesiastical parties, although the clergy oscillated between positions.[3] These rivalries can be seen to be played out in the directions taken by the French government, notably in its stance over the schism and its relationship with England. When Duke Philippe inherited Flanders in 1384 his attitude towards England was strongly mediated by his economic interests which were firmly connected to the Anglo–Flemish wool trade.[4] While France and England discussed peace and Richard II in particular sought a rapprochement with Paris, the French nobles' positions on England were less of a point of friction.[5] Nevertheless, the disputes over the schism and the governance of the kingdom during King Charles's illnesses were sufficient to accentuate the rift between Burgundy and Orleans. The course of these disputes can be mapped out in line with the preferences of the head of the government.

The schism provoked a wide range of issues, from the rise of non-orthodox theologians such as John Wyclif, and movements such as the Lollards and the Hussites, which affected the geopolitical alliances across the continent. In France, most of the French nobility, led by Louis of Anjou, king of Naples, Louis, duke of Orleans, and the French king, when lucid, demonstrated a firm adherence to Clement VII and, initially, to his successor Benedict XIII. In contrast, the French clergy appeared determined to show a measure of independence by debating the matter. Royal commands suppressing ecclesiastical debate were relaxed in time, and the notion of subtracting allegiance from the Avignon pope gained prominence. Benedict was from Aragon and a seemingly abrasive character, and friction soon arose between him and the French, aiding the campaign to abandon him in the pursuit of healing the rift in the church. In tandem, Philippe of Burgundy controlled the French government; he envisaged a certain path for France. In 1398 therefore, the French withdrew their allegiance and sent troops to besiege Benedict at Avignon.[6] The fact that the besieging army was commanded by Geoffrey de Boucicaut, brother of one of the two Marshals of France, reveals that the Burgundian party was directing the French court at that time. Perhaps to underline this Burgundian domination of court, rebellious vassals across the southern lands most often associated with Louis of Orleans's hegemony were brought to heel by royal armies led by Marshal Jean de Boucicaut, a Burgundian loyalist.[7] The fact that Geoffrey de Boucicaut would serve the Orleanist and Burgundian camps betrays the shifting adherences of the French nobility. However, by 1402, Louis of Orleans had assumed lead of the government, during which time he and his ally, Waleran, count of St Pol, issued personal challenges to Henry IV, and a more aggressive policy towards England was defined.[8] Consequently, the crown's position on the schism also changed; the siege of Avignon was eased and finally lifted in 1403 after Benedict's escape into the hands of Robert de Braquemont, a Norman Orleanist, was effected in March of that year.[9] French obedience to Benedict XIII resumed in May 1403 while the court and the government were directed by Louis. Although he never returned to Avignon, Benedict retained staunch Orleanist support, which benefitted his cause while they remained in control in Paris.[10] Although Louis's dominance only lasted a few short years, this provided the window of opportunity exploited by both sides in this French–Welsh alliance. The Orleanist ascendancy forms the critical backdrop to the connection with Owain Glyn Dŵr and they appear to have wasted no time in undertaking joint actions.

However, this is not to represent Owain Glyn Dŵr as an Orleanist creation; he had come to wider prominence by virtue of his military successes and diplomatic efforts. By the end of 1402, Owain had won a number of small but significant military victories which enabled him to command a sufficient number of Welshmen to cause the English administration in Wales to stall. French sources identified revolts against Bolingbroke's accession as being pro-Ricardian counter-revolutions.[11] While that was the case with the Epiphany rising in 1400 and the Percy revolt of 1403 evoked Richard's name, it is incorrect to label the violence in Wales as such. Although this justified French interest in England, for Richard was Charles's ally and son-in-law, the revolts by senior nobles opposed to Henry demonstrated significant and more complex discontent among England's elite.[12]

Before Glyn Dŵr had clearly established his noble credentials and demonstrated his military worth, initial contacts between him and Charles VI's court were understandably clandestine. Louis of Orleans had maintained a unit of Welsh mercenaries and deserters for several years and they likely facilitated numerous contacts, perhaps exemplified by the efforts of Dafydd ap Ieuan Coch. It is also possible that Louis's Welsh troops assisted the French and Bretons who landed near Kidwelly in October 1403, as well as Jean d'Espagne. These expansive pulses into Welsh waters and across the width of the Channel region were supported by sustained and effective campaigning on land by the French, including the capture of Mortagne and Corbefin, as well as widespread advances in the Limousin.[13] The French, Bretons and Castilians were demonstrably engaged with the Welsh rebels after Louis of Orleans came to prominence at court. French gifts of wine, weaponry and advice offered to Glyn Dŵr, combined with the enticement of a military alliance with France, is clear evidence of the French wisely, seductively, deploying a soft power policy in the first years of the fifteenth century.[14] The French perceptibly invested resources into this Welsh connection. In order to give their union a conception of legitimacy, and to enable the French to consider overtly fuelling the revolt, this growing relationship required the mechanism of an alliance.

Glyn Dŵr's embassy was led by his Chancellor, Gruffudd Yonge, Doctor of Canon Law and his acting bishop of Bangor, and John Hanmer, Owain's brother-in-law. Although Hanmer was only a minor English noble, in the treaty he is ranked as being of same blood as Owain who, for the first time, overtly described himself as *Owynus, Dei gratia princeps Wallie*: Owain, by the grace of God, prince of Wales. They led a larger party in which one clerk, a legally trained notary, identified himself as 'Benedict Comme, clerk of the diocese of St Asaph, notary public by apostolic authority'. He noted that he had delegated the document to be written by another since he was busy elsewhere, demonstrating that unnamed others were also present. The more important ambassadorial missions of the period comprised a leading noble, preferably one of the royal blood, and a cleric of equivalent rank, usually a bishop, who was either the keeper of the king's privy seal or a chancellor. They were empowered to act in place of their leader. Late medieval embassies commonly comprised a number of legal specialists to conduct and conclude the important diplomatic business at hand. It is therefore noteworthy that the Welsh,

although apparently excluded from such high-ranking affairs since the fall
of Gwynedd in 1282, clearly knew the appropriate methods and requirements for diplomatic parties of the time. It is perhaps more striking that
they were able to assemble a team capable of treating with and, by consequence, impressing the French sufficiently to conclude the alliance.[15]

The treaty text reveals that Yonge and Hanmer were empowered to
discuss, agree and confirm a treaty with the French. They were also given
leave to write any necessary documents required and to act in Owain's
stead in the case of any special circumstances arising during negotiations. Remarkably, the commission appears to reveal the French as the
instigators of the alliance; it mentions the ongoing affection shown by
the French towards Owain and the Welsh, before declaring Glyn Dŵr's
desire for union with Charles. This infers that there was already a positive
relationship between the two leaders or their representatives. It is plain
that the memory and the connection between Owain Lawgoch, the well-
remembered *Yvain de Galles* to the French, and Owain Glyn Dŵr was
evoked at this time. The same chronicle which recalled that previous
Welsh–French link also revealed that Glyn Dŵr's ambassadors made two
requests when given an audience. These were to purchase as many arms as
the French were willing to sell and transport to Wales, as well as seeking
military support for their cause. Although the Saint-Denys chronicler
dressed the embassy in terms that stressed the bravery of the French, he
also included mention that Glyn Dŵr lacked troops – a point he first raised
with the Scots and the Irish in 1401. The tenor of the commission and the
resultant treaty appear in keeping with the expected form of the time and
perhaps demonstrate an evolving diplomatic style. The arrival of higher-
level clerics to Owain's side in 1404 no doubt helped and it seems likely
that the surviving treaty document was the result of guiding discussions
with agents of the French crown. Perhaps to emphasise his legitimacy and
confidence, the 1404 exchange also marks the first overt record of Owain
presenting himself as 'Prince of Wales'. Simultaneously, Owain decried the
name of 'Henry of Lancaster' and attacked his legitimacy to rule. Since that
was an issue at the heart of the dispute which began the Hundred Years'
War, any nobleman who might detract from the Plantagenet assertion of
legitimacy would surely meet a favourable hearing at the French court.[16]

The French treaty signatories present an intriguing picture of
strained unity at the French court in summer 1404. However, close
examination of the traceable personalities suggests Orleanist motivations

played a strong role in making this alliance and drove subsequent events. The rank and eminence of the French party conducting negotiations with Yonge and Hanmer show that the French took Glyn Dŵr extemely seriously indeed and that they were intent on impressing that idea upon the Welsh with a substantial charm offensive.

The first stage of the main treaty document was dated 14 June 1404 and confirmed the parameters of Glyn Dŵr's ambassadors' commission from the previous month and, more importantly, defined the terms of the alliance. It also named young Jacques de Bourbon, count of la Marche, and Jean Montagu, bishop of Chartres, as the principal negotiators on the French side. Montagu was an illegitimate son of Charles V, and therefore half-brother to the king and Louis of Orleans. He was an opponent of Jean, the new duke of Burgundy. This agreement was copied and ratified in the French chancellor's house in Paris on 14 July. Present at this final concord were Arnaud de Corbie, chancellor, and no fewer than three bishops, Jean of Arras, Philippe of Noyon and Pierre of Meaux, as well as Charles VI's secretary and notary, Jean de Saints, who completed the named ecclesiastical contingent and appears in numerous documents of Charles VI's reign. In contrast to Montagu, Jean Canard, bishop of Arras, was the long-serving chancellor of Philippe the Bold's court and a lifelong Burgundian. The other clergymen are less easily traceable, so their allegiance cannot be verified with as much certainty as Montagu and Canard, and, as Benedict Comme alluded, others were present but remained anonymous.[17]

Leading the nobles were Jacques de Bourbon, count of la Marche, and Louis de Bourbon, count of Vendôme. The imposing presence of two counts of Bourbon is noteworthy. As princes of the blood, the Bourbons were connected to the crown itself, as well as to the houses of Orleans and Burgundy. Louis, duke of Bourbon, these counts' uncle, along with Jean, duke of Berry, openly acted as a counter to the ambitions of both of the vying houses, intervening militarily to block open conflict between them. The other significant nobles involved in the treaty were lords Robert de Braquemont and Robert d'Amilly, both 'knights of the chamber', and a long-serving knight, Arnaud de Corbie.[18] Robert de Braquemont was the Orleanist lord who received Benedict XIII on his escape from the siege of Avignon in 1403, and whose family long served the dukes of Orleans. Robert d'Amilly and Arnaud de Corbie were supporters of the dukes of Burgundy, although the latter also served the crown before declaring openly for the Burgundians during the looming civil war.[19]

Therefore, this extremely impressive French ambassadorial party balanced the interests of the two ascendant ducal factions, Burgundy and Orleans, as well as the crown, represented through the officials and the counterweight of the Bourbon counts. This group might have presented a vision of a united court, or ensured that each faction had a stake in all ongoing negotiations. Although Jacques de Bourbon openly held Burgundian sympathies throughout his life, Count Louis de Bourbon's principal territory, Vendôme, was an appanage held of the duke of Orleans. However, in view of its innately aggressive stance against Henry IV, this alliance should be considered Orleanist in drive and interest.[20] It is noteworthy that France made no such overtly hostile moves against England while Philippe the Bold was alive. His death in April 1404 allowed Louis of Orleans to acquire more control over the government. The alliance with Glyn Dŵr was a clear statement of his intent to make war on Henry IV. In addition, Louis demonstrated a personal commitment to this alliance by sending along men from his own household on the ensuing mission, paying for their equipment from his own accounts.[21]

It is noteworthy that in spite of the disparity in the allies' power and their apparently long absence from international diplomacy, the composition of Glyn Dŵr's embassy mirrored the form, if not the size and eminence, of that of the French by containing men of the blood and the cloth, as well as legal specialists. Nevertheless, these documents paint a scene of several meetings between the envoys, to discuss the direction of the alliance, attended all the while by numerous scribes, whose identities are lost. In the treaty, the ambassadors exchanged promises, swearing for their masters on the holy gospels of God. The alliance was then born in principle; and its details defined its nature and limits.[22]

Following the usual *politesses*, in which the French generously addressed 'the illustrious and most dreaded lord', 'the magnificent and powerful Owain, Prince of the Welsh', the treaty comprised eleven clauses to bind the Welsh and French leaders. The first gave the reason for this alliance:

> In the first place, that the said lords the king and the prince shall be mutually joined, confederated, united, and leagued by the bond of a true covenant and real friendship, and of a sure, good, and most powerful union against Henry of Lancaster, adversary and enemy of both parties, and his adherents and supporters.[23]

This reveals the unambiguous motivation for the treaty; it specifically targeted Henry and his adherents. Although this is unsurprising, it is noteworthy for two reasons. Such treaties appear to be often made for specific, immediate reasons, and not at times when there is no threat or need for mutual protection or engagement. This treaty, however, did not permanently bind the signatories, their heirs and successors, as did other contemporary alliances, indicating a measure of caution on the part of the French. The reason for Owain's hostility towards Henry is evident, but this clause indicates French interest in removing Henry from the throne. One factor for this was French ire over Henry's treatment of Charles's daughter, Isabella. His treatment of her, Richard II's bride and still a teenager in 1404, caused her uncle, Louis of Orleans, to challenge Henry to a duel. Louis's ally, Waleran, count of St Pol, also issued a similar defiance to Henry.[24] The second and probably main reason was a perception that the new king's tenure on the crown was weak enough to challenge. In signing this treaty with Owain, the French were preparing to openly breach the twenty-eight-year truce with England signed in 1396. This shows a different policy direction within the French administration from that of previous years and clearly under-lines the Orleanist influence in government. It also demonstrates that they recognised Owain as a strong, suitable ally with whom to intrigue and that he presented an exploitable opportunity to damage or remove Henry. Also of import is that the treaty does not mention England or its people anywhere. Henry and his adherents are identified as the enemy, and therefore this was not necessarily intended to start a war against the English in general, but rather an aspiration to decapitate the English regime. Nevertheless, this personal element and aggressive new direction were indisputably Orleanist in flavour.

The next three articles of the treaty covered predictable promises that they would help one another against Henry, that they would be 'true and faithful friends' who would warn the other if they became aware of Henry plotting against them, and also act to hinder those plans. Next, the terms of the treaty made clear that each lord would 'punish in such manner that shall give an example to the others' any of their people who aided Henry in any way, even if either leader were brought to peace. Although the latter might appear to have been aimed at the Welsh who had served in their thousands in English armies, Frenchmen in English territories also served England, and French princes of the blood, notably Louis of Orleans, had previously sought Henry's friendship.[25] This clause also suggests an Orleanist drive to sever ties to England, whereas Burgundian financial interests were firmly connected to English trade with Flanders.

The sixth clause determined that each party would discuss any peace moves and give the other one month to respond. Inclusion in peace negotiations with the enemy has precedence in a number of other alliances, notably those between France and Scotland.[26] This apparently formulaic but bonding clause became significant at a critical point later:

> Again, that one of the lords, the king and the prince aforesaid, shall not make or take truce nor make peace with the aforesaid Henry of Lancaster, but that the other might be included if he had wished in the same truce or peace, unless he is united or did not wish to be included in the same truce or peace, and he shall determine, concerning such refusal or rejection, who wished to treat for the said truce or peace, within a month after the one shall have signified the said truce or peace, by his letters patent, sealed by his seal.[27]

Next, the French agreed to seize shipping in their ports which did not carry letters of testimony from either lord. While this measure might help the French to easily acquire mercantile goods and shipping, the removal of a number of English ships from the Channel would also likely give them the upper hand militarily. Shipping also served a role in spying on the other side's ports, coasts and particularly on other shipping, such as the gathering of invasion fleets. This was evident in late 1404 when Henry's government received ample warning of the fleets in Sluys and Harfleur which prepared to invade Wales that year.[28] Therefore, controlling movements from ports was another way of controlling the flow of information as well as weakening the enemy's commerce. Without such intelligence, England's coastal defence depended on news from ships from its own ports and shore-based watches. Such a purely reactive defence is less efficient and would disadvantage England.

The next two clauses appear formulaic; the first is a promise of redress, stating that should the two lords or their subjects fall out, then this should be resolved amicably and their quarrel ended peacefully. In addition, this covenant was binding and sealed with promises, and both parties were reminded of that. The penultimate clause empowered the ambassadors to make promises and vows in their lord's place and, having touched holy relics, the union was final and binding. Then followed a clause which seemed to absolve all men, no matter their 'race or subjection', of previous pledges to Henry:

> However, all those who by reason of their race or subjection, while subjects of the aforesaid Henry of Lancaster, shall not appear, or by pretext of former treaties previously federated, shall be excepted from these covenants and leagues.[29]

This can be construed as touching both parties, those friendly to them and those they hoped to engage; this clause served as a release from any oath and legitimised actions henceforth taken against Henry. For Louis, Henry's ally during his exile at the French court, this served as an official renunciation of that tie, had the duel challenges not reached a wider audience. Also, this clause absolved the Bretons, many of whom had served the English crown prior to its withdrawal from Brittany in 1397. By this time, apart from supporting French, Castilian and Welsh attacks, the Bretons were clearly in conflict with England at sea and on land. England had finally relinquished its last stronghold in Brittany in 1397, leaving a bitter legacy. Although their candidate, Jean de Montfort, had triumphed over the French-supported duke, Charles de Blois, in 1364, English captains *in situ* had exacted a heavy financial toll from the Bretons since that victory.[30] Jean de Montfort died in 1399 and his son Jean, the new duke, owed England less than his father. Henry machinated to prolong English influence in Brittany by marrying Jean V's mother, Joanna of Navarre, in 1403.[31] The Bretons showed active opposition to the marriage and opened a maritime conflict against the English – largely a spectacle of coastal raids and counter-attacks.[32]

Since legality and legitimacy were highly important matters to establish prior to military action, this clause releasing them from oaths is significant. The allies were then free to engage others in this contest. In light of this, it is probably significant that Breton fleets and soldiers were involved in the conduct of attacks on English interests in Wales, England and at sea at this time. The Bretons comprised notable elements of the force assembled following the conclusion of this treaty, as well as being instrumental in the 1405 invasion. It might also be that the previous clause pertaining to the seizure of shipping would appeal to the Bretons, whose naval power might be augmented by the removal of English vessels from the Channel.

However, even before the second signing of the alliance document in Paris on 14 July 1404, the French demonstrated their intentions to engage their allies in this venture by seeking Castilian support. On 7 July 1404, the senior Bourbon, Duke Louis, wrote to the king of Castile and Leon requesting ships for the mission to Wales while the French simultaneously gathered their own fleet in Channel ports. The letter began with a warm, friendly passage which showed that Louis knew the king and his relations well. He then asked for forty armed ships because:

> The king has ordered my very dear and well-beloved cousin, the Count of March, to proceed shortly to Wales with one thousand lances and five hundred crossbowmen; who will set out shortly to embark in Brittany, and from thence to Wales.[33]

A lance was a medieval military formation centred around a well-armoured and mounted man-at-arms. Although the complement of a lance varied according to its leader's status, typically he would have a well-armoured sergeant alongside him and usually three archers. It was common for a page or another servant to be present to assist the man-at-arms, although the latter were sometimes non-combatants. All those counted in the lance were mounted. An army of a thousand lances represented a fighting force of at least 5,000 men, but possibly with up to 2,000 more, some of whom fought. Given that the number of sailors in the fleet usually equalled the tally of soldiers, and they could also fight, this army was a significant force. Added to the French numbers, of course, were the Castilians who arrived with up to thirty warships laden with troops and sailors. In total, the army of 1404 was a highly significant force, well over 10,000 strong.

The French requested the Castilians to rendezvous with the count of la Marche in Brittany on 15 August that year and then to accompany him to Wales. There, Louis revealed that the force 'will find a good entry aided and assisted, in order to attack, harass, and injure the English, our enemies'. Seemingly, Louis then threatened the Castilians: 'And in this may you not fail us.'[34] Louis then finished with an amicable flourish. Nevertheless, this letter demonstrates French diplomatic style in action; far from being a jumble of polite, inconclusive phrases, the expedition organisers expected Castilian support and showed no timidity in making that plain.

A contemporary Castilian account eulogising one of its noblemen, Pero Niño, records the arrival of a letter from France that largely replicates the intentions declared by Duke Louis de Bourbon. The account of the Castilian expedition renders a beautiful description of the journey, from the Spanish court to that of France, detailing their camaraderie, giving tales of battles, victories and repulsions by local forces during the mission which ravaged England's southern coast. During one descent onto English soil they discovered that the land had been emptied of men by Henry IV who had summoned them to go and fight Owain in Wales. In a noteworthy addition, Pero Niño's tale recalled how the duke of Orleans was in charge of the government at that time and he paid the Castilians to become his men and wear his livery. Moreover, Pero was recruited by Louis of Orleans to replace the fallen Breton champion, Guillaume du Châtel, and stand with six of Louis's men in a combat against seven Englishmen, in a reproduction of a previous fight between seven of Louis's men and seven of Henry's.[35]

The Welsh–French alliance came to life in summer 1404 with the French mustering an invasion force to be led by Jacques de Bourbon, who had been involved in the treaty. Henry's diplomats and spies were crucial in passing on intelligence of the build-up of the 1404 fleet. The fleet gathered slowly, so slowly that the English had the opportunity to attempt to burn vessels idling in Brest harbour. In September, they wrote that the French were stalling ongoing diplomatic discourse due to the likelihood of a diversionary attack to assist the Welsh rebels and, shortly after, they reported that the forces were instead intending to invade Wales. They identified Louis of Orleans and Waleran of St Pol as active obstacles to the peace process.

On 6 October, Henry was informed that the fleet for Wales had mustered but still not moved. Five days later the startling news arrived that a substantial army, reportedly comprising 15,000 men and horses, had assembled in Sluys in order to make the journey to Wales. Soldiers from France, Flanders and other nations, including Prussia, stood ready to make the assault. On 14 October, Nicholas de Ryssheton, one of Henry's ambassadors in Calais wrote to the mayor of London informing him that Wales, Sandwich and Calais were threatened. Further intelligence revealed that the attack fleet had moved to Harfleur, where the army size of 15,000 men and horses was reconfirmed. Their shocking purpose was announced: they were to travel to Wales, occupy and repair its castles, and from there inflict as much harm on England as possible.

However, the weak link in this invasion was its leader. The troops summoned were apparently left waiting while Jacques de Bourbon vainly pursued some love affair in Paris. When he finally arrived in port in mid-November, he proclaimed he could not go to Wales and so took to the sea in pursuit of merchant vessels. He made an ineffective landing near Dartmouth, swiftly withdrew and then slunk back to port.[36] The entire affair wasted an exceptional opportunity and the French threat of 1404 evaporated; the weather had been fair, the troops assembled and prepared, and the Castilians had arrived. The blame for this shameful failure fell squarely on Count Jacques, who was described venomously by the Saint-Denys chronicler:

> I am ashamed to have recounted the crossing of the French to Wales; by the fault of the count of la Marche, the course and end of the expedition, far from appearing as it did at the beginning, became dismal for them … this retreat covered the count with infamy and left an indelible stain on his name. The princes of the fleur de lys did not forgive him for having forgotten that he was the issue of royal blood, and of having sullied his honour by his culpable negligence.[37]

Nevertheless, an alliance between Charles VI and Owain Glyn Dŵr was given life and, according to the Saint-Denys chronicler, Owain received the gift of arms and armour subsequently sent by Charles thus:

> The king [Charles VI], in order to give pleasure to the Prince of Wales [Glyn Dŵr], gave to the ambassador, at the moment of his departure, an all gold royal helmet, a cuirass and a sword, and charged him with delivering them from him to his brother. I learned from the Frenchmen who found themselves there when these presents were given to him, that he humbly received them on his knees covering them with kisses, as if he had received the king in person.[38]

A Castilian Account of the Conflict in Wales[39]

How Owain, Prince of Wales, Rose and Refused to Recognise the Earl of Derby, who the English had made King

As I have recounted above, that the English had deposed King Richard of England, Owain, Prince of Wales, was his close relative.[40] He refused to recognise the earl of Derby as king like the rest of the kingdom; before, although it grieved him, he declared a great war against the king and London, where he was residing.

Wales is a faraway land, on the fringe of the kingdom, to the north. It is a very strong land, and mountainous, it is well-populated and has good fortresses. There are at the borders some passes they call the Marches; there is no other way to enter than that. The prince saw that there would be a long war with the king: he threw down all of the fortresses of his land, and left only five castles, that are in the strongest part of the land, near each other, and he made all of the people of his land live around those castles.

They say it is a very healthy and fertile land, of beautiful people. And he had there many of King Richard's knights, and many other people, and they all fought on horseback.[41] And each one had his horn; and so they used that, when it became necessary, they understood one another so well upon using it, it was like a man's voice or word. And when the king came to his land, he allowed him to enter the Marches, and he put himself in other places where he could not be found, and he defended other passes. And when they overran his land, that was his advantage; that the prince and his men were such warriors, that at night they captured and killed many of the king's people. And afterwards, when the king turned to leave, the duke [*sic*; the prince] still went at him with swords, causing him great harm. If the king retreated to London, he would leave and pass the Marches to the plain, and robbed the land: and returned, and passed the Marches. And the king had already gone to the country of Wales three or four times.

The king sent his ambassadors, saying that it was great madness, and that it could not last; and that he desist from that opinion, and that he would grant him mercy. And he responded, that he would do the best he could, that of three noblemen that would be appointed in London, one of them would be his. The king of France always sent him help in the form of crossbowmen, weapons, and wine of which there is none in England.[42]

And if the captain of the Castilian ships had come to England in the fleet of Pero Niño, because that coast had very few people at that time, they would have captured places, and made many rescues, and many other good things; and come back from those places with honour, and also with much booty. And because captain Pero Niño did not have more of his countrymen, he should be lauded even more and all the good things he did be more widely recounted; since there were no more than three galleys and two ballingers in his company. And if he took twenty galleys, as others had taken before and since, it can be believed that he would have done remarkable things.[43]

CHAPTER SEVEN

An Orleanist Coup?

My lords the dukes of France, who controlled the government, wished to keep the promise of aid made to the prince of Wales, and at the same time repair the shameful failure of the count of la Marche by some notable feat of arms.[1]

While the treaty of alliance was being signed and the fleet being assembled, the conflict rumbled on in Wales. Owain's first parliament that summer no doubt discussed the course of the conflict as well as diplomatic initiatives, particularly those with the French. Harlech and Aberystwyth had fallen to the Welsh and, in a strategic development, the rebels garrisoned them. It is possible that Beaumaris also went to the rebels following the defeat of crown forces on Anglesey by Welsh and French troops. Perhaps to allow them to consolidate their hold in the west, border castles in the east, such as Montgomery, came under attack. The government responded by strengthening its forces along the border, rather than trying to retake the fortresses lost to the rebels. In the south, the Welsh, led by William Gwyn ap Rhys Lloyd, again captured and burned the town of Kidwelly in late summer, destroying its recovery from the siege involving the French and the Bretons the previous winter. Further west, the region around Haverford fell into rebel hands. They returned to besiege Coity and once again attacked a reconstituted Cardiff. It was eventually taken and ransacked, with Owain reportedly giving an example of his caustic wit to the friars who asked for the return of the goods they had put in the castle for safe keeping. This successful assault on Cardiff revealed that the rebels had no intention of holding it at that stage, as they did with Aberystwyth and Harlech. Rather, they wanted to plunder it and had obliged the government to repeatedly defend and reinforce it, lessening Henry's ability to act elsewhere. In June, the Welsh thrust into Archenfield in Herefordshire and returned to mount a longer campaign into the county in September. As summer turned to autumn, English border communities made truces with the Welsh, acts which plainly demonstrate rebel dominance in the region. The government could only accept the truces, thus demonstrating that at that time, Wales was lost to them and a new state, governed by its native people, had appeared. In these turbulent months, the men of Somerset and Devon made an unsanctioned landing in Glamorgan and rounded up as much livestock as they could carry in their boats. The government's control over its populations in the counties adjacent to Wales appeared to be inconsistent, at best. However, the crown was not entirely absent from Wales during the year; as 1404 drew to a close, it sent sizeable forces to relieve Coity and reinvest Cardiff.[2]

On 12 January 1405, in his new castle of Llanbadarn (Aberystwyth), Owain ratified the treaty documents signed in Paris the previous summer and returned his assent to France. It was in these treaty documents with the French that Owain gave an indication of his vision of his reign. His commission to Yonge and Hanmer of 1404 and the ratification of 1405 referred to those years being the fourth and sixth years, respectively, of his 'principate', outlining Owain's name for this period. There were other machinations afoot; Constance, Lady Despencer, kidnapped the Mortimer heirs, Earl Edmund's nephews, from Windsor and tried to deliver them into Glyn Dŵr's hands. She was the widow of the earl of Gloucester killed in the 1400 Epiphany Rising against Henry, and sister of the duke of York, whose loyalty to the king was questionable. It seems impossible that this scheme was undertaken without conspiratorial premeditation. The attempt was made in February 1405 and was thwarted at Cheltenham, close to the Welsh border. The Mortimer minors were returned to the king. The crown's investigation into the matter revealed that Thomas Mowbray, Earl Marshal, had known about the plot but played no active part in it, and was therefore pardoned. The duke of York was sent to the Tower for his alleged, but peripheral, involvement. He was released after a few months and restored in 1406. Nevertheless, the plot is indicative of unseen connections between Glyn Dŵr and the very highest echelons of the English nobility.[3]

February 1405 witnessed the drafting of another alliance, probably by proxy, known as the 'Tripartite Indenture', or three-party alliance. This leagued Glyn Dŵr, Edmund Mortimer and Henry Percy, earl of

Northumberland. The aim was to form a military alliance purposed to dethrone Henry, giving Percy control of the northern English counties, Mortimer the south and Owain an expanded realm of Wales. The treaty text does not seem to have survived in its original form, but a document summarising its contents describes the following articles:

In the first place that the lords – Owain, the Earl, and Edmund – will henceforth be joined, confederated, united and bound by a true league and a true friendship and a sure and good union.

Furthermore, each one of the same lords will pursue and also procure the honour and welfare of the other, and will, in good faith, prevent any losses or damage which come to the knowledge of one of them, intended to be inflicted on any of them, by anyone whosoever. Each of them will also act and do with one another, each and everything which ought to be done and suffered by good, true and loyal friends, to good, true and loyal friends, laying aside all deceit and fraud.

Also, if at any time one of the said lords knows or learns of any loss or injury intended by anyone against any of them, he will notify it to the others as swiftly as possible and he will help them in that matter, so that each may be able to take those measures against such malice as he is able.

Each lord will act in good faith to prevent any damage or injury to any of the other lords, and each will help the other in time of need, as far as he is able.

Also, if, by God's will, in the fullness of time, it appears to these lords that they are the same persons of whom the Prophet speaks, between whom the governance of Great Britain should be divided and shared, then each of them will strive to his utmost to effectually achieve this.

Also, each of them will be content with that portion of the aforesaid kingdom, as defined below, without any further demand or claim to superiority, indeed each will enjoy equal liberty in his allotted portion [of the kingdom].

Again, between the same lords, it is unanimously covenanted and agreed, that the aforementioned Owain and his heirs will have the whole of Cambria or Wales, within the borders, limits, and boundaries written below, from Leogria, which is commonly called England; namely from the Severn Sea, as the river Severn leads from the sea, going to the north gate of the city of Worcester, and from that gate directly to the ash trees, commonly called *Onnenau Meigion* in the Cambrian or Welsh language, which grow on the highway leading from Bridgenorth to Kinver; then along the highway, which is commonly called the old or ancient road, directly to the head or source of the Trent; then to the head or source of the river, commonly called Mersey, thereafter, as that river leads to the sea following the borders, limits, and boundaries mentioned before.

The aforementioned Earl of Northumberland and his heirs will have the counties written below, namely, Northumberland, Westmorland, Lancashire, York, Lincoln, Nottingham, Derby, Stafford, Leicester, Northampton, Warwick and Norfolk.

The lord Edmund will have the remainder of the whole of England for himself and his successors.

Also, should any battle, riot or discord arise between two of these lords, may it never be, then the third of these lords, after good and faithful counsel, will duly rectify such discord, riot, or battle, and the quarrelling parties are bound to obey his endorsement or condemnation.

Also, they will loyally defend the kingdom against all men, except for the oath on the part of the aforementioned lord Owain, given to the most illustrious prince, Lord Charles, by the grace of God, king of the French, in the league and covenant made between them.

And so that all of the aforesaid [articles], each and every one, are well and faithfully observed, these lords – Owain, the Earl, and Edmund, now continually contemplating the sacred body of the Lord and the Holy Gospels of God which they have personally touched – have sworn to inviolably observe to their utmost, each and every one of these statements and they have caused their seals to be mutually affixed to this document.[4]

Although the treaty summary likely borrows heavily from the original text, its ultimate accuracy is difficult to ascertain. In addition, it has been indicated elsewhere that the Tripartite Indenture bears textual similarities to the 1404 treaty of alliance between the French and the Welsh, as well as a treaty from 1398 between the Charles VI and Jacques I de Lusignan, king of Cyprus. In all, this infers a French guiding hand to these documents rather than a Welsh one.[5] The Indenture contains formulaic clauses from its time; the first four articles make for a standard opening. They announced the union and guaranteed that the parties would protect, inform and assist one another in good faith. The fifth clause hesitantly referred to their designated destiny to rule Britain, according to words of the Prophet, probably Merlin in this case. The next announced the intention to divide Britain between them and held them to their assigned territories. Articles, 7, 8 and 9 defined the geographical limits of the three, united territories. While the lands intended for Percy and Mortimer were easily defined by the northern shire names, in Percy's case, and the rest going to Mortimer, the bounds of an enlarged Wales had to be described using a different method. The use of rivers, roads, towns and geographical features, such as the ash trees, to precisely demarcate the border seems entirely practical. The tenth clause sought to guarantee that discord between the parties would be peacefully resolved for their mutual benefit. The penultimate statement swore unity between them in the face of all enemies, although dispensation was made exempting Glyn Dŵr from fighting against Charles VI, his acknowledged ally. Glyn Dŵr was then publicly Charles's ally in *Britanniæ Majoris* or 'Great Britain', as they described this new kingdom. The final article assured that each party had made a sufficient, appropriate declaration to God as well as to his new allies that he would remain faithful to his word.

This treaty is the first firm proof of an alliance between Glyn Dŵr and the Percys. No evidence other than tarnishing rumour has emerged regarding a union prior to Hotspur's fateful revolt in July 1403.[6] In fact, the contemporary evidence plainly demonstrates that Glyn Dŵr and his forces were campaigning in south-west Wales. The plethora of extant letters from local commanders described the Welsh moving south-westwards, exactly the opposite direction from Percy at Shrewsbury, and therefore it seems impossible for their forces to have combined at that time.[7] The letters from the garrison commanders passed through many pairs of hands en route to the king, making it perhaps inevitable that news of the Welsh attacks would reach Hotspur before he announced his defiance. Although some Welshmen fought alongside Hotspur at that bloody encounter, there is no indication that they were present as part of a Glyn Dŵr–Percy rebel alliance.

Spring brought a renewed impetus on the part of the government to reverse its spiralling fortunes in Wales. At last, there appeared to be good news for Henry, with a letter from his heir announcing a military victory in March. Prince Henry, who had established his household in the borders the previous summer, claimed a substantial victory, but his report must only be accepted with extreme caution. The prince described being with Lord Talbot, the knights William Newport and John Greyndour, and a small company of retainers in, to use his words, 'only a very small force'. He wrote that they fought an 8,000-strong rebel army assembled from various parts of Gwent and Glamorgan, which had burnt four houses at Grosmont. The future King Henry V also claimed to have killed between 800 and 1,000 rebels, capturing one of their leaders, who was not named and did not subsequently appear in any records. Although a proclamation announcing Prince Henry's news was issued in London, this letter also seems to have been treated in a measured way at the time, there being no parades or festivals to celebrate Prince Henry's, or Henry IV's, first battle victory against the Welsh since revolt broke out there in 1399. The supporting evidence is also lacking; in 1403, a similar-sized Welsh army could be tracked by the letters of fearful castle commanders in the area. They reported its muster, its leaders, its advance and the sacking of Carmarthen. In addition, there were reports of the same army devastating the region around Carmarthen before returning up the Tywi valley. There is no comparable evidence exposing any of this alleged force's details or movements. Equally, for a similar reported death toll, the battle of Bryn Glas left two mass burial sites, yet Grosmont produced none. Also, there is no wider knowledge of the battle reported in chronicles, as there was with Bryn Glas. Nor is there any imprint of the event in local folk legend, although the latter is rarely entirely reliable, it can give an indication of activity. In all, Prince Henry's account is not supported by any contemporary sources or the physical evidence on the ground.[8]

Parliament and the government designed a strategy to wrest back parts of Wales from the rebels, and provided the funding for substantial forces to carry out the task. The plan would involve two armies thrusting into rebel territory, with the king leading forces in the south, while the prince would advance into the north. In late April, the prince was given command of 3,500 soldiers for the operation, more than 2,000 more were raised to reinforce seven key castles, while the king would have sizeable forces for his drive into south Wales. As the king moved to Hereford, forces in advance of his won a fight at Usk in early May. Although Welsh losses overall were relatively light, a number of significant personnel were killed. Glyn Dŵr's heir, Gruffydd ab Owain, led a party into Usk. Near the castle they were confronted and scattered by forces under Richard of Codnor and Sir John Greyndour. In the skirmish, Tudor ap Gruffydd, Owain's brother, was killed, Gruffydd ab Owain was captured and sent to Nottingham castle. One of the priests killed that day was, in the eyes of the Scots chronicler Walter Bower, a rabble-rousing legend named John ap Hywel (John Powell), the revered abbot of Llantarnam. According to Adam Usk, who was away on the continent at the time, 300 rebels were beheaded by Codnor's troops after the battle, although this too is uncorroborated elsewhere and must be viewed with suspicion. While the casualties sustained were numerically light, the impact of having family members killed or captured possibly affected Glyn Dŵr's strategic planning in the months which followed. Even more bad fortune befell Owain and his supporters in the following weeks. His secretary, Owain ap Gruffydd ap Rhisiart, was captured in May and John Hanmer, Owain's brother-in-law, also found himself in chains in June.[9]

Elsewhere in Europe, that grand continental power, France, was exerting its power beyond its borders. The great French adventure for 1405 envisioned the capture of Rome, no less, and the campaign had been openly building since April. Once the Holy See had been seized, Benedict XIII would be installed and he would name one of the French dukes, either Orleans or Anjou, as Emperor. Although statements supporting the campaign were issued in the king's name, the initiative clearly favoured Benedict's cause, which, for some time, had also been that of the duke of Orleans. The plan was for French troops under Duke Louis of Bourbon and Duke Louis II of Anjou, claimant to the kingdom of Naples, to advance through the French-allied states of the Ligurian coast to Pisa and from there to strike for Rome. The rival pope, Innocent VII, fled the chaotic popular revolt which broke out in Rome that summer, in which several members of his entourage were cut down by the mob as he made his escape. The moment had arrived, Rome was to be taken, and the court despatched Louis of Anjou for Genoa with significant forces. Benedict had arrived in Genoa in May, where Marshal Boucicaut, the French governor of the territory, was attempting to negotiate alliances and secure routes for an advance on Rome.[10]

In addition, the striking failure of the Bourbon-led mission to Wales in 1404 slighted the honour and reputation of the French. Therefore, apart from fulfilling promises of assistance made to their new Welsh ally and consequently taking the war to the king of England, a mission in 1405 would redress the self-inflicted insult to the considerable honour of France. This was certainly the mood of the moment among the lay chroniclers:

> Marshal de Rieux and the lord of Hugueville, considering the great dishonour there would be to the king if we did not go and help the Welsh, seeing as though the king had promised it, deliberated and

decided to go there, and in fact they went there. In going they had a
series of encounters at sea, as well as when they arrived in Wales, from
where they returned with their honour.[11]

The religious commentators appeared to be of the same mind: 'My lords
the dukes of France, who controlled the government, wished to keep the
promise of aid made to the prince of Wales, and at the same time repair
the shameful failure of the count of la Marche by some notable feat of
arms.'[12] In parliament, even the Burgundian spokesman drew attention
to England's 'redoubtable enemies, the Scots and the Welsh'.[13] Therefore,
with their pride wounded, the French determined to send an army to
Wales during the 1405 campaigning season and assembled a fleet in Brest
harbour.

A *via facti* strategy to take Rome and end the schism was in favour;
the forces to achieve that were being assembled and an expeditionary
force was en route to Wales. Simultaneously unbalancing England by
causing trouble in Wales might gain additional time to press the main
offensive in Rome or end the long conflict with England by inserting
a weaker or French-supported king on the English throne. Mid-late
summer 1405 was no doubt an exciting time at court in Paris; with the
desirable prospect that a victory in either theatre would hugely favour
French interests.

* * * * *

Meanwhile, with royalist forces poised to simultaneously invade north and
south Wales, news broke in June of a serious rebellion centred on York.
Although his movements during this period are difficult to ascertain,
events would reveal that Henry Percy, earl of Northumberland, had
been plotting against the king.[14] This large-scale, widespread northern
revolt was nominally led by Richard Scrope, the archbishop of York,
Thomas Mowbray, Earl Marshal and earl of Norfolk, Henry Percy, earl
of Northumberland and Thomas, Lord Bardolf. Scrope and Mowbray
appear to have risen too early and were too distant from the alleged
military commanders of the movement and their additional troops.
Duped into parley with Ralph Neville, earl of Westmorland, they were
seized and summarily executed a few days later.[15] The extraordinary deed
of executing an archbishop was roundly criticised; the Roman pope, to
whom England adhered, vented his fury on the English ambassadors who

related the event to him. The majority of the rebels dispersed, returned home and were eventually pardoned, according to distant Adam Usk, after removing their trousers, prostrating themselves on the ground and humbly begging. Percy and Bardolf retreated to Scotland. Others loyal to Percy resisted militarily and held towns such as Berwick against King Henry, eventually meeting brutal execution as traitors.

The following year Percy and Bardolf were tried for treason and condemned in their absence. Although it is difficult to ascertain to what extent the treason charges contained general defamations and slanders against the accused, there are several articles of note. They recounted the actions and movements of the York rebels in May and June 1405, justifying the execution of many of them for treason, and used the same evidence against Percy and Bardolf.[16] Trial articles seven and eight categorically connected Percy to the Scots and French ambassadors in alliance, presenting written evidence in Percy's name and bearing his seal. Article nine is particularly compelling: a letter from Henry Percy to Louis of Orleans, whom Percy addressed as 'most high and most powerful prince, the duke of Orleans'. The letter tells how Percy's ambassadors had approached the king of France's envoys in Scotland to discuss an alliance between them. It also announced Percy's intention and will, along with his allies, to continue the fight for King Richard, if still alive, and to avenge him if dead. Percy also said that he intended to continue the 'just quarrel' of the queen of England, 'your niece' Isabella, Richard's widow, and to make war on Henry of Lancaster. Percy then acknowledged that Louis had sustained this quarrel and others against Henry, so he requested aid in his conflict against Lancaster and offered his support to the king of France. The letter is not dated and, being situated among other evidence from summer 1405, it is tempting to assume it was written at that point. However, it seems perhaps axiomatic that such an effort to attract Orleanist support would have been planned long in advance and, consequently, it would predate the moment when the rebels found themselves in the field. Irrespective of the unsure dating, the letter demonstrates that Percy's connection to France was not solely and vicariously through the Welsh. In addition, treason trial articles twelve and thirteen explicitly connected Percy to the rebels in Wales, in adherence, counsel and alliance. This therefore suggests that the Tripartite Indenture was more widely known in contemporary circles than has previously been supposed. It is unknown whether a bond was formed between Louis and Henry Percy at that point. Northumberland's apparently key role in the betrayal and capture of Richard II might have gravely damaged his chances of attaining instant or profound amity within the French court. Nevertheless, this letter showed that an alliance between Percy and Orleans was in the air.[17] This is further supported by a letter written by Charles VI in 1406 in which he admonished Henry Percy and the English rebels for not having risen with enough men when the French had come to Wales:

> They should know that, if recently, when we sent an army to Wales, we had been sure that the partisans of the just cause and the friends of the legitimate heirs to the throne would welcome our people favourably and would hasten to join them, we would have had at our disposal far greater forces, but we are still ready to help them in the aforementioned cases.[18]

The York revolt stands out for two reasons, the first being the unusual fact that the leaders issued a manifesto, which was read out by the archbishop to the assembled thousands on Shipton Moor. The second is the brutal fate suffered by Archbishop Scrope and the Earl Marshal. The intriguing factor is that several manifesto articles mentioned the Welsh, despite there being no overt link between Scrope and Glyn Dŵr, but through Northumberland. Percy's alliance with the Welsh can only be formally dated to late February 1405; the manifesto for the June revolt is likely to have been written after that point, demonstrating that the York uprising and Welsh actions for that summer were coordinated to some degree. Without the connection between Northumberland and Glyn Dŵr made in the Tripartite Indenture, there seems no reason to include mention of the Welsh within the ambit of a northern rebellion seemingly centred on York and the Percy-held Scottish border towns and fortresses, such as Berwick.[19]

As a document, the manifesto read out by Scrope appears a fiery, rebel-rousing defiance of the king against whom it levelled ten accusations. After each one, Henry and his adherents were thunderously excommunicated for their crimes. The articles described Henry's proposed duel with the duke of Norfolk, the Earl Marshal's late father, and subsequent exile in 1398. The consequence was Henry's return under arms to reclaim his inheritance but, having gained substantial support, he contravened his promises and seized the crown. He was also accused of robbing and killing nobles, clergy, merchants and members of virtually all other strata in the kingdom. His false seizure, deposition and murder of King Richard, son of the noble Edward, also earned Henry Archbishop Scrope's excommunication. The next treason charge elaborated Henry's brutal treatment and slaughter of many clergymen, which proved to be a recurrent accusation throughout his reign. Then, he was condemned for his execution without trial of the earls of the Epiphany Revolt of 1400 and of the Percys, the brother and the son of the apparently approaching earl. He was also charged with crimes against the church, Rome and the universities. Scrope then criticised the military expeditions and harm caused during Henry's reign up to that point, which had damaged and impoverished the kingdom through intolerable exactions. The final article of the manifesto reassured the audience that the York rebels did not seek to bring widespread changes, but had three specific aims. The first was to put the 'rightful heir' on the throne. Although no name is offered here, bearing in mind the context of the time and the Tripartite Indenture, the Mortimer heir is the only credible candidate. Secondly, the rebels wished to make peace with the Welsh and other enemies of the kingdom. The general pacific appeal might echo sentiments common towards the end of Richard's reign. It is noteworthy that the Welsh were mentioned in first place, and the Scots and the French not named at all, but covered by a blanket term referring to other enemies of the kingdom. The final intention, perhaps inserted tactically here to guarantee a rousing cheer at the end of the reading, vowed to do away with Henry's exactions and promised the grant of an indulgence.[20]

Although this revolt was swiftly crushed at York, and the remainder chased over the border or besieged within northern castles, the timing and connectivity with the Welsh is particularly noteworthy. This was a revolt that had been planned well in advance. Given the confirmed connections between all parties engaged in the endeavours intended for the summer of 1405, there seems little doubt that this was a coordinated effort: an attempted coup in England, backed by the Orleanists. It is unlikely that reports of the defeat and dispersal of the rebels at York reached France before the fleet set sail for Wales.

During July and early August, Owain convened his second parliament, this time held at Harlech. Two Flintshire landowners, David Whitmore and Ieuan ap Maredudd, acted as spies for Sir John Stanley of Cheshire, one of King Henry's trusted men in the region, who duly reported it to the king:[21]

as fortune would have it, one David Whitmore and Yevan ap Meredith, two of the more influential persons in the county of Flint, were come thither to talk to me ...And also they have also told me how that Owen Glyndwr has summoned a Parliament at the present time, being held at Harlech, where there will be four of the more influential persons of each commote throughout all Wales, being in his obedience. And also, most dread Lord, the said David and Yevan have informed me that, as far as they have been able to learn up to this time, the said Owen, provided that he can be assured at his said Parliament of having a very great force and considerable aid out of France, doth propose to send to you, most mighty Lord, after this his Parliament above mentioned, for a treaty; and the same David and Yevan are gone to the said Parliament for to know therein all the purposes and results thereof, and to meet me again at the County Court to be held on Tuesday next in Chester, to certify me as to all the truth thereon, and the purpose of the said Parliament.[22]

There seems no reason to dismiss this report as fanciful. While it confirms the occasion of the parliament, it also gives other valuable information. Perhaps most importantly, it reveals that Owain wanted a treaty with Henry. No further details are known, but it would certainly have proposed peace of some kind. It seems probable that the treaty would have sought some form of recognition of Owain and his position in Wales, but also, it seems highly likely that Glyn Dŵr would have pursued a prisoner exchange for his son, brother-in-law and others who had fallen in to English hands. In addition, this shows that the Welsh knew that the French were coming that summer, which proves further unseen communications between Wales and France. However, because of Stanley's spies, Henry IV also knew of the imminent French arrival. The fleet arrived in Welsh waters just a week after Stanley wrote his letter to the king and were therefore probably already at sea when the letter was written. French evidence claimed that Glyn Dŵr was present to greet the expeditionary force as it came ashore; if correct, the second parliament could not have lasted more than a few days into August. David and Ieuan's evidence also sheds light on the composition of the Commons element of the parliament; 'four of the more influential persons of each commote throughout Wales' would attend, no doubt alongside the nobles and the clergy. This would have been a sizeable assembly and shows that Owain engaged equitably with all Welsh communities under his rule. Stanley's letter also makes plain that the English knew and accepted that areas of Wales were under Owain's obedience; this implies that oaths to him were common knowledge and, in receiving them, he was acting typically for a ruler of his time. In keeping with other parliaments of the period, Owain's assembly gave representation to contemporary society's three estates; the clergy, the nobles and the commons. Owain's second parliament appears to have discussed the impending arrival of their French allies and the intention to treat with Henry IV. The king was likely armed with this intelligence before Owain made contact with him that summer.

With the rest of the French court focused on the drive for Rome and on the fleet bound for Wales, Jean, duke of Burgundy, an adherent of the Roman pope and ally, economically at least, of England, chose that moment to attempt a coup d'état of sorts, or at least to gain control by attacking the policies of the government under Louis of Orleans. The quarrel escalated rapidly and, in light of the deepening dispute between the ducal factions, Louis of Anjou was recalled before he reached Genoa, and the duke of Bourbon was not permitted to leave Paris for the Italian campaign, his influence being required at court. The two adversarial dukes issued a series of condemnations of one another and, with their respective allies, gathered thousands of troops around Paris from August onwards. Amid the spiralling tension and manoeuvring forces, the government effectively ground to a halt. After a period of high tension, Burgundy was obliged to withdraw his appeals to parliament. His actions pushed Queen Isabeau and the venerable Jean, duke of Berry, into the Orleanist camp; these three made a tripartite alliance in December that year.[23] Perhaps in shock, most of the other great magnates appeared to retain positions of indecisive neutrality. While Boucicaut was establishing a safe path for the advance, Benedict's army was ravaged by a plague which erupted in the region. This bold initiative to take Rome withered as the toll of plague victims rose, the forces France had assembled were no longer strong enough for the task. Benedict had retired from Italy to Nice by October, where he learned that Innocent VII's position had become so weak that he was dependent on the military backing of Ladislas, the rival king of Naples, who in turn had negotiated a pact with the influential Colonna family, who commanded the forces holding the Vatican at that time. France's decisive opportunity in Italy had been lost through squabbling in Paris and for subsequently failing to advance when the chance arose. Nevertheless, preparations for the expedition to Wales would have been too far advanced to halt for any reason save royal command; the French were about to invade Henry's domain.[24]

CHAPTER EIGHT

The Two French Invasions of 1405

Consequently, following their orders, from Brittany and Normandy, they mustered with six hundred crossbowmen, one thousand two hundred lightly armoured sergeants and eight hundred chosen fighting men, who were to be transported to Wales in two large warships and thirty medium-sized vessels.[1]

At about this time, the marshal of France and the master of the crossbowmen, by orders from the king and at his expense, collected twelve thousand fighting men, who came to Brest in Brittany to help the prince of Wales against the English. They had six score sailing ships that they found there.[2]

On 7 September 1405, Robert Mascall, bishop of Hereford, recorded that a procession was held for the king's expedition against the duke of Orleans, who, according to the bishop, was with 144 armed ships in Milford in support of the Welsh rebels.[3] Although Louis was not present, it seems clear that in contemporary England, the invasion of west Wales was believed to be the duke of Orleans's enterprise.

English sources are suspiciously quiet about the matter; only Thomas Walsingham appears to have mentioned it in any detail. His *Chronica Maiora*, which can be dated to 1422 or slightly earlier, largely denigrates the deeds of the mission.[4] Although its absence in English records might suggest that the invasion was a minor event of little relevance, this is extremely unlikely. The insertion of hostile land forces by the French adversary into a region of mainland Britain claimed by the English crown can only be a highly noteworthy event. Moreover, the territory in question was designated as the prime, titular appanage of the heir to the English throne and had been held militarily by a large, incredibly costly spread of garrisoned castles for over a century. In addition, Henry IV's reaction on learning of the French landing demonstrated the gravity he attributed to the event. It is striking that for months, this French army was able to campaign against the king of England on the British mainland, and remained unchallenged by the warrior-king, Henry IV. In light of these factors, it seems reasonable to raise the idea that this important event was downplayed in English sources for political reasons.

However, despite only fragmentary evidence in English sources, there are two contemporary French accounts of the expedition. One was written by the Burgundian soldier and courtier, Enguerrand de Monstrelet; the other comes from the Chronicle of Saint-Denys, which was probably written by Michel Pintoin. Although Monstrelet's chronicle was published in 1444, it was begun around 1413 and the first book, from which this evidence comes, was probably completed by 1422, the same year the Saint-Denys chronicle ended.[5] These two main sources appear to be the root of all other French accounts. Certainly, the chronicler Jean Juvenal des Ursins rehashed that of Saint-Denys, while Pierre Cochon appears to have borrowed from Monstrelet when passing comment on the matter.[6] This is unsurprising, as des Ursins wrote his work in Paris and apparently copied large tracts directly from nearby Saint-Denys, whereas Monstrelet's and Cochon's chronicles were both composed in Burgundian territory.[7] Monstrelet and the monk of Saint-Denys offer somewhat different tales of the mission; however, both regale seemingly credible, detailed accounts and both discernibly contain errors.

The Chronicle of Saint-Denys Account of the 1405 expedition[8]

The Deeds of Marshal de Rieux in Wales

My lords the dukes of France, who were the principal governors of the kingdom, wished to fulfil the promise of aid made to the prince of Wales and, at the same time, to repair the shameful failure of the count of la Marche, who had previously been commissioned with this operation, by some notable feat of arms. They resolved to send to that country soldiers under the renowned knights, Marshal de Rieux, lord de Hugueville, the Master of the Crossbowmen of France, and the lord Borgne de la Heuse. Consequently, following their orders, from Brittany and Normandy, they mustered with six hundred crossbowmen, one thousand two hundred lightly armoured sergeants and eight hundred chosen fighting men, who were to be transported to Wales in two large warships and thirty medium-sized vessels. And, after a month waiting for the sea to turn calm, they all embarked around the end of July and finally arrived in the port of 'Willeforde' [Milford], in the county of 'Pennebroc' [Pembroke]. There, ten thousand Welshmen sent by the prince duly met them to help the army freely enter the principality, and if any obstacle were met, they could help them.

Then, the French with the Welsh captured and destroyed the fields of the country, and the fire voraciously consumed them, and went straight to the town of 'Heleford' [Haverford], from whose heavily fortified castle, immediately sallied many archers closely followed by three hundred men armoured from head to toe, resolved to make a stand and began fighting. Soon, many were vanquished, and they captured sixteen, killed forty and compelled the rest to flee. Thereafter, they reached the town and made many assaults; and indeed seventy of the garrison were killed, but because of the strength of that place they were unable to take it and having ordered their siege engines to be transported by sea to another place, they abandoned the siege. However, although ever so few of the French fell in these assaults, nevertheless a famous knight called 'Patrouillart de Tries' went to his grave, whose loss was solemnly suffered by all of the French.

The same day, a selected group of foragers set off to a castle named 'Picot' [Picton] to take control and they forced it to come to surrender at the first assault. Consequently from this place, laden with plunder, they withdrew, and through the surrounding countryside, leaving none unhurt by this event, with fire and sword harmed all that they could, and arrived at a walled coastal town called 'Canneby' [Tenby], the army, by common agreement assented to besiege, encircle and manfully take it by surrounding it with archers and the assembled siege engines. However, although they industriously pressed, they had not yet started the first assault, when in the distance they saw a fleet of thirty ships approaching, with armed men and well-provisioned, that had been launched to come to the aid of the inhabitants.

When they learned the truth from their scouts, so much fear and terror rushed over them, and death seemed imminent, and because most of the boats they had were on the sand, and they were not able to push them to the sea, having no means of saving themselves in their boats, soon they had evacuated the beaches and consumed the ships with fire, so they did not fall into the enemy's hands. Next, with no one as yet in pursuit, they completely lost heart, choked by fear and fled in such confusion and with such speed that they abandoned their siege engines and most of their ammunition, and scattered their baggage, although at that time, they had with them two thousand Welsh horsemen.

After this shameful flight, they burned villages, as was their way, until they reached the very strong castle of 'Sancti Clari' [St Clears], where they established a siege. But at last they promised to come to terms if the inhabitants of the good town of 'Callemardin' [Carmarthen], nearby, came to their obedience. From this well-populated town, surrounded by a strong wall, the king of England perceived many opportunities and from here archers with armed forces often made sorties causing the Welsh much harm.

Consequently, the prince firmly swore not to depart from there, until his men had captured it. There, the French positioned themselves in one place and the Welsh in another, after spending four days besieging it, with shovels and picks made of iron they undermined the walls in that place, so that they could fight hand-to-hand in the open. There, many of the enemy were wounded and killed, a second assault was repeated, when the French attempted to take possession of the tops of the walls, the townsfolk requested a mutual peace treaty to be arranged.

They agreed, both, that they would stay in the town and, with the exception of their arms, keep as much of their chattels as each person could carry – thereby the prince's oath would be observed – and that he and the French would be given a free entry. Then the prince and the Welsh, who had not yet reached the foot of the walls, accepted this offer, and praised the vigour of the French and, as was agreed, the prince and his men freely entered the town. From that town the Welsh brought out plunder, with a bountiful burden of loot, the surrounding walls having been for the most part destroyed, and set fire to every street in the town and the suburbs. Thereafter both armies reached the ramparts of the fort of 'Cardinguan' [Cardigan], and due to the inauspicious outcome for their neighbours, the terrified townsfolk swiftly surrendered.

And finally, the French, who had advanced sixty leagues across hostile territory, requested of the prince to divide them on account of the sterility of the surrounding countryside, and to allocate them to suitable places to inhabit, while a fleet was sought to repatriate them. And therefore they remained in three places until the feast of All Saints, and then the knights and squires arranged to return in six small ships, leaving behind one thousand two hundred lightly armoured sergeants and five hundred archers in Wales, over whom a Picard squire named 'Blesum de Belay' was put in charge, who all obeyed, until ships to return them would be sent.

They returned in dishonour, on account of how they thus abandoned those who had fought for their glory and were always first in the assaults, and who had frequently pulled them out of many dangers. However, those nobles were praised who faithfully remained with them, kindly helped them and saw to their needs, and gathered ships from wheresoever at their own costs and brought them back around Lent.

Therefore, the monk of Saint-Denys recorded a short campaign by a large force that struggled to demonstrate its superiority over a small number of castles and towns in south-west Wales. The chronicle identified three leaders who ranked among the highest echelons of French military leadership of their day, indicative of the importance placed on this mission. The Breton lord, Jean de Rieux, was a career soldier and one of two marshals of France, which was one of the most senior appointments in French forces of the time. The other marshal of the day, Jean le Maingre, usually called Boucicaut, was the governor of Genoa, a possession which gave France a major territory in Italy and consequently allowed them to play an influencing role in Italian affairs. Given the proposals for the leaders of the 1404 invasion force to take and hold castles in Wales, the marshal's presence is noteworthy and a similar role as a French representative in Wales is possible to envisage. The de Rieux family served Louis, duke of Orleans, as marshals of his forces before and after the elevation of Jean to the post of Marshal of France. Jean de Hangest, was lord of Hugueville and, more significantly, he was the Master of the Crossbowmen of France, which was also a senior military appointment. Jean de Hangest was a Picard officer appointed by the crown who had previously served as a chamberlain to the king. In that role, his chief responsibility was the control and payment of the king's domestic budget; an important position given to a trusted servant of the crown. Through family lands held in Genlis, de Hangest certainly had connections to the Burgundian court. However, he faithfully served the king and was a devoted Orleanist in the civil war against the Burgundians, eventually dying at Agincourt. He brought a great deal of military and diplomatic experience to the campaign, as did Jean de Rieux. In the case of Jean de Hangest, this also included siege skills and artillery knowledge, which was an increasingly important and common factor in period warfare. The third leader identified was Robert de la Heuse, also known as 'le Borgne' or 'Strabo'. Both nicknames indicate an injured or missing eye and, although he served the king, he was also an adherent of

Louis, duke of Orleans. These men consistently figured in contemporary chronicles and documents; they were among the most experienced and highest-ranking military leaders France could have sent.[9]

The Saint-Denys chronicle detailed the size of the army; 800 elite men, 600 crossbowmen and 1,200 lightly armoured sergeants in a fleet composed of two large warships and thirty medium-sized vessels. It added that these troops were raised in Brittany and Normandy which, at the time, were under Orleanist influence, though not necessarily governance. The army size is worthy of comment here; the better-known army sent to Scotland in 1385 under Jean de Vienne comprised 1,300 men-at-arms and 250 crossbows. This has been described as 'a major French army', yet it was only just over half of the size of that sent to Wales. With that in mind, the relative obscurity of the Welsh expedition seems curious, although this might identify an area in which the Saint-Denys chronicle is incorrect.[10]

The chronicle tells that the French waited for a month for the sea to turn calm, but set sail before the end of July; the timing is relevant if a midsummer rising been plotted with Northumberland. While a more common season to sail, it contrasts notably with the mustering and November launching of the 1404 attack fleet. When they arrived at 'Willeforde' (Milford), they were allegedly greeted by a Welsh force of 10,000 sent by the man the French recognised as the *principi Wallie*, the prince of Wales, Glyn Dŵr. The chronicle then related how the French and Welsh devastated the country in their path, and marched on 'Heleford'(Haverford). There was a battle in front of Haverford, followed by a brief siege. Although the French and Welsh reportedly inflicted scores of casualties on the enemy, they failed to take the castle. In the fighting, the French lost a knight from a famous family, 'Patroullart de Trya' (Patrouillart de Tries). The casualties caused, forty in the battle and seventy in the assault, seem believably low, although denote a significant fight. However, the defending force, identified as 300 armoured men plus a large number of archers, has not been traced in English sources. It is noteworthy that the artillery had been sent elsewhere, presumably on ships with other men, and this implies that the French had split their forces. From there, French foragers or scouts took 'Picot' (Picton) in a swift first assault. They ravaged the countryside as far as 'Canneby' (Tenby), once again putting all to fire and sword, 'as was their way'. Here, they prepared to assault the walled, fortified town, encircling it with crossbowmen and bringing up artillery, implying that the forces had been reunited, at least in part, by this point. The operation was apparently disrupted when a thirty-strong fleet was spotted, packed with English soldiers coming to relieve the town. It is unclear how the chronicler or the observers could know that these soldiers were furnished and well-provisioned, and this perhaps indicates another hole in this version of the campaign. This oncoming English fleet apparently caused an uncontrollable panic among the French, who abandoned the siege and their artillery. As their ships were stranded, they unloaded and torched them in order to deny the enemy. The French then fled in terror, despite the fact that there was no one in pursuit and they were reportedly accompanied by 2,000 Welsh horsemen. If the original estimation of 10,000 Welsh troops was accurate, this would indicate that the Welsh had split their forces, or that the Saint-Denys account is inconsistent. One English source possibly refers to part of this incident, Walsingham reported that Thomas Berkeley and Henry Pay had burnt fifteen French ships in an unspecified harbour, although Milford Haven could perhaps be presumed from the context. However, Walsingham does not mention the French army in flight nor any other details helpful to understanding the land campaign, except that Carmarthen fell to the allies. Walsingham's chronicle appears inconsistent and intriguing in other details. He identified the French fleet as having 140 ships, yet it seems difficult to envisage such a powerful naval force fleeing from the thirty English ships proposed by the French monk. The Saint-Denys chronicle proposed a force comprising just thirty-two vessels, which would be inadequate to transport the army of around 2,600 soldiers, as well as their equipment, a comparable number of sailors, supplies or horses. In this area also, the Saint-Denys chronicle seems inaccurate. Walsingham wrote that at this time and later, English naval forces intercepted French ships attempting to reach Wales.[11]

Having recomposed themselves and after attacking villages in their path, the French prepared to attack 'Sancti Clari' (St Clears) whose residents promised to surrender if the French took 'Callemardin' (Carmarthen). When the allied force arrived there, Glyn Dŵr, who was again recognised as *princeps Walensibus* or prince of the Welsh, swore not to leave until he was master of the place. The chronicle then described a four-day siege of the well-populated, strongly walled town. The French sapped the walls, forming a breach that would allow them to fight hand-to-hand. The first assault apparently inflicted numerous casualties on the defenders. The

French almost gained possession of the wall parapets and overran the breach in the second assault. Consequently, the inhabitants sought parley. They offered terms to the French and the Welsh, on condition that the allies allowed the inhabitants to live and to remain in the town. Due to the fact that they consented when Carmarthen was theirs and would have been easy to garrison, this suggests that the French were not intending to stay this time, in contrast to the evidence which reported the aims of the 1404 mission. The Welsh also agreed to the deal struck between the French and the town's inhabitants, and then ransacked the town. They set fire to the streets and suburbs, and eventually left the town with significant damage to the walls. This action underlines the fact that neither of the allies intended to garrison the town, but had largely destroyed it, perhaps aiming to deny the enemy its use. It should be recalled that Carmarthen was the most heavily-populated English borough in Wales at the time. Therefore, a notable gesture can be discerned by the French and the Welsh taking it, plundering it, partly destroying it and then discarding it. From there the allied army marched to 'Cardinguan' (Cardigan) which, fearing the same fate, capitulated. According to the Saint-Denys chronicle, the expedition then appears to have wound down its military activities after having covered an estimated sixty leagues. This seems to be an inaccurate figure, since sixty leagues seems significantly too far for the described tour around Pembrokeshire.[12]

The chronicle claimed that the French asked the Welsh prince to station them in three different areas, in order not to suffer privation until they could return to France. Glyn Dŵr did this and the French remained in Wales until the feast of All Saints, 1 November, when six vessels arrived and returned the knights and squires to France. The monk of Saint-Denys tells us that they left the 1,200 troops and 500 crossbowmen under the command of a Picard squire named 'Blesum de Belay' in Latin, or 'le Bègue de Bellay' in French, until further ships could be sent to them. This claims therefore that the French crammed into the six small ships mentioned the 800 chosen fighting men and the 100 crossbowmen from the original army muster, minus any casualties, but adding their equipment, supplies and horses, as well as the expedition's leaders. This appears to be a further inaccuracy in the monk's account.

The Saint-Denys chronicle commented, in its frequently scathing tone, of the disgrace and dishonour of the nobles of the expedition who had, in the chronicler's view, abandoned those who had faithfully served under them. However, it reassured the reader that some nobles remained true to their word and brought the men back to France towards Lent, 1406. The Scots chronicler, abbot Walter Bower, wrote that the French stayed in Wales for nearly a year and were sent home by Owain in honour.[13] However, in perhaps another mark against the Saint-Denys account, none of the expedition leaders appears to have suffered in terms of honour, appointments or reputation, in a way that Jacques de Bourbon's name temporarily declined in the aftermath of the 1404 mission.

The contingent commander, 'le Bègue de Bellay', has proved quite an enigma, but from a list of the knights and squires of the realm from 1400 emerge three credible candidates. One who, despite seeming to have the correct surname, only comes to prominence after 1415 and does not appear to have the same martial pedigree or Orleanist connections as the other men. Therefore, Jean de Bellay, while still a possibility, is probably ruled out.[14] The other two, 'Monseigneur le Besgue de Villaines' and 'Monseigneur de Bellauges', both campaigned together in the royal army sent against Guelders in 1388. Although 'Monseigneur de Bellauges', and variations of that name, remained active around court during the relevant period, due to his rank and wealth, he also seems less likely than the final possibility.[15] The only candidate bearing the unusual nickname 'le Bègue', or 'the stammerer', is Pierre de Villaines, commonly referred to in a variety of contemporary sources as 'le Bègue de Villaines'. Due to the rarity of that nickname, this man was probably more memorable than most. In addition, a number of the Villaines family, similarly to the lord of Bellenges, fought for the Orleanist cause throughout this period. Pierre de Villaines senior was connected to the Marmouset government favoured by Charles and Louis, and escaped the worst persecution of Philippe of Burgundy when he regained power, suffering imprisonment rather than execution. He had campaigned with Bertrand du Guesclin in Spain, losing an eye fighting the English and, perhaps notably, appears to have fought in a number of battles on the same side as Owain Lawgoch. As sub-commanders in du Guesclin's forces, it seems likely that Lawgoch and le Bègue knew each other well.[16] He was also associated with known Orleanists such as Jean Montagu, bishop of Chartres. In addition, he served in the government of Touraine, Louis's first duchy. Moreover, le Bègue can be found in Brittany and La Rochelle during the relevant period, in the company of Robert de la Heuse and Villaine's family had marriage connections to the Hangest family. However, Pierre de Villaines senior held a number of titles, particularly in western France and Spain, and might have already died by this time. While alive, he moved in the highest circles of court and government, therefore he was too well known and too highly ranked to be confused with a squire. However, it is worth speculating that one of Pierre's sons had his father's affliction, a stammer, and was known by the same nickname. Further source evidence supports this assertion, because if le Bègue was marooned in Wales, he can be traced in records after the expedition's return. In 1406, he appeared in Malicorne, one of Pierre de Villaine senior's lordships, in western France. He served as governor of La Rochelle and can be traced in the Orleanist west until 1410.[17] One of Pierre de Villaines sons, also Pierre, died at Agincourt. The cautious conclusion is that the mysterious leader left behind with the troops in Saint-Denys's account, if this event ever happened, was one of the sons of the well-known Pierre de Villaines. As staunch Orleanists, they were exactly the sort of dependable servants to charge with such a commission.

The Saint-Denys version of the invasion paints a picture of cowardly troops led by unworthy nobles, destroying the fields and villages of west Wales and achieving little, either in their own names or to assist their ally. It should be noted that the Saint-Denys chronicler frequently and manifestly had an axe to grind against the behaviour of the nobility and should be considered as a highly political source. This should not affect his ability to present facts and details, but it clearly gave his account, indeed his chronicle at large, a certain flavour. The other record of the expedition, that of Enguerrand de Monstrelet, was also politically flavoured, but differently to the monk's account.

Enguerrand de Monstrelet's Account of the 1405 Expedition[18]

The Marshal of France and the master of crossbows, by order of the king of France, go to England to the assistance of the prince of Wales.

At about this time, the marshal of France and the master of the cross-bowmen, by orders from the king and at his expense, collected twelve thousand fighting men, who came to Brest in Brittany to help the prince of Wales against the English. They had six score sailing ships that they found there, and due to the wind, which was against them, they stayed there for fifteen days. But when they had a wind which was favourable for them, they arrived at the port of 'Harfort' [Haverford] in England, which they took swiftly, and killed the inhabitants except those who turned in flight; and wasted the surrounding country. Then they came to the castle of 'Harford', where the earl of Arundel was and several men at arms and men of war. And when they had burned the town and the suburbs of the said castle, they left from there, destroying all the country before them by fire and by sword.

Then they went to a town called 'Tenebi' [Tenby], situated eighteen leagues from the said castle, and there the aforesaid French found the aforesaid prince of Wales and wholly ten thousand combatants who were waiting for them there. So, they all went together to 'Calemarchin' [Carmarthen] twelve leagues from Tenebi, and from there, in entering the 'pays de Morgnie' [Glamorgan], they went to the Round Table, namely the noble abbey, then they took the road to go to 'Vincestre' [Worcester]. They burned the suburbs and the surrounding country, and three leagues further they encountered the king of England who was coming against them with a large force; there they drew up, the one facing the other, and openly put themselves in battle array, each one of these parties on a mountain and there was a wide valley between the two hosts. They each wished that the opposing force would mount an attack, but this was not done. And they were this way for eight days, that each day, in the morning, they arrayed themselves for battle, the one against the other, and there they remained all day until evening. During which time there were several skirmishes between them, in which around two hundred were killed from the two sides and several wounded. Among them, on the French side, three knights were killed, namely my lord 'Patroullart de Troies', brother of the aforesaid Marshal of France, the lord 'de Mathelonne' and the lord 'de La Ville'. Moreover, with this, the French and the Welsh were hard-pressed by famine and other discomforts. Because with great difficulty could they gather food because the English closely guarded the crossing points. Finally, when these two forces had been the one facing the other has been said, the aforesaid king of England, seeing that his adversaries would not attack him, withdrew to 'Vincestre' during the evening. But he was pursued by some of the French and the Welsh who robbed him of eighteen carts laden with food and other baggage.

And these French and Welsh withdrew to Wales. While this journey was taking place, the French fleet was at sea and in it were a number of men at arms to guard it. This fleet approached Wales, to a port to which they had been directed, and there they found the French, namely the admiral of France and the master of the crossbowmen who, with their men, put to sea and sailed until they arrived without mishap at Saint-Pol de Leon. When they had disembarked and visited their men, they found that they had lost a good sixty of them, of whom the three knights mentioned above were foremost. And afterwards they left there and returned to France, each to their own places, except for the two royal officers, who went before the king in Paris, and the other princes of his blood, by whom they were received with much jubilation.

The account written by Enguerrand de Monstrelet differs from that of Saint-Denys on several critical details, although in places the two accounts also tally. Similarly to the Saint-Denys description, Monstrelet made errors which detract from his version of the expedition. First, Monstrelet placed the expedition among other events of 1403, but it occurred in 1405 – although the entry began with the vague proviso of 'around this time', indicating his uncertainty. It is probable that Monstrelet confused the 1405 French–Breton expedition with the attack of 1403: both missions landed troops in south-west Wales and combined with Welsh forces under a known leader. In 1403, that Welsh were led by Henry Don, but in 1405 Glyn Dŵr appears to have been present.

Both chronicles agree that the expedition leaders were the Marshal of France and the Master of the Crossbowmen; however, Monstrelet identified 'Patroullart de Troies' as the brother of the marshal leading this expedition. This would make 'the marshal' Renauld de Tries, who was an admiral of France until he died shortly after this expedition. Ducal records show that the de Tries family were servants of the dukes of Orleans throughout this period, further emphasising the Orleanist backing for this project. 'Patroullart' had served Louis as chamberlain. It is possible that an admiral would lead such an expedition, just as the mission to Scotland in 1385 had been commanded by an admiral, Jean de Vienne. However, this more likely informs us of who commanded the fleet, rather than disputing the force's leadership.[19]

The figure of 12,000 soldiers is obviously inaccurate and even Thomas Johnes, the chronicle's original translator, corrected it to 1,200 men, which would be an entirely more credible number. However, this might also be a confusion with the reportedly 12–15,000-strong army raised in 1404 for Jacques de Bourbon's humiliating failure. Also, the fleet sizes are radically different in the two accounts. Monstrelet described it as six score sailed vessels, as opposed to the thirty-two suggested by Saint-Denys. Walsingham's chronicle and the bishop of Hereford's evidence support Monstrelet's figure.[20]

Both chroniclers agree that the fleet was delayed by contrary winds. Monstrelet's fleet left Brest and arrived in 'Harfort', where the French slew several inhabitants and then made for the castle. Monstrelet incorrectly claimed that the earl of Arundel was present, but his description of the burning of the suburbs and devastating the area with fire and sword tallies with that of Saint-Denys. On a point of geographical likelihood, Milford seems a more credible place to land than Haverford; however, Monstrelet might simply have named the region after the nearest sizeable castle to feature in the campaign account. Next, Monstrelet also concurred that the French went to 'Tenebi', where he claims that the French found the 'prince de Gales' and 10,000 soldiers waiting for them. In slight contrast, the monk's chronicle placed these Welsh troops at Milford, where he believed that the French landed. It is noteworthy that both versions of the expedition describe this Welsh force as 10,000-strong. In translations of Monstrelet's chronicle, 'Tenebi' is described as eighteen miles from 'Harfort', which is almost accurate geographically. However, the original French text says 'eighteen leagues', which is much too far, as one league is roughly three miles.

Monstrelet gave no description of any attack on Tenby, so does not corroborate or dispute the tale of fear and flight related by Saint-Denys. Instead, the two armies met there and headed directly for the regional capital, 'Calemarchin' or Carmarthen. This was described as twelve leagues from Tenby which, avoiding modern bridges and the like, is close to being accurate. Monstrelet gave no account of a siege there, despite a variety of sources agreeing that the allies took Carmarthen. Instead the armies then entered 'pays de Morgnie' or Glamorgan, and went to a holy place associated with the round table. This demonstrates the power and lure of Arthurian myth in this period. That such an army might direct itself somewhere with such a legendary association is a statement on French claims to Arthur's constructed chivalric legacy. The abbey connected to the round table has been presumed to be Caerleon, although Monstrelet gave no names or details that lead to that conclusion, and there is no compelling reason to believe this modern supposition.

From there, the French and the Welsh are said to have taken the road to 'Vincestre', which has reasonably been suggested means Worcester, and certainly cannot be confused with anywhere in Wales. At Worcester, they allegedly burned the suburbs and the surrounding countryside before encountering Henry IV and his army, three leagues from the town. Here, Monstrelet recounted how the two armies adopted battle formations, each on a hillside with a broad valley between them. This stand-off was said to have lasted eight days, during which there were numerous skirmishes between the two probing armies. These were said to have resulted in over 200 dead, among them 'Patroullart de Troies', along with 'monsieur de Mathelonne' and 'monsieur de La Ville', and many wounded. The three named seem to emerge in the records, once more the connections lead to western France and Brittany, and appear to have Orleanist links. According to Monstrelet, the alleged stalemate outside Worcester ended when Henry IV withdrew behind the town's walls one evening when he perceived that the French and the Welsh, hard pressed by hunger, would not attack. As he retired, some French and Welsh are said to have taken eighteen carts laden with food. The loss of baggage from Henry's army is in part corroborated by Lloyd, although the number is higher at forty carts, and swollen rivers were the supposed cause.[21]

Then, they returned to Wales and the French embarked on the ships that had previously received intelligence on which ports to use. This last point correlates with evidence from the Saint-Denis chronicle that Glyn Dŵr had provided the French with a map of Wales's accessible ports. The French returned to Saint-Pol de Léon without incident and the two leaders went to Paris where they were feted by the king and the princes of the blood. The influential churchman, Pierre Cochon, concurred with or perhaps copied from the Saint-Denys chronicle, writing that they returned at 'Toussains', or All Saints', but Monstrelet inferred that all returned to France and went to their homes at the same time, with no reference to any men left behind in Wales.[22]

It is worth pondering briefly why the French and the Welsh attacked south-west Wales, instead of landing in the north where Owain had a firmer hold, and then clearing out the remaining castles in Gwynedd. For the Welsh, the English-held castles seemed to have been reduced to mere presences and no longer fulfilled their original hostile role. Aggression against the south-west might mark an attempt to expand Owain's territory to fully encompass the region, once more bringing the native Welsh kingdom of Deheubarth, as it was before English invasion, within its traditional orbit of power: under the rule of Gwynedd. In addition, the immense haven at Milford offered an appropriate, perhaps better, anchorage for a large French fleet than anywhere in the north. Owain therefore intended the French to fulfil a notable military role for him, a task they appear to have attempted to achieve, at least.

For the French, there was perhaps a different reason for an Orleanist-inspired mission to attack south-west Wales: personal vendetta. The lands of Pembroke, Tenby, Cilgerran and others including St Clears had been given for life to 'Isabel, the king's consort' as part of her dower in 1396. Shortly after his coronation, Henry IV distributed these lands among his supporters, William Beauchamp, Francis de Court, John Norbury and Thomas Percy 'and his heirs male'. The bitter feud between Henry and Louis makes this aspect of the expedition worthy of consideration. It is noteworthy that the French went to those places granted to Louis's niece, Isabella. While the French no doubt intended to deny Henry the lands and revenue they perceived as part of Isabella's right, it might also be that they were assessing the region for support, either against Henry or in favour of Isabella or Henry Percy senior. Intelligence passed to Henry's government during winter 1404 clearly reported that the French were planning to occupy and rebuild castles in Wales, from where they would be able to do as much harm as possible to England. Links between the French presence in west Wales and on Isabella's former lands which also had a Percy connection, in the same year as the Tripartite Indenture seem impossible to ignore.[23]

CHAPTER NINE

Invasion and Truce?

They have told me that Owain of Glyndyfrdwy has presently summoned a parliament, to be held at Harlech ... the said Owain, if he can be sure of having from his parliament, a very great force and substantial help from France, he intends to send to you, most powerful lord, after his said parliament, to ask you for a treaty ...[1]

The two French chronicle accounts present a common core of a story, and then diverge to the point where either one omits a large section of the tale, possibly through ignorance but perhaps for political gain, or the other invents a significant part of the account, doubtless for similar, if opposing, political reasons.

Certain common elements help construct a credible narrative. First, although the invasion fleet was sanctioned by the court and the government, and supported by the dukes, those named enacting the mission appear to be predominantly of Orleanist adherence. This demonstrates that this expedition was not simply a surprising escalation of Louis's quarrel with Henry which demonstrated the duke's personal strength and ambition, but it also represented an impressive articulation of French power by inserting, and later extracting, a campaign army onto the British mainland in support of a significant rebel force fighting against the king of England.

The bulk of the army appears to have been raised in northern and western France, as well as in Brittany. While the nobles and more experienced soldiers of both sides were likely able to converse in French, the bulk of the Welsh and Breton troops could speak to one another in their own languages, since Breton derives from Welsh. The army's size remains undetermined; the fact that Monstrelet's claim was wildly incorrect for 1405 does not make the troop numbers proposed by the monk any more accurate. However, the latter's precisely detailed army appears quite large by contemporary standards, but remains feasible, even plausible. The force which deployed to Scotland with Jean de Vienne in 1385 seems comparable to other similar armies and would tally with Thomas Johnes's translation of 1,200, rather than the unusually large army of 12,000 found in Monstrelet's original French. While almost certainly incorrect for 1405, this high number is close enough to be accepted as a later confusion with the army reported by Henry's spies and ambassadors in France for the invasion force mustered in 1404.

Monstrelet's estimate of the fleet size of 120 sailing ships seems entirely more credible than that of the monk, who wrote of two warships and thirty medium-sized vessels. In addition, Monstrelet's figure is largely and independently supported by Mascall and Walsingham who claimed the French fleet numbered 144 ships. Consideration of the basic logistics of the operation further support Monstrelet's assertions. The army described by the monk of 2,600 fighting men, carried by a fleet of thirty-two ships works out at an unlikely 81 soldiers per vessel. Applying the generally accepted maxim that the number of sailors required was usually equal to the fighting contingent being transported, the total adds up to the improbable complement for each ship, without adding horses, equipment, artillery or supplies, of over 160 men per vessel.[2] To compare the other mathematical possibilities of this case, Monstrelet's improbably large army of 12,000 carried by his proposed fleet works out to 100 fighting men per vessel if the fleet were 120-strong, or eighty-three men if there were 144 ships. If Johnes's interpretation of the army size as 1,200 was accurate, then this equates to ten or eight fighting men per vessel, depending on the fleet size. If Monstrelet's fleet carried the army identified by the monk, each vessel would carry eighteen or twenty-two soldiers, according to the fleet being 144 or 120 vessels respectively. English naval records of the period supply reasonable force numbers for comparison. The English fleet of 1377–8 sailed with twenty retinues totalling 4,000 men-at-arms and archers in 100 ships manned by 3,600 mariners, an average of 40 soldiers per vessel. In 1385, Sir Thomas Percy and Sir Baldwin Raddlington took to sea with approximately 2,000 soldiers and the same number of sailors in forty-three vessels, or 46 and a half soldiers per vessel. The 51-ship fleet used by the earl of Arundel in 1387, in which Owain Glyn Dŵr served, carried 2,381 soldiers and 2,600 sailors, an average of 47 fighting men per vessel. Doubling the number of soldiers per ship to account for the sailors gives a rough total complement. Other period studies offer similar examples where English fleets listed a highest average of forty-five soldiers per ship, to a low of fewer than fifteen troops per vessel on other occasions. While the French favoured larger ships, these comparisons are still instructive.[3] In terms of their design, there was only a certain load that contemporary ships could carry. There were also command factors to consider, focusing on the reality that ships sank and took their entire complement with them. Therefore, losing ships crammed with men rendered the eventual landing force far less effective or likely to succeed than a force spread out over a higher number of vessels. Therefore, while the army size remains unknown, the fleet described by Monstrelet is far more likely than that of the Saint-Denys chronicle.

The army embarked at Brest and, after being delayed by adverse winds, the fleet departed towards the end of July, probably arriving in Milford Haven in the first week of August. Walsingham commented that the French army's horses died of thirst during the crossing, but he is the sole authority for this and, in reality, there no reason to trust his claim because he had no way of knowing if this were true. They attacked Haverford and laid waste to the surrounding area, but failed to take the castle. The artillery appears to have been shipped elsewhere, they did not press the siege and moved on. They went to Tenby, by which time both sources agree that they were with Glyn Dŵr and a Welsh force estimated at 10,000-strong, although Owain might have been present to welcome them ashore initially. This large number is almost certain to be exaggerated, but both accounts give the same high figure. However, this also underlines the probably inaccurate troop figures offered by the chronicles which would otherwise mean combined French–Welsh forces of between 12,000 and 22,000 men: this army did not wield that much power in the field. Due to differences in the accounts, it is unknown whether or not they attacked Tenby or simply passed it by. Other evidence shows that some of Tenby's townsmen assisted the French and the rebels, so it might have been viewed as a friendly town and therefore escaped attack.[4]

The Saint-Denys chronicle consistently derided the actions of many of the French nobility to the point of it becoming polemical in places, whereas Monstrelet's text was written by a low-ranking noble and war captain with a generic vested interest in describing such an operation by his peers in a positive light. The final point on which both chronicles concur was that the combined army went to Carmarthen. Although the Saint-Denys chronicle gave the only account of the assault on Carmarthen, supporting evidence shows that they did take the town and castle. Monstrelet only acknowledged that the allies went there, subsequently, the two chronicles dramatically diverge. The army in the Saint-Denys account turned north-west and headed to Cardigan before dividing and settling into winter quarters. At that point, the monk opined that the majority of the nobles treacherously abandoned their loyal troops. According to Monstrelet, after the allies left Carmarthen they struck east, visiting iconic, though rumoured, Arthurian sites, before confronting the king of England outside Worcester. Although Monstrelet is sometimes viewed as a less reliable source than the monk of Saint-Denis, there are indicators favouring the Worcester standoff theory.[5]

The passage of armies tends to leave traces; primarily physical and sometimes cultural. Although the French–Welsh army of 1405 appears to have left an imprint on vernacular folk-tales and places names of western Worcestershire, due to the inherent unreliability and susceptibility to manipulation of such stories, it is sufficient to draw attention to the fact that the Welsh–French army of 1405 appears to have a presence within local English lore.[6]

Any army of the estimated size of the allied force, or even a contingent thereof, should leave traces on the landscape and historical record of the area as it foraged for food and suppressed opposition. This appears to be the case with the southern and northern approaches to Hereford and Worcester; this cautiously advanced theory is founded on the taxation records for the border, as well as other supporting evidence.[7]

The tax records give snapshots of the economic state of the border shires during the revolt, detailing how much money was raised and which places were granted exemptions from paying. Extant records detail the situation in 1404 and again in late 1406 and 1407. The first observation, supported by contemporary letters, is that the Marches had sustained considerable destruction and impoverishment by warfare up to the first measuring point in December 1404. The evidence presented by the appeals for exemption and tax collection highlights a surge in claims between 1405 and the next tally in 1407, strongly suggesting that the area experienced an event to cause this rise. Allowing for natural occurrences of poverty, a declining economy perhaps, and other unrecorded smaller-scale rebel attacks in the border regions, the level of successful claims for tax exemption due to war damage still appears to have risen more steeply than the prior rate of attrition caused by Welsh troops. Although this number is higher than previously, it has been suggested elsewhere that these figures probably mask a more extensive record of damage since people had returned to the area by the time of the levy in 1407 and some areas, while damaged, were not deemed to have sustained sufficient destruction to warrant exemption. Therefore, at some point between January 1405 and the next occasion exemptions were permitted, 1407, the border region of Herefordshire, along with southern and western Shropshire endured an event which caused destruction and depopulation. Due to the fact that all sizeable incursions ceased from the Welsh side for several years after 1405, the only candidate for this activity, outside the other possible but undeclared economic and unrecorded military factors, is the passage of the allied army in late August and early September 1405.[8]

Border communities sought tax exemption due to impoverishment through war damage, this information was collected by the authorities. The information furnished by Bishop Mascall's register appears to further corroborate Monstrelet's claim that the army went to Worcester. The places seeking exemption, apart from a general north–south spread of afflicted communities, can be perceived as presenting southern and northern ingress/egress routes heading towards and away from Worcester along established roadways. The southerly approach leads from west to east, from Monmouth and Hay towards Hereford. The army might not return by the same route if it needed to forage, Monstrelet claimed that the army needed food, and this was common among contemporary campaigns. The possible north-westerly egress runs away from Worcester through the chain of communities from Leominster, Ludlow, towards Montgomery but likely encompassing Clun, then through to Caus and Shrewsbury. These routes also follow established roadways and appear to use the easier hill passes between Wales and England. It seems probable that some of the settlements mapped were damaged before and perhaps during the summer of 1405, nevertheless, on this evidence, although not decisive, Monstrelet's account seems credible.[9]

The presence of the French in the border area was specifically mentioned by a letter from the inhabitants of Shropshire to the king. The letter, sent from Shrewsbury, contains noteworthy information on the state of the shire and reveals the palpable fear felt by the inhabitants.

The author addressed this begging letter to the king, humbly but clearly in tones of desperation. They feared that 'the Welsh rebels and their adherents' were poised to overrun and waste the county with 'their very great power' to the despair of the king's loyal lieges there. The letter pleaded for troops from elsewhere to come and protect them. Tellingly, the plaintiff wrote that news of the rebels and the French had arrived, and he believed that the enemy was aware that Shropshire contained fewer troops than the rest of the border shires and, armed with that knowledge, they were planning a *chevauchée* into the county. The author added that a third of the county had been destroyed by the rebels and that those living in the devastated areas had left to 'earn their meat and sustenance elsewhere in your realm'. The letter displayed a state of near-panic at the seemingly imminent and great threat posed to the county by the Welsh rebels and the French. It bears the date of 21 April but no year is given, although it has been cautiously suggested and equally cautiously accepted as dating from 1403.[10]

Although it is possible that the Welsh rebels alone had wrought such extensive damage to the county by then, however, dating this letter to spring 1403 seems too early. Critically, this letter clearly associated Welsh and French forces, yet it mysteriously predates the Welsh–French alliance by over a year. In addition, although the French put troops ashore at Kidwelly in October 1403 and later still at Caernarfon, the Shropshire letter was written in April and cannot refer to them. Also, both landings were followed by coastal sieges, too distant to threaten England's inland border counties. Similarly, there was no French threat to the border in April 1404 or April 1405. In fact, the first and only potential French threat to the border came in late summer 1405. It seems highly unlikely that the inhabitants feared a French invasion of rural, inland, western Shropshire before they had even arrived in Wales. While it should be kept in mind that the letter's author might have inserted generic mention of the French to invoke the fear of the king's most powerful enemies, the terror expressed needed to be credible to the king, if it were to stand a chance of receiving crown aid. However, if the letter expressed a genuine, realistic concern of a French–Welsh incursion, then this plainly fearful letter should be considered for April 1406. The only realistic possibility of a French threat to the Welsh–English border arose in late summer 1405. If the Saint-Denys chronicle were correct about any part of the French force overwintering in Wales into 1406, then this further

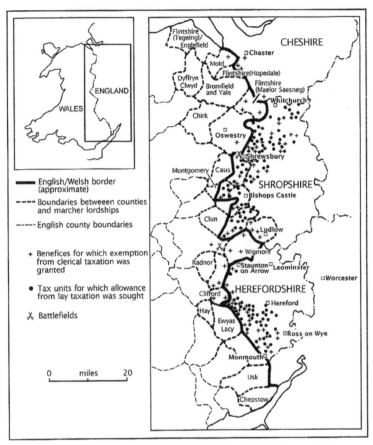

Figure 12 Tax units affected by the rebellion.

supports the idea that this letter can only date to April 1406 or possibly, but less likely, April 1407 shortly before Prince Henry invaded Wales in May that year. Ongoing rumours concerning the presence of the French in Wales might well have been in the air during the following spring when they broke camp. The English of the border shires were unlikely to have been privy to news of their departure around that time. However, August and September 1405 would be good months for incursions into the agriculturally productive border areas; the harvests would be ripening and would help feed a foraging army. It seems likely, therefore, that some of the damage done to the county occurred in summer 1405 and was recorded, in part, in the survey of 1407.

If present in the border areas in 1405, the allies appear to have left before the end of October. A letter from the countess of Hereford, although writing remotely, revealed that there were only rumours of them in the Worcester area by 28 October.[11]

Therefore, government and local sources demonstrate that there was a notable volume of destruction wrought upon the area at the right time, the French were clearly identified by local inhabitants and there were no noticeably large-scale attacks recorded anywhere in this region afterwards within the time frame surveyed. Certain opinion holds that the conflict began to sour for Glyn Dŵr from 1405 and, if this analysis is correct, this also isolates 1405 as the only candidate year for the destruction which befell the March between 1404 and 1407.[12] Although the theory of decline in 1405 is challenged below, the physical evidence demonstrating the presence of a hostile force in the region during summer 1405 appears compelling.

However, there is a further suggestive source which supports Monstrelet's story concerning Worcester; the movements and orders of King Henry IV. The king had suppressed the York revolt and was demonstrably present at Pontefract between 6 and 12 August 1405.[13] On 7 August, still at Pontefract, Henry learned of the French landing, writing orders to the following effect to the sheriffs of sixteen counties, indicative of a large, immediate threat:

> Order, as he loves the king and his honour and desires the safety and defence of the realm and the marches thereof, upon sight etc. to cause proclamation to be made that all knights, esquires, yeomen and other fencible men of the sheriff's bailiwick upon their allegiance and under pain of forfeiture shall make ready, array and furnish themselves with arms, every man as his estate requires, and hasten to draw to the city of Hereforde, to march with the king and manfully resist the malice of his enemies; as now newly it has come to the king's ears that the seigneur de Hugevyle and great number of his other enemies of France with a fleet of ships have landed in Milforde haven to reinforce the Welsh rebels, and with them are purposing to invade the realm and the marches of Wales, and to do what mischief they may to the king and his lieges; and his will is to resist their malice, and take order for defence of the realm and marches and of the said lieges.[14]

The profound shock at this bold French move seems palpable within this and subsequent messages that season. However, in this order the king had to call upon affection for him, threaten forfeiture and raise the prospect of the French and the Welsh invading the march and the kingdom at large. Also, in this erupting crisis, Henry summoned as many troops as he could, not just the knights and squires, but also the yeomen and anyone else who could bear arms: the urgency and gravity that the king felt is evident in this short warning order. In addition, this note identified Jean de Hangest as foremost among the French. However, Henry's surprise seems out of line with the intelligence at his disposal. In July, commissions were issued to raise troops to counter the French who were going to attack English interests in Picardy and then 'to go to Wales to strengthen the rebels there'. In the same month, Thomas Berkeley was commissioned to raise troops in Gloucester, Bristol and Somerset because it was said that the Welsh were going to invade that area 'with a great force'. Henry had been told that the French and the Welsh were coming, but when it arrived, the news still appeared to shock him.[15]

Henry can then be tracked travelling across the country, moving from Nottingham to Leicester, arriving there by 16 August at the latest.[16] Records place him at Leicester until 19 August.[17] He then proceeded to Worcester, covering the seventy or so miles by 23 August, from where he ordered the sheriffs of seven counties 'under pain of the king's wrath' to meet him at Worcester the following Monday. These messages again exuded tones of fear and threat – highly suggestive of the stress provoked by an immediate and sizeable danger.[18] Henry can be shown to be present at Worcester until 31 August. Although Enguerrand de Monstrelet gave no precise dates, this evidence places Henry in the area and within the timeframe declared by Monstrelet, and for precisely the right amount of time, eight days, during which the stand-off between the armies was alleged to have occurred.[19] This is the first opportunity for the confrontation. However, the king's actions show that he was still preparing for military action. While in the Worcester area, Henry summoned more troops, binding named individuals as well as reissuing the orders of array to seven surrounding counties to meet with him at Hereford:

> Strict order, in consideration of the peril which threatens, and the damage which may happen to the king and the whole realm by insufficient resistance, and of the king's high confidence in the estates and persons of that county, to cause all knights, esquires and other fencible men thereof able in body to travail to come to the king's presence, so that they shall be with him at Hereforde on Friday next, furnished and arrayed, every man

as his estate requires, to march with the king to resist his enemies, bidding them upon their allegiance not to delay, refuse or omit to do so; as the king has particular information that his enemies of France have landed in Wales with no small power to reinforce the Welsh rebels.[20]

The French and Welsh allies were plainly identified by Henry and the threat they posed was credible and large enough to warrant this further, urgent call for more troops. By 4 September Henry had advanced to Hereford where he tried to raise a loan and recorded his intent to march against the French in Wales.[21] Here, Bishop Mascall celebrated the expedition the king was about to launch against the duke of Orleans who had invested a force into Milford.[22] His trail of orders shows that the king remained at Hereford at least until 10 September after which point, though it is unclear when, he left the city. The king resurfaced in the records on 28 September, in Worcester, less than thirty miles to the east.[23] It is not known what Henry did during this eighteen-day period, which offers another window of opportunity for the reported eight-day stand-off to have occurred. It is unlikely that he marched the army directly to Worcester at a speed of approximately one and a half miles per day, so it is reasonable to assert that this army was involved in some event or action during this time, and this is perhaps the best opportunity for the alleged stand-off between the three armies.

It is possible that Henry made some effort to advance west but for reasons unknown, such as failing to find the enemy or being deterred by adverse weather conditions not mentioned in any other source anywhere, he returned to Worcester.[24] Both of these seem extremely unlikely; if present, thousands of men and horses are easy to track and there is a lack of any corroborating reference concerning weather conditions. It is also possible of course, that Henry did not attempt to attack, track or harass the allies, but this raises questions and invites speculation. Records reveal that he remained at Worcester for the first week of October, from where he returned to Westminster, arriving there by 14 October.[25] His return to the capital far to the east, with no other orders of array being issued en route, intimates that some sort of resolution for the substantial, panic-inducing threat of the previous month had been found. Henry was clearly in the place indicated by Monstrelet at the right time of the year and, most compellingly, for the precise amount of time claimed. It seems difficult to discredit Monstrelet's accurate claim, implying that this aspect of his account is, at least in part, correct.

* * * * *

According to the Saint-Denys evidence, the higher-ranking nobles and their better-armoured troops did not return to France until All Saints, and so were available for battle until November. According to the same chronicle, the majority of their sizeable army which reportedly overwintered in Wales was, until Lent 1406, also present and therefore theoretically occupying part of the domain claimed by Henry.[26] If this account is correct, they were divided into three groups, and, logically, would have been easier for Henry to engage and destroy, had he the will.

This poses a problem. Henry clearly knew that the French were in Wales and he hurriedly raised significant forces from across England to go and meet them. Yet the government records fail to reveal a confrontation between English and French–Welsh forces at the time. In addition, during the following year, the king did not go and reassert his power in those places where the French were or had been. The conclusion that Henry shied away from battle is troubling, particularly against the French adversary on the British mainland. One of the signal features of Henry's reign is that he readily and hastily rushed to battle, as his suppression of the weaker revolts, such as Percy risings of 1403 and 1405, clearly demonstrated. Not only this, but Henry appears to have deliberately projected an image of being a king who would deal with dissent resolutely, either in face-to-face dispute or in mobilising troops and hastening to a confrontation. He led all of the previous expeditions to Wales from 1400 onwards and had stood poised to invade again in May 1405, prior to the York rebellion. While it is feasible that in this case he decided not to risk himself on campaign, this distinctly runs against the record of his reign and previous martial career as a crusader, soldier and tourney fighter. This also fails to explain why he did not send an army under a subordinate, such as Prince Henry or the earl of Arundel.

Henry's lack of activity in Wales during and after the French invasion is so uncharacteristic that it requires further consideration. This might indicate that Henry accepted that he had lost control there and ceased efforts to retake it or reassert himself there, but this stands in marked contrast to the annual expeditions and sustained efforts of previous years. Perhaps, his reticence to act reflects that the French army had returned to France in the uneventful manner described by Monstrelet, leaving only the Welsh to attack, although this explanation also seems unsatisfactory and incomplete. After the Welsh sacked Carmarthen in 1403, Henry journeyed there in person, installing his half-brother, the earl of Somerset, as garrison commander for a time. He also reasserted his authority by showing the flag in west Wales following the sack of Carmarthen in 1403. However, the king did not pursue and confront the allies in Wales at the moment of crisis in late 1405 or at all the following year. This significant deviation in behaviour and career *modus operandi* strongly implies that something had changed from previous years.[27] For roughly a year after the events of late summer 1405, the king of England and the native prince of Wales appear to have conducted themselves as if a truce were in force.

Weaved into the story of 1405 is the curious tale of the English of Pembrokeshire paying off the Welsh with the significant sum of £200 of silver around November 1405. This is suggestively supported by Privy Council records and might indicate that a truce was secured in that area. English border communities had been making truces with the Welsh for a number of years and so such arrangements had become a feature of the conflict by this point.[28] In addition, there is a notable flurry of evidence concerning hostage exchanges, exemplified by a curious paper trail of permissions, safe conducts and licences to treat with the rebels concerning the case of Thomas Roche, constable of Pembroke castle. He was captured by the Welsh sometime during the latter half of 1405 and was eventually exchanged for four Welsh prisoners.[29] It is also noteworthy that Roche was rewarded with legal protection by Henry in regard to his custody of Carmarthen, which probably identifies where, when and why he was taken by the Welsh.[30] However, Roche's liberty does not appear to have been easily arranged. Henry personally issued a firm command to Reginald, Lord Grey, to see to it that a number of seemingly unknown or rankless rebels were released so that Roche could be freed.[31] The negotiations for Roche's release dragged on until the following summer.[32] The process of negotiation with the rebels might be dismissible as a locally worked solution had the king not been consistently involved. His personal hand in the matter could be taken as a legitimisation of the rebels' territorial claims, as he could be viewed as ensuring that truce terms were honoured. In this matter, post-invasion, both sides in Britain acted as the English and French conducted themselves in exchanging prisoners during times of truce. The assertion made here is that a truce was agreed between Henry and Owain, backed by the French, during late summer 1405.

It should be borne in mind that, according to the English spies at Glyn

Dŵr's parliament in July and August 1405, Glyn Dŵr intended to present himself before Henry with the French behind him and discuss peace.[33] Owain Glyn Dŵr certainly appears to have been a man of his word and, in that light, it seems probable that he proposed a truce to Henry during summer 1405, exactly as he said he would. This fleshes the current image of Glyn Dŵr with a degree of compassion and humanity; Henry held Owain's son and heir, Gruffydd, his brother-in-law and ambassador, John Hanmer, along with others close to the Welsh leader. Therefore this moment, shortly after their capture and while Owain had significant forces at his disposal, offered an opportunity to propose a truce and to conduct negotiations aimed at securing their release. It seems likely, were such a truce proposed, that it contained some recognition of Owain's position in Wales and the territorial integrity of that claim.

To examine this suggestion from the crown's perspective, a truce would explain several ambiguities. If Henry made such an agreement, no matter how insincerely, that would explain why the king and the sizeable army he frantically gathered in August and September made no decisive move into Wales, that season or the following year. Evidence from March the following year implies that the king had not managed to resupply Coity castle in the Vale of Glamorgan since he 'was last in Wales' in late 1404.[34] This suggests that Henry was expected to have entered Wales in 1405, but did not even go the seventy or so miles from Hereford to Coity across the gentle open landscape of Glamorgan during his eighteen-day sortie from Hereford. It should be borne in mind that Henry IV's previous expeditions to Wales had covered significantly more terrain in a similar or shorter period. Therefore, his inactivity across the border and the plight of Coity are highly noteworthy.

The military activities arranged shortly before Henry's departure for London were not indicative of mounting a campaign westwards. In that first week of October 1405, he ordered Richard, baron Grey of Codnor, and Thomas, earl of Arundel, to hold commissions of *oyer* and *terminer* in Hereford, Gloucester and the king's own lordship of Brecon. This empowered Arundel and Codnor to pass judgement on cases such as treason and felonies, which would encompass revolt and assisting the enemy in any fashion. Arundel was also commissioned to hold sessions of *oyer* and *terminer* in Shrewsbury and Shropshire. In so doing, Henry appears to be attempting to cleanse the border of rebel influences or affiliations; the crown was firmly re-establishing its jurisdiction in the

English border shires. It evidently believed that it had to do so, but also that there was opportunity to carry out the task without threat of attack from Wales. However, the king appears to have been free to act in the English border shires, but not at all in Welsh areas, demarcating a distinct boundary of his authority. Also, Arundel was made keeper of Shrewsbury which authorised him to do whatever was required to secure the county of Shropshire. Within these documents are orders to muster troops for the care and keep of the castles of the border regions, but nowhere is there mention of offensive action against the rebels.[35]

These are clearly security measures designed to stabilise and secure the English side of the border. This implies a threat to penetrate the border, and supports the redating to 1406 of the Shropshire tenants' letter who feared that the French would return. On 7 October, local officials were appointed to raise a force of 200 men-at-arms and 600 archers to muster in November – so in no apparent hurry. Their task was to accompany Codnor 'for the safe-keeping of the castles and fortresses of those parts (South Wales) and the counties of Gloucester and Hereford adjoining'. A comparable force was to be raised to assist Arundel also. While this intends an advance into 'South Wales', judging by the letter of the orders, this force was raised to secure and stabilise the English side of the border and bolster nearby castles such as Brecon, an estate held by Henry Bolingbroke since 1384, technically on the Welsh side but in proximity to English centres of power. It is questionable whether these forces of 800 men would have ventured too deeply into Wales if there were no truce in force because, even combined, they were smaller than either the Welsh or French force individually and each was smaller than the probable number of casualties sustained by Mortimer's army at Bryn Glas. Since the Welsh could kill that number on their own, it seems evident that such forces would be at notable risk of destruction at the hands of these significant allied forces unless they believed attack unlikely. Later that month, Codnor was appointed as the king's lieutenant in Brecon and Hereford for a period of forty-nine days. Again, this seems unhurried and short-term; hardly indicative of a counter-strike by crown forces or in fear of an expected enemy attack. Finally, the force ordered to be raised in early October assembled at a seemingly leisurely pace and, six weeks later, on 24 November 1405, it was commissioned to serve Lord Codnor until 1 February. At the same time, Henry ordered another session of *oyer* and *terminer* to be held in Gloucester and Hereford, as people there were reported to have been supplying the rebels with 'victuals, armour and other harness'. The sum of these actions appears to be a reimposition of law, order and the king's authority over Hereford, Gloucester, Shropshire and Brecon. These are clearly defensive security measures, carried out at will, rather than under the threat of an immediate attack. They stand stark in comparison with Henry's hurried summoning of troops from so many counties during the late summer and early autumn. Once more, these later measures imply the existence of a truce, rather than a state of war and fear of invasion.[36]

The following year, parliament debated a strategy for the Welsh war and demanded action; it voted funds for Prince Henry to raise a sizeable army of 5,000 men that year, yet they did not enter Wales at all and were not redeployed to cover another emergency, as happened the previous year. He was granted ample money during the year and a second force was funded in September 1406, yet it never mustered or moved against the Welsh.[37] The fighting that occurred in 1406 was peripheral; indeed it might be just to limit English military operations that year to the completion of the isolation and invasion of Anglesey. The two other references to fighting in Wales that year appear confused or simply fictitious. One claimed that 1,000 Welshmen including one of Owain's sons were killed in a battle which conveniently took place on St George's Day. The claim, if not a confused inflation of the previous year's battle at Usk, fails to mention any details such as identifying either army's commanders, the place of battle, the identity of the alleged son or any corroborating evidence. In addition, there are no supporting mentions in other records, neither are any of the mundane facts of warfare evident elsewhere, such as orders for array and muster, a payment trail, the logistical provisioning of these forces, and so on. The other claim, once again made by the garrulous Adam Usk who, in his own words was 'wandering through Flanders, France, Brittany and Normandy' for two years, alleged that Northumberland and Lord Bardolf were defeated by Usk's patron when he later rewrote his chronicle, Edward Charlton, lord of Powys.[38]

Without the conclusion of a truce, it is difficult to explain or dismiss Henry's passivity, given his martial career up to that point and the extraordinary challenge posed to any king of England by a French army, allied with powerful rebel forces, present on lands he claimed and were held in the name of the royal heir. The conclusion of a truce might also explain the de-escalation of the conflict for a period thereafter, as well as the hostage negotiations, such arrangements being common following truces. In addition, this tallies with Glyn Dŵr's stated intentions at the Harlech parliament.[39]

A truce might also explain French actions following the campaign in Wales. Assuming that the Saint-Denys chronicler was correct, the return of the French nobles was legitimate and possibly a term of the truce: that they quit Wales. The army left behind would have been safe from attack from the English, or acted as a guarantee of powerful opposition should Henry return. Assuming that Monstrelet was right, the unmolested departure of all of the French was entirely feasible and in keeping with a truce being in force. In either scenario, the French had recovered their honour, tarnished by the count of la Marche in 1404. They had either invaded and ravaged one corner of their enemy's domain, or they had confronted him and shown him their colours on his own soil, possibly assisting in negotiating a truce for their Welsh ally. Their shame erased, they were free to return home to be feted.

Glyn Dŵr's desire for a truce seems merited for several reasons. First, this would seem to be an understandable reaction of a father whose son and several close companions had been captured that summer. To view it more coldly, several key personnel were missing but retrievable. Next, as recorded by a good independent contemporary source, that was exactly what Glyn Dŵr said he would do when the French arrived. Also, the manner in which this appears to have been done seems to fit with the normal contemporary native cultural and diplomatic practices in terms of conflict resolution.[40] Meetings at border points to settle disputes and to seek redress are documented throughout the medieval period. The form and typical clauses used in such 'agreement meetings' appear consistently in examples from 1354 to 1498.[41] These meetings were often followed by a period of truce during which the different sides sought to fulfil the obligations to which they had committed themselves. Such an agreement between nobles giving their word on a given matter might explain Henry IV's personal involvement in pursuing the release of seemingly unknown, low-level Welsh hostages whose captivity was controlled or in the sway of Reginald, Lord Grey, the man partly responsible for the Glyn Dŵr's central role in the eruption of the rebellion. These 'agreement meetings' were not solely native practices, but were adopted by the Normans and the English in their dealings with the Welsh. Recognising the protagonists acting within the cultural customs of their day appears to ground their actions in a more realistic way. Finally, had the French assisted in winning peace for Glyn Dŵr, it might help explain the clauses of the Pennal Declaration of March 1406, which is viewed as a document detailing key elements of a Welsh state. State construction is far more likely during a truce won after a series of apparently successful military and diplomatic campaigns, not during a war, particularly one which some believe was in decline for the Welsh after 1405. The declaration of 1406 appears to give an idea of Glyn Dŵr's peacetime intentions, to create a stable Welsh state, sustained with support from his French allies. The extent of the French–Welsh army's campaign reach and the reasons why Henry declined to face the allied army in combat remain, for now, unclear. However, both parties behaved differently after the French expedition and, if anything can be read into their actions, then a truce seems a plausible explanation.

The expedition to Wales should be considered within the context of other French activities beyond its borders that year. Indeed, it seems that this mission formed one integral part of a broader strategy, with this element enacted in 1405. In a similar time frame, Charles de Savoisy commanded a force that launched from Saint-Mathieu in Brittany in late August and conducted a bloody attack on England's Channel coast, between Portland and the Isle of Wight, in the company of Bretons and Castilians.[42] This was part of a strategy, evidently enacted during 1403 and 1404 also, which was designed to give the French and their allies supremacy at sea and to terrorise the English coast. Charles VI's letter from November 1406 to Henry, earl of Northumberland, establishes grounds to tie the York rebellion to the expedition to Wales to part of an attempted coup, fuelled by Louis of Orleans, all of which aimed at dethroning Henry IV.[43]

> They should know that, if recently, when we sent an army to Wales, we had been sure that the partisans of the just cause and the friends of the legitimate heirs to the throne would welcome our people favourably and would hasten to join them, we would have had at our disposal far greater forces, but we are still ready to help them in the aforementioned cases.[44]

In addition, from spring to midsummer 1405, there was a plan to forcibly instal Benedict XIII into Rome.[45] Although that drive foundered well before completion, the fact that France was able to articulate its external power so forcefully in 1405 demonstrates not only its perhaps unexpected military capabilities, but also its less frequently discussed political and strategic will to exert itself in such a way.

CHAPTER TEN

The Pennal Declaration

Again, that the lord Benedict shall brand as heretics and cause to be tortured in the usual manner, Henry of Lancaster, the intruder of the kingdom of England, and the usurper of the crown of the same kingdom, and his adherents, in that of their own free will they have burnt or have caused to be burnt so many cathedrals, convents and parish churches; that they have savagely hung, beheaded, and quartered archbishops, bishops, prelates, priests, religious men, as madmen or beggars, or caused the same to be done.[1]

The 'Pennal Declaration' concerned Wales's papal allegiance at this stage of the schism. It comprised two documents; a short preamble and the main document which focused on the course of the schism and culminated with Owain's requests to Pope Benedict XIII. The longer document also acknowledged receipt of a French letter, which reached Owain on 8 March 1406, showing that this initiative also originated in France. Owain's responses were both dated 31 March 1406. This firmly dates Owain's 1406 parliament, which was held between the arrival of the French proposition and the completion of the reply. Within the body of the main document, the declaration, Owain explicitly says as much: 'Following the advice of our council, we have called together the nobles of our race, the prelates of our Principality and others called for this purpose.' They engaged in 'diligent examination and discussion', after which they threw their support behind Benedict as the true pope, in contrast to the anti-pope in Rome.[2]

There is no record of the original letter to Owain, although its contents are clearly rewritten within his reply. Owain's declaration gave no exact composition date for the French proposition, although the text offers clues which help establish an approximate time frame for its composition as well as the identity of the French hand guiding this policy. The documents show that the move came from Charles VI's court, appearing to fall during a period of regency under the queen and the duke of Orleans during one of the king's absences, but at a time seemingly denoted by Louis's weakening grip on power. The pressures to govern prudently were evident even in the literature of the time. In this period, Christine de Pizan wrote 'The Book of the Body Politic', a moralising discourse emphasising the virtues of a good prince were, among others, to treat all with kindness; to protect the people and the land, ensuring the discipline and restraint of the armies; to act as a good shepherd of the people and not as a tyrant.[3]

The original letter was brought from France by 'Hugh Eddowyer, of the Order of Predicants, and Maurice Kery, our friends and envoys'. Eddowyer was therefore a member of the Dominican Order, his presence is noteworthy due to the order's influential role in Benedict's personal council, including holding the position of the pope's confessor. The Dominicans provided a conduit for Owain which ran directly to Benedict. Little further emerges on these two envoys, except through the incarceration and release of a Dominican friar named Hywel Edwere in north Wales in 1410, while the other might have been connected to Richard Keri, who had been associated with Glyn Dŵr for many years.[4]

It is telling that the Welsh were invited to declare their allegiance for the pope commonly, though not entirely accurately, regarded as the French candidate. Benedict was from Aragon and had a fiery, undulating relationship with the French factions. However, the party then dominating Charles VI's court regarded the Welsh as a legitimate power and a desirable ally. The 1404 alliance transferred Wales's temporal allegiance to France. One of the stated aims of the French initiative which arrived in March 1406 was to secure Wales's spiritual allegiance to the French king also. Clearly, by the time it was written, the Welsh had sufficiently demonstrated their liberty from England to conduct their own political, military and diplomatic affairs, and were therefore legitimate to induce further into French influence. This overt acquisition of the full allegiance one of England's British dominions was a significant and aggressive measure by the French, proving their intent to expand their power and influence into Britain.

According to the Saint-Denys chronicle, the bulk of the French–Breton expeditionary force overwintered in Wales and returned to

France around Lent 1406, which began in April that year. If correct, then it seems likely that the documents signed at Pennal were taken to France with that returning army.[5]

In diplomatic terms, the preamble is a relatively brief note which gave a précis of the longer document it accompanied. It is valuable for a number of reasons, perhaps most notably for its use of the first person, which strongly suggests that Glyn Dŵr dictated this part of the declaration. Although it is reasonable to believe that Gruffydd Yonge or any of Owain's ecclesiastical entourage wrote the religious parts of this response, for they understood the mechanics of church business, the document gives another example of Owain Glyn Dŵr's voice: an apparently angry one that used repetition and colourful, violent phraseology. To illustrate that point, he referred to English barbarism three times in this short note and again described them as 'Saxons'. The preamble mentions the 'fury of the barbarous Saxons' and the 'barbarous fury of those reigning in this country' as well as referring to them as 'barbarians'. As discussed previously, the description of an enemy as barbarian was used to recount the unwarranted destruction of something innocent, perhaps holy. Italian writers of the period refer to descending German armies in a similar manner. Such phraseology undoubtedly connects Owain's response to other comparisons of barbarism in contemporary French, Italian and Scottish literature. The Pennal voice spoke of the violence and oppression suffered by 'my nation' as well as that wrought upon the church in Wales, which it described as 'the metropolitan church of St. David's'. The preamble wrote of it being 'violently compelled, by the barbarous fury of those reigning in this country, to obey the church of Canterbury, and de facto still remains in this subjection'. It called for French support to 'remove violence and oppression from the Church and my subjects'.[6]

These denunciations of Henry and his violent methods were not simply Glyn Dŵr venting against injustice. The original French approach, contained within Owain's longer reply, regaled the pro-Avignon account of the schism, using certain similar expressions to illuminate the efforts Clement and Benedict had made to heal the rift in the church. The language of the French letter described in detail the mob violence which had forced the election of Urban VI on the grounds that he was Italian, and how the Roman pontiffs had usurped the Holy See. Owain appropriated the same terms and, by mirroring that language, appears to have been attempting not only to relate to the issue in hand and demonstrate his fervour in this important matter, but also to reflect the similarities between Henry's and Urban's conduct. Moreover, Owain's condemnation of Henry and his allegedly unjust, unchristian and barbarous ways would likely have been music to the ears of those French nobles who bore Henry ill will. In writing this, Owain was speaking directly to Louis of Orleans who detested Henry and was Benedict's most fervent advocate at court. In a period where personal relations played a major role in high-level politics, Owain appears to have been addressing his audience wisely.

In this short letter, Owain appeared humble and addressed the French king with the correct words of esteem. Perhaps most importantly to the French faction whose support he hoped to elicit, he made plain his answer regarding Benedict: 'confident indeed in his right, and intending for me to agree with you as far as is possible for me, I recognise him as the true Vicar of Christ, on my own behalf and on behalf of my subjects.' For the Welsh rebels, it was paramount that he expressed his desire to retain French support and to seek their aid in simultaneously resurrecting and liberating the Welsh church from Canterbury's yoke. In realising this, it seems clear that the Welsh were constructing a state, not grasping for military support. This would seem appropriate for a nation at peace rather than one at war, especially if they were losing that conflict, as has been previously written.

Owain closed by requesting that the French presented the letter to Benedict XIII and supported their cause. Therefore, the Pennal Declaration was a letter to the French court, not a direct approach to Pope Benedict. However, this short preamble contains the classic elements of an address by Owain Glyn Dŵr: a structured argument, repetition of key ideas, violent language and emotive appeal. In this note, he displayed a subtle, even gentle side to his language: 'as you deemed us worthy to raise us out of darkness into light'. In this brief letter, Owain's intelligence seems perceptible.[7]

The main document in the Pennal Declaration comprises two sections. By far the greater part discussed the schism and justified Benedict as the true pope, while a short final section presented a number of points and requests Owain wished to make in order to revive the Welsh church. While the greater part of the document has been largely passed over in preference of the Welsh clauses, the longer section reveals noteworthy points. The main themes of the message are valuable: the French sought Owain's declaration of support for the French-backed pontiff and

Wales desired to strengthen ties to France by offering over its spiritual allegiance to French guidance. It is also of interest due to its contents and the style points it revealed.

First, the document gave the names of the two more envoys, 'Hugh Eddowyer' and 'Morris Kery', who formed part of Glyn Dŵr's entourage. It also provides the dates of the parliament, probably Owain's third, which sat sometime between 8 and 31 March 1406. Although the date range of this assembly is now clear, most writers have assumed that it was convened at the place named on the document, Pennal. While this is possible, it might simply denote that Owain signed the document in the church there, in the presence of French messengers, according it with befitting sanctity. Other period documents, such as the Tripartite Indenture, were often validated by the touching and swearing on the Gospel and holy relics. To repeat such a ceremony while creating a document on the subject of a people's spiritual allegiance would seem appropriate and, perhaps, be expected. It is also worth recalling that Owain held his 1404 parliament at Machynlleth and that of the following year at Harlech.[8] Pennal is just outside Machynlleth, and it is quite possible that Owain was varying his councils between southern and northern strongholds, in a manner comparable to other contemporary rulers. Similarly, the English Parliament was not yet irredeemably rooted at Westminster; several parliaments were held around England in places as diverse as York and Winchester.

One short passage in the declaration reveals the composition of Owain's parliament: clergy, nobles and the most prominent men of each commote.[9] Therefore, Glyn Dŵr's court, government and parliaments were constructed and conducted entirely in keeping with the norms of his time.

The main thrust of the French letter described the events which 'violently and through an infamous riot' raised 'Bartholomew de Prinhano' to the highest Christian office. The description of the election, the aggression of the Roman mob and the withdrawal of the cardinals from Rome is unremarkable fare. It does, however, neatly exemplify Italian opposition to the French dominance of the papacy during much of the fourteenth century. The declaration text then renders a largely routine justification of the deliberation over the rightful election of Clement VII and subsequently that of Benedict XIII. Within this part of the letter there is also a defence of the efforts made by Clement and Benedict to heal the schism, and contrasting revelations are made of the actions of the Roman candidate, described as the *intrusi,* the intruder or anti-pope, to deepen the crisis. This section also contains a notable tactic of French persuasion; the listing of all those temporal princes who freely supported Benedict.[10] They were all lords of French territories, or rulers connected to the French crown by blood, marriage or alliance. Superficially, this resembles a weak list of pro-French puppets and relations. However, it seems to have been proposed as a subtle, seductive invitation to join that club. The lure of accepting would be to stand in liberty in a similar manner to Scotland, Cyprus and Genoa, whose political independence against larger, aggressively acquisitive neighbours was powerfully upheld by France. Viewed in that light, the French approach to Owain should be perceived as one of intelligent diplomatic seduction. That point can be directly underlined by the paragraph preceding Owain's demands; in this telling section, the French offered to acquire or arrange many of the requests Glyn Dŵr subsequently made.

It seems to our said lord the king that this [agreement of Welsh support] shall be to the safety of his [Owain's] soul, of his subjects, and the safe-keeping of his realm. Concerning this, the same lord the king, who sincerely zealous, prays heartily for his [Owain's] safety, the prosperity and conservation of his honour, his state and himself, under the bond and treaty of friendship, and of a singular love which he has for him. He [Charles] requests that he [Owain] indicate this himself, because if he puts the aforesaid into action, he [Owain] will give the same lord, the king, great satisfaction, and he [Charles] will consider himself very well pleased and to his greater obligation. If, by chance the said lord prince [Owain], the prelates the other ecclesiastics of his land, and his subjects dread, because from this kind of restoration, that certain prelates and other beneficed clergy, appointed by the anti-pope and his predecessors, and other favours of whatsoever nature granted on behalf of future occasions to his subjects may be unsettled, or that the lord Benedict may wish to change anything. On that account, our lord the king offers that he will, procure from the said lord Benedict that all the prelates and beneficed clergy shall be confirmed, and all favours, dispensations, etc., shall be ratified and conceded to them in secure and proper form. Also the lord Benedict shall provide, that when prelacies and other benefices are vacant, or shall be vacant, those persons only who are sufficiently in the faith and good will of the said lord the prince [Owain] shall be appointed, and not rivals or suspects.[11]

This manifestly promised that Charles would have a greater obligation towards Glyn Dŵr and detailed those things that he would initially secure from Benedict on Owain's behalf. Therefore, many of the points that comprise Owain's articles originated from this French suggestion. Indeed, there seems little point in pressing the originality and breadth of the vision supposed in Owain's declaration, that would be to ignore the real value of the document. If it is essential to praise the declaration, then the strength and intelligence of the Pennal Declaration are that there is nothing entirely new or visionary in it. In fact, all of its articles can be related to other events either in Wales or contemporary Europe, and therefore all of the Welsh requests were theoretically grantable on grounds of precedence. Requests founded on established precedent would be far more appealing to those in the largely conservative society of the time, rather than a rash of radical, new ideas from an unfamiliar corner of Europe, as some characterise Owain's declaration.[12]

In the final section, that of primary interest to Welsh historians, the same aggressive voice identified in the preamble again becomes apparent. Owain forcefully described English behaviour as that of *barbarorum Saxonum*, or barbarous Saxons. Yet elsewhere, the letter uses other terms, such as *monasteriis et collegiis anglicorum* or 'English monasteries and colleges', and *regni Anglie*, the 'kingdom of England', where there was no Saxon reference.[13] Owain was specifically repeating the point about the English being Saxons and all that went with that allusion. Similar terms describing the English as Saxons, and therefore likening them to pagan barbarians, also appeared in contemporary European literature. One of the French ones, *Traité A Toute La Chevalerie*, further described why the English were perceived in this manner:

> They [the English] make continual deadly war ... where they have made themselves spread, and spilled more human blood, ravaged with fire, raped women, destroyed churches, hospitals and other holy places [than all the other Christian nations] as witnessed in France, Spain, Scotland, Wales and Ireland. ... and those Scots and the Welsh, the Spanish and those from Ireland who have been consulted, indeed all of the other neighbours of the said English, bear witness that the said English are harsh and intolerable people, and are hated by their neighbours.[14]

Within the Pennal Declaration, Owain used clever linguistic ploys, weaving French terminology into his reply. The French letter to Owain

identified the Roman pope as *intrusi*, 'the intruder' and, in a repetition
of the preamble's appropriation of French terms, Owain's articles refer
to *Henricum Lencastrie intrusorem*, 'the intruder Henry of Lancaster'.[15]
Throughout, it appears that Owain was astutely communicating with his
interlocutors, borrowing the terms they used and relating them to his
circumstances.

Demands made by Glyn Dŵr in the Pennal Declaration have been
identified as political as well as ecclesiastical, and likened to a civil
programme for an independent church within an independent state.[16]
Owain's articles were the following:

> First, that all ecclesiastical censures against us, our subjects, or our land,
> by the aforesaid lord Benedict or Clement his predecessor, at present
> existing, the same shall by the said Benedict be removed.[17]

The simple request for the lifting of any censures made by the Avignon
pope against Owain, his subjects and lands would be simple to achieve.
The French promised that they could procure this as well as many of the
other subsequent requests.

> Again, that whatsoever vows and of whatsoever nature given by us or
> whomsoever of our principality, to those who called themselves Urban
> or Boniface, lately deceased, or to their adherents, shall be absolved.[18]

This second clause acts in tandem with the first, annulling the obedience
to Benedict's papal adversary, who was Innocent VII at that time. This too,
would have been simple to grant.

> Again, that he shall confirm and ratify the orders, collations, titles
> of prelates, dispensations, notorial documents, and all things
> whatsoever, from the time of Gregory XI, from which, any danger to
> the souls, or prejudice to us, or our subjects, may occur, or may be
> engendered.[19]

The next clause appears as a cautious next step, following the removal
of censures by Avignon and the annulment of vows to the Roman pope,
returning to the established state of affairs immediately prior to the
schism. This also would be simple enough to decree in writing or in a
public audience.

Again, that the Church of St David, archbishop and confessor, was a metropolitan church, and after his death, twenty-four archbishops succeeded
him in the same place, as their names are contained in the chronicles and
ancient books of the church of Menevia, and we cause these to be stated
as the chief evidence, namely, Eliud, Ceneu, Morfael, Mynyw, Haerwnen,
Elwaed, Gwrnwen, Llewdwyd, Gwrwyst, Gwgawn, Clydâwg, Aman, Elias,
Maelswyd, Sadwrnwen, Cadell, Alaethwy, Novis, Sadwrnwen, Drochwel,
Asser, Arthwael, David II and Samson; and that as a metropolitan church
it had and ought to have the undermentioned suffragan churches, namely,
Exeter, Bath, Hereford, Worcester, Leicester, which is now translated to
the churches of Coventry and Lichfield, St Asaph, Bangor, and Llandaff.
For being crushed by the fury of the barbarous Saxons, who usurped to
themselves the land of Wales, they trampled upon the aforesaid church
of St David's, and made her a handmaid to the church of Canterbury.[20]

This is the first clause of any Welsh significance. The reason for presenting
these twenty-four names, established through the proper consultation of
chronicles and books, proved a precedent for native control of the church
and a long Christian heritage. The broader claims to ecclesiastical sovereignty over those English dioceses named was also founded on established
precedent and a belief, supported by manuscript and myth, that St
David's had once counted those parts of England within its influence.[21]
This clause also allows for that angry voice, railing against the 'barbarous
Saxons' to once again be heard. However, it should also be borne in mind
that the terms of the 1405 Tripartite Indenture had also laid a Welsh
claim to areas of England, and this 1406 declaration could be viewed as
a continuation of that assertion; the spiritual and administrative layers
of control, to accompany the temporal of the previous year. It seems
likely that the French would support Owain's territorial claims to areas
of England, for this would weaken their long-term adversary while
strengthening an ally. If there were still plans afoot to invade England
and combine with English rebels to dethrone Henry, as King Charles's
letter of November 1406 blatantly stated, then this statement by Owain
appears to connect with desires expressed in England and France.[22]

Again that the same lord Benedict shall provide for the metropolitan
church of St David's, and the other cathedral churches of our principality, prelates, dignitaries and beneficed clergy and curates, who know
our language.[23]

This fifth clause has drawn particular interest from writers whose mother tongues were Welsh, notably Lloyd and Davies.[24] However, as shown above, the notion of selecting clergy favoured by Owain was proposed by the French. Equally, the call for priests able to freely commune with their flocks was not new, since Gerald of Wales raised the same issue in a letter to the pope in 1201 and again by others on numerous occasions thereafter, particularly during the fourteenth century. Nor was it a uniquely Welsh issue, as other peoples such as the Bretons and the Flemish had raised similar complaints.[25] This should also have been simple enough to agree, although anointing an entire national clergy, however small, would have required considerable effort.

> Again, that the same lord Benedict shall revoke and annul all incorporations, unions, annexions, appropriations of parochial churches of our principality made so far, by any authority whatsoever with English monasteries and colleges. That the true patrons of these churches shall have the power to present to the ordinaries of those places suitable persons to the same or appoint others.[26]

Equally, the transfer of the oaths of allegiance away from English institutions in lands under Owain's influence would have been easy to announce, but harder to enforce. The second part of this, regarding locally appointed candidates, would also have been an easy clause with which to concur, and would have granted Owain's church a measure of control over its personnel. In theory, the pope might not have wished this, since pontiffs traditionally played a role in candidate selection; to grant this would be to lose a measure of power. However, this and the following clause mirrored movements within the French church at that moment; the appropriation of control over the national church by the secular authorities. This 'Gallican' attitude appears entirely appropriate considering a recent conflict between the French government and Benedict over appointments and taxes. In making this and the following point, it seems that Owain was shrewdly relating his state of affairs to those of his audience at the French court. In matching their political environments and using phraseology with which his audience was comfortable, since they wrote similarly to him, Owain shows impressive diplomatic guile.

> Again, that the lord Benedict shall concede to us and our heirs, the princes of Wales, that our chapels, etc., shall be free, and shall rejoice in

the privileges, exemptions, and immunities in which they rejoiced in the times in the times of our forefathers the princes of Wales.[27]

This request concerning the control over the garnering of ecclesiastical taxes in Wales would have been resonant with the French court. It made a claim to rights similar to those then in the air in France and, once again, it was loosely attributed to historical precedence. This would certainly benefit Owain and clergy loyal to him. As with all of the preceding clauses, this would have been easily, though theoretically, granted by papal decree, with the harder task, its practical application, being left to those *in situ*.

> Again, that we shall have two universities or places of general study, namely, one in North Wales and the other in South Wales, in cities, towns, or places to be hereafter decided and determined by our ambassadors and nuncios for that purpose.[28]

Many places across Europe, such as Rome, Turin and St Andrews, were petitioning for and establishing universities. Therefore, this clause is only original in the Welsh context, but not so in a contemporary British or continental one.[29] It does however signal Glyn Dŵr's intention to train an independent administration for which universities played a key role in producing the essential personnel. This is a measure of an administration at peace, not one struggling with a militarily superior enemy. Therefore, this is a sensible and constructive measure, but considering the number of other such institutions inaugurated around the same time, it is not a revolutionary proposal. It is perhaps noteworthy that this is aired as a future intention, their locations seemingly undecided. In addition, the fact that there were to be two might indicate that divisions between north and south forced Owain's hand on this matter, rather than there being a wealth of candidates in both regions.

> Again, that the lord Benedict shall brand as heretics and cause to be tortured in the usual manner, Henry of Lancaster, the intruder of the kingdom of England, and the usurper of the crown of the same kingdom, and his adherents, in that of their own free will they have burnt or have caused to be burnt so many cathedrals, convents and parish churches; that they have savagely hung, beheaded, and quartered archbishops, bishops, prelates, priests, religious men, as madmen or beggars, or caused the same to be done.[30]

The two final clauses were certainly connected. The penultimate article, above, demanded, in the rich, colourful language attributable to the document's originator, how the enemy should be declared heretics and tortured in riposte to their many violent crimes against clergymen and the church at large. Indeed, this call would certainly have been presentable as valid at the time because up to 1406, Henry IV's reign had produced a staggering body count of society's upper echelons. Among the nobility, this included a king, the earls of Gloucester, Huntingdon, Kent, Salisbury, Wiltshire, Worcester, the Earl Marshal who was also earl of Norfolk, along with dozens of knights and an unknown, but high number of lower-born men.[31] His large-scale killing of clergymen has been described as a 'peculiar characteristic of Henry IV's retributive policies', the death toll among Britain's religious community was only surpassed by Henry VIII.[32] Although a precise figure has proven impossible to calculate, Henry's regime presided over the often brutal despatch of considerable numbers of all ranks of cleric, from friars through to the archbishop of York.[33] So, in the same fashion that the first Welsh clauses acted as related stepping stones for those that followed, so the penultimate article prepared the ground for the subsequent call for a crusade against Henry. Once declared heretics, the armies of the Christian faithful could legitimately overrun them in just wars.

> That the same Lord Benedict shall grant to us, our heirs, subjects, and adherents, of whatsoever nation they may be, who wage war against the aforesaid invader and intruder, as long as they hold the orthodox faith, full remission of our sins, and that the remission should continue as long as the war between us, our heirs, and our subjects, and the aforesaid Henry, his heirs and subjects shall endure.[34]

There seems no doubt that these last two clauses established the justification for holy war against Henry, his heirs and his supporters – not against England, it should be noted.[35] This undisguised call to arms repeated Owain's request for foreign troops first made in 1401, perhaps revealing his most significant weakness: having insufficient men to effectively and universally oppose the larger forces of the crown.[36] This promised another long war against the common enemy. Given Orleanist control of court at the time of the approach to Owain, and their powerful presence there even when not directly at the helm, these last two articles appear to be a counter-seduction on Owain's part by appealing to that which they wished to see. In so doing, also by reflecting terms written originally by the French in his reply, and by using similar linguistic ploys, Glyn Dŵr emerges as engaging and intelligent.

However, apart from being appealing to the faction controlling the French government, this call was also based on recent precedent. The Roman popes Gregory XI and Urban VI had used crusades as weapons against French and Italian opponents. Gregory called for a crusade against Milan in 1372, while Urban VI had declared crusades against the Clementists in 1373 and 1384. The first of Urban's attacks on the French induced the raid on Flanders by English forces under the bishop of Norwich in 1373, while the second caused conflict with Louis of Anjou.[37] Many of the targets attacked by papal aggression, Milan and Louis of Anjou, for example, had close personal connections to Louis, duke of Orleans. Therefore, in this time of personality politics, a call to crusade might not only have been personally appealing but also based on just, retributive precedent. There might be another, more elusive, example of a holy war being called at this time – allegedly by Archbishop Arundel against the Welsh in 1404.[38] This clause in Owain's reply might be in response to that, as well as engaging with the intense enmity between Louis and Henry, as well as that which existed between the papal candidates.

In addressing an appeal for a holy war to the Avignon papacy, Owain was not issuing a desperate call for help or attaching a seemingly overblown religious appeal to an otherwise regional feud between temporal princes; he was displaying his knowledge of his interlocutors. The Orleanists and others in France no doubt welcomed wider support in their struggle with Henry IV. They might have legitimately sought a crusade as a counter to Roman-inspired crusades against them, their allies and adherents. The papacy had been aggressive in its pursuit of such campaigns since its translation to Avignon, particularly against Christian lay rulers.[39] In seeking such a campaign against Henry, Glyn Dŵr again appeared to be using the correct language to the correct audience. The Avignon papacy had sought to flex its muscles at the beginning of the fourteenth century by supporting campaigns throughout the eastern Mediterranean, aimed at those Christian princes requiring correction in the region, as well as the faith's Muslim enemies. Many of the proposed crusades were to support embattled Christian allies, particularly Armenia, as well as to reclaim or expand the territories of nobles favoured by the Curia, and the French ranked highly among them. However, crusades were not solely sent east. Grand campaigns in Spain not only supported the *Reconquista* of the peninsula from the Moors of Granada, but the papacy also lent its weight to the political and dynastic struggles between Castile and Aragon, allies of France and England. Although the papacy also encouraged often large-scale campaigns against pagans in Eastern Europe during this period, it also conducted a notable number of smaller, political actions too, particularly in Italy. Certain of the crusades called against Christian rulers appeared to contain a strong element of personality politics between the pope and the noble or region in question. A notable example was the designation as a heretic of Bernabò Visconti, by Urban V in 1363. This was followed by a military campaign against Milan. Despite the enduring Anglo–French conflict and the terrifying mortality caused by the century's plagues, most calls for crusades were made during the second half of the fourteenth century, during the lifetimes of Glyn Dŵr and his allies. Whether on a grand or small scale, the Avignon popes were practiced exponents of crusades against European lay rulers whom they deemed as heretics. Usually, they recruited troops or mercenaries locally or from nations uninvolved or adjacent to the conflict area. Similar campaigns were conducted against the Serbian king, Italian territories and in numerous Spanish conflicts. With those campaigns in mind, the rallying of England's neighbours in the treatises mentioned, appears pointed towards alliance and violent action, rather than just being fine prose. The fear of drawing papal sanction was exemplified by the thoughts of Jean Gerson, chancellor of the University of Paris, who was aware of an increased possibility of English attack should the French be branded as heretics: 'since they might attack us all the more freely [considering us] to be on a par with schismatics, heretics and Saracens'.[40] This shows that the Welsh authors of these clauses were well aware of the political form and uses of crusades, as well as the willingness of the Avignon popes to use them as a mechanism to attain their goals. Therefore, these two, final, more aggressive requests in the Pennal Declaration had demonstrable foundation on recent events and were justified, if required, as counter-strikes to the belligerence of the Roman adversary and his heretical adherents. In that light, they seem far from being unlikely or extreme, but entirely within the known actions of the Avignon popes, and therefore they form an astute request.

The Pennal Declaration also reveals clues to the timing of the drafting of the original letter delivered to Owain by Kery and Eddouwyer. The text clearly states that Benedict had been to Italy and that he was still in Genoa at the time it was written.[41] This correlates with the proposed campaign of 1405 which aimed to advance on Rome and have Benedict crowned as the sole and true pope. Benedict arrived in Genoa in May 1405 and retired from Italy to Nice by October. The possible composition dates for the French approach to Owain therefore fall between May and October 1405, with some leeway for the slow passage of the news of Benedict's withdrawal to reach the letter's author.

* * * * *

The impact and broader significance of the Pennal Declaration are difficult to measure, this is partly because of the paucity of surviving documentation on connected matters. Moreover, the matter is further confused by hindsight of the civil war which was about to erupt in France, which obscures or corrupts as complicit all which happened before it. Due to the lack of a written response or confirmatory report, there is no incontrovertible proof that Benedict ever saw the letter, which remains stored in French archives. However, Benedict's actions demonstrate that he either received a copy or a full summary, for he certainly knew of the Welsh allegiance to him and the articles requesting his pronouncement. This is evidenced by his provision of Welshmen to Welsh bishoprics from June 1406 to John Trefor, Lewis Byford, Gruffydd Yonge and Adam Usk, as well as a grant to Maredudd, Glyn Dŵr's son.[42] Benedict also appears to have designated St David's as a metropolitan church.[43] In addition, within Benedict's records are Welsh-specific rolls, in which Welsh clergy are provided with benefices in Wales. The names cited in the Welsh Rolls include 'John Boughton', 'Matthew ap Jevan Lloyt', 'Griffin ap Jevan' and 'Philip ap Ll'. issued from Savona in July and November 1406. From Marseille in January and February 1407, Benedict similarly made provisions for 'Gregory ap Ivan', 'Jorwerth ap David ap Jorwerth', 'Roger ap Jenn' and 'Mereuduth ap David ap Gruffuth'. Certain Welsh records are also mixed in with the Scottish Rolls of the time, for in January 1407, Benedict gave dispensation to 'Meredith ap Oweyn ap Gruffuth', Owain's son, to remain married to 'Ellyw verch Rhys ap Gruffuth' despite being related in the fourth degree, which likely made them first cousins, and declaring their past and future offspring legitimate.[44] The confirmation of titles, provision of benefices and the designation of St David's as the metropolitan church all correlate to articles three and five of the Pennal Declaration. Without the creation of that document, Benedict would not have taken such measures. Therefore, it seems that Owain's requests were enacted by the pope, and therefore it is reasonable to believe that many of the other articles were consented to, at least in principle, at the same time. At that point in time, the Pennal Declaration could be perceived to have been another successful diplomatic effort on Owain's part. These must have been exciting times, the Welsh were in the process of resurrecting their own native church, they had contact with the pope unfettered by Canterbury, they held territory and castles, they were running their own political affairs and in contact with other powers, they had a firm alliance with France and there were possibly still French troops in Wales to offer support: all appeared to be going well.

However, perhaps the primary significance of the declaration has so far been missed. Superficially, it declared Owain's desire to support one of the papal candidates. Within the text, it is plainly stated that the French king wished to be bound closer to Owain and in riposte the Welsh leader expressed a reciprocal sentiment.[45] However, due to the fact that the House of Burgundy consistently supported the Roman pope, this is clearly an Orleanist initiative, though one with oscillating degrees of royal and ducal backing. Therefore, this is an alliance document further binding Glyn Dŵr to France, but more specifically to the Orleanists who backed Benedict XIII at that time. Overtly, the declaration concerned papal adherence, but in substance, it tied Owain to Louis.

However, by the time Owain's letter reached Paris, the mood at court was shifting again. King Charles recovered his senses in December 1405 and reviewed the alarming escalation of hostile posturing between Orleans and Burgundy of that autumn. On 27 January 1406, Charles decreed that the government was to be a council of the princes, and not one commanded by a regent alone. By July 1406, a new council was formed, albeit dominated by Orleanists for the moment, but no longer with Louis at the helm. Thus, Louis, who had firmly held power up to midsummer 1405 and retained it but slowly, decreasingly by degrees thereafter, lost clear, personal control of the government at that point. Although he remained a powerful, instrumental member of the council, his gradual decline in power, not always perceptible at the time of its slide, would also affect his allies and their causes.[46]

Therefore, by the time Glyn Dŵr's reply reached Paris, at the end of April 1406 at the earliest, it arrived in an altered environment to that in which the question was first posed. This, of course, would have been impossible for Owain to gauge or affect. However, military preparations were under way for offensives against the English in the south-west and north-east of France. The duke of Burgundy was to reduce Picardy, while the duke of Orleans was to take key areas of Aquitaine.[47] En route south, Louis, consistent with his policy of alliances, made a treaty with Jean, the seventeen-year-old duke of Brittany.[48] While the two rival dukes were blatantly sent to the opposite ends of France, a calmer environment was restored to the capital. With that, came renewed debate on the most effective means of ending the schism. At that time, the consensus of court, the universities and the clergy favoured another withdrawal of obedience and proposed a plan for the mutual cession of both popes. The court referred the debates to parliament which discussed the matter through the summer and autumn of 1406. Eventually, parliament also proposed to withdraw obedience once again.[49]

Louis's efforts before Bourg were wholly ineffective, earning him the acidic criticism of chroniclers. Likewise, Jean the Fearless appears to have achieved even less in Picardy, and might not have even moved his troops out of their quarters. Henry Percy, earl of Northumberland, appeared in Paris during the year looking for support in his fight against Henry.[50] King Charles replied by letter, giving an answer which could be viewed as a response of sorts to the Pennal Declaration.[51] While calling on the English to overthrow Henry and giving an ongoing assurance of French support to that end, Charles's letter also appeared to rebuke them for not turning up to support the French army when it arrived in Wales. Percy left with no army, and went to try to raise one in Scotland, with no material, but probably with verbal French and Welsh support.[52] By the time Louis of Orleans returned to Paris in early 1407 his star appeared to have waned.[53] While this was unlikely to remain the case for long, this moment perhaps offered his enemies a transient window of opportunity in which to move against him.

PART FOUR

Fall

CHAPTER ELEVEN

English Diplomatic Manoeuvring

[the duke of Brittany's] ... admiral, his marshals, captains, constables ... and all others will conform to these orders ... [for a] ... truce and abstinence of war [with the English] for the term of the coming year.[1]

Clearly, while the Welsh and the French were conducting business in their own interests, their opponents were not idle. English military efforts in Wales in the first five years of the fifteenth century had largely proved unimpressive across a number of theatres. Successive, serious internal revolts such as those of 1400, 1403 and 1405 describe an environment in which the king's enemies dared to tread. Although Henry's brutality against his opponents increased throughout his reign, this was clearly insufficiently fearsome or effective enough to fully control the kingdom.[2] In the advent of Louis's more aggressive position towards England from 1402, the French had enjoyed successes against English possessions in France, such as the capture of Mortagne, Corbefin and several places in the Limousin.[3] In addition, Breton, French and Castilian fleets had carried the war directly onto English soil and appeared to narrowly hold the balance of power in the Channel during these years. Although the Scots had been comprehensively beaten in September 1402 at Homildon, they continued to harass English interests on sea and land, and appear to have provided logistical support in the form of sea-going transport for the Welsh and French.[4] More embarrassingly, Henry IV had personally derided the Welsh as a people 'of little repute' and parliament scorned them as 'bare-footed idiots', yet in the long years of their damaging, costly and humiliating revolt, Henry, his commanders and their forces met with successive defeats.[5] Whether on the battlefield, as at Ruthin or Bryn Glas, or in the storming of great fortresses such as Carmarthen, Conwy, Harlech and Aberystwyth, crown forces were consistently inferior to those of Glyn Dŵr.[6] Although the English won a victory at Usk near the border in May 1405, notable for the importance rather than the number of casualties, this was a negligible return for the scale of their military efforts, reputation and financial outlay to that point.[7] Wales had been lost to the natives.

In addition, the revolt exposed the feebleness of those castles which remained nominally under crown control. Their assault and seizure does not appear to have been a key part of the rebel strategy and there is no evidence of a concerted effort to seize any but a key few. This is understandable since the rebels would need to commit men to garrison them, losing all mobility advantages. Evidently, if the Welsh could take the largest and best-defended ones, such as Harlech and Carmarthen, the smaller, more isolated castles posed the rebels far fewer problems. In addition, decades of experience in France meant that crown forces were well able to conduct sieges; however, they were demonstrably less effective in the wilderness of fifteenth-century Wales. Those crown commanders who retained keep of castles in Wales conducted remarkably few operations against the rebels during the revolt, and their allegiance appears to have moved towards a position of neutrality, or perhaps self-interest, in certain cases.[8] Although crown control was extant in a number of locations in Glyn Dŵr's Wales, in some cases it appears to have been largely notional. The parlous state of English fortunes in Wales at that time provides perhaps the best example of a seemingly dire general situation for English power. However, 'military conquest was a traditional means of acquiring new territory, although it was seldom used on its own'.[9] So, while England's military efforts lacked success, its diplomatic ventures proved more fruitful, in time.

The actions and skills of England's diplomats, the largely unsung servants of the crown, who embarked on numerous missions to the continent improved England's fortunes where its armies had proven inadequate. While many of the ambassadors' letters are of limited value individually, as a whole they help construct a useful corpus showing their form, style and political direction. Two additional points emerge from these letters: the grindingly slow pace of medieval diplomatic processes and the private thoughts the ambassadors shared with the Privy Council. Henry's ambassadors often denigrated their counterparts in letters to England, then greeted them in person with blustering pleasantry.[10] From the mass of these discussions, the intriguing and critical evidence emerges of a diplomatic strategy that was so effective in rescuing England's cause. The names of England's ambassadors are largely unfamiliar, but appear to follow the seemingly typical composition for ambassadorial parties of the time, with nobles, clergy and clerks.[11] Concerning England's ambassadors who undertook the relevant missions to France, the nobility was represented throughout by a small group of knights. They were Richard Aston, John Croft, William Hoo, Hugh Lutrell, William Lyle, Thomas Swynford and Thomas Swynborne, few of whom are well-known, though the latter is most easily traced due to his other military activities. The only clergyman who consistently featured in the critical meetings was Nicholas de Ryssheton, Doctor of Laws. John Urban seemed to be a permanent member of these embassies, although his designation is unclear. At times he had no defined title, at others he was described as an ambassador or the 'Lieutenant du Maire de l'Estaple [a Calais]', which was a role focused on the co-ordination of military activities there.[12]

Lutrell, Croft, Ryssheton and Urban made representation to Philippe of Burgundy in December 1403, addressing complaints to him and France's Great Council against the aggressive actions of the duke of Orleans and Waleran, count of St Pol.[13] These referred to the various recent probing attacks which England had suffered along the entirety of its south coast and had also reached as far as Kidwelly in west Wales in October that year. This approach probably had a more profound purpose, as subsequent discussions would reinforce.

The English were aware of the divisions and struggles within the French court during the king's illness. Philippe of Burgundy was therefore the right choice for them; he had consistently been the senior noble at court since the death of Charles V in 1380, he enjoyed a commercial relationship with England, and Orleans was his adversary. Shortly after, the same English ambassadorial team opened discussions with the Flemish deputies, as well as with Duke Philippe, regarding Anglo–Flemish trade. The stratagem seems to have borne fruit immediately; the count of St Pol was summoned to Paris to account for his actions. A number of letters passed between Henry, his ambassadors at Calais and the Privy Council. These dispatches reported on progress, but also showed Henry's will to support and encourage the ambassadors in their tasks.[14]

The English made an intelligent concession during winter 1403–4. The previous summer was remarkable for the level of maritime violence witnessed, as well as the better-known coastal attacks. Repaying such violence in kind would have seemed justified and was perhaps expected. In contrast, the English offered to extend the previously agreed safeguard to French and Flemish fishermen. This was a significant gesture, not just of goodwill but one which few, if any, of their opponents could attack. Gesture, goodwill, adherence to notions of good conduct and apparent good faith appear to have been essential to the art of successful diplomacy at the time. From this point, early 1404, Henry's ambassadors can be seen raising and addressing grievances regarding the seizures of goods and vessels, commercial advantages and talks on peace. These were undertaken with the Flemings, therefore the House of Burgundy also, along with separate missions to the Hanseatic League. There is no need to further develop the undulating course of all such commercial negotiations, but solely to acknowledge the diligent efforts and intelligent strategy of Henry's diplomats; engaging partners and adversaries alike in discussions encompassing hostility and redress, peace and trade, with a view to achieving mutually beneficial commerce, which strongly advanced England's interests at that time.[15]

Aston and Ryssheton delivered a strong complaint to Philippe of Burgundy in March 1404. Their French ambassadorial counterparts included the bishop of Chartres and Jean de Saints, who would be so closely involved with the Welsh alliance negotiations in May of the same year, as well as with the Pennal Declaration of 1406. The noble envoy was Jean de Hangest, one of the 1405 expedition leaders. The letter is an excellent example of the English strategy towards the French court. Aston and Ryssheton recognised but disputed the degree to which outrages and reprisals had been committed by the English side, noting that they were contrary to the extant truce. They countered de Hangest's accusations regarding English actions in Picardy and Boulogne citing murders and robberies committed on Alderney. They furthered this with an attack on de Hangest for profiting from these activities and inferred French meddling in Anglo–Scots affairs. Henry's ambassadors also recalled the actions of the Bretons, who they identified as subjects of the French crown in the obedience of the Admiral of France, who had landed in England, burned and plundered Plymouth, where they robbed, murdered and carried off the people of the area. All of this had been done contrary to the oaths they had sworn and the responsibility for adherence to these promises lay with the French court. Not only that, the Bretons had also attacked Jersey and Guernsey where they committed similar atrocities. Henry's representatives then complained that the count of St Pol had maintained fleets on a war footing in Flanders. While this ran contrary to the spirit of the truce and oaths sworn by him and others of the royal blood, they went on to point out that these fleets had been used to attack all kinds of vessels, during which the cowardly practice of hurling projectiles at those trying to save themselves by swimming away had been witnessed. Not only that, these ships had been involved in landings on the Isle of Wight where they had molested poor fishermen and overrun sheep pens.[16]

While clearly a slight against the nobility and behaviour of those involved, the English repetition of the importance of the sworn oaths, the truce and the responsibility of the French court to control its subjects, reinforced their position. In short, they expected better from the French. They went on to make that very point, with recognition that the correction and punishment of the 'Duc d'Orliens' who was making war in contravention of the oaths made by his king, fell to the French court. They did not ask for reparations, and cited the formulaic but relevant phrase about seeking to avoid the spilling of Christian blood, but asked that the court obliged Louis to remain faithful to the oaths of peace that all of the French nobles had sworn. In a parting shot, Henry's men added that they were unaccustomed to such behaviour from the French, and could not recall previous reigns where the king had such disobedient subjects.[17]

The letter is an excellent example of shrewd diplomacy; it made clear England's complaint in black and white, but at the same time sought to isolate the activities of Orleans and St Pol from those of the rest of the French nobles. In asking the French court to set its house in order, it showed that Henry did not blame Charles's court as a whole – and the implication here regarding war was clear – but identified the unfaithful, disobedient Louis as the malefactor by whose actions France's collective honour was tarnished. Asking the French to settle the matter was a masterstroke, since it helped set the factions further against one another and, by deploying the arguments of precedent, norm, honour and standards, Aston and Ryssheton had appealed to factors consistent with the time and familiar to the target audience. This letter probably also assisted Louis's opponents at court, the Burgundians, in pointing out the abnormality of his behaviour and the advantages of removing him from power in order to pursue a course of peace and commerce.

The death of Philippe of Burgundy the following month weakened Henry's cause in the French court. With Louis in control, hostility to England increased rapidly. The ambassadors at Calais continued to play vital roles however, maintaining a level of discourse with the court and monitoring enemy activity in France. In the first case, they continued negotiations with Margaret, duchess of Burgundy, who continued to run many of the duchy's commercial affairs in the months following her husband's death. She in turn influenced the Flemings to maintain peace with the English and, over the summer months, it appeared as if a new treaty between England and Flanders would be signed. As Louis of Orleans took up the reins of government, peace negotiations with the French ambassadors, usually led by Jean de Hangest, visibly stalled. English relations with the Burgundians and Flemings also soured and then turned hostile, probably in adherence to the leaning of the court's dominant faction, and their previously hopeful discussions ground to a halt. The English diplomatic style of the time did not simply rely on the fine intellects of the king's envoys. They sought to quicken the prospects of a truce by conducting an attack on Sluys that year. On this occasion, underpinning the truce offer with the threat and use of force utterly failed.[18]

Henry's diplomats were crucial in passing on intelligence of the build up of the 1404 fleet. In September, they wrote that the French ambassadors were stalling due to the likelihood of a diversionary attack to assist the Welsh rebels, and identified Louis and Waleran as the main adversaries in attaining peace. Shortly after they learned that the fleet and its staggeringly large army of 15,000 had orders to invade and occupy Wales, rebuild the castles there and do as much harm to England as possible.[19] As intelligence was passed to England regarding the build-up of French and other forces and the eventual movements of the fleet westwards along the Channel coast, Henry's ambassadors tried a new tack as the situation appeared to be sliding towards war; they threatened to withdraw from discussions. This appeared to provoke a reaction from the French who immediately dispatched a full ambassadorial party composed of Jean, bishop of Chartres, Jean de Hangest, Guillaume Boisratier and Jean de Saints, who proposed a venue for discussions with the English. As the mission under Jacques de Bourbon launched, faltered and slunk back to port, the French returned to the idea of negotiations with Calais, allowing Swynford and Ryssheton their opportunity to stall in turn.

The French threat in 1404 had evaporated, and discussions on where or whether to meet went on throughout the winter.[20]

Others joined Henry's men in Calais, adding their names to the documents describing their exchanges with the French. Their meetings were to no avail and the diplomatic stalemate between the royal courts remained throughout 1405. This lean period in relations coincided with Louis's brief domination of government. Within that time frame, the Kidwelly landing in October 1403 took place. Subsequently, Jean d'Espagne launched his mission to the waters off Caernarfon in early winter 1404. Jean d'Espagne's efforts notably resulted in castle assaults and the allied capture of Anglesey after killing the deputy sheriff and all of his men in one fight. With a background level of ongoing French–Welsh military and diplomatic contact, the 1404 fleet and army was gathered. French activity peaked, but did not culminate with the fleet of July–August 1405.[21] Henry's diplomatic service was still active during this time, however, demonstrating how when one source of opportunity ran dry, others were devoted more time and occasionally bore fruit, such as relations with the Hanseatic cities, the Prussians and Portugal. These missions, in particular, helped improve England's trading relations which in turn helped Henry's finances. Consequently, a wealthier English government found itself with a greater ability to act across a broader spectrum of interests. Anglo–Scots correspondence also suggested that the latter was a nation split between factions, similarly to France. While the powerful duke of Albany maintained publicly cordial relations with Henry IV, James of Douglas clearly did not, and troops under the earl of Orkney accompanied Lord Bardolf into Berwick as the York rebellion flared in June 1405.[22]

Diplomatic contacts with the French were not entirely abandoned during 1405 however, and connections with Flanders and the Burgundians in particular, grew from May onwards. News of the count of St Pol's ineffective attack on Marck was passed on, and his failure was recorded with scorn in French records.[23] Then, Henry's ambassadors reported the breakthrough that had appeared long in coming. News from Calais brought by John Urban revealed that the knights Richard Aston and William Hoo, and squires Perin Lorraine and Richard Oldington, had brokered a trade treaty with the duke of Burgundy on 6 March 1406. While this was good news from a financial perspective, it also demonstrates the successful exploitation of a factional fissure in the French court. Jean *Sans Peur*, 'the Fearless', the new duke of Burgundy, was rising in power and was clearly engaged in mounting a challenge to Louis of Orleans. Strengthening the Burgundian cause would assist England and simultaneously weaken Louis, in turn harming Glyn Dŵr. That a major court party had established links to England indicates that control of the direction of the French government had partly slipped from Louis's grasp at that point. While this change in position might have been temporary, with Duke Jean's friendship and Louis's weakness both being transient, the English took advantage of this opportunity. The records demonstrate highly lucrative trade between England and Flanders during the rest of 1406. Louis and his allies were far from beaten though; the Bretons put 2,000 troops onto Alderney in July that year. However, the English now had a supporting role within one of the courtly factions and therefore, they then had a role in the French power struggle. This subtle but significant victory had been won by Henry's ambassadors alone.[24]

Another arena where English diplomacy eventually fared well, perhaps unexpectedly, was in Brittany. English successes here can be identified as openly bearing fruit during and after 1406. In 1402, Philippe of Burgundy gained the tenure of the duchy during the last year of Jean V's minority, and entered into alliance with him.[25] With Philippe's aid, Henry IV married Jean de Montfort's widow, Joanna, in 1403; a move which provoked resentment among much of the duchy's nobility.[26] That anger was vented in the previously described attacks on English interests and, in part, were a statement on Brittany's perception of its independence, but mostly in reaction to the harsh, even punitive, English governance of the duchy which had ended in 1398. Openly, Anglo–Breton relations from 1406 onwards witnessed a remarkable transition from hostility to truce in little over a year. Breton involvement in the aggressions against England was undeniable; from its greatest lords, such as the du Châtel, to its common soldiery and mariners. In the wake of these years of attacks, Henry IV acted against them. While there were military efforts, such as the attack on Saint Mathieu, Henry's main effort appears to have been economic and diplomatic. Between December 1405 and March 1406, Jean V's records reveal notable diplomatic traffic between the duke and his mother, who is described as '*la reyne d'Angleterre*'. It seems reasonable to believe that Henry would engage his new queen in assisting discussions: peace and commerce worked in their mutual interests, while war between her husband and her son only benefitted their adversaries. This exchange began in the aftermath of the 1405 mission and, if the monk of Saint-Denys was correct about the army spending the winter in Wales, then they were holding discussions while Breton troops occupied lands claimed by Henry. These letters appear to coincide with a slight thaw in relations; the duke assented to the collection and payment of ransoms for notable Bretons held by the English. The fine balancing act played by the Breton dukes was never a simple task, and equally, Jean V was obliged to engage with the crowns of England and France without rousing either. The young duke maintained excellent relations with the French court, sending embassies to discuss a potential marriage with Charles VI's daughter, Jeanne, although other matters of import were surely debated on these occasions as well.

England's treaty with Flanders had been brokered by March 1406 and lucrative commercial intercourse swiftly followed. In May that year, Henry ordered the expulsion of the Bretons and the French from London, and the seizure of their ships and merchandise soon after. In riposte, the Bretons initially maintained their hostile stance and conducted attacks, such as that on Alderney in July. In addition, in September, the duke entered into a personal alliance with Louis as well as sending a fleet and troops south against the English in Bordeaux to aid the king of France. Nevertheless, during 1406, Anglo–Breton relations had shifted from a position close to open warfare to one of reduced, though ongoing, hostility, but then with burgeoning dialogue.[27]

The early months of 1407 saw Louis return discredited from campaigning in south-west France. Perhaps in consequence to his loss of prestige, the Anglo–Breton rapprochement gained pace. The Breton ducal records reveal significant numbers of cross-Channel prisoner exchanges from March to May 1407. These ransoms and exchanges involved sizeable numbers of men on each side, the largest being the trade of 120 English prisoners for 'Hugues de Kaerenmanach' who was held by Thomas, Lord Berkeley. It is impossible to distinguish whether these men were seized on land, at sea or in port, and therefore Walsingham's claims concerning the English disrupting military convoys to Wales are impossible to prove or refute. However, these diplomatic exchanges between both courts and a general decline in fighting appear to be indicative of a truce being held. English records mention truce talks at the end of May. Jean V declared a guarantee of safety for English merchants in June 1407. It is noteworthy, but perhaps coincidental, that ducal military officials were ordered to ascertain the obligations of Jean, son of Jean d'Espagne, around that time. Peace appeared to be in the air.[28]

This careful process appearing to lead towards the conclusion of peace cannot have been unplanned or undertaken without mutual contact. These documents appear to have been lost, were they ever written, but seem to begin with Queen Joanna's letters to Jean V. The final result of this unseen discourse was achieved on 11 July 1407, when Jean V signed a full year-long truce with England. The terms of the agreement appear to reveal Jean's mother as the instigator. Within it, Jean named his mother, the queen, before any others such as Henry, disclosing that he accepted a year-long truce and in so doing ordered his admiral, marshals, captains, constables and all others to respect the agreement and to abstain from war with the English.[29] The Bretons, therefore, were lost to the Welsh cause until at least midsummer 1408, but had probably been disentangling themselves for some time prior to the truce. Without the use of Breton ports, ships and manpower, an expedition to Wales suddenly became a far less realistic proposition, and presented the English with a smaller front on which to concentrate. The diplomatic prising of Brittany from hostilities effectively cut off French–Welsh maritime connections while the terms of the Anglo–Breton truce were honoured. In addition, the Flemish ports used to gather the 1404 fleet were now friendly and trading with England. These significant advances won by his diplomats provided Henry and his government an opportunity to press their cause in Wales.

A further good example of Henry's envoys causing division between the French factions was seen in 1407. By June, Aston and his colleagues had concluded with the duke of Burgundy a 'general security' on sea and land which was to last three years. The peace agreement's proclamation throughout Burgundy was confirmed in another letter to Henry; the Burgundians were, openly and publicly, England's partners in France.[30] A major court faction had therefore made peace with England, and concluded a treaty which ensured a degree of co-operation. English diplomatic actions in these years describe a classic and effective 'cultivate and eradicate' strategy: bolstering and inflating their allies' power, they not only strengthened him but this strategy outlined the attraction of amicable relations with England, while eroding the power and, subsequently, the appeal of their adversaries evidently hostile and discredited policies. Henry's diplomats can be seen to further exploit their position of strength and that of weakness of the other parties involved by giving favourable trading conditions to the Flemish alone, while insisting on excluding the French from any measure of benefit from Anglo–Burgundian peace and trade. This ploy of favouring one partner to the detriment of other less friendly parties was used elsewhere by England during the Middle Ages and, in this case at least, can be perceived as the deployment of a version of 'soft power' by Henry's government.[31] With the Burgundians apparently positively disposed towards England, and the Bretons assuming a neutral posture, the English position was much improved. While they strove to recover England's diplomatic and financial position generally, one consequence of these missions was to effectively close the sea lane to Wales and the ports from which the armies which threatened English power there had launched. With a better financial position and the rebels isolated from their allies in France, a major window of opportunity opened in the west. In addition, with France's eastern and western Channel regions neutralised for a time, an attack on the centre of the enemy's coast, Normandy, also became a considerable possibility.

CHAPTER TWELVE

Ailing France, Rising England

... without the said Owain being included in it [the proposed Anglo–French truce] ... the said Owain must not be named ... because the said Owain must be subject to the Crown.[1]

While the diplomatic intercourse engaging France, England, Brittany, Scotland, Wales and others was ongoing, towards the end of 1405, the University of Paris returned to the question of healing the schism in the church. With Benedict's strongest ally, Louis, weakened following the events of late 1405 and the king's insistence on rule by council from January 1406 onwards, the matter of another withdrawal of obedience resurfaced.[2] The debates quickly led to an abandonment of the *via facti*, which intended a forceful military solution, and moved in favour of the *via cessionis*, which would see both popes resign.[3] These sessions took place throughout 1406 and by November it was largely, though not unanimously, agreed that such action was required. Although mutual cession by both popes was preferable, action against Benedict was deemed necessary by those loud voices opposed to him in council. While unilateral cession might prove potentially harmful to France, since its immediate central influence over the papacy would drop sharply in the short term, the appeal of withdrawing obedience was improved by the plan to seize ecclesiastical taxes, tithes and benefices for the French state. Perhaps with that lucrative incentive in mind, a partial withdrawal of obedience was projected to follow.[4] When Innocent VII died on 6 November 1406, Jean Gerson proposed that the Roman cardinals should recognise Benedict and thus heal the schism, giving hope to his cause, as well as to the Orleanists and their allies.[5] However, the idea was overborne by turbulent arguments in council and, in March 1407, the French sent ecclesiastical ambassadors to Rome where they realised that, despite his encouraging words, another recently elected Roman pope, Gregory XII, had no intention of resigning the papal crown unilaterally or mutually, thereby bringing union to western Christianity.[6] Although the University of Paris dominated the discussions in the capital, Benedict XIII was able to outmanoeuvre those ambassadors sent to hold talks with him. The University had required them to pronounce France's intention to declare neutrality, should Benedict fail to publish Bulls on the steps he would take to resolve the division in the church. He did not do so, but apparently conducted himself with such skill and diplomacy that, at the end of discussions in May 1407, he was able to stall the declaration of neutrality.[7] An agreement for both popes to meet at Savona was agreed by both parties, with differing levels of enthusiasm.[8] Roman politics once again disrupted the already troubled course of events. Ladislas of Durazzo, king of Naples, chose that moment, June 1407, to attempt to seize Rome. He took a number of the surrounding territories; however, he failed to gain full control of Rome but improved his connections with local notables, such as the Orsini family.[9] The fighting in the papal states and the kingdom of Naples broke out repeatedly, surged unpredictably, receded then erupted again over a generation, at least, and these conflicts formed the essential political landscape on which the interests of other powers, particularly France, played out in these regions. Although Duke Louis II of Anjou was still an important figure in the area, during these key years, 1404 to 1408, Ladislas was the prevailing regional strongman.

Ambassadors and other churchmen continued to plan and arrange the projected meeting at Savona, intended to oversee the cession of popes Benedict XIII and Gregory XII. Benedict duly obliged and presented himself there in good time, from where he continued his papal business while awaiting his rival.[10] Gregory proved reluctant and concocted a series of excuses and stalling tactics, insisting on the insecurity of his passage to the venue, and ultimately failed to attend.[11] This temporarily strengthened Benedict's otherwise precipitous position as he had, after all, attended in good faith. Therefore, for this key period, the focus and energies of France's ruling elements were engaged and, from a Welsh perspective, distracted from all but the most critical matters of the schism, internal factional squabbles and trade relations. While inadvertent, the French church's overriding interest in its own affairs over the needs and desires of the temporal government and its allies also harmed Glyn Dŵr's regime.

Henry IV's diplomats had, to a certain degree, secured England's finances and overseas trade. This not only calmed and then improved relations with England's partners, raising its standing, but more importantly assured a flow of finance critical to any government. Linked with these agreements was the liberty for its fishing fleets to ply their trade which, in their unofficial capacity as coastal sentinels, bolstered England's actual and imagined security. This equally benefitted the continental fleets, from the Bretons to the Hanse traders. However, the potential threat posed by a recovering England overshadowed that of all of its neighbours except France. As the country's strength returned, it would enable Henry's government to investigate other opportunities to improve England's position by interfering with its neighbours' politics; the treaty with Burgundy in March 1406 and the truce with Brittany the following year were crucial to this. A further significant step in England's drive to disrupt its hostile neighbours also came in March 1406, when a stroke of luck brought the heir to the Scots' throne, James, into English hands. En route to France, his ship was captured by English pirates off the north-eastern coast of England. His capture and the death of King Robert III the following month obliged the Scots to appoint a regent. The king's brother, Robert Stewart, the powerful duke of Albany, took that role and maintained a passive stance towards England. This guaranteed that the ongoing hospitality to James and Albany's son, Murdach, taken at Homildon in 1402, would be sufficient to keep them alive. However, this also effectively made Albany king in James's absence. Albany is often portrayed as a divisive schemer, whose politicking ensured the fruition of a factional struggle similar to that of the French court which damaged the possibility of harmony and unity among Scotland's nobles. A truce between England and Scotland was made and subsequently renewed over the following years of relevance.[12]

This period of recovery and largely peaceful relations with Flanders and the Hanseatic states continued into 1407, creating an environment in which England was better able to move against its enemies in Wales. Prior to early summer 1407, the English record in Wales during the revolt was poor. The widespread, multi-seated rebellion had erupted and eventually coalesced, under Glyn Dŵr and his commanders, into an effective fighting force which developed its own political programme and established an international presence through diplomacy and alliance. The first English victory of any significance came at Usk in May 1405, while 1406 saw a notable lack of activity by either side. While a number of Welshmen hedged their bets and sought rapprochement with the government, they were so few that they all appear to be known by name. Parley with or submission to the authorities was no guarantee of loyalty to the crown in any case, as many of the Welshmen who sought royal pardon in 1400 and thereafter, returned as rebels in subsequent fighting seasons. Such actions appear symptomatic of a populace troubled by the context in which it finds itself, and this sort of behaviour is not uncommon in similar conflicts. Although the struggle for Anglesey was fought and won by crown forces in 1406, the suggestion that areas of mainland Wales, such as Glamorgan, submitted in 1406 come from an unreliable source uncorroborated by other evidence.[13] Even if correct to any degree, the return of rebel power would likely see these areas return to rebel allegiance. Although submissions would follow in subsequent years, 1406 is remarkable for its seeming lack of activity of any kind in Wales.

While many of the rebels in the border county of Flintshire, the last predominantly Welsh-speaking area to revolt, began submitting in late March and April 1407, such apparent improvements in the government's influence in Wales represent non-aggressive means of advancing Henry's cause. It is noteworthy that neither before or after were troops rushed to the county to cause, enforce or secure the submissions in Flintshire. This further supports the existence of an unpublicised truce delimiting military action. This sort of nibbling around the fringes of an area under a truce appears consistent with behaviour typical of the period. The move against Anglesey, notably not part of mainland Wales, began in 1405 prior to the French expedition and the proposed truce. That initial attack on the island was made by English troops based in Ireland, with the further, decisive operations conducted during 1406. It was only early in 1407 that the crown was able to instal a military commander there, and he still required a personal guard of a 100 men. The killing of a rebel captain, Hywel Gwynedd, in March on a mountain on the border also fell within the common probing and testing of a truce's boundaries, arguably without technically infringing it. If local forces were engaged in the fight, rather than royally commissioned troops, it became a moot point rather than a breach. It seems equally likely that, during this period, similarly small numbers of Welshmen crossed into the English border shires to make mischief and acquire plunder too.[14] A truce agreed in late summer 1405 would have benefitted Henry, giving him time to improve his position with continental partners and rebuild his strength at home. It is worth recalling that England had again been torn by serious internal revolt in the summer of 1405 and, to any government, internal security was essential before considering other matters. In that time, crown strategists had determined that a strike against Llanbadarn (Aberystwyth) would be the most productive way of ending the revolt.[15]

Therefore, within the environment of improving and peaceful relations with the Bretons and a growing amity, underpinned by a treaty, with the Burgundians who controlled Flanders, the English gathered forces to strike at Glyn Dŵr's Wales. In preparation, Prince Henry issued orders to Thomas, Lord Berkeley, to attain timber for siege engines, much of it to be acquired from the lands of former English rebels.[16] With the removal from the conflict of the Flemish and, in particular, the Bretons, there would likely be no French fleet arriving in Wales for as long as the truces held. Improved international relations would provide England with the opportunity of extending those agreements before any French-sponsored fleet could launch. With the Welsh isolated for at least a year, this afforded the opportunity to recommence hostilities and to press that attack.

In May 1407, the operation to recapture Wales was led by Prince Henry, then aged nearly twenty, at the head of an army equipped with numerous siege engines and even cannon, along with a fighting force of 600 men-at-arms and 1,800 archers.[17] They promptly began the attack on Llanbadarn, but the prince's troops failed to win a swift victory and one of the huge siege guns, called *messager* or 'messenger', even exploded during the siege.[18] The siege proved more difficult to prosecute than expected, and a truce was negotiated for the crown by Richard Courtney, the chancellor of Oxford University: it came into effect on 24 September 1407.[19] The well-known account of Owain appearing at Aberystwyth and delivering a threatening display of his power, in effect ordering his commander to fight and die there or Owain would decapitate him on the spot, also derives from the dubious Annals source and, while it provides anecdotal interest, remains unproven. It seems likely that Prince Henry had left the siege long before its conclusion or the unreliable Annals evidence would suggest that Owain defeated him before Aberystwyth. Since there is no evidence to suggest, refute or corroborate this, it seems reasonable to assume Henry's and Owain's absence. Whatever the true account of the truce negotiations, the Welsh did not surrender at the appointed time and the fighting recommenced shortly after. The siege of Aberystwyth would be bitterly contested for another year but other events, propitious to England's causes, occurred in Paris in November 1407.[20]

The conflict between the dukes of Burgundy and Orleans had largely been a bloodless political feud over government control, finance and territory. Equally, the other ducal Houses of Anjou, Berry and Bourbon also manoeuvred and machinated to improve their respective positions, and this often required them to ally or to neglect to support one faction or another on a given matter. Their allegiances were not necessarily fixed, making the political picture a complex, multi-factional one of shifting positions and temporary, issue-based alliances, nevertheless anchored to traditional amities and expected behaviours. However, Philippe of Burgundy had largely, but not entirely, dominated the government since the death of Charles V, his brother, in 1380. During the 1390s his nephew Louis, brother of Charles VI, had risen to prominence, as duke of Touraine and then Orleans, and challenged Philippe's supremacy. During the king's illness, the two leading dukes in particular had enriched themselves on the wealth of the kingdom, and competition over the size of their claims to that resource gave rise to conflict between them.[21]

With that as an originating factor, their quarrel took on political and territorial dimensions, incorporating allies and other factions into their competition for control of France's wealth. One example of their alliances comes in the form of the Visconti of Milan. Philippe supported that branch which included Bernabò Visconti, and by consequence his grand-daughter, Isabeau of Bavaria and her other principal family, the German Wittelsbach dynasty. Louis of Orleans married into Giangaleazzo's side of the Visconti family, and naturally leaned towards the other German factions. Their political manoeuvring had resulted in Philippe and Isabeau, once she was queen of France, investing their candidate in Genoa after persuading the king to compel Louis to sell his stake in the territory.[22] It was their obstruction of his Italian ambitions that obliged Louis to look elsewhere for expansion. Therefore, he began acquiring territory and allies in north-eastern France from 1398 onwards, but with impetus from 1401. It seems probable that this drive was personally motivated by Philippe's thwarting of his ambitions to the south. The clearest sign of this was his alliance with Philippe's regional enemy, the duke of Guelders, and Louis's acquisition of Luxemburg in 1402.[23]

Philippe of Burgundy's death in April 1404 obviously helped Louis's cause. From September that year, Louis and the league of German minor princes he had recently cultivated, moved against Metz, Lorraine and the surrounding regions. The city recognised Rupert as Emperor, obliging him to defend it. In the late summer of 1405, the massed forces of Louis and Jean the Fearless manoeuvred around Paris causing great fear; however, no notable fighting took place.[24] Although both sides were pacified at conference by the other dukes and the queen, a notable secret alliance was formed between Louis, the queen and Jean, duke of Berry. The conflict in the north-eastern border region was indecisive during 1405 and gave way to negotiation and posturing throughout the following year. By May 1407, Louis's allies had reformed their league and again threatened Metz and Lorraine. In July, they were decisively crushed at Champigneul, with most of the German nobles and Louis's general, Guillaume de Braquemont, being captured. The duke of Lorraine and the Messines went to Paris to submit to arbitration; however, matters were not satisfactorily resolved and Louis prepared a new military solution the following month in alliance with the marquis of Pont-à-Moussons. The fear of a wider conflagration engulfing the region, dragging in the German Imperial parties and the French ducal factions, was palpable during the late summer and early autumn; these actions risked sparking a major conflict.[25] The rivalry between Burgundy and Orleans had finally been brought to the battlefield at Champigneul where the defeat of Louis's allies there handed the initiative to his enemies. The use of their temporary advantage was swift and surprising.

Louis, duke of Orleans, brother of King Charles VI, was murdered on a Parisian street on 23 November 1407 by a gang led by Raoul d'Anquetonville, acting under the orders of Jean the Fearless, duke of Burgundy.[26] This was a highly significant event within the struggles of the courtly factions; members of the French royal family were not supposed to kill their brethren. It also acted as the trigger event for France's slide into civil war. Initially Jean denied it, then admitted it and was sent from Paris in disgrace while the outraged court decided what action to take. While his banishment and disgrace only lasted a few months, his act provoked a bitter enmity among many of the nobles of France. However, for the moment, the Orleanists were in disarray and were unable to act decisively. Louis's heir, Charles, was just thirteen years old at the time, so the Orleanists turned to Bernard, count of Armagnac, for leadership. Politically, he was well connected to the Houses of Berry and Orleans, but his actual loyalties were undoubtedly to Louis. Bernard was constable of France, son-in-law of Jean, duke of Berry, and his sister had married Valentina Visconti's brother. He also married his daughter, Bonne, to Charles of Orleans in 1410 and Bernard helped shape Charles's early career. In addition, Bernard was a respected member of court and was a good choice to lead the opposition to the Burgundians; the Orleanists soon became known as the Armagnacs.

While there is no evidence directly connecting Henry IV's government to Louis's murder, this news would have undoubtedly been welcomed at Westminster. Given that Owain had allied himself to France under Louis's leadership, effectively to the Orleanists, and agreed to adhere to his papal ally, the duke's assassination would evidently damage Glyn Dŵr's power and standing in France.

This dramatic step by the duke of Burgundy provided England an opportunity to press its interests in the ensuing turmoil. This is proved by the orders issued at the Privy Council in December 1407 to Henry's latest team of ambassadors; Thomas, bishop of Durham, Sir Thomas Erpingham, Hugh Mortimer, squire, and legal expert John Cateryk.[27] The inclusion of Hugh Mortimer, a kinsman of Edmund Mortimer, is unlikely to be a coincidence, and was likely designed to show the French that the Mortimers supported the king. These men were empowered to treat with France regarding a truce and a royal marriage between the two crowns. Within these orders were clauses critical to the French–Welsh alliance. While the usual formula regarding the accepted inclusion of allies was mentioned, the instructions explicitly required that the French agreed that Owain was not an ally and the truce should be made specifically excluding Owain.[28] The ambassadors' line threateningly maintained that Owain must be subject to the crown.[29] The Anglo–French treaty documents contain no mention of these machinations, of course, but spoke airily of France being entitled to include their 'allies, friends, confederates, kingdoms, subjects, lands and lordships or their people' within the terms of a perpetual peace between France and England. The treaty terms therefore appear to allow France to represent the Welsh, in keeping with the clauses of the 1404 alliance. The French–English treaty of late 1407 explicitly stated that the French could declare and discuss for its allies on all questions, quarrels and wars, irrespective of their circumstances and dependency.[30] Theoretically, therefore, Owain stood close to inclusion in a treaty of perpetual peace and, had Wales been part of the ensuing truce, it would have formally become an established entity, independent from England. Conversely, the fact that the subject of Wales was not even permitted to be discussed demonstrated three crucial points. The English government was determined to defeat Owain and retain Wales as a territory and, therefore, the conflict with Wales would continue until one side had been defeated. Thirdly, critically, France was in too weak a position to argue otherwise. Consequently, with no foreign support, it appeared that the writing might suddenly and unexpectedly be on the wall for Glyn Dŵr's Wales.

During the same negotiations, peace was also agreed for Aquitaine and other areas of France through negotiation with the agents of Jean, the aged duke of Berry. The new embassy holding discussions with the English were Gerard de Puy, bishop of Saint Flore, Lord Guillaume de Morevyll, known as l'Ermite de la Faye who had served as chamberlain to the king and had campaigned at sea with Marshal Boucicaut, Casyne de Seremuller, squire and chamberlain of the duke of Berry, and Master Johan Hue, secretary.[31] It seems probable that this ambassadorial team also conducted the negotiations relevant to Wales, but nowhere is there any mention that they argued for Glyn Dŵr's inclusion in peace negotiations with the English. Even if they were non-aligned factionally, the probable goal of the French ambassadors was to swiftly remove any threat England could pose to a France in disarray. However, these men who concluded the truce for Aquitaine, appear to have been under the aegis of the duke of Berry, showing that the Orleanists were no longer conducting affairs. Shortly after, Christine de Pizan's 'Lamentation on the Evils that have Befallen France' appealed to the duke of Berry as the senior noble of the moment to heal the rift and avert the decent into fratricide.[32] It seems just to suggest that the concession over Owain might not have sat comfortably with the French, but circumstances dictated that their security considerations came foremost. The French abandonment of their ally, though an entirely disreputable act, was perhaps understandable within its context. The fact that the English were able to insist on such terms demonstrates that England was momentarily ascendant. Nevertheless, this stood in plain, direct breach of their treaty of alliance with Glyn Dŵr:

Again, that one of the lords, the king and the prince aforesaid, shall not make or take truce nor make peace with the aforesaid Henry of Lancaster, but that the other might be included if he had wished in the same truce or peace, unless he is united or did not wish to be included in the same truce or peace, and he shall determine, concerning such refusal or rejection, who wished to treat for the said truce or peace, within a month after the one shall have signified the said truce or peace, by his letters patent, sealed by his seal.[33]

Considering the grand, binding terms of the 1404 treaty, and the barely noticed discarding of Glyn Dŵr during these negotiations, it seems difficult to conceive other than that Owain was bargained away as a point to safeguard France. It is unlikely that he would learn of his exclusion until the French and the English had completed their negotiations; the news likely came as a surprise and a bitter disappointment.

Duke Louis's murder caused grave problems in France, not only among the nobles, but also the clergy. When the Burgundian theologian Jean Petit delivered a speech defending the act, he justified it by portraying Louis as a tyrant and that the killing of a tyrant was beneficial to France. This caused revulsion in many, notably in Jean Gerson who, although a Burgundian-sponsored cleric for many years, fully transferred his allegiance to the House of Orleans and harangued Petit on the matter for the few remaining years of his life. While Gerson and others abhorred political assassination out of principle, Petit's discourse was also biased and implied a proximity between Burgundy and Isabeau, suggesting that Duke Jean was intriguing with the queen as well as using clergy in his employ as tools to further his temporal interests. It was known that Giangaleazzo Visconti deposed Isabeau's grandfather, Bernabò Visconti, in order to take possession of Milan. At the time it was justified by the claim that Bernabò was a tyrant, and removing him was legitimate, even a duty. In addition, it was also claimed that Bernabò's fragmentation of Milan among his sons weakened it and benefitted her enemies; therefore his downfall was essential to maintain Milan's power. A further point of friction aligned the unproven accusation that Louis's wife, Valentina Visconti, had poisoned Charles VI, with the similar allegation that Giangaleazzo had poisoned Bernabò. The closeness between the defences of both killings, considering the family connections, is unlikely to have been coincidental and this ongoing dynastic rivalry had brought its woes to the heart of the French court. Louis's murder threatened to provoke a downward spiral into a substantial conflict. Duke Jean's machinations had the potential to reach far beyond the verbal involvement of the French clergy in debates on political assassination by royal cousins who had often sworn themselves to peace. It risked embroiling Italian powers and Imperial factions in this element of the feud being played out in France. For those who ran France, this situation was the dominant concern of the moment.[34]

The projected papal conference at Savona had failed and the issue of the schism dragged on exhaustingly. Benedict had increased in credibility from his presence at Savona and Genoa during 1407, and by April 1408 he had regained a modicum of French support. The Roman papacy had lost credibility the previous year and, it was determined, might be ripe for invasion. The notion of reasserting the claim of Louis, duke of Anjou, over Naples was again given life. In Italy, Benedict plotted with Marshal Boucicaut for Genoese galleys to assault the papal seat, and both men had some degree of amity with Paolo Orsini, leader of the papal guard in Rome. They moved to muster in late April 1408 and put to sea shortly after, but Rome's vulnerability had been noticed by Ladislas in Naples, who attacked and took the city as well as Ostia, its port, probably with the connivance of the Orsini. Just as in 1405, Benedict's military plans for Rome had been thwarted by circumstances beyond his control. However, Gregory's papacy was in chaos, largely due to regional military instability and, more importantly for a spiritual ruler, the disaffection spawned by his failure to live up to his promises regarding the schism. At that moment, most of his cardinals abandoned him, fleeing to Pisa; the Roman papacy seemed as if it would fall, given even the lightest push.[35]

Although this presented an opportunity to win those cardinals to Benedict's cause or to advance on chaotic Rome, the murder of Louis had robbed Benedict of his most powerful support in the French court. Since then, Benedict's opponents in Paris had worked assiduously to promote their solution to the schism; a pronouncement of France's intention to declare neutrality by Ascension Day in May. Although Charles VI wrote to Benedict to that effect on 12 January 1408, he did not receive the letter until mid-April. At the same time, truces were signed between England and other regional powers such as the Breton and Burgundian dukes, as well as the Scots. Events appeared to be turning towards a restoration of peace in the Channel region and between the thrones of England, France and Scotland. However, Benedict countered the French court's letter by sending a Bull written in May 1407. The papal order would excommunicate any who threatened withdrawal from the pope, challenged papal decisions or hampered the healing of the schism. This policy had possibly been concocted with the connivance or at least knowledge of those ambassadors sent to Benedict in 1407, although they now risked falling foul of it. Excommunication was to be followed by interdict.[36]

With hindsight, this appears a rash course of action. However, Benedict's previous contests of brinkmanship with the French court had ultimately proved successful, and the prior subtraction of obedience had been fully reversed. Benedict still had friends at court, and although Louis was no longer alive, there remained a strong possibility that their mutual friends would soon regain control. With those salient points in mind, there seems little reason to suppose that Benedict's methods and obstinacy would fail to return France to his cause once again. However, the University of Paris was leading the debates at court, Benedict's letter was denounced and his supporters jailed or hounded out of France. Marshal Boucicaut was commissioned to seize Benedict, who fled to Perpignan, where he held council, and thereafter he retired to safety in Aragon. France declared neutrality in May 1408.[37]

The Pennal Declaration thereby became not only irrelevant, but a threat to Welsh–French relations. It might be appropriate to ponder whether the Pennal Declaration finally resulted in a bittersweet moment; some of the requests appear to have been agreed by Benedict, such as absolving the Welsh of their oaths to Canterbury, appointing Welsh bishops loyal to Owain, making St David's a metropolitan and providing benefices for Owain's clergy, in effect, the Welsh church had been resurrected by order of a pope. However, following that pope's path would tear Owain from the French, which he could not afford. Owain's actions concerning France's withdrawal of obedience are unknown; however his ambassadors, probably Yonge and Trefor initially, were in Paris in 1408, and Yonge repeatedly appeared in records for a decade thereafter.[38] The French certainly included the Welsh ambassadors, along with a host of other connected parties, in the discussions on the matter held at the University of Paris. It seems certain that Owain would have been willing to jettison Benedict and adhere to Charles. Militarily, the cause did not appear lost in France. According to Monstrelet, during the course of the debates in Paris which began in April 1408, the king himself agreed to pay for an army to go to Wales to assist France's Welsh allies. Robert 'le borgne' de la Heuse was commissioned to lead 300 men-at-arms and 200 crossbowmen to Wales. In addition, Jean, duke of Brittany formed an alliance with the Orleanists in May 1408, theoretically, the western sea lanes were open again. This evidence appears in the same year Walsingham described combat at sea during which English fleets defeated troop ships bound for Wales. A French relief force combined with Welsh troops might well have broken the siege at Aberystwyth, once again throwing Henry's plans for Wales into disarray and his armies into retreat.[39] Charles VI certainly said that he would send more military aid to Wales and to English rebels, and there is no overriding reason to dismiss this promise.[40] If Monstrelet and Walsingham were correct, then the third substantial French fleet bound for Wales was stopped at sea. On such fine margins conflicts are often won or lost. When viewed in this light, despite their moment of weakness during the negotiations in December 1407, in the shocked aftermath of Louis's murder in Paris, the French were still faithful to their Welsh allies. However, continental affairs once again dominated, European powers withdrew obedience from both popes and began organising a conference to be held in Pisa which would finally end the schism.[41]

The diplomatic victory ensuring a truce with France enabled the English to press their sudden ascendancy in Wales, placing another siege under Gilbert, Lord Talbot, before Harlech, Owain's northern stronghold, in early 1408. The winter of 1407–8 was noted across Europe as a hard one – 'the worst for five hundred years', according to the monk of Saint-Denys – causing many animals to die and water sources to freeze solid for months. Shortly after Louis's murder, the Percy threat was finally extinguished in February 1408 when Northumberland and Bardolf were slain attempting to regain their northern estates. Lewis Byford, one of Glyn Dŵr's bishops, was captured in their company in this brief fight in the snow on Bramham Moor. In little over six months the landscape of the revolt had dramatically changed from a picture of an apparently settled native rule under a popular, skilled leader with a progressive plan for a stable state, with notable foreign allies, to the nightmarish vista of complete isolation, articulated by two seemingly decisive strangleholds firmly placed around Glyn Dŵr's urban centres. Without these, Owain might lack legitimacy internationally and be more easily denigrated as one of a number of rebels or pretenders who plagued

Europe's thrones throughout the period. In addition, parliaments held in the woods perhaps lacked the required majesty or appeal for envoys of foreign crowns, whereas safely held ports and castles told those powers that they would be able to extract their forces when required. Without urban sites, Glyn Dŵr perhaps lacked a measure of the grandeur and credibility required by successful leaders, as well as the logistical necessities to receive allied armies by sea. Perhaps as a consequence of the failure of the French relief army to arrive, the pressure on Aberystwyth became unbearable. After resisting English assault and siege for more than sixteen gruelling months, Aberystwyth appears to have capitulated towards the end of 1408, perhaps in September.[42]

This allowed Henry's forces to focus on the last urban stronghold, where another winter proved enough for the trapped garrison at Harlech, which surrendered no later than March 1409. Edmund Mortimer died in the siege, but his wife and children, who were Glyn Dŵr's daughter and grandchildren, were captured at its fall, along with Owain's wife. They were taken to London as was Owain's heir, Gruffydd, where they were all eventually killed. It is noteworthy that Glyn Dŵr's family was kept alive for so many years at the crown's expense. Gruffydd died during 1411, perhaps of disease, perhaps of starvation, while the women and children were only allowed to starve to death in December 1413. The horrors that the women and children endured as they faced death *à huis clos* can only be imagined. Yet had they not been required by Henry IV and Henry V for some purpose, such as for bargaining with Owain, then there seems no reason for the king to have paid to sustain them for these five or so years. Henry IV had, after all, shown no timidity in despatching a large number of people, whether on the scaffold or in prison. It should be clarified that it was Henry V who had the captive women and children killed. Therefore, their continued existence raises the question whether their lives were sustained as a check on Owain, only being discarded to die of starvation as punishment or when his power had sufficiently dwindled. While this underlines the cold brutality of the politics of the day, it is also noteworthy that no evidence claims that Owain killed any of his prisoners, even his arch-enemy, Lord Grey. Killing prisoners was an option deliberately chosen by the captor.[43]

However, during this period, characterised elsewhere as an advanced stage of the slide to defeat, Welsh ambassadors were active in the courts of France and Scotland. To the Welsh of the time, there still seems to have been a war to fight. Their efforts appear to have earned continued support among the French, who raised forces for Wales which appear to have been mostly blocked by the English at sea. Shortly after the capitulation of Harlech in 1409, two French carracks, the 'Sancta Maria' and the 'Sancta Brigida' were seized off Milford. Other than being connected to the revolt, there is no credible explanation why these two, probably with support vessels, were at the 1405 expedition's point of entry into Wales. It seems likely that their presence proves Monstrelet's claim that the French continued their efforts to engage with Glyn Dŵr and the rebels. Moreover, the revolt went on, but at a different rhythm to before. Although rebel operations became less frequent and damaging, the Welsh were still a notable military force within Wales. In addition, they remained well able to mount attacks across the English border. The king himself reprimanded leaders and communities in the English border counties for making truces with the Welsh for some time after the fall of Harlech in 1409. The fact that judicial sessions were held in Wales from this point onwards and that Welsh communities began paying fines and pledging allegiance at spear point and under threat of further financial penalty, did not mean that the grievances which led them to revolt had been resolved. The course of similar conflicts, historically, demonstrates that a forceful return to an area by significant insurgent forces often causes an area to once again rebel. The government did not restore loyalty to the crown by punishing the natives, it managed to persuade them that they were the ascendant power in the area, not the rebels. By such suppressive means, peace is temporarily bought. While the government sought to re-establish its authority in several areas of Wales following the fall of Harlech, letters recently redated to the summer of 1412 suggest a new Welsh leader was in command.[44]

However, events far away would pull victory further from the rebels and closer to the English crown. First, a general council was agreed across Europe and was convened at Pisa, sitting between March and June 1409. Although the Roman and Avignon popes were declared deposed and an alternative candidate elected, it proved a disaster.[45] Neither of the two schismatic popes – or indeed their supporters – in reality accepted their depositions, so then there were three popes rather than two. The schism went on, in some respects worse than before.

In France, the conflict between the ducal parties grew in the years following Louis's murder. Jean actively sought to keep the agreement with

England, personally intervening in restoration disputes in Normandy and Picardy, as well as dealing with a serious revolt against him in the Low Countries during 1408.[46] As his power rose, Jean the Fearless seized control of the government of France in 1409. His consolidation of power in Paris was a bloody affair; he set about persecuting his opponents, many being killed while others fled. Jean Montagu, the bishop of Chartres, who had been involved in the treaty of alliance with Glyn Dŵr in 1404 and who was a notable Orleanist and former Marmouset so hated by the duke's father, was publicly beheaded. Such was Duke Jean's grip on power that some adherents of his enemies sought his amity. The perfect example of this is the treaty of alliance with the duke of Brittany in July 1410, who had made a series of alliances with those princes of the Orleanist cause shortly prior to the Burgundian coup. The venerable but ailing duke of Berry, the count of Alençon and others who had been unengaged if not neutral, appalled by Jean of Burgundy's excesses, declared themselves Orleanists, making a larger conflict inevitable. By mid-1410, France's slide to civil war was inexorable.[47]

Meanwhile, Henry's ambassadors in Calais announced that the peace with the Burgundians was still holding in May 1410, and that negotiations for its prorogation were due. Elsewhere that summer, mutual safe conducts were agreed for Castilian and English ships. In November that year, Henry IV approached Albany, the regent of Scotland, with a view to negotiating a final peace or a long truce between the kingdoms.[48] While all of these agreements and understandings could be reversed by one act or declaration, they are indicative of a trend supporting England's diplomatic ascendency at that time.

In 1411, circumstances dealt the English another fortuitous hand, which they played well. In the north, two armies of Scots fought each other, distracting them for the rest of the year.[49] More importantly, probably as a consequence of French factional warfare that year and in view of the mounting alliance against him, the duke of Burgundy approached the English at Calais and requested military aid. Henry responded swiftly, despatching a force of 300 lances and 1,000 archers under the command of the earl of Arundel.[50] While a coup for Jean, who could show he had the powerful military support of England at his back, this was clearly a more significant development for the English. The friendship with Burgundy had worked a fissure in the edifice of the French court. This new, military alliance had turned into a breach through which they could push troops into France. The Burgundians and their allies closed on Paris in September, fighting an action at the bridge of Saint-Cloud on Paris's western boundary in early October. The Orleanists were forced to give up the bridge; they fell back on Paris and fled south. The Burgundians and their English allies took the capital shortly after. Jean the Fearless and the earl of Arundel dined with Charles VI at the Louvre.[51]

Probably in reaction to this development, the duke of Brittany agreed to a ten-year continuation of his truce with England at the end of October, again closing the door on possible French exploits in Wales.[52] The Burgundian leader took control of the king and his children at that point, and in the last action of the season, led them to the siege of the town of Etampes, which his impressive array of troops took before returning to their quarters for winter. With the fighting season over, Arundel and the English contingent retired to Calais. The financial accounts of the new duke of Orleans, Charles, show that Welsh adherence survived the murder of Duke Louis. Welsh troops, most notably Madoc Howell, drew annual wages from the ducal treasury during these difficult years.[53] With the passage of English troops through Paris and their alliance to the de facto leader of France cemented in agreement and on campaign, Glyn Dŵr's cause was no longer of interest to those then leading France. Internationally at least, Owain Glyn Dŵr died as a figure of significance at the fall of Saint-Cloud.

In Wales, however, Owain Glyn Dŵr was still a force to be considered. He demonstrated as much by capturing and ransoming Henry's main stalwart in Wales, Dafydd Gam, in April 1412. Although Owain seems to have faded after that final public act of defiance and personal vendetta, it appears likely that he passed on the mantle of leadership to his son, Maredudd ab Owain.[54]

However, the actions of 1412 saw the final defeat of French ambitions in Britain for decades to come. During the winter, the Orleanists approached the English and tried to persuade Henry to support them militarily rather than the Burgundians.[55] This request marks the complete opening of France to the English. When both warring factions solicited England's aid it handed the balance of power to Henry. This demonstrated that England had recovered to the extent that it was strong enough to influence the outcome of the French civil war. It also allowed the English the opportunity to play both factions, which they did brilliantly. In addition, this allowed the English to fully understand the weaknesses of their French adversaries before prosecuting an invasion of their territory.

The Orleanists offered Henry all that England had ceded at Brétigny in 1360, as well as Poitou on the death of the new duke of Berry, and also Périgord and Angoulême on the death of the young duke of Orleans, in return for 1,000 men-at-arms and 3,000 archers. In contrast, the Burgundians discussed a marriage alliance between Prince Henry and one of Duke Jean's daughters. Having helped the Burgundians drive their opponents from the north the previous year, in 1412 England supported the Orleanists. In June, one of Henry IV's sons, Thomas, duke of Clarence, and the renowned warrior, Sir John Cornwall who was also Henry IV's brother-in-law, landed in Normandy with an army of at least 4,000 and pressed inland, prospecting to advance towards the French factional conflict near Bourges. This expedition, inserting a large English army into France, was the fruit of a political masterstroke which aimed to confuse and weaken the French factions.[56]

Meanwhile, the French warring parties held talks and agreed peaceful terms, including the renunciation of all foreign alliances. Peace was brokered, largely at the intercession of Louis, duke of Guyenne, Charles VI's heir, as the king slipped back into illness. Embarrassingly for the French, the invited English army arrived after the nobles of the warring factions had all declared their unity and affection for one another. After some testy negotiations, the English were bribed 150,000 crowns to leave. They departed via Bordeaux, having played a role in cleaving the loyalties of France's magnates but also having gathered intelligence on the enemy's strength and posture, as well as on his territory.[57]

In November 1412, a treaty was made at Buzançais, which obliged all of the dukes to write to Henry and renounce all and any agreements with him. This appears to have been well received in general, with Christine de Pizan penning 'The Book of Peace' in celebration of the apparent blossoming of peace and unity among the nobles. However, the fact that this was a necessity carried out by royal command demonstrates the depth of the fractures within the French court and how far the English had been able to exploit them. So, the dukes duly sent their honourable renunciations to Henry. It is noteworthy, though, that Clarence rejected them and, secretly, Charles of Orleans made another agreement promising amity with the English in contravention of his king's orders.[58]

The close of 1412 did not see an end to the conflict with the French and the Welsh, but arguably it brought the conclusion of respective phases. In France, England had held the balance of power between the warring French factions and received ambassadors from both parties. For the ailing Henry IV, this was an extremely positive outcome that reversed England's position of the previous decade. As a consequence, neither French faction was able or probably willing to support a conflict in Wales in any form. In Wales, the tempo of the conflict reduced, but continued. Maredudd ab Owain seemed to be leader in his father's place, and the ransom of Dafydd Gam in 1412 appears to be Owain's last act of note. The actions which led to the English expedition of summer 1412 and culminated in the inter-French treaty of Buzançais made it appear as if Owain had therefore finally been abandoned by the French. In all probability, they had abandoned him, but they had not yet given up on the Welsh rebels, who were to have one final swansong at Constance in 1417. However, as a figurehead or representative of Wales in Europe, Owain Glyn Dŵr's moment appears to have disappeared at that point, for reasons entirely beyond his control.

CHAPTER THIRTEEN

Constance – A Last Stand for Wales?

It is really remarkable that such educated men would want to write that Wales, Ireland or even Scotland are not part of the English nation, because they do not do what the king of England tells them to do. If that point were granted, which it is not, it is irrelevant ...[1]

In an effort to finally heal the schism in the Western church, the European powers determined to hold another ecclesiastical conference to make amends for that of Pisa in 1409. The ongoing schism had gnawed at Europe since 1378 and had resulted in a number of popular movements which questioned the direction and leadership of the Western church. Founded on the writings of John Wyclif and others, movements such as the Lollards and the Hussites rose, garnering mass support and posing tangible challenges to religious and secular authorities. To the established order, the schism and the movements that it spawned sought to change the power structure of the age, as well as causing considerable disruption to the continent's usual political and commercial intercourse. Therefore, Europe's nobility and clergy were obliged to act. The resulting conference, the Council of Constance, met in a number of sessions between 1414 and 1418. It was populated by delegations from western and central European states which followed the Catholic rather than the Orthodox faith. The most influential delegations at previous such gatherings were traditionally from France, Germany, Italy and Spain. Although the German and Italian parties were generally cohesive, they were affected by the secular politics of the time as well as the positions of their allies and enemies. The Spanish were delayed in attending the Council of Constance due to internal divisions; a number of the Spanish kingdoms were in conflict with one another as well as being allied to either France or England. The French were riven between their temporal courtly factions and their religious leanings for the different papal candidates, leaving them a weakened presence. In the absence of the Spanish, the English delegation took their place as a major party, termed 'nations', at Constance, much to the vexation of the French.

Although its main purpose was to seek a solution to the schism, a number of other issues were also fought out at Constance, one of which explicitly included the Welsh rebels. Arguably, the best-known event saw church authorities renege on their promises of safe conduct to Jan Hus who was imprisoned, tried and then burnt alive on 6 July 1415.[2] Also of great importance were the English campaigns in northern France in 1415 and 1417 which evidently destroyed the possibility of peaceful or constructive relations at Constance.

Despite the restoration of peace amid the fine words of amity committed to parchment at Buzançais, factional warfare continued in France. The citizens of Paris revolted in 1413, but were crushed and their preferred leader, the duke of Burgundy, was swept from power. The expulsion of Duke Jean and the suppression of the Cabochien Revolt, as the Parisian rising was called, allowed the Orleanist-Armagnac party to regain control. Except for one brief interlude, from 30 May 1418 to 19 September 1419, the Armagnacs assumed control of the government, whether in Paris or in exile in Bourges, for the remaining period relevant to this study. This would be important to the Welsh rebels in 1417.

However, the broader context of the time is important, as is an acknowledgement that the temporal and spiritual politics of the period were intertwined. During 1414, there was talk of the new king of England, Henry V, raising armies to invade France. The same year, Jean, duke of Burgundy, offered to form a treasonable compact with Henry V, by promising to act against France in England's favour. Irrespective of his stated intention to the other French princes, Jean made no effort to assist them or to advance against Henry V's invasion the following year. Despite sending two of his brothers and a number of prominent Burgundians to their graves at Agincourt, he kept his significant military power out of the entire affair. Burgundy was not entirely alone in this; the duke of Brittany also failed to reach Agincourt – his truce with England no doubt influenced his actions. Peace with the Bretons and the Burgundians who controlled Flanders gave the English a distinct advantage in the Channel and allowed them to focus their land-based efforts on Normandy and Picardy.[3]

The short campaign which resulted in the battle of Agincourt has provided England with political and cultural capital ever since and requires no lengthy description here. Before departing for France, Henry V had to deal with the Southampton Plot which sought to kill and replace him with the young Mortimer heir, Edmund, earl of March. Once revealed, Henry quickly seized, tried and had the three ringleaders beheaded. They were Edmund Mortimer's brother-in-law, Richard, earl of Cambridge; Henry Scrope, baron Masham and nephew of Richard Scrope, the archbishop of York executed in the 1405 York Rising; and Sir Thomas Grey, a Percy loyalist and Cambridge's son-in-law.[4] Henry V and his army landed near Harfleur on 13 August 1415, which they besieged and took in late September. Those Harfleur residents who swore allegiance to Henry were allowed to keep their possessions, the rest, some 2,000 men, women and children, were expelled. Casualties and dysentery seriously depleted Henry's army, and even at this early stage of his expedition, he appears to have lost over a third of his fighting force. Many were sent home to England to recover, including Henry's brother, the duke of Clarence, the earl of Arundel and Edmund Mortimer, earl of March, and perhaps 5,000 troops. To that point, Henry's campaign had been extremely costly with little to show for it. As disease threatened to ravage his army further and having installed Thomas Beaufort, earl of Dorset, in Harfleur along with 1,200 troops for its defence, on 8 October 1415, Henry V set out to march along the coast to Calais with a greatly reduced force.[5]

The famous clash with French forces led by the Constable of France, Charles d'Albret and one of the two Marshals of France, Jean le Meingre, also called Boucicaut, took place on 25 October, 1415 near Agincourt. Prior to the battle, Henry appears to have offered terms – reparations for damage caused by his forces and the delivery of prisoners taken up to that point, in return for unmolested passage to Calais. Boucicaut and d'Albret advised allowing Henry's request, as with previous English *chevauchées*, French forces would shadow them to ensure they left French territory as agreed. However, younger French nobles seemed to have been impetuous enough to have insisted on battle, to their cost. At Agincourt, Welsh troops fought on both sides. The tale of the battle is well known, with perhaps the key features including good English positioning, the role of the archers behind stakes, the sodden ground and the apparent lack of control over the French troops who piled into each other, all of which contributed to Henry V's signal victory. Although the French lost thousands of men that day, they also lost over 120 high-ranking nobles. Perhaps the best-known were the dukes of Brabant, Alençon and Bar, along with the counts of Nevers, Marle, Vaudemont, Blamont, Grandpre, Roucy and Waleran of St Pol. In addition, Charles d'Albret the Constable of France, Jean de Hangest and Jacques de Chatillon, admiral of France, also fell.[6]

One feature of the battle was the fate of the prisoners who were taken and killed en masse on Henry's express orders. The issue of the slaughter of the prisoners has provoked debate in recent times; however, few contemporary chronicles recounted it with distaste. Certain of the best-known French ones, notably those of Enguerrand de Monstrelet, Jean le Fèvre, Pierre Fenin and Jean de Wavrin, attribute actions by French troops led by Isambart d'Azincourt and Robert de Bournoville in attacking the English baggage park as provoking Henry. Fearing he was under attack from the rear, he might have been compelled to make that well-known decision.[7] It is worth speculating that killing them might also have been a ploy to dissuade the French who were forming up for another attack on the exhausted English. If so, it proved an extremely effective one. Several of the highest ranking prisoners were spared and taken to England. The principal French magnates who survived being taken prisoner were the dukes of Orleans and Bourbon, the counts of Eu, Richemont and Louis of Vendome, who had been prominent in making the alliance with the Welsh in 1404, along with Marshal Boucicaut who was also captured alive. Some were ransomed, but others were refused their liberty at any price under strict order from Henry V, even ignoring papal intercession. Their fate was simply to die in captivity, such as Marshal Boucicaut in 1421. Others spent long years as hostages, such as Charles, duke of Orleans, finally released at the intercession of his Burgundian enemies in 1440.[8] As if to compound the trauma of 1415 for the French, Louis of Guyenne, the heir-designate of Charles VI, died of an illness in December that year.[9]

Agincourt provided the English with a fine tactical victory; however, it was of limited strategic value, since Henry did not take Paris or leave a significant military footprint in France on the back of that campaign. Instead, in its aftermath, he swiftly made for the coast, reaching Calais by 29 October.[10] The true cost to France was not in losing a battle or an army – the French population of the day could easily sustain the loss of a few thousand men – but it was in the toll of the nobility who commanded French forces who were killed or captured there. The heavy defeat suffered at Agincourt had a bearing on the eventual French victory in the Hundred Years' War. Having lost a notable portion of its army commanders, the French inevitably looked to others to lead their troops. While maintaining some high-born commanders and ennobling others who served well, they turned to professional soldiers and former merce-naries, such as Etienne de Vignolles, known as 'la Hire', who employed different methods to most noble commanders. Capable minor nobles, such as Jean Poton de Xaintrailles were also given the opportunity to lead forces and shape France's military future. In addition, the French forces annihilated at Agincourt were all men of some status: lords, knights and squires. The military reforms which followed, particularly those of Charles VII's lifetime, provided France with forces which were finally capable of consistently defeating the English. Within a generation of this defeat, the French had begun to construct forces recognisable as a national army, rather than sending into battle men of a certain noble's estates under his leadership. These new forces engaged men of all social classes and experimented with mobile, flexible forces as well as artillery superior to that of their adversaries. Within another generation of Charles VII's reforms, the French had cleared the English out of all of France, except Calais.[11]

With the temporal affairs of all nations inevitably affecting matters at the Council of Constance, the task of resolving the schism became increasingly difficult. During the course of the council, English diplomacy, perhaps combined with a poor approach by their French counterparts, managed to win an alliance with the host, the German Emperor Sigismond, in August 1416.[12] In February 1417, the English began preparing for another invasion of France. With relations deteriorating between several of the nations at the council, the French raised an argument which encompassed French–Welsh affairs. The debate in question pitted the French and English delegations against one another during the twenty-eighth and thirty-first sessions of the Council, held on 3 and 31 March 1417. Although it constituted only a minor feature of the proceedings at Constance and had no bearing on its outcome, this episode nonetheless marks the last international act relevant to the last Welsh rebellion.

To complicate the matter further, by 1417, the French ambassadorial party was engaged in its own internal conflict between the envoys of

Armagnac or Burgundian adherence, along with those who balanced the interests of the crown, the church and the other dukes. While no doubt compelled by their own self-interest, during the twenty-eighth session of the council, on 3 March 1417, the French raised the issue of the legitimacy and sovereignty of the English nation at Constance. Within the context of that, they evoked the plight of the Welsh and others, and demanded their ecclesiastical liberty. When the French delegation tried to deliver their *protestatio*, their representative, Jean Campagne, delivered a few lines before being jeered and booed into silence by delegates from several nations. Irrespective of the message, those opposed to France, namely the Italians, English and most of the German delegates, along with their allies, formed the bulk of the audience at Constance, so such hostility towards Campagne's speech is unsurprising. The protest was then formally submitted in writing. Within the riposte offered to the French protest by Thomas Polton, Henry V's ambassador, the tenor of the original French claim is revealed. The aim of the protest was to reduce the size and weaken the influence of England's representation within the church council. Complicit with that, the French sought to strengthen England's adversaries, by winning ecclesiastical independence for Wales and others.[13]

The English response was delivered in writing by Thomas Polton at the thirty-first session on 31 March 1417. Polton's response listed and then rebuffed at length three principal French arguments. The English reply was a skilful but exhaustively long rebuttal, combining a variety of apparently well-researched, incisive points with verbose, misleading statements and humorous comments denigrating the French. When combined, this method produced a compelling defence against Campagne's *protestatio*.

The first French point was founded on a papal decree named *Extravagans, Vas electionis*, made during the reign of Pope Benedict XII (1334–42). Their argument was that the decree divided Catholic obedience into four groups known as 'nations'. The four primary nations were France, Germany, Castile and Italy. Other nations were classed beneath these four and thus came into their obedience ecclesiastically, for example, Navarre to France, Portugal to Spain, the eastern Mediterranean Latin possessions to Italy and England to Germany. Europe's universities divided their students into those groups also, for administrative, teaching and logistical purposes such as accommodation. The Council of Constance had also followed that established arrangement. However, in the absence of the Spanish delegation, the English had assumed the Spanish position and voting rights. The French asserted that since England came within Germany's obedience it was not an ecclesiastical nation in its own right. Just as other nations such as Hungary, Scotland, Wales and many others had no individual representation at the Council, then England did not deserve the level of representation it enjoyed at that time, which put it on an equal footing to the four principal nations mentioned.

The second French argument further detailed the divisions agreed during Benedict XII's reign. He divided the papal obedience into thirty-six parts and counted York and Canterbury as just one province. The French underlined the fact that since Benedict was born in Bordeaux, and therefore under English influence, he was in essence favourable towards England. The fact that he determined England to be just one thirty-sixth of the papal obedience should therefore stand and be applied to their level of representation at the council.

The third main French point challenged England's geographical size and made a comparison of the two nations' ecclesiastical provinces, concluding that England was far smaller than France and therefore should not have equal representation on the Council. England only had two provinces, York and Canterbury, whereas France had eleven provinces and 'one hundred and one wide and spacious dioceses'. Moreover, the French claimed that their Christian pedigree, in terms of the length of time they had been obedient, and to whom they had been obedient, made them superior to the English. Also, that the kingdom of France was composed of several duchies and counties, each being larger and richer in terms of 'lands, cities, castles and walled towns than the kingdom of England'. Therefore, they argued that it was 'ridiculous and unreasonable' that England should enjoy an equal number of delegates as France on the council, and that the French should have at least six times England's representation.

The French made a number of demands to accompany their three points of protest. The first was that the council should await the absent Spanish delegation before continuing with its business. Within that demand they added that England, the fifth nation, should simply return to being part of the German nation, as established by Benedict XII's decree. Their second demand offered an alternative to this too: that if the English were to retain their representation, then the other nations be divided also, creating new nations in the same manner that England had acquired its unofficial, unsanctioned high position within the council. The French insisted that failing to do so would be insulting to them because of the justifications presented in the three points of their protest. The third French point reiterated that if the other delegations did not agree to an expansion of the nations represented, then they should reinstate the original arrangement of four nations; Italy, France, Spain and Germany.

To a certain degree their points appear fair and balanced. Indeed, the call to await the return of the Spanish, a major force in political and religious terms, but also allies to the French, seems wholly reasonable. The absence of such a major faction due to domestic matters certainly disrupted the business of the council. The French questioned England's right to the same level of representation on apparently reasonable grounds; historical precedence, ecclesiastical tradition based on papal decree, as well as on a practical comparison of size, population and wealth. Their inference was that with the future of the church at stake, it was important that the right people were leading the debate towards resolution. Superficially, the French stance seemed generous to those without a voice and appeared to have been designed to promote a fairness of representation at the conference called to heal the schism. French success in this ecclesiastical forum to elicit support for its causes would certainly have benefitted many nations such as the Scots, Irish and Welsh.

Thomas Polton's reply appears to take the air of an experienced school master comically yet forcefully rebutting one of his less capable students. The French position was utterly demolished by the lengthy English reply. In the first case, it seems evident that Henry's representatives had an intimate knowledge of *Extravagans, Vas electionis*, and used that in-depth insight to deny that its author intended it to be a map of the divisions and obediences in the way the French claimed. They gave examples to illustrate their points, citing passages from the papal decree that put holes in the French case. One example was that the English provinces of York and Canterbury were listed among Occitan provinces, which they felt proved that England was not viewed as part of Germany and that the document was a convenient list of groupings, rather than a firm decree. On the point that England comprised only one province in the kingdom of England, and therefore should only have one place in council, Poulton replied: 'It is the worst sort of argument. For in much of what they have written they argue from the kingdom of England alone to the whole

English nation. These chaps write a lot of stuff like this.' The riposte then built a case regarding the peoples of 'the English or British nation'. Polton frequently repeated that phrase, cleverly blurring the edges of the terms in use to an audience which was probably unsure and largely disinterested in determining the precise details of these definitions. The reply qualified how the English nation was composed of eight kingdoms: England, Scotland and Wales were those of 'greater Britain'; Man and the four Irish kingdoms comprised the rest. The English argument destroyed that of the French, minutely picking apart Campagne's protest which seemed, in contrast, to have been airily composed on matters of general principle and with inadequate knowledge of the documents they cited. As the response dealt with the French points in a detailed way, it also took the opportunity to ridicule the authors of the protest and their argument, using terms such as 'feeble' and denigrating their points 'as these scribblers pretend'.[14]

So the argument ran, skilfully infusing well-made points with references, comparisons and ridicule, but also with flagrant untruths which broadened the argument to a degree that to pursue it would be fruitless, pointless and demand a great deal of time and energy. In response to how the French decried the size of England and its various regions, Polton gave a list of those places which belonged to the English or British nation, replying: 'and there is the famous principality of John, prince of the Orkneys and about forty other islands. Even these islands are equal to or larger than the kingdom of France.'[15] While of course they are not, to pick on every English assertion and respond to the high number of deliberate inaccuracies would be impractical and exhausting, which was probably their point. This discourse of stylish equivocation and solidly made points easily bettered the French protest. The relevant passage responding to the French protest about Wales is riven with ambiguity, misdirection, fact and insult. On the whole, this is an excellent sample of the tenor of the English reply:

> These people claim that Wales and the prelates and clergy of those parts do not pay any attention to the king of England, nor do they want to be part of the English nation, as is manifest here in this council. Always remembering the earlier disclaimer, the answer is that they can blush for putting out such a flagrant untruth. For the whole of Wales is obedient to the archbishop of Canterbury, as its primate, in spiritual matters and

to the most serene king of England in temporal matters, peacefully and as a matter of routine. That is evident on the spot and in this council, where many venerable doctors and other graduates and clerks from Wales are participating in this famous English nation. Similarly, they are just as clearly mistaken about Ireland, which embraces four provinces and sixty spacious dioceses. It is well known and undoubted that these provinces are recognized parts of the English nation.

When they go on to propose that the suffragan bishops of Scotland are not and have no wish to be in the English nation, always with the same disclaimer, the answer is that they are undoubtedly, and ought to be, part of the English nation, since they have no way of denying that Scotland is a part of Britain, though not so large a part. The whole world knows that. Also they have the same language as the English. It is really remarkable that such educated men would want to write that Wales, Ireland or even Scotland are not part of the English nation, because they do not do what the king of England tells them to do. If that point were granted, which it is not, it is irrelevant. It is obvious that the point whether any nations obeys merely one prince or several does not apply. Are there not several kingdoms in the Spanish nation which do not obey the king of Castile as chief among the Spaniards? It does not follow, all the same, that they are not part of the Spanish nation. Are there not Provence, Dauphiné, Savoy, Burgundy, Lorraine and several other territories, which have nothing to do with the adversary of France and yet are included in the French or Gallican nation? And it is the same with other nations.[16]

This English passage dismantled and dismissed the French argument with some style. The French decision to withdraw obedience from Benedict evidently obliged the Welsh to do the same, setting aside his decrees on the re-establishment of the Welsh church. This consequently rendered undeniable the English statement that the Welsh followed Canterbury in spiritual matters, especially since there was no French alternative. The excerpt also reveals that the French had given a voice to the Welsh members of their ambassadorial team, such as Gruffydd Yonge, and the English had done likewise in their party, notably in the form of Philip Morgan. The inclusion of Welshmen in the English delegation was unlikely to be a coincidence, and was doubtless intended to refute the claims of France, its allies and the Welsh rebels present in the French delegation that there was universal opposition to the king of England. The threat to Scotland, that Polton believed that it was and ought to be part of England, was tangible. Equally, the English point on the irrelevance that certain nations were not obedient to the temporal leader was a skilfully delivered argument. It is noteworthy though that Polton did not give a detailed refutation of the assertion that the Welsh did not obey the king of England, but flowed past it in his discourse. Therefore, despite the ongoing and partially successful efforts to reintegrate the Welsh into the government's tax and judicial systems, by 1417 it was widely known that the Welsh were still a force opposed to the English king. News of the rebellion must, therefore, have spread across Europe in previous years. However, another part of the English response included Wales and convincingly trumped the original French protest:

> Where the French nation, for the most part, has one vernacular which is wholly or in part understandable in every part of the nation, within the famous English or British nation, however, there are five languages, you might say, one of which does not understand another. These are English, which English and Scots have in common, Welsh, Irish, Gascon and Cornish. It could be claimed with every right that there should be representation for as many nations as there are distinct languages. By even stronger right ought they, as a principal nation, to represent a fourth or fifth part of the papal obedience in a general council and elsewhere ... It should not be overlooked how these scribblers are working towards inequality between nations.[17]

By accepting the French point and deflecting it to England's advantage, such as suggesting that each language group should have representation at the council, the argument forwarded by the English delegation simply outclassed that of their adversaries. It was not in the interests of the larger powers to allow every language group within their obedience to have an equal say: they would likely use the occasion to protest against their treatment by the central authority. The geopolitical realities faced by all of the larger states were similar in this respect; in order to expand their power and influence to compete with the other large powers, they had to acquire new territories and peoples to tax and recruit to their purposes. The application of this French notion of fair representation would have to apply to all groups and territories, not just those in the English or British nation. Failing to do so would, as Polton said, be unfair, but it was also not in the interests of any of the significant powers, including France. In this manner, each point of the French protest was dealt with and compellingly defeated. The righteousness of the principles involved seems to have been buried in the form and style of the exchange. There would be no further ecclesiastical debate over the fate of Wales; the argument was lost, largely thanks to a loquacious, dissembling reply by Thomas Polton and in the avalanche of other, more dominant political, military and even ecclesiastical matters. As an issue of continental relevance, rebel Wales was lost in a sea of words at the Council of Constance.

CHAPTER FOURTEEN

Owain's Last Days?

Very many said that he died; the seers maintain he did not.[1]

Meanwhile, Wales was still problematic to the English crown; the revolt, though significantly weakened and reduced to episodic convulsions, was still ongoing. The notion that the revolt withered after 1405 and finally died at the fall of Harlech in early 1409 seems largely inaccurate; however, the crown gained the upper hand with the fall of the last fortress, although garrisoning castles had not been a core element to the rebels' strategy. Peace would take a number of years, decades in some cases, to spread across Wales and become the norm. There was no final battlefield defeat and, as with so many popular insurgencies, there was no neat or clichéd ending either: no grand surrender, no marriage union and no killing of the leader. Even after Henry's armies had eventually brought to capitulation the two principal Welsh fortresses in 1409, English commanders complained that 'this cuntre of North Wales shall nevere have peese', and a joint French–Scots attack on Wales was predicted for that summer. The capture of the two French carracks, the 'Sancta Maria' and the 'Sancta Brigida', off Milford in 1409, lends credence to this view.[2]

Undeniably, the tenor and tempo of the conflict changed following the sieges of Aberystwyth and Harlech. The fall of those two removed Owain's main urban centres; however, the king recognised that the Welsh were not finished. In May 1409, warnings of renewed revolt reached fever pitch, resulting in orders eventually being issued to the earl of Arundel, Roger le Strange, Edward Charlton, and Lord Grey of Ruthin to go in person and make war on the rebels. Officials and communities continued to make truces with the rebels, one case from September 1409 saw a representative of Hopedale lordship making payment to

Owain Glyn Dŵr in person. However, certain functions of governance had returned to the more anglicised border lordships such as Brecon, Chirkland and on recaptured Anglesey; some places were able to hold judicial sessions in the towns and collect a level of rent revenue. However, by 1409, even these areas were only yielding approximately a third of the pre-revolt level and the bulk of that payment was raised from the English burgesses and tenants. This must be considered along with the fact that there were negligible returns from some areas, such as Merioneth, Caernarfon and northern Cardigan, into the 1420s. While it is certainly the case that numerous areas were, by this stage, too badly damaged by the passage of the conflict to yield previous sums to the tax collectors, in the more hostile areas this should also be considered as deliberate disobedience. These are indicative of an ongoing conflict of some nature between government and populace.[3]

The pattern for the following years is similar; reports of uprisings and disturbances provoked the government to pay for a naval patrol to operate from Chester to Anglesey, and raise a 900-strong force on the land to deploy for four months. The south-west flared again during summer 1411, with Cardigan becoming the focus for the government. Crown authority, in the sense that the population was not consistently in arms and some degree of revenue was raised from a particular area, returned across Wales asymmetrically, with each region offering different challenges to crown officers. At some point between 1410 and 1412, Rhys ap Tudor was captured while attacking in the borders, and executed in Chester. The following year, Gwilym, his brother, received another pardon. Similarly, Gruffydd ab Owain, heir of the rebel leader, died in captivity in London in 1411. In 1412, parleys intended to induce rebel submissions were still ongoing. The king's chief stalwart in Wales, Dafydd Gam, was seized by Owain Glyn Dŵr and ransomed for 700 marks. In all, the events of these years present a curious landscape of neither outright warfare, nor peace or submission. At the same time, a 180-strong force was posted to Bala to attempt to suppress rebel activity in the area. In addition, the Welsh appeared to have a new leader, Maredudd, Owain's son. The first evidence linking him to some overt form of power comes from June 1412, where men wishing to hold discussions with the English were obliged to operate under his protection. Since they required his permission to move between areas and to treat with the authorities, they evidently considered themselves primarily obedient to him. This was made explicit in letters written to English officials in Wales, where it was recorded that a particular man was able to come to parley because he was 'under the protexion of Mered' ap Owein'. In these respects, the conflict in Wales still bore certain of the hallmarks of an insurgency and therefore, in contrast to the notion that the revolt was something that could die, this was a quarrel that could run for years in some form and be reignited if similar perceived injustices persisted.[4]

The year 1413 saw the publication of a statute which recognised that the conflict was ongoing, and that the English in Wales and the border shires were at risk. It described a situation in which blood feuds conducted by the relatives of recently slain rebels were so common that judicial remedy was deemed necessary. In July that year, officials serving the new king, Henry V, announced fears that the French and the Welsh were about to launch an attack on England. In December that year, Margaret Hanmer, Owain's wife, Catrin, his daughter, and her four children by Edmund Mortimer were starved to death in prison by the crown. It seems likely that Owain was alive long enough to learn this news.

South-west Wales featured prominently in the records from early 1414, describing troop movements and hastily reinforced garrisons from Aberystwyth to Kidwelly. A significant submission by some 600 diehard rebels from Glyn Dŵr's heartland came in March at Bala, more than five years after the fall of Harlech. The crown's officers, Thomas, earl of Arundel, who led Henry V's forces into Paris as a contingent in the Burgundian army, along with Edward Charlton, Lord of Powys, and Sir David Holbache, made the supplicants drop to their knees and agree that they deserved death for their treacherous actions, and that they should be grateful of the clemency of their new king. Such methods would not easily buy peace. Also in 1414, parliament heard how the rebels were regularly entering Shropshire, Herefordshire, Gloucestershire and other parts adjoining, not only causing damage but abducting the king's loyal subjects from their houses, the towns and the roads. While a few of the English hostages were killed, most were held for ransom, with some unfortunates remaining captive for half a year or more. At that point, the rebels were not the same force which held Aberystwyth and Harlech, but were still able to mount a significant threat on both sides of the border and, notably, menace the king's subjects in their own homes. In the same year, Sir John Oldcastle, the Lollard leader, raised a revolt drawing thousands of soldiers to his banner. He was linked to the Welsh and the Scots, and had connections in the Welsh March where he was rumoured to be seeking to ally himself with the Welsh rebels. The Lollards formed an additional factor in the instability in the west during these years. Over the next three years Oldcastle's forces withered, rose again, then dispersed causing him to go into hiding. By 1417, he was known to be in the Welsh borders, where it was believed that he had gone to hold talks with Maredudd ab Owain. English officials fell foul of their new king for holding discussions with the Welsh rebels without permit. Troops were hurriedly sent to the south and messengers called garrisons to alert.[5]

Despite oaths being sworn to English officials and fines being paid by communities in certain parts, many proved more recalcitrant than submissive. In the absence of the open warfare of the previous decade, the environment in Wales could be described as a threatening one, and a number of Englishmen and crown administrators were attacked and murdered. Even as Henry V launched the first stages of his great French adventure, Wales appeared to be smouldering towards ignition once more. In 1415, the king sent another detachment of troops to Wales to help provide additional security. Officials held discussions with rebels in local initiatives, and were fined for so doing by the king. Gilbert Talbot was commissioned to locate and discuss peace with Owain: 'Appointment of Gilbert Talbot, *chivaler*, to treat with Owin Glendourdy of Wales on certain matters declared to him by the king and to receive Owin and other Welsh rebels to the king's obedience and grace if they seek them.' The entire parameters of Talbot's brief are unknown, but he was unsuccessful in his efforts to persuade Owain to submit. Talbot was again appointed 'to treat with Meredith ap Oweyn, son of Oweyn de Glendourdy, on certain matters declared to him by the king and to admit the said Owin and other Welsh rebels to the king's obedience and grace if they offer'. This shows that the authorities were attempting to use Maredudd as a conduit to Owain, to mediate his persistent intractability. It is worth speculating that there might have been a human element to Owain's apparent stubbornness. His wife, Margaret, his eldest son and original heir, Gruffydd, his daughter, Catrin, and his grandchildren through her and Edmund Mortimer, had all died in crown custody between 1411 and 1413. In light of that, it seems reasonable that he would refuse to make peace with those responsible. However, this commission to Talbot also demonstrates that Owain could be contacted with relative ease and that he was believed to be alive in February 1416. If this is correct, he did not conveniently die on the feast of Saint Matthew, 20 September, 1415, as peddled by Gruffydd Hiraethog.[6]

Although Sir John Oldcastle was captured in 1417, then tried and brutally executed that December, thus eliminating that potential foe, the Welsh appeared to be ready to rise again during the year. The constable of Harlech wrote to the chamberlain of North Wales warning him that an alliance had been forged between Maredudd ab Owain, the Scots and the men of the Outer Isles. A landing of Scots was expected between Mawddwy and Dyfi and the Welsh were preparing to meet it:[7]

> This is the credence by mouth that is to say howe John Salghall constable of Harglagh certeified and warned by lettre to the chamberleyn of Carnarvane howe that a gentell man of Walys that most knewe and pryueist was with Mereduth ap Owyn in grete specialte warned hym of an accorde made betwene the same Mereduth and men of the owt yles and of Scotland throgh lettres in and owt as he enfourmed hym that they sholden come a lond and aryve at Abermowth and Eve betwix this and midsommer neghst with her power and that the same Mereduth shold priuely do warne his ffrendes to make hym redy with hors and harneys again the same tyme, for which warnyng the same gentell man dar noght passe the toun of Harglagh etc. And likest hit semeth to be soth be cause of the gouernance of the Walsh peple, for they selleth her catell and byeth hem hors and harneys. And sume of hem stelleth hors and sume robbeth hors and purveyen hem of sadles, bowes and arowes and other harneys etc. And other recheles men of many dyuers cuntreis voidem her groundes and her thrifty gouernance and assemblen hem in dissolate places and wilde and maken many diuers congregaciones and mee[t]ynges pryuely, thogh her counsaile be holden yit secrete fro us, wherthogh yong peple ar the more wilde in gouernance.[8]

According to this local, English source, the Welsh were once more preparing for war in summer 1417. Similarly to the evidence describing Owain's cavalry raid or *chevauchée* in 1400, it is instructive how this force was also equipping itself as cavalry, offering a possible insight of how the Welsh prosecuted some of their campaigns in this period. Henry V's government sought to defeat this rising by offering Maredudd ab Owain a broad, all-encompassing, pre-emptive pardon:

> 30 April 1417: Pardon to Meredith ap Owain of Wales for all treasons, insurrections, rebellions, felonies, trespasses, misprisions, extortions,

offences, conspiracies, confederacies, congregations, negligences, contempts, concealments and deceptions.[9]

Maredudd refused, but the timing and its proximity to the proposed rising in league with the Scots and the diplomatic efforts at Constance of the previous month are noteworthy. This offer by the crown should be seen as an effort to neutralise any threat in west and perhaps an effort to prise the son from the father, rather than a demonstration of even-handedness and magnanimity, albeit calculated, as inferred elsewhere. In light of this stirring revolt, in May 1417, absentee lords were ordered to return to their Welsh estates, to fortify and prepare to defend them with Englishmen. The notion in government circles was clearly that the Welsh rebellion had been revitalised with foreign alliances in 1417; another war was on the horizon.[10]

Discounting the weakened and largely extinguished Lollards, this is a credible assertion. The Scots, revived after a number of bleak years following Homildon, had again begun to act beyond their borders. While small numbers of Scots mercenaries had earlier found their way into continental retinues, notably those of Jean of Burgundy, by 1417 the government was able to deploy Scots forces outside Scotland. Traditional northern targets such as Penrith, Roxburgh and Berwick were assaulted with no success during 1415.[11] The hope or fear of a Scots landing in Wales in 1417 was entirely credible; however, it did not materialise. It seems implausible that there was no connection between the French mention of Wales and Scotland at Constance and the diplomatic intercourse between them which stoked fears of another uprising in 1417. Although there are no extant written connections between the Welsh, French and Scots at this time, it is clear that Gruffydd Yonge acted as a French envoy to Scotland during this period. He is the most obvious conduit between these three powers and his career enjoyed a measure of elevation even as the Glyn Dŵr regime dwindled. He had been with the French delegation at Constance, and was translated to the bishopric of Ross in Scotland in 1418, and this position is likely to have been initially supported by the French and the Scots.[12] He appears in the detailed accounts of Jean of Burgundy's government of 1418–19 as a bishop and an ambassador. He played the same role in France during the previous years of more chaotic governance and fewer records there.[13] Certainly by 1418, the dauphin Charles was openly casting about for foreign allies in his fight against the Burgundians and the English. His approaches to the Scots and Castilians, as well as others such as the Lombards and the Savoyards, are well known.[14] Within the context of these diplomatic initiatives, it is entirely credible to believe that these and earlier discreet efforts included contact with the Welsh.

While certain administrative functions gradually returned to Wales following the fall of Harlech, it is also possible to chart the orders for garrisons to be maintained, troops to be sent in haste and castles to be repaired throughout the period 1409–17. Although events in France again dominate contemporary chronicles and records, a sufficient amount of evidence detailing persistent though smaller-scale conflict in Wales exists, demonstrating the continuity of the rebellion in some form. It is also clear that while the crown sought and received the submissions of many Welsh rebels, at times, these men were able to negotiate with the authorities in terms which favoured them.[15] Reports of the demise of the revolt, in military terms at least, prior to 1417 are premature.

However, events on the continent would surely have caused the Welsh great concern. After the heavy defeat sustained by their allies at Agincourt and the failure of the French diplomatic initiative at the Council of Constance, Henry V reinvaded France in August 1417 and pressed further inland than during the largely coastal sortie of 1415. Burgundian troops won a grand sweep of towns and castles during 1417 and although they fought no set-piece battles and the final military picture of the year remained unclear, it appeared predominantly favourable to Duke Jean. His diplomatic initiatives also appeared to be flourishing; Jean made alliances with Brittany and the German Emperor that year, and another with Queen Isabeau early in 1418. In May that year, the Burgundians seized Paris and many of the Armagnacs fled, including the new dauphin, Charles. Jean then proceeded to massacre perhaps 2,000 Armagnacs in the capital. In a calculated counter-stroke, when he arrived at a parley, the Armagnacs murdered Jean, duke of Burgundy, on the bridge at Montereau in September 1419, causing a further descent into bitter civil strife in France.[16] Later, a story arose that visitors would be shown the skull of duke Jean, complete with the hole left by Tanguy du Châtel's axe. They would be told that this was the hole through which the English entered France. This was of course incorrect, that was the breach worked by Henry IV's diplomats in previous years. Also, Duke Jean's murder proved to be the catalyst for a full Anglo–Burgundian alliance. The resulting treaty of Troyes in May 1420 promised the French crown to Henry V on the death of the aged, infirm Charles VI.[17]

On 9 January 1420, John, duke of Bedford, soon to act as the English regent of the Anglo-Burgundian dominated regions of northern France, was commissioned to persuade Maredudd ab Owain to serve the king in Normandy, in the company of the many other Welshmen already fighting there for the crown. The fact that a man of such esteem and rank as John of Bedford, Henry V's brother and perhaps the second most important man in England, was sent to treat with Maredudd demonstrates the respect and gravity with which the government treated the matter at that point. In July the same year, the king authorised the sheriffs of Caernarvon and Merioneth, as well as Thomas Walton, the chamberlain of North Wales, to treat with the Welsh rebels.[18] In 1420 therefore, the rebels were clearly still a force powerful and worthy enough to be approached by Bedford, one of the most senior and respected English nobles of the age, as well as by the crown's governors in Wales.

Although Maredudd and his supporters maintained their defiance, Henry V might well have been satisfied with his progress in France. His forces, when combined with Breton and Burgundian territories, held perhaps as much as the northern fifth or even quarter of the country. At that time, his alliance with Burgundy had great potential and the Breton truce was still in force. With this view dominating the horizon, with the English seemingly triumphant in northern France and the French retreating further south, deep into central France, the possibility of them returning to support the rebels in Wales had faded and a reconsideration of the Welsh position seems natural. The end of this second phase of the same 'Glyn Dŵr' revolt, under Maredudd, came in early 1421. This conclusion seems to have been, in part, caused from below, rather than solely an action decided by the leader. Certain evidence suggests that the Welsh communities determined how they should be organised and led, and more importantly, how they should be brought to peace.[19] It seems probable that the opinions of the native communities served as a mediating influence on Maredudd's thinking and they possibly forced his hand towards peace. Certainly, the native culture in which he lived was one which engaged numerous elements of society in the decision-making processes, particularly those involving war, peace and their laws. Whatever his motivations, letters patent to receive the rebel leader date from April; Maredudd ab Owain submitted and was granted a pardon on 8 May 1421. The author of this pardon was convinced that Owain Glyn Dŵr had died by this time:

> Pardon to Meredyth son of Owyn de Glendordy of Wales for all reasons, felonies, insurrections, adherences to the king's enemies, trespasses, rebellions, contempts, deceptions, misprisions, ignorances, conceal-ments, and other offences; as on the testimony of holy writ the son shall not bear the iniquity of his father nor for the offence of one is another to be punished but each shall bear his own burden and receive reward as he has done, whether it be good or evil, and although Owyn rebelled against the king and the crown, prodigal of his honour and forgetful of his due fealty, nevertheless Meredyth after his father's death did not follow his malice but having it in hatred dwelt peaceably among the king's subjects and came as soon as he could to the king's presence in spirit of humility and demeanour of a penitent, and the king has inclined ears of pity to his supplication on that account.[20]

The mystery surrounding Owain Glyn Dŵr's final years, including when, where and how he died, currently seems unlikely to ever be solved. Perhaps this is just as well, for this adds a mystical nuance to the story, as the poet, Rhys Goch Eryri, wrote in the years after Owain's disappearance:

> Let the work of the heavenly lord be unquestioned,
> And let the little world be sad
> Because earth has been placed
> On a naked sword as gleaming as snow.
> I do not know why, unless it were madness,
> (A rightful man is free of deceit)
> The serpent went to a dwelling beneath Heaven
> Where there is no death.[21]

The 'serpent' in question here embodies Owain, and represents the heroic deliverer from the prophetic traditions, and must not be confused with the biblical snake with negative connotations.

However, the weight of chronicle opinion assumes that Owain died at some point during the second decade of the fifteenth century and, while this might well be accurate, most sources claiming this post-date the event by decades or even centuries. However, one source from 1430 could conceivably be connected to Owain's passing, when he would have been approximately seventy years old. Curiously, during the reign of Henry VI, a statute was published reaffirming Henry IV's indictment against Owain and those of his bloodline. This was an unusual measure for a government to undertake unless it was prompted to do so. While possible that Owain had been dead for up to fifteen years, it is also plausible that he lived until shortly before this statute's reaffirmation, and that his passing impelled the government to reissue the proclamation to ward off challenges for his estates by his numerous kin. The original recipient of Owain's estates was John Beaufort, earl of Somerset, who died in 1410 without ever taking possession of them. However, none of Beaufort's offspring died shortly prior to the 1430 reaffirmation of the indictment against Owain, so the publication of the statute seems unlikely to have been connected to them.[22]

Whether he lived a few short years after Maredudd appears to have taken over by 1412 or longer as the above might imply, it is worth touching upon the manner in which he lived his final years. Despite the various rumours, myths and legends, there is no established record detailing where he lived after he emerged from the woods in 1412 to capture Dafydd Gam. There is no proof of his lifestyle and nothing which gives the cause of his death or the place of his burial. While the seers who proclaimed his immortality were obviously incorrect, those who later wrote of his death were also guessing or, at best, recording anecdotes which had passed through several reinterpreting mouths. A tradition arose among English sources claiming that Owain lived out his final years in misery, that of a hunted, starving fugitive on the run. However, with the exception of Adam Usk who was pardoned in 1411 and reintegrated into English circles thereafter, all other evidence for Owain's death was put to parchment much later by people with no connection to him or his entourage. Also, Adam was separated from and probably ostracised by Owain's followers after 1411, so his account is equally problematic. Other sources wrote on the matter decades and, commonly, centuries later. It seems clear that these works denigrating this part of Owain's life are at variance with the established facts and were evidently politically motivated. One such author, the Italian, Tito Livio, was commissioned to write his account by Henry V's brother, Humphrey, duke of Gloucester, in 1436. Portraying the death of a traitor to his paymaster in terms of misery, loneliness and starvation seems predicable and baseless. Although Owain had been indicted for treason, with a royal pardon on the table after 1415 there was no reason to hunt him, and no one is documented as attempting to do so. Negotiations were occasionally held between high-ranking crown officials and Owain or his representatives; his approximate whereabouts appear to have been known. With those salient points in mind, it is reasonable to condemn as ill-willed fantasy the writings of those who imagined that he lived out his final years as a fearful, hungry fugitive. There is no contemporary evidence to sustain such a line.[23]

In contrast to the English sources which described him so negatively, the significant corpus of post-revolt Welsh poetry demonstrates that his countrymen held Owain in enduringly high esteem. It should be remembered that none of the later poets were in Owain's pay, and so their praise was likely motivated by genuine affection, possibly reflecting their patron's desire to be publicly connected with Owain, or that they espoused the popular views of their audiences in the taverns and courts. There is a remarkable consistency in the respect and affection given to Owain after the revolt had failed. This ranges from those who knew him and likely served with him – for medieval Welsh poets were warriors too – such as Llywelyn ab y Moel, Rhys Goch Eryri and Guto'r Glyn, through to the next generation of poets who created compelling verbal imagery of Owain, calling him *Arth y Sycharth*, 'the Bear of Sycharth', and describing him as a wolf at the head of his warriors. While they lauded his martial prowess, he was also praised for his kindness and gentleness, and connected Owain to a variety of impressive historical figures, such as the mythical giant king, Bendigeidfran, and Uther Pendragon.[24] Arthurian-style allusions about Owain being able to return when roused for a moment of need also sprinkle the poems of the age. As the Tudors rose to prominence and then to power, they proudly and openly recalled their bloodline connection to the rebel, Owain Glyn Dŵr. Extant poems by Lewis Glyn Cothi, Llawdden and Ieuan Gyfannedd demonstrated that claiming kinship with Owain remained desirable throughout the fifteenth century while others, such as Gutun Owain, Tudur Aled, Lewys Môn, Gruffudd Hiraethog and Siôn Tudor, did the same during the sixteenth century. By the time Owain was sympathetically incorporated into Shakespeare's iconic works, the pinnacle of English literary output, the survival of a positive memory of him was assured.[25] Moreover, the lack of any disparaging works from Owain's native adversaries' bards in subsequent years is highly noteworthy: even his enemies avoided speaking ill of him. His chief native opponent, Dafydd Gam, was less fondly remembered by a later poet:

Dafydd Gam, misfortunate wanderer in battle,
a traitor to King Richard,
utterly did the devil, angrily pressing his claim,
such was your state, turn his finger in your arse.[26]

However, the disappearance of Owain Glyn Dŵr and the other factors which affected the Welsh, the transition from war to peace and the return to the uncomfortable, reluctant accommodation of English rule in Wales, determined that the people needed to act. When combined with the opportunities offered by the renewed fighting in France, change on a social and cultural level appeared essential. The medieval Welsh expressed themselves through poetry, and those which have survived help assess the social health of a people. Such a perspective of their popular culture, hopes and everyday frames of reference cannot otherwise be revealed by the drier methods of measuring the state of a nation, such as tax revenues or judicial sessions. While the poets carried forward an emotional element of Owain's memory, one poem in particular seems to encapsulate the post-revolt reactions of the Welsh, and it only briefly mentioned Owain. Although Llywelyn ab y Moel wrote a poem on 'the Battle of Mare's Heath' or *Brwydr Waun Gaseg*, some time during the later years of the revolt, it seems likely that it gained wider popularity after the wars in France once again took Welshmen abroad. One reason dating it to that period could be that Llywelyn described 'an odious French badger-keeper' among the enemy, whereas in his and in other Welsh poems of the time, the English are consistently referred to as 'Sais' or 'Saesson'. Although earlier chronicles consistently refer to the English leaders as 'the French', this was not so during this later period, and it might identify an effort to vilify the French rather than the English, perhaps to legitimise or normalise going to war against their former allies.[27] The poem regales the tale of how a band of Welshmen set out to fight the enemy, boasting that they would share the spoils and swore oaths that they would never run from an attack. However, when the enemy suddenly appeared and hurtled towards them, with over a 100 of them on horseback, Llywelyn and his companions all broke and ran, leaving their spears in the grass. Llywelyn readily claimed the ignominy of being the first to run and the fastest in flight, swearing that he would never return to Waun Gaseg.[28] However, this poem patently describes a society coming to terms with its recent past. They were evidently at ease with the course of events to a sufficient degree that they could see humour in their defeat, they were not wallowing in self-pity or recalling prophecies of vengeance, but were clearly moving on.

In addition, the message of the poem, regaled by the poet in taverns and at gatherings, could only have been delivered to an accepting audience by someone of standing in the community, and not by someone recognised as a coward.[29] As such, 'the Battle of Mare's Heath' gives a snapshot of a robust, mature society successfully coming to terms with itself, its recent conflict and the notion of defeat. If this were a typical reaction to the demise of the struggle for independence, then it is little wonder that Welshmen were able to engage more thoroughly in the politics and military affairs of the kingdom in the rest of the fifteenth century. The next generation saw numerous Welshmen knighted, including Rhys Gethin's son, Richard, while others such as Matthew Gough served as army and garrison commanders. As the Hundred Years' War ended in French victory and the Wars of the Roses raged in England, this unprecedented rise in social standing of Welshmen in England continued. Although the process was not a simple one, a small number of Welshmen rose to become earls. Of those, a descendant of the Tudors, so obviously involved in the conflict at the beginning of the fifteenth century, would even ascend the throne of England as Henry VII. This level of engagement in the life of the kingdom and the successful elevation of so many Welshmen and their families was unheard of in any previous generation, but particularly since Edward I's invasion of Gwynedd in 1282. The revolt had catalysed change, although the improvement in their status slowly evolved over a generation. However, if the healthy self-deprecating attitudes expressed by Llywelyn ab y Moel were typical, then, as a people, the Welsh appeared ready to confront the rest of the fifteenth century and engage more fully in the military and political life of Britain.

Conclusions

The environment in which this Welsh insurgency took hold had been created by a number of contributory dynamics, founded on the significant social and legal disparity between Wales's Welsh and English populations. The rebel movement certainly had the right kind of people, although evidently too few to permanently overpower such a huge enemy, and their diplomatic drives proved that they were aware of that. The insurgency had a number of leaders, political, military and ecclesiastical, who were capable of binding together the loose groupings which found themselves in revolt, constructing a credible political programme and winning sufficient military victories to give this rebellion the air it needed to thrive. In addition, the combination of these elements, was sufficient to draw recruits and non-military supporters into the conflict, from peasants to clergy to nobles from Wales, France, Brittany, Spain and England. The native and the French elements certainly had sufficient political and personal grievances to persuade them to commit themselves to this revolt. In addition, the extent to which medieval Wales was a highly martial culture is little appreciated. A significant degree of that society's surviving literature, its poetry, describes a culture keenly focused on battle prowess and association with a lineage of similarly military figures. Perhaps its prime method of distinguishing a man's worthiness and reputation was connected with his deeds in war. This sort of culture alone would have been sufficient to give rise to revolt – and the Welsh were not unique in having such a society. However, when added to the ideology of the oppressed, as they clearly and correctly perceived their condition, this created a potent level of discontent which was likely, at some point, to ignite. They also had the materials to do so, many had years of military service, armour and weaponry. Once those leaders with the intent and the capacity to lead such a group had emerged, the next stage, the development, dissemination and application of a doctrine was also clearly perceptible. Given those prime ingredients, this Welsh rebellion was likely to pose significant difficulties to those tasked with suppressing it.

During the course of the conflict, the classic characteristics of a flourishing, puissant insurgency became identifiable. One of the key features concerns freedom of movement. Evidence from crown commanders in Wales, written as early as the end of 1401, showed that they feared going out against the rebels. When crown forces did move, they restricted themselves to marching in sizeable numbers along designated routes between the castles and walled towns. In contrast to this almost agoraphobic outlook, the Welsh enjoyed practically total freedom of movement. It seemed that the only partial check to them was the annual, short-lived royal expedition which lumbered expensively and pointlessly through predetermined regions. In addition, transport of people and victuals to castles appears to have been frequently undertaken by boats from south-west England, Chester and English-controlled parts of Ireland.

For much of this conflict, the rebels enjoyed almost universal popular support in Wales, and they were able to connect with those discontented with King Henry in England, France and elsewhere. Perhaps most importantly for a popular insurgency, virtually none of the natives opposed them. The number of Welsh adherents to the crown was so miniscule that most appear to be known by name and to have been connected to key figures, such as Dafydd Gam's family adherence to Bolingbroke in Brecon, or to have been personally opposed to Glyn Dŵr, such as Gwilym ap Gruffudd ap Gwilym from Flintshire. There simply was no pro-government movement among the Welsh beyond two or perhaps three minor strongmen and their personal retainers, along with small numbers who served in castle garrisons. There is, of course, a subtlety in distinction between opposition and varying degrees of support. Nevertheless, those committed enough to fight found themselves moving in a highly permissive environment.

The rebels evidently knew the terrain better than their enemy, which is a common but not universal feature of insurgencies. They used that knowledge to affect the outcome of their campaigns, whether it was the ambush at Ruthin which captured Lord Grey, or the choice of an advantageous battlefield at Bryn Glas. They also engaged more successfully with the Welsh populace, in their own language and with cultural sympathy; whether to attend funerals of those killed by the king's men or to evoke popular prophecies. In contrast, English armies, several thousand strong, marched through areas, destroying crops, executing individuals they found and imposed indiscriminate communal punishment for acts of rebellion. Although there was no media in this period in the modern sense, the rebels dominated the narrative of the revolt in Welsh ears. There is no known dissenting literature, yet numerous examples of poetry sympathetic to the revolt and its leadership have survived. With this broad spread of advantages in intelligence, from geographical knowledge, to popular support, to having better information on the enemy's position, posture and movements, the Welsh were better able to manage the battle space to their advantage and project their power far beyond their actual field strength.

There is nothing which reveals whether Owain taxed the Welsh once he became the dominant force in the land. However, it is plausible that he did, to fund his projects and to fully behave as a ruler, as suggested by his letters and actions, such as summoning nobles and taking oaths of allegiance from communities. In that regard, it is difficult to determine whether the authorities or the rebels dominated economically during this conflict; however, it is well established that crown revenue from Wales effectively stopped entirely for several years. There is no dispute that long before Maredudd ab Owain accepted a pardon in 1421, the crown was collecting revenue in Wales. However, it would not be accurate to equate the payment of taxes and a level of civil obedience with allegiance to the authorities. One of the key conclusions arising is the fact that the rebels were able to bring down the taxation and governance structures through disobedience and violent action, as well as conducting their own political affairs independently, beyond the grasp of the authorities, can only be viewed as a significant rebel success.

Perhaps the most popular of these boundary interactions concern the military actions which disputed the ground. The fact that the Welsh enjoyed almost unrestricted freedom of movement in the field demonstrates that they controlled the territory through which they moved and campaigned, and not the garrisoned forces which were reluctant to venture forth and were reliant on support from across the English border or by sea. Without accurate figures of combatants and clashes, it is impossible to fully discuss loss exchange ratios between these opposing forces. However, a conclusion presenting an overall picture of Welsh dominance in combat is axiomatic. The conflict went from a position where there was no fighting, to a more fluid environment of a few disparate eruptions of violence, to a concluding position where the rebels won battles, stormed fortresses, some of which they garrisoned, conducted grand military sweeps, held parliaments, and brokered an alliance with the French. To resurrect, even reinvent, a long-buried state, they had to be more successful than the enemies who initially controlled them. To only consider the casualty numbers is also to miss a vital point. Those small-scale contacts which were recorded, along with those which went unrecorded, but must have taken place because one side receded, were sufficient to hand the rebels dominance in the field. The actual and psychological effects of brief engagements, ambushes and threats to supplies caused the English to physically retreat into their castles and adopt a siege mentality. This empowered the rebels but also demonstrated their territorial control of the majority of Wales.

Studying a map of the areas in which combat took place would also reveal highly significant points. Given the wide reach of the rebels and their interconnectivity with Wales's communities, it is understandable why there was no fighting in some areas. This shows that in these areas there was no substantial threat to their control, and the same maxim can be applied to those areas under crown influence. Their effective frontlines can therefore be determined as being those places where each side rubbed against one another and contested control. This assists the demarcation of rebel territory, implying a boundary which encompassed all within a zone from Flint to Shrewsbury, and Montgomery to Hereford as its eastern border. Enduring crown presences in Wales, such as Cardiff and coastal southern Pembrokeshire, formed some of the few breaks along the rebels' southern boundary, while Caernarfon, Rhuddlan and Conwy protruded into the rebels' northern frontier.

The relationship between the rebels and those castles which nominally remained loyal to the crown during the conflict remains a point of intrigue. It is clear that certain of the English constables who governed the castles had fluid loyalties, such as Thomas Barneby, Chamberlain of North Wales, based in Caernarfon. While he apparently retained control on behalf of the king of England, he does not seem to have taken offensive action against the Welsh and, between 1405 and 1410, he appears complicit in the release of high-value rebels delivered into his custody. Research into the actions of other constables might well yield similar stories of duplicity, matched by compliance with the strongest local power at a given moment. It seems probable that accommodation was made between the rebels and at least some of the English commanders because, as the captures of Harlech, Conwy, Aberystwyth, Carmarthen and others proved, the rebels had the power and know-how to take the fortresses and walled towns. If the English and French sources, which independently estimated Welsh armies, on different campaigns, as numbering between 8,000 and 10,000 men, were generally accurate, then the Welsh had sufficient men to also instal sizeable garrisons in each castle. However, they did not and, in the absence of written proof from the time, speculation forwards the notion that the garrisoning of the castles was not a key feature of their strategy during that period. While it is possible that this was out of fear of exposing their comparatively limited numbers to conventional siege attack by England's powerful, experienced forces, other options merit consideration. In the first instance, fear of being besieged seems to have been absent: Harlech and Aberystwyth fell to the Welsh in 1404, yet no move was made against either for more than three years. The Welsh were likely aware that, in the climate in which they took those castles, the threat of counter-siege was, temporarily perhaps, non-existent. However, other possibilities allow for agreement being reached between the rebels and a number of the constables, in which no substantial attacks were brought to bear against either side. This would induce a state of negotiated neutrality where final victory by Owain or Henry would decide the allegiance and conduct of the more malleable commanders. Another possibility is that the castles were reduced to near irrelevance, having little bearing or impact on the rebel state. An adjunct to this avenue is that the Welsh were perhaps expecting the French to arrive and garrison the castles, as English intelligence claimed was proposed for the immense force of over 10,000 troops assembled and wasted under Jacques de Bourbon in 1404. The annual assaults on Kidwelly seem to have been mostly carried out by local Welsh leaders engaged in the sort of violent personality politics typical in the medieval world. The English there were contained, however, and Kidwelly was not used as a staging post for military adventures in the region, even once the tide had turned against the rebels. Similarly, south Pembrokeshire experienced a few large attacks by Welsh forces, most notably shortly prior to the arrival of the French. This seems likely to have been either out of a need to reassert rebel influence there or, on one occasion, to ensure that the region was ready for the arrival of Jean de Hangest and the 1405 expedition. Whatever the precise details of the situation between the insurgents and the garrisons, the latter do not appear to have posed a significant threat to the territorial control and integrity of the rebel state.

The results of all of these boundary interactions were those typically associated with insurgencies in full flood. Most obviously, there were military and civilian casualties on both sides. In addition to this, there was physical and economic damage; whole towns and villages were burnt, and remained in disrepair decades after the demise of the revolt. The rebels not only attacked the local economic apparatus, such as mills or fairs, but they also managed to bring down the civil governance structure. However, the psychological impact of the rebellion has perhaps been underestimated. The climate of fear and insecurity produced by insurgent action was palpable in the panicking letters from the castles in Wales and the repeated calls for help in England's border shires. Although there are no records to confirm it, the fear of visitation by a royal expedition likely had the same terror effect on Welsh communities. All parties concerned produced propaganda of one sort or another, whether praise poetry for Owain, the words of ambassadors brokering treaties, or the corpus of English, French, Scottish, Spanish and Welsh literature which denigrated one side in favour of the other. The course of the revolt saw the insurgents rapidly develop their military strategies and political programmes. Their dynamism and flexibility were key factors in their dominance over government forces, which tinkered with and repeatedly imposed the same inadequate plan. The efforts of Henry's envoys on the continent demonstrated English diplomatic prowess in action, and they were essential in cultivating the conditions which allowed England to prevail militarily in a conflict it showed no signs of winning previously. The insurgency therefore catalysed doctrinal evolution as well as obliging both sides to develop their military and political programmes in order to contest and prevail. Also typical of insurgencies is that they give rise to social dislocation and further grievances, and this conflict was no different. The letter written by the Shropshire tenants from April 1406 revealed how a third of the population of the county had left due to rebel pressure. Other examples include the residents of Carmarthen being given free passage elsewhere, which is reminiscent of Henry V's treatment of the people of Harfleur in 1415, and the burgesses of Kidwelly fleeing to England in boats. The course of any conflict creates a fertile seedbed in which animosity and further grievances can be grown. While the various court cases and vendettas pursued during and after the rebellion's demise show some degree of furthering grievances, it could also be argued that Welsh–English relations suffered in the aftermath of this revolt. To some degree, they remain a feature of those multifaceted relations to this day.

Late fourteenth-century Wales contained the essential ingredients to see an insurgency seed and grow. The reasons for the rise and fall of that regime can be refined into military, diplomatic, political and external factors. Events and issues arising in Wales, England, France and other countries were all causative, as were the processes of social change which occurred during the period. Although a Welsh rebellion in this period was not inevitable, in view of the factors at play within that particular historical and cultural backdrop, it is not surprising that there was a significant revolt. However, the swift rise of the rebels surprised many, and the scale of their successes were even more of a shock. The principal surprise came in the realisation of just how capable the rebels were: they formed into a cohesive yet flexible fighting force which was also engaged in ambitious, yet realistic political and diplomatic initiatives. The fruits of their efforts were perhaps the largest shock this rebellion delivered: not just the reconstruction of a state that had been long lost to a more powerful neighbour, but also the fact that, for several years, England lost Wales to the natives.

Militarily, the Welsh conducted an extremely effective insurgency campaign. From its seemingly chaotic inception, they performed well, whether rescuing comrades from the gallows, sacking towns or taking fortresses and holding out against siege by crown forces. Once they had coalesced into a loose but largely unified movement, they were able to make the government's planners appear militarily amateurish.

The disparate nature of the outbreak of the revolt provided the first series of problems. Small-scale attacks did not present a challenge to governmental authority in Wales and could be dismissed as irrelevant to the government's distant seat of power. However, their widespread and highly localised nature revealed a large number of societal issues that needed to be overcome in order to restore order and stability. This is notably different from the return of peace and the spread of happiness, leading to common harmony and prosperity. Simply put, the govern-ments in question were focused on the needs and interests of the ruling elite and only appear to have addressed the issues of the lower-born when they seriously infringed or disrupted the life of the upper strata.

That elite required only obedience, revenue and the provision of anything that supported the realisation of their grand schemes: soldiery, taxes, food, shipping, other forms of revenue such as communal fines and so on. In that light, events in a place derided in parliament and dismissed by the king himself were clearly of no interest to a new, unstable regime in London. While this clearly refers to the establishment of Henry IV's government in 1399, this could equally apply to the reigns of his predecessor, Richard II, and the reigns of those who followed – all of which saw revolts against the monarch or his method of governance. This was not therefore solely a failing of Henry IV's government, but a feature of the ruling mindset which for centuries ignored the desires and needs of the many in favour of the few. This elitist, dismissive approach to governance led to generational revolts.

In terms of the outbreak of violence in Wales, Henry's administration failed to grasp the fact that small actions were significant. While attacks often only caused a small number of casualties, in each instance the local balance of power tipped in favour of the victors. The indisputable fact that the insurgency grew in scale and success implies that, in most cases, the rebels prevailed in these fights. The gradual changing of a population's loyalties was a subtle process of small shifts in their perception of who was in charge in their area. This applied to this conflict just as it does to modern ones. The effects of these small gains were often more psychological in nature than military. However, they can be seen in full fruition when, before the end of 1401, the usually loyal tenantry of the king's own lands in Brecon refused to pay their taxes and other dues unless the crown sufficiently suppressed the rebels in that area. Due to its history of English control and settlement, the records for Brecon are more complete than for other areas. Even so, it appears that the insurgents did not target Brecon as frequently or with the same vigour as they did other areas, such as the borders, Kidwelly and Cardiff. In that light, it is reasonable to believe that matters were worse in areas where the loyalty of the populace was initially lower and where there was more conflict. Therefore this example of direct disobedience in the king's own estates was indicative of an extremely potent revolt developing.

Achieving numerous small victories, seemingly irrelevant perhaps when viewed in isolation, brought more substantial gains to the insurgents as the rebellion developed and consequently enlarged the tasks and the difficulties faced by the authorities. In contrast to these small steps taken by the rebels, the crown conducted massive, costly military expeditions as the cornerstone of its strategy to suppress the rebellion. This style of the annual, gestural invasions would never bring either a set-piece battle nor, consequently, could the king's impressive displays of military might bring victory or peace. Such large-scale military responses were not fit for purpose and proved to be inappropriate methods of suppressing insurgencies, even in this historical period.

Swift, decisive and multifaceted action followed by a strategy which guaranteed long-term support and continual reinforcement of that plan were required to stanch the revolt before it developed into something truly troublesome. In comparison to the energy with which the rebels engaged in the conflict, the government's slow and ineffective responses made it appear arthritic, even incompetent.

One notable issue was the terrain; the Welsh knew it intimately, the English did not. Even those resident in the walled towns and the boroughs in their lee knew comparatively little of the land beyond their economically privileged limits. The Welsh language and culture was, and still is, largely a mystery to its closest neighbours. Those English nobles who held estates in Wales were usually absentees and had to be ordered by parliament to go to the front lines once conflict erupted there. This put a disproportionate amount of responsibility onto the shoulders of commanders at their posts in Wales. The resident garrisons and local tenant-militia forces had provided a continuity of cover in a restive but not necessarily rebellious region for a century. However, the system of rotating commanders and troops evidently led to inefficient occupation, and this imperfect method is still used in modern conflicts. In this case, it led to near-mutiny among English troops who did not wish to be in Wales. In contrast, the Welsh wanted to be nowhere else. In terms of this conflict, the English failed in the basic requirements of knowing the terrain, physically and culturally, and in being present beyond the castle walls.

In the first year of the conflict, local commanders such as Hotspur and Charlton would readily take to the field to pursue enemy groups. By the end of 1401, they complained that they did not have enough Englishmen with them to venture out of their castles to attack Glyn Dŵr. This reluctance to engage the rebels demonstrates that even though written examples of engagements are relatively few, more fighting took place than was recorded. As a result of those clashes, in the minds of the English in Wales, the rebels were already a force to fear fighting except on terms which significantly favoured the defenders. This reluctance to act not only handed to the rebels the countryside beyond the castles, it ceded them the initiative which, in counter-insurgency terms, is all-important. In addition, this allowed the rebels freedom of movement and demonstrated that crown troops were restricting their own movements and actions unless certain criteria were fulfilled. The fact that the crown insisted on relying on 'men born beyond the Severn' to fulfil all roles automatically divided Welsh from English, even those Welsh who had faithfully served the authorities for generations. While the garrison contingent lists prove that some exceptions were made, where this rule was applied, it could only hamper English prospects in Wales. Inevitably, this division, although enshrined in legal ordinance, would be set aside when convenient to the defenders.

This provided just one of many examples illustrating the way in which the government had incorrectly diagnosed the problem. The core issue was not one of ethnicity, but one of treatment of the Welsh; their daily economic and legal reality, as well as a perception of their conditions and opportunities. The simplistic and inaccurate diagnosis that Welshness was akin to treachery could only enflame and entrench the issues which gave vent to the rising. The Welsh did not violently rebel because they loved or hated either candidate for the English crown, the mass did not rise in protest against the harsh treatment of Owain Glyn Dŵr. One of the main reasons that they rose was because Bolingbroke's seizure of the throne distracted the powers which held them down long enough for the Welsh to vent their anger against those who had oppressed them for so long.

Combined with this seriously flawed identification of the problem was the failure to provide an effective remedy. This was a phrase recurrent in the literature of the time, whether from Richard Kingston in Hereford, the tenants in Breconshire or garrison commanders around Wales, all of whose letters indicated that the government's strategy was widely recognised as ineffective. The plan seemingly depended on the castles and grand tours with sizeable forces, neither of which were adequate. While it seems axiomatic that the latter might have demonstrated the impressive military power at Henry IV's disposal, in themselves they could not bring peace except for the few days that the army was present in any district. Their actions in driving off cattle, looting towns and churches as well as executing people, could only exacerbate the revolt.

The public execution of Llywelyn ap Gruffudd Fychan at Llandovery earned the rebels honour and cost King Henry prestige, even among the English chroniclers who reported the event. The way Llywelyn met his death showed that the fear of repression and even that of death had gone, and that the Welsh leader was someone for whom his people were willing to die. With these factors in mind, government control would also be lost unless it acted with intelligence and empathy. The government's brutal response to Llywelyn's proud gesture strengthened the rebels and reduced the credibility of crown forces. The government's reactive strategy of bolstering standing garrisons and slowly sending large armies to scenes of rebels attacks further empowered the Welsh, who created more flashpoints to which the authorities had obliged themselves to respond. While the government was reinvesting Cardiff or Carmarthen and responding to pillaging attacks in Shropshire, the Welsh were able to take and garrison Harlech and Aberystwyth, which were their more likely targets from the beginning. One of the recurrent insights this study reveals is the high level of the rebels' strategic skill; they were highly intelligent, experienced men of war executing an effective, flexible and evolving plan.

Rebel successes might also have been assisted by the crown's archaic plan for the suppression of the native Welsh. The reliance on castles and garrisons was outdated; when the Welsh tilted into disobedience, the castles proved ineffective in reversing that position. Their psychological impact was negated for the Welsh no longer feared them and realised that they could overrun them. When the insurgency strengthened to the point where the local balance of power appeared to have swung to them, the populace favoured the rebels more than the authorities. Rather than dominating the landscape as they had previously, the castles became isolated outposts too weak to affect the conflict. Another of their prime purposes had been a punitive one; soldiers launched missions against the Welsh from them, enabling the domination of the surrounding territory. This revolt became too powerful for that and the sources reveal that commanders and troops were unwilling to venture out against the rebels or to stay in Wales beyond the limits of their contractual obligations – clearly a psychological coup for the rebels. Although a few dozen soldiers, reinforced with armed English tenants, would often be enough to defend a castle against all but the most determined sieges, they had no enduring offensive impact in this conflict. Their role became more one of armed observation than any other. Recognition of their redundancy also comes from the English counteroffensives in 1407–9; the armies which besieged the rebels at Aberystwyth and Harlech marched from England to their targets without visiting, needing or being supplied by any of the castles in Wales. While some rebels sought pardons at castles in the later years of the revolt, some of the more notable submissions, such as at Bala in 1414, took place in the open air of the Welsh communities. Although the rebels eventually lost this conflict, they had proved the castles largely irrelevant when dealing with this sort of popular insurgency.

A further deficiency of the crown's strategy for Wales was its inflexibility. The government reorganised its military structure for Wales on several occasions and replaced its commanders equally frequently. The problem was not that the commanders were necessarily incapable, they were seeking to implement an inadequate strategy. In fact many of the commanders sent to Wales are perceived as being among the best of their generation, with perhaps Prince Henry, Henry Percy junior and Thomas, earl of Arundel as the most widely lauded. To some degree this was another flaw in the English system which placed dependence on a commander's position within a strict social hierarchy, rather than on his proven abilities. While this might be an acceptable approach in conventional wars against similarly structured enemy armies, insurgencies are no respecter of rank or privilege, and peasants can topple kings. Not one of the Welsh war leaders was even a knight, none were ranked higher than squire according to the English system of social rank, although several enjoyed far higher status in native Welsh hierarchy. However, these mostly low-born men outfought, outmanoeuvred and outthought all strata of England's nobility sent against them, including a king, princes, dukes, earls, lords, barons and knights. It is little wonder that perhaps two of England's most consistently effective commanders in Wales were relatively low-ranking nobles, but were capable soldiers. The first, Richard, baron Grey of Codnor, was a highly talented soldier, as was a border gentry knight, Sir John Greyndore, who also knew Welsh terrain well. Their abilities and knowledge enabled them to stand out among those of higher social status.[1] However, the staggering fullness of the Welsh victory at Bryn Glas demonstrated the disparity in ability between the leaders of the opposing forces. This is characterised by their choice of battlefield, the drawing of their adversaries into terrain disadvantageous for them, and then swiftly executing decisive tactics. In the case of Bryn Glas, this probably involved ambushing the enemy in plain sight from within their own ranks, having infiltrated a rebel unit into the enemy army, and then breaking Mortimer's forces with a downhill charge. This martial capability and ruthlessness – as the Welsh destroyed the entire force opposing them – demonstrated a level of mastery significantly beyond that of the experienced English command team opposing them.

However, for much of the revolt, the Welsh were more successful in the field than crown forces. Superficially, this might seem a surprise; but many had served in England's armies in France, Scotland and Ireland, others had gone on crusade, while some had served under French colours. While England could field equally experienced forces, fighting for the kings of England had given the Welsh perfect insight not only into how the English military system functioned, but also which enemy tactics had posed them the greatest difficulty. Having an understanding of how the English conducted operations, including invasions, *chevauchées*, garrisoning and supply methods, handed the Welsh an advantage. During the years when the Welsh fought, up to autumn 1405, they clearly employed a version of asymmetric warfare appropriate to their context. This entailed unseen movement, intimidation, the mounting of rapid, surprise attacks where the enemy had to defend or was not expecting them, and drawing the enemy to terrain advantageous to the rebels. A good example of attacking the enemy's weak points was the repeated, successful raiding of the royal expeditionary forces' baggage trains, where the army kept its food and treasury. On one occasion the rebels helped themselves to Prince Henry's personal wardrobe, stealing his clothes and jewels. While this harassment was useful, another more potent example was the systematic targeting of the enemy's food stocks, evidenced by the damage wrought in England's agriculturally productive border counties, as well as the burning of the fields around Kidwelly, Milford and Carmarthen. Infiltration was another classic guerrilla tactic in which the Welsh were highly effective. It appears as if Glyn Dŵr was able to turn or infiltrate the personal retinue of his local nemesis, Reginald, Lord Grey of Ruthin. He was lured out by a feint against his castle only to fall captive in a prepared ambush, having apparently been led there by Welshmen in his entourage. Similarly, but on a larger scale, the rebels also appear to have executed a startlingly effective ploy by infiltrating a unit of archers into Mortimer's army of the March shortly before the battle of Bryn Glas. This Trojan Horse moment appears to have been a decisive factor in their victory in open battle against a significant English force. On an even larger scale, the work of insurgent infiltrators seems to have been funda-mental in turning a county to declare itself for the rebels. The fact that they caused the anglicised, well-controlled border county of Flintshire to turn red in 1403 was a striking success.

As a guerrilla movement, the Welsh rebels proved to be a more than competent force. Moreover, they clearly showed the ability to evolve strategically, which was something that crown forces struggled, even failed to do. While their non-conventional warfare methods had gained them the upper hand before the end of 1401, during the next year they were able to win a small battle at Ruthin, capturing Lord Grey, and annihilated Mortimer's army in open battle, causing shockwaves which reached the king. That battle was later recalled by Shakespeare and earned a place, however small, in England's cultural fabric. The following year, the Welsh rebels behaved more like a conventional army in the field; the leader wrote letters of array, summoning nobles and their troops to join him on campaign. They mustered at a given place and marched against a sweep of enemy castles, suppressing crown forces, taking castles and storming Henry's regional capital and the English borough with the highest population in Wales, Carmarthen. Around the same time, the rebel leader took oaths of allegiance from other native leaders and the people of entire regions, clearly acting as the ruler of those areas. This might be the earliest identifiable point where the revolt could be said to have reached a critical mass; even if the authorities returned Owain's estates at that point and passed laws integrating the Welsh as social, legal and economic equals, this revolt was highly likely to run its course irrespective.

Had the French army of 1404, which English and French sources independently described as being between 12,000 and 15,000 armoured men and horses, landed in Wales and occupied the castles as proposed, then a different and much larger conflict would have been fought in Wales. There was a strong possibility that Wales would have become a French-supported territory for a time, similar perhaps to contemporary Scotland or Genoa. The margin of the eventual Welsh defeat might have been as thin as Jacques de Bourbon's whimsical pursuit of a love interest. The convergence of the rebels' military and diplomatic efforts came in the form of the 1405 French expedition; the physical expression of the alliance between Glyn Dŵr and the French. Up to that point, the rebels had proven to be an impressive, well-led, mobile, flexible guerrilla and conventional force, capable of developing and adapting militarily, politically and diplomatically.

It was in the political and diplomatic spheres that the resolution would be found, as with any conflict. Initially, the rebels also performed unexpectedly well in this sphere too, but it would be due to successes in these domains that the English would eventually gain sufficient advantage to enable them to asphyxiate the revolt. Similarly to its military efforts, the government's political solutions in Wales were woefully inadequate. The diagnosis of the problem and the possible attendant solutions led to the king deploying on an annual, two-week procession of a Welsh region as a vain effort to resolve the conflict. Politically, the scapegoating of Owain and two of the Tudors, as well as the knee-jerk reaction of confirming the harsh anti-Welsh legal ordinances, were catastrophic decisions in a quest for an early and an easy peace. Despite these measures, Owain appeared tractable for a number of years, but opportunities to deal intelligently, leniently or fairly with him were repeatedly spurned by a dismissive, arrogant parliament. While seeking resolution with the crown, Owain also looked further afield, attempting diplomatic links with the Scots and the Irish. While these initially bore no fruit, they show that Owain and his council could make connections outside Wales. He certainly had help in the pursuit of diplomatic ties, but in his missives to Welsh nobles and to foreign powers, the same voice, Owain's voice, appears consistently distinguishable. Therefore, it seems likely that Owain directed the diplomatic wording of his letters throughout the revolt. In Wales, the rebels attracted numerous clergymen from the beginning, and their connections likely enabled Owain to directly contact both popes. Equally, churchmen facilitated contact between the various noble courts. Owain also obtained support, perhaps unexpectedly, from English nobles and clergy disaffected with Henry. The Welsh also received notable support from the upper echelons of French society. While the patronage of the powerful duke of Orleans was evident, the less direct but also effective backing of writers such as Jean Creton or Michel Pintoin also assisted the Welsh cause in the French court. During the early years of the revolt, as the Orleanists grappled their way to power, the movements in French politics also helped the rise of the rebels, as did English political division and weakness. The negotiation of an alliance with the faction which would eventually prevail in the French civil war, and consequently roll the English out of France, was another pinnacle of rebel success. It also presented a significant danger to England, for while the Welsh could not invade, the French could.

Perhaps the Welsh–French alliance was the catalyst for a series of remarkable performances by Henry's diplomats. In their dealings with the French they seemed to act precisely in the ways that they failed to do in Wales. They correctly assessed that Louis of Orleans and his allies were their key adversaries and they worked assiduously to weaken the duke's position while strengthening that of England and its friends on the continent. The English ambassadors in France appear to have been given more freedom and trust to conduct affairs than their counterparts in Wales. While remaining in close contact with Henry and his council, they also reached out to other elements in the French court with whom they could do business, notably the Burgundians. This use of an interagency approach, within the context of the period, included building relations with those who could influence affairs or were somehow connected with the issues of the moment. These groups included French nobles, wealthy Flemish traders, Channel fishermen and surrounding powers such as the Bretons and the Hanseatic states. These actions and their largely positive conclusions all significantly helped Henry's ambassadors make their arguments credible in France. Their successful inducement of those who could speak in the French parliament and at Charles VI's court marked a critical success for the English.

In their other roles, Henry's ambassadors in France were also able to return significant intelligence on affairs of interest to England. In Wales, however, the government also engaged in intelligence gathering with mixed fortunes. On occasions it worked excellently, as the forewarning of Owain's plans to sue for a truce in 1405 demonstrated. No doubt it also gained valuable information from the small number of Welshmen who stayed in the service of their local English nobles, irrespective of the legal ordinances declared by parliament. At other times, these efforts were less successful, with locally hired scouts leading troops into ambushes. Overall, within Wales, the rebels had the upper hand in matters concerning intelligence, military and political affairs. To some degree, this was due to the willing collaboration of English nobles and clergymen who opposed the new king. In the absence of progress in Wales, successes on the continent likely persuaded Henry's government to focus its efforts on France; they were clearly correct to do so.

There, they appeared to adopt a long-term strategy based on flexibly engaging with their adversaries. When they suffered setbacks, they tended to avoid making dramatic knee-jerk reactions, as showed by the offer to extend the safety agreement for fishermen despite Orleanist attacks on the Isle of Wight and the adjacent Channel coast. Although parliament still issued ordinances against the 'aliens', notably the French, Bretons and Genoese, found in England, particularly in its ports, these matters were introduced at a beneficial moment for the English cause. These small, perhaps easy successes helped build towards an advantageous position in France, just as this approach had served the rebels well in Wales.

Another factor which led to overall Welsh success prior to 1407 was the crown's insistence on imposing a strategy which only appeared to have one main thrust: seeking a single decisive confrontation. In contrast, the rebels conducted a campaign which targeted the enemy's strategy, rather than his forces. England's strategy for Wales rested on the castles, with repeated royal expeditions intent on seeking a forceful resolution. By isolating the castles and attacking them across the length and breadth of Wales, the government was obliged to spend its limited financial resources and spread out its forces. When combined with the withdrawal of civilian obedience and the rise in rebel military strength, which in turn led to the collapse of revenue from Wales, the castles soon proved to be expensive drains on the royal coffers, offering a negligible return for continuing to support them. The rebels effectively rendered useless the annual invasions, by avoiding or even leading them vainly around the countryside. They too became expensive, pointless and ultimately humiliating for the king of England. The Welsh also sought to construct a series of alliances with foreign powers and English rebel factions violently opposed to Henry. In France, Henry's ambassadors emulated this approach by befriending and assisting one belligerent courtly faction against another, and similarly brokering alliances with the relevant powers, the Burgundians and the Bretons. By successfully augmenting friction between the natural divisions in the French court, and by exploiting those cracks further, the English brilliantly reduced the French ability to project its power overseas. Although the English did not cause the French civil war, they did assist the descent into fratricidal conflagration. Once the civil war was on in earnest, Henry's envoys were able not only to combat the French adversary's strategy, but they could even influence its direction in that conflict; the rebels had no means of influencing Henry's court from within. England's ambassadors performed remarkably well in this task, and certainly created and shaped a solution for the French problem which suited Henry. When a truce with the Bretons was in place and the French courtly factions were busy seeking alliances with England and fighting one another, Henry's diplomats had created a window of opportunity enabling the government to assault the Welsh fortresses. With uncharacteristic speed, the authorities gathered and thrust an army under Prince Henry against Aberystwyth. There, they found the Welsh garrisons prepared to defend themselves against conventional siege warfare. Perhaps here, the English had the military edge, at last. Earlier, they had failed to adapt their forces to resemble the flexible, fast-moving and highly effective Welsh, but at Aberystwyth, the enclosed rebel garrison was more akin to those they were used to fighting in France. Even so, the Welsh held out for almost a year and a half. Although Harlech succumbed more quickly, helped in part by an extreme winter, the campaigns needed to wrest two fortresses from the Welsh still took almost two years to prosecute. The rebels continued to resist, however, and the failure of the English to adapt their forces to those of the enemy and the terrain allowed the revolt to continue, occasionally demonstrating its power. In opposition to the ongoing, if withering, revolt, the crown was able to flood areas with troops to forcefully compel communities to pay fines and swear oaths of allegiance to the crown. Whether genuine or contrition, repeating these methods helped to deter rebel cohesion and consequently assisted the slow fracturing of rebel influence, although this approach failed to address the causes of the rebellion. This style of attritional suppression helped bring about a submission of 600 rebels in a key district around Bala in 1414; a full five years after the fall of Harlech, the rebels were still around in significant numbers. In restructuring the political and economic environment to its pre-revolt state, returning to the pattern of near-total English dominance through privileges based on ethnicity, the rebel state was displaced and pushed into the shadows. This reimposition of previous conditions was supported militarily and order was restored slowly and asymmetrically over decades. However, such a settlement would only prolong the animosity between excluded native and privileged settler.

External factors had certainly helped England improve its position in Europe and in Britain, most obviously, the French civil war. The Great Schism also helped polarise European powers and, in France's case, led to it diffusing its power into a number of projects centred on northern Italy and Rome, but also including Britain, the region where the German Empire bordered north-eastern France, and in the low countries. This also dissipated French power at a key moment. The rise of Owain Glyn Dŵr was effected by a plurality of factors, including his own intelligence and leadership skills, powerfully supported by a talented group of warriors and ecclesiastics, encouraged by French amity. The fall of Owain Glyn Dŵr was largely occasioned by events outside his control: French in-fighting and English diplomatic success. The French proved to be highly honourable allies, just weak at key moments. Owain had backed the right faction; the Armagnacs would eventually prevail under Charles VII. Even before Maredudd ab Owain accepted a pardon, slight, perhaps imperceptible, changes were taking place that would reorganise and consolidate the French forces which would begin to decisively push back the English. Within a decade of Maredudd's submission, the French had won a string of battle victories, Charles VII had been crowned king of France at Reims, Paris had again fallen to the French and Joan of Arc had briefly played her part in the Hundred Years' War. The Welsh had narrowly missed out on the decisive French resurgence by a handful of years.

The aftermath of the revolt has been substantially covered elsewhere, most notably in Rees Davies's *Revolt*. However, the overall picture painted is one of the imposition of crushing financial penalties and stringent application of the anti-Welsh legislation. While this was no doubt true, it cannot be ignored that in the years which followed, Welshmen gained lands, wealth and titles through their military efforts in France and then during the Wars of the Roses. It appears that more Welshmen were knighted in the generation after the revolt than had been during the whole of the fourteenth century. This is indicative of a change in English attitudes also, which must be connected to the revolt. Subsequently, a small number of Welshmen became earls and one of the Tudors famously became king of England. While all of the tangible elements of the rebellion, such as the parliament and that fledgling independent state, had been washed away by the restoration of English authority over Wales, the Welsh folk memory of Owain, a warm and enduring one, has lasted the centuries. He remains a figure of striking historical significance to this day.[2]

Notes

Acknowledgements

1 *Welsh Records*, pp. 23–54, 103–6, 108–10; *OGC*, pp. 431–4, 497–550.

Introduction

1 *Revolt*, p. 229.
2 R. Griffiths, 'Prince Henry's War: Armies, Garrisons and Supply during the Glyndŵr Rising', *BBCS* 34 (1987): 165.
3 Marchant, *Chronicles*, pp. 121–3.
4 Although this tallies with one of the thrusts of Rees Davies's work, notably in *The Age of Conquest, Wales 1063–1415* (Oxford, 1991), p. viii; also described in Robert Bartlett, 'Heartland and Border: The Mental and Physical Geography of Medieval Europe', in *PIMA*, p. 23.
5 *Glendower,* pp. 37–9, 80–2, 126–46; Davies, *Revolt*, pp. 98, 103, 151, 193, 199, 263, 293; T. Pugh, *Henry V and the Southampton Plot* (Stroud, 1998), pp. 40–1; D. Moore, *The Welsh Wars of Independence* (Stroud, 2005), pp. 169–85, 264, 269; H. Pryce, *J. E. Lloyd and the Creation of Welsh History: Renewing a Nation's Past* (Cardiff, 2011); G. Brough, 'Owain's Revolt? Glyn Dŵr's Role in the Outbreak of the Rebellion', *Studies in History, Archaeology, Religion and Conservation* 2:1 (2015): 1–30.
6 *Glendower*, p. 146.
7 D. Kilcullen, *Counterinsurgency* (London, 2010), p. 30.
8 The term, 'The Winds of War', while appropriate, is also an acknowledgement of my initial mistranslation of *'wynt o ryvel'* in relation to *Glendower*, p. 150.
9 The English translation in *OGC*, pp. 154–7, is a translation of Bellaguet's inaccurate French text, not of the troublesome Latin original.
10 J. Beverley Smith, 'Distinction and Diversity: The Common Lawyers and the Law of Wales', in *PIMA*, pp. 139–52.
11 Davies, *Age of Conquest*, pp. 372–4, 385–8, 408–12, 419–21, 431–43; *Revolt,* pp. 173, 217, 224, 290.
12 R. Frame, 'The Bruces in Ireland, 1315–18', *Irish Historical Studies* 19 (1974):

3–37; Davies, *Age of Conquest*, pp. 387–8, 437; Carr, *Owen of Wales*, pp. 72–3, 78–9; Carr, *Medieval Wales*, p. 89; Barrell, *Medieval Scotland*, pp. 119–20, 124.

13 Carr, 'Welshmen and the Hundred Years' War', pp. 26–7; Davies, *Age of Conquest*, pp. 410–11, 437, 445; Carr, *Owen of Wales*, pp. 78–9; Walker, *Medieval Wales*, pp. 163–4; Carr, *Medieval Wales*, pp. 91–2; *Revolt*, pp. 82–6; Moore, *Welsh Wars of Independence*, pp. 165–6.

14 E. Owen, 'Owain Lawgoch – Yeuain de Galles: Some Facts and Suggestions', *The Transactions of the Honourable Society of the Cymmrodorion* (1899–1900): 6–105; A. D. Carr, *Owen of Wales: The End of the House of Gwynedd* (Cardiff, 1991); Spencer Gavin Smith, 'What Does a Mercenary Leave Behind? The Archaeological Evidence for the Estates of Owain Lawgoch', in J. France, ed., *Mercenaries and Paid Men: The Mercenary Identity in the Middle Ages* (Leiden, 2008), pp. 317–29.

15 *Glendower*, pp. 18–27; A. Goodman, 'Owain Glyndŵr before 1400', *WHR 5* (1970–71): 67–70; *Revolt*, pp. 144–50; Ll. Smith, 'Glyn Dŵr, Owain (c.1359–c.1416)', *ODNB*, 2008.

16 L. Thorpe, trans. *Gerald of Wales: The Journey Through Wales / The Description of Wales* (Harmondsworth, 1978), pp. 182, 230–1; *OGC*, pp. 12–33, 71–3, 263–97, 315–20.

17 R. Loomis and D. Johnston, *Medieval Welsh Poems: An Anthology* (Binghampton, 1992), pp. 115–17; D. Johnston, trans., *Iolo Goch: Poems* (Llandysul, 1993), pp. 34–8.

18 Webb, 'Creton', pp. 104–6, 113; Williams, *Chronicque de la Traïson et Mort de Richart Deux roy Dengleterre* (London, 1846), pp. 211–12; Clarke and Galbraith, 'Deposition', pp. 125–81; Given-Wilson, *Chronicles*, pp. 137–52, 155; Bennett, 'Richard II and the Wider Realm', in Goodman and Gillespie, *Richard II: The Art of Kingship* (Oxford, 1999), p. 199.

1: The Outbreak of Revolt

1 F. S. Haydon, ed., *Eulogium Historiarum*, vol. 3 (London, 1863), p. 388 (L. *'Et illi de parliamento dixerunt se de scurris nudipedibus non curare'*).

2 *Glendower*, pp. 28–41; *Revolt*, pp. 1, 102–7; *OGC*, pp, 36–9, 74–5; Marchant, *Chronicles*, pp. 219–20, 225–6, 229–31, 237.

3 A. G. Bradley, *Owen Glyndwr and the Last Struggle for Welsh Independence, with a Brief Sketch of Welsh History* (London, 1901), pp. 110–29; *Glendower*, pp. 28–4; J. D. Griffith Davies, *Owen Glyn Dŵr* (London, 1934), pp. 28–42; D. Walker, *Medieval Wales* (Cambridge, 1990), pp. 169–70; G. Williams, *Owain Glyndŵr* (Cardiff, 1993), pp. 25–6; *Revolt*, pp. 88, 102–3, 199; A. D. Carr, *Medieval Wales* (Basingstoke, 1995), pp. 108–15.

4   Given-Wilson, *Chronicles*, pp. 36–7; *CAU*, pp. 58–9. See also B. Williams, *Chronicque de la Traïson et Mort de Richart Deux roy Dengleterre*, pp. 188–9; J. Sherborne, 'Richard II's Return to Wales, July 1399', *WHR*, 7 (1974–5), pp. 389–402; Preest, *Chronica Maiora*, p. 307.

5   Clarke and Galbraith, 'Deposition', pp. 125–81; Given-Wilson, *Chronicles*, p. 155.

6   Given-Wilson, *Chronicles*, p. 122; Preest, *Chronica Maiora*, p. 309.

7   Pugh, *Henry V and the Southampton Plot*, p. 39; Given-Wilson, *Chronicles*, pp. 129, 141, 149.

8   Williams, *Chronicque de la Traïson et Mort*, p. 211.

9   Webb, 'Creton', pp. 1–433, 104, 105, 204; Hutchison, *Henry V*, pp. 38–53; J. Taylor, 'Richard II in the Chronicles', in A. Goodman, and J. Gillespie, eds, *Richard II: The Art of Kingship*, p. 34; Given-Wilson *Chronicles*, pp. 7, 134, 138.

10 Webb, 'Creton', pp. 104–6, 113; Given-Wilson, *Chronicles*, pp. 137–52.

11 Williams, *Chronicque de la Traïson et Mort*, pp. 211–12; M. J. Bennett, 'Richard II and the Wider Realm', in Goodman and Gillespie, *Richard II: The Art of Kingship*, p. 199.

12 Webb, 'Creton', pp. 177–8.

13 *Welsh Records*, pp. 104–5, 112–13.

14 P. McNiven, 'The Cheshire Rising of 1400', *BJRL*, 52 (1970): 375–96.

15 *Glendower*, pp. 33–4; Walker, *Medieval Wales*, p. 170; Davies, *A History of Wales*, p. 198; G. Hodges, *Owain Glyn Dŵr and the War of Independence in the Welsh Borders* (Logaston, 1995), pp. 37–42; *Revolt*, pp. 102–3, 237; R. A. Griffiths and R. Thomas, *The Making of the Tudor Dynasty* (Stroud, 1997, orig. 1993), p. 21; C. Barber, *In Search of Owain Glyndŵr* (Abergavenny, 1998), pp. 51–4.

16 H. Ellis, *Original Letters Illustrative of English History* (London, 1827), pp. 3–7; *Glendower*, p. 29; *Revolt*, pp. 102–3, 237.

17 *Revolt*, p. 304.

18 *POPCE*, vol. 1, p. 134 (F. 'de petit reputacion'); Haydon, *Eulogium Historiarum*, vol. 3, p. 388; *Revolt*, p. 107; *CAU*, pp. xlvi–xlvii.

19 *PROME*, vol. 7, p. 403; *PROME*, vol. 8, pp. 3, 7, 9–92 (69, 77–8), 93–153, 403.

20 *Fœdora*, vol. 8, pp. 163–4; *Glendower*, pp. 28–35; *Revolt*, pp. 65–93, 102–6, 153–4; *OGC*, pp 74–5.

21 B. Smith, 'Owain Glyn Dŵr's Raid on Ruthin (1400)', *Transactions of the Denbighshire Historical Society*, 10 (1961): 239–41; R. Ian Jack, 'Owain Glyn Dŵr and the Lordship of Ruthin', *WHR*, 2 (1964–5): 310–11; G. A. Sayles, ed., *Select Cases in the Court of the King's Bench under Richard II, Henry IV and Henry V*, vol. 88 (London, 1971), pp. 114–17; Thomas, 'Oswestry', pp. 117–26; *OGC*, pp 36–43; Marchant, *Chronicles*, pp. 229–31, 237.

22 *Fœdora*, vol. 8, pp. 159–60; Webb, 'Creton', pp. 104–7, 176–8; Ellis, *Letters* pp. 3–4; *CPR 1399–1401*, p. 357; *Revolt*, p. 304.

23 C. A. J. Armstrong, 'Some Examples of the Distribution and Speed of News at the Time of the Wars of the Roses', in R. W. Hunt, W. A. Pantin and R. W. Southern, eds, *Studies in Medieval History Presented to Frederick Maurice Powicke* (Oxford, 1948), pp. 431, 439; *Revolt*, p. 102; G. Brough, 'Owain's Revolt? Glyn Dŵr's Role in the Outbreak of the Rebellion', *Studies in History, Archaeology, Religion and Conservation*, vol. 2:1 (2015): 1–30, 15–16, 19–21.

24 *Welsh Records*, pp. 23, 103–6, 111–14 (L. *'Owynus, Dei gratia princeps Wallie'*, 10 May 1404); *Revolt*, pp. 102–6; *CAU*, pp. 100–1, 148–53, 158–61; *OGC*, 62–7, 82–3. Note: there is a typographical error in the article Brough, 'Owain's Revolt?' where it says that Usk did not mention this, p. 17.

25 Sayles, *Select Cases*, pp. 114, 116–17; Thomas, 'Oswestry', pp. 118, 120, 123.

26 *POPCE*, vol. 1, pp. 173–9; *ANLP*, pp. 308–9; *Revolt*, pp. 106, 182–5; A. Bell, 'The Fourteenth Century Soldier, More Chaucer's Knight or Medieval Career', in France, ed., *Mercenaries and Paid Men*, pp. 301–11; *OGC*, pp. 36–9, 58–60, 68–9.

27 *Fœdora*, vol. 7, p. 540, vol. 8, pp. 113, 125–6, 144–7, 149–50, 155–8; J. Strachey, ed., *Rotuli Parliamentorum ut et Petitiones, et placita in Parliamento tempore Edwardi R. III*, vol. 2 (London, 1776), pp. 147, 362; N. H. Nicolas, *History of the Royal Navy* (London, 1847), vol. 2, pp. 83, 155, 309–10; J. L. Kirby, ed., *Calendar of Signet Letters of Henry IV and Henry V (1399–1422)* (London, 1978), p. 28; Sayles, *Select Cases*, pp. 213–15; *CAU*, pp. 94–5; *PROME*, vol. 4, p. 372, vol. 6, pp. 31, 70–1; *OGC*, pp. 36–7; B. Lambert and W. M. Ormrod, 'Friendly Foreigners; International Warfare, Resident Aliens and the Early History of Denization in England, c. 1250–c. 1400', *English Historical Review*, vol. 130, no. 542 (2015): 14–21.

28 *CFR, 1399–1405*, pp. 129–30; Sayles, ed., *Select Cases*, pp. 114–17; *Revolt* (use of the term 'ethnic' to distinguish Welsh from English), pp. 173, 217, 224, 290; P. Morgan, 'Cheshire and Wales', in *PIMA*, pp. 208–10.

29 Thomas, 'Oswestry', pp. 117–26.

30 Brown, 'The English Campaign in Scotland, 1400', in Hearder and Loyn, eds, *British Government and Administration*, pp. 40–54 (Henry IV managed eight miles per day in Scotland in 1400); D. Green, *Edward the Black Prince: Power in Medieval Europe* (London, 2007), p. 35; H. J. Hewitt, *The Organization of War under Edward III* (Barnsley, 2004), pp. 40–7 (this puts twenty miles per day as an acceptable high-end figure for unarmoured movement by foot in peacetime); R. A. Griffiths, 'Crossing the Frontiers of the English Realm in the Fifteenth Century', in *PIMA*, p. 212; Brough, 'Owain's Revolt?', pp. 14–16.

31 Clarke and Galbraith, 'Deposition', pp. 175–6 (where fighting at Welshpool

appears to occur in 1401, not 1400); *Glendower*, pp. 31–2; *Revolt*, pp. 102, 343, nn.1, 2; Thomas, 'Oswestry', pp. 117–26.

32 Brown, 'The English Campaign in Scotland, 1400', in Hearder and Loyn, *British Government and Administration*, pp. 40–54; C. J. Neville, 'Scotland, the Percies and the Law in 1400', in G. Dodd and D. Biggs, *Henry IV: The Establishment of the Regime, 1399–1406* (Woodbridge, 2003), p. 73.

33 *CPR 1399–1401*, p. 555; *Glendower*, pp. 32–5; Thomas, 'Oswestry', pp. 117–26.

34 *Fœdora*, vol. 8, pp. 163–4; *OGC*, pp. 34–7.

35 *Fœdora*, vol. 8, pp. 163–4, 181–2; Clarke and Galbraith, 'Deposition', pp. 173–4; *CPR 1399–1401*, pp. 392, 451; *CAU*, pp. 86–9. Note: Lloyd also believed that there were other Welsh risings before September 1400, *Glendower*, p. 29, n. 2.

2: Rebels and Risings

1 *CAU*, pp. 144–5.

2 *POPCE*, vol. 1, pp. 151–3, 166; *CCR 1399–1402*, p. 389; *ANLP*, pp. 294–5; *Revolt*, p. 105; *CAU*, pp. 144–5.

3 *Revolt*, pp. 282–7; *PROME*, vol. 8, pp. 93–153; *OGC*, pp. 44–52.

4 Marchant, *Chronicles*, pp. 152–82.

5 *Revolt*, pp. 222–7; *OGC*, pp. 50–3.

6 *POPCE*, vol. 1, pp. 147, 150; *Glendower*, pp. 37–9; *Revolt*, pp. 52, 103–4, 199; Marchant, *Chronicles*, p. 238.

7 *Fœdora*, vol. 8, p. 209; *CPR 1399–1401*, pp. 447, 475.

8 *Glendower*, pp. 37–9; *Revolt*, pp. 52, 103–4, 199; *CAU*, p. 128. Repeated in the 'Dieulacres Chronicle' which borrows from *CAU*, although the number executed is given as eight: Clarke and Galbraith, 'Deposition', pp. 173–4 and Marchant, *Chronicles*, p. 238.

9 *CAU*, pp. 128–33.

10 *CPR 1399–1401*, pp. 518, 520; *CFR 1399–1405*, pp. 84, 94; *Glendower*, p. 40; Hutchison, *Henry V*, pp. 71–83; CAU, pp. 128–33; *Revolt*, pp. 64, 82, 226.

11 *POPCE*, vol. 1, pp. 152–3; *CCR, 1399–1402*, pp. 389–90; *Glendower*, p. 40; Kirby, *Calendar of Signet Letters*, p. 28; *Revolt*, p. 190; *OGC*, pp. 54–7.

12 *CAU*, pp. 148–51; *OGC*, pp. 64–5.

13 D. Watt, ed., *Scotichronicon by Walter Bower* (Edinburgh, 1996), vol. 1, pp. 27, 31, 33, 37, 45, 55, 67, vol. 2, p. 273, vol. 3, p. 173, vol. 4, pp. 143, 183, vol. 7, pp. 448–51, vol. 8, p. 103; *Revolt*, p. 189; *CAU*, pp. 147, 151, 199–210; Marchant, *Chronicles*, pp. 164–70.

14 N. Grèvy-Pons et al., *Jean de Montreuil, Opera* (Paris and Turin, 1964) vol. 2, pp. 96, 113, 201–2; E. R. Chamberlin, *The Count of Virtue: Giangaleazzo*

Visconti, Duke of Milan (London, 1965), p. 71; Watt, ed., *Scotichronicon*, vol. 8, pp. 106–9; *CAU*, pp. 147, 151, 199–210; Marchant, *Chronicles*, pp. 164–71.

15 H. Fulton, 'Owain Glyn Dŵr and the Use of Prophecies', *Studia Celtica*, 46 (2005): 105–21.

16 *CPR, 1401–5*, p. 22; *CAU*, pp. 148–9, n.2.

17 *POPCE*, vol. 1, pp. 151–3; *ANLP*, pp. 292–3; *OGC*, pp 54–7.

18 *Glendower*, pp. 39, 150–1; *Revolt*, p. 266.

19 *CAU*, pp. 144–5.

20 *POPCE*, vol. 1, pp. 151–3; *CPR 1399–1401*, pp. 518, 520; Clarke and Galbraith, 'Deposition', pp. 175–6; *ANLP*, pp. 294–5, 301–2; *Glendower*, p. 44; *Revolt*, pp. 105, 278, 333; *CAU*, pp. 144–5; R. Griffiths, 'Owain Glyn Dŵr's Invasion of the Central March of Wales in 1402: the Evidence of Clerical Taxation', *Studia Celtica*, 46 (2012): 115; *OGC*, pp. 74–7.

21 *Glendower*, pp. 40, 42–4; *Revolt*, pp. 56, 104–6, 238, 310; *CAU*, pp. 144–5; *OGC*, pp. 76–7.

22 *CAU*, pp. 146–7; *OGC*, 58–63.

23 My adaptation of *ANLP*, p. 281 and *OGC*, pp. 58–9.

24 *CAU*, pp. 150–3; *OGC*, pp. 64–7.

25 *Revolt*, pp. 181–5.

3: 'Owen ... the Rod of God's Anger'

1 *CAU*, p. 161.

2 R. Griffiths, 'Prince Henry, Wales and the Royal Exchequer, 1400–3', *BBCS*, vol. 32 (1985): 202–13; R. Griffiths, 'Prince Henry's War: Armies, Garrisons and Supplies During the Glyndŵr Rising', *BBCS*, vol. 34 (1987): 165–73; H. Watt, '"On Account of the Frequent Attacks and Invasions of the Welsh": The Effect of the Glyn Dŵr Rebellion on Tax Collection in England', in G. Dodd and D. Biggs, *The Reign of Henry IV: Rebellion and Survival, 1403–1413* (Woodbridge, 2008), pp. 48–81; R. Griffiths, 'Owain Glyn Dŵr's Invasion of the Central March of Wales in 1402: The Evidence of Clerical Taxation', *Studia Celtica*, 46 (2012): 111–22.

3 *Glendower*, pp. 48–9; *Revolt*, pp. 106–7; *CAU*, pp. 154–61; *OGC*, p. 77; Marchant, *Chronicles*, pp. 56–7, 220–1, 226–7, 233–4, 237–8.

4 *CPR, 1401–5*, pp. 155–6, 171; *Revolt*, p. 233.

5 Griffiths, 'Owain Glyn Dŵr's Invasion', p. 113.

6 Note: There appears to have been two, perhaps three men named Rhys Gethin. They came from Nantconwy, Builth and, possibly, Gower. The former and the latter also had well-known brothers, Hywel Coetmor and

Morgan Gethin, respectively. See *Glendower*, p. 66 and *Revolt*, pp. 58, 199, 205; C. Fychan, *Pwy Oedd Rhys Gethin?* (Aberystwyth, 2007).

7 http://www.historyofparliamentonline.org/volume/1386-1421/ member/ [accessed 29/07/15].

8 *Glendower*, pp. 50–2; *Revolt*, p. 102; Griffiths, 'Owain Glyn Dŵr's Invasion', pp. 116–17; *OGC*, p. 79; http://www.historyofparliamentonline.org/ volume/1386-1421/member/bere-kynard-de-la-1402; http:// www. historyofparliamentonline.org/volume/ 1386-1421/member/whitney-sir-robert-i-1402 [accessed 06/08/15]; Marchant, *Chronicles*, pp. 221–2, 234–5, 239–40.

9 P. J. Lucas, ed., *John Capgrave, Abbreuiacion of Cronicles* (Oxford, 1983), p. 219; Preest, *Chronica Maiora*, p. 322; *OGC*, pp. 78–9; Marchant, *Chronicles*, pp. 44, 53–4, 65, 105, 107, 158–61, 216, 221, 235, 239–40. Note: 'Rees a Gythe' is more likely to be 'Rhys Gethin' than 'Rhys ap Gruffudd' as it appears in the *OGC*/Marchant translation.

10 *POPCE*, vol. 1, pp. 185–6; Griffiths, 'Prince Henry's War', pp. 165–73; D. H. Evans, 'An incident on the Dee during the Glyn Dŵr rebellion', *Denbighshire Historical Society Transactions*, vol. 37 (1988): 5–40; *OGC*, pp. 66–9; Marchant, *Chronicles*, pp. 222, 224, 227, 236, 239.

11 *Revolt*, pp. 114–15, 276; Griffiths, 'Owain Glyn Dŵr's Invasion', p. 112.

12 *CAU*, p. 161.

13 *Glendower*, pp. 54–4; *CAU*, p. 161; Griffiths, 'Owain Glyn Dŵr's Invasion', p. 117.

14 Bower, *Scotichronicon*, vol. 8, pp. 42–9; *Revolt*, pp. 180–6.

15 C. Given-Wilson, '"The Quarrels of Old Women": Henry IV, Louis of Orléans, and Anglo–French Chivalric Challenges in the Early Fifteenth Century', in G. Dodd and D. Biggs, eds, *The Reign of Henry IV: Rebellion and Survival, 1403–13* (Woodbridge, 2008), pp. 28–47.

16 *POPCE*, ii, pp. 59–60; *Glendower*, p. 58; *OGC*, pp. 68–9, 313. Lloyd's and Livingston's dispute of Nicholas's 1401 dating for the Percy envoy to Mortimer seems accurate.

17 N. Saul, *Richard II* (New Haven, 1997), pp. 424–9; A. Tuck, 'Richard II (1367–1400)', *ODNB*, 2004 [accessed 06/08/15]; *OGC*, pp. 70–1.

18 R. Griffiths, 'Some Secret Supporters of Owain Glyndŵr?', *BIHR*, vol. 37 (1964): 77–100; *Revolt*, pp. 185–6; J. Ross, 'Seditious Activities: The Conspiracy of Maud de Vere, Countess of Oxford, 1403–4', in L. Clark, ed., *The Fifteenth Century: Authority and Subversion* (Woodbridge, 2003), pp. 25–41.

4: Owain, Prince

1 *Welsh Records*, p. 113.

2 *Glendower*, pp. 60–2; *Revolt*, pp. 111–15, 280; *OGC*, pp. 80–3.

3 *Glendower*, pp. 31–5, 40–1, 53, 64–7, 76, 131, 140–2 (Note: There is confusion over the identity of 'Rhys Ddu': Lloyd names Rhys ap Tudor, p. 34, and three other men named 'Rhys', pp. 67, 131, n. 2; *Revolt*, pp. 199, 205 favours Rhys ap Gruffydd ap Llywelyn ab Ieuan as 'Rhys Ddu'); Griffiths, 'Prince Henry's War', p. 165; *OGC*, pp. 84–7.

4 *Welsh Records*, pp. 105–6, 113–14. Note: I have included Owain's spelling of his own name and changed Matthews's 'behoved' to 'suited'.

5 *Glendower*, pp. 63–9; *Revolt*, pp. 25, 111–12; *OGC*, pp. 84–9.

6 Marchant, *Chronicles*, p. 1.

7 R. Griffiths, *Conquerors and Conquered in Medieval Wales* (New York, 1994), pp. 125–6; Marchant, *Chronicles*, pp. 124–31, 152–61, 227.

8 *Revolt*, pp. 180–6; A. L. Brown, 'Percy, Thomas, earl of Worcester (*c.* 1343–1403)' (2008); S. J. Lang, 'Bradmore, John (d. 1412)'; Simon Walker, 'Percy, Sir Henry (1364–1403)' (2008); A. L. Brown, Henry Summerson, 'Henry IV (1367–1413)' (2010), all entries in *ODNB*, 2004; online edn, January 2008 and 2010, www.oxforddnb.com [accessed 10/09/15].

9 *Saint-Denys*, vol. 3, p. 359; *Revolt*, pp. 188–9; Griffiths, 'Prince Henry's War', pp. 170–3; *OGC*, pp. 80–1, 88–91, 102–3.

10 *POPCE*, vol. 1, pp. 217–18, 270–4; *CPR, 1401–5*, p. 26; *CPR, 1405–8*, pp. 285, 298, 311, 438; *Revolt*, pp 114–15, 240–1.

11 *Glendower*, pp. 63–76; *Revolt*, pp. 111–15, 230–1, 238–9; *OGC*, pp. 88–91.

12 *Revolt*, p. 275.

13 *Revolt*, pp. 273–5.

14 W. H. Bliss and J. A. Twemlow, eds, *Calendar of Entries in the Papal Registers Relating to Great Britain and Ireland, Papal Letters, Volume 5, AD 1396–1404* (London, 1904), pp. 30, 44, 623–4.

15 *Revolt*, pp. 211–14; *CAU*, pp. xxi–xxxvi, xlvii–l, lv–lvii, lxxix–lxxxvi.

16 *Revolt*, pp. 115–18; Griffiths, 'Prince Henry's War', pp. 166, 169–70; Watt, 'On account of the frequent attacks and invasions of the Welsh', in Dodd and Biggs, *The Reign of Henry IV: Rebellion and Survival*, pp. 48–81; Griffiths, 'Owain Glyn Dŵr's Invasion', pp. 111–22; *OGC*, pp. 80–1, 88–103.

17 *Fœdera*, vol. 8, pp. 356–8; Johnes, *Monstrelet*, p. 102; *Saint-Denys*, vol. 3, pp. 170–81, 197–201; Riley, *Ypodigma Neustriæ*, pp. 403–5; Douët-d'Arcq, *Monstrelet*, pp. 80–1; *Revolt*, pp. 192, 231; Preest, *Chronica Maiora*, pp. 349, 361; J.-C. Cassard, 'Tanguy Du Chastel l'homme de Montereau', pp. 83–104, and M. Jones, 'Les Du Chastel au sein de la noblesse bretonne', pp. 105–23,

in Y. Coativy, ed., *Le Trémazan des Du Chastel: du château fort à la ruine* (Brest-Landunvez, 2006).

18 *POPCE,* vol. 1, 221, vol. 2, pp. 83–4; *CPR, 1401–5,* p. 319; *Glendower,* pp. 77–82; J. Gwynfor Jones, ed., *The History of the Gwydir Family and Memoirs* (Llandysul, 1990), p. 118.

19 R. Blanchard, *Lettres et Mandements de Jean V, duc de Bretagne* (Nantes, 1890), vol. 5, p. 46; Lannette-Claverie, *Collection Joursanvault,* pp. 11, 33, 38, 90, 199, 206, 209, 260, 313.

20 *POPCE,* vol. 1, p. 221, vol. 2, pp. 83–4; *RHL Henry IV,* vol. 2, pp. 15–17, 22–4; *Glendower,* pp. 80–2; *Revolt,* pp. 193. Note: Lloyd and Davies disagree on the year of these events in Anglesey.

21 *Glendower,* pp. 71–6; Griffiths, 'Prince Henry, Wales and the Royal Exchequer, 1400–3', pp. 202–13; Griffiths, 'Prince Henry's War', pp. 165–73; *Revolt,* pp. 112–16; Watt, 'On Account of the Frequent Attacks and Invasions of the Welsh', in Dodd and Biggs, *The Reign of Henry IV: Rebellion and Survival,* pp. 48–81; Griffiths, 'Owain Glyn Dŵr's Invasion', pp. 111–22.

22 *Glendower,* p. 82; *Revolt,* pp. 163–4.

23 Ellis, *Original Letters,* p. 43; Hingeston, *RHL Henry IV,* vol. 2, pp. 76–9; *Glendower,* p. 101; *Revolt,* pp. 164, 220.

24 Vaughan, *Valois Burgundy,* pp. 3–13, 48–161, esp. 95–122.

25 Vaughan, *Valois Burgundy,* pp. 25, 98, 100, 108; J. H. M. Salmon, *Society in Crisis, France in the Sixteenth century* (London, 1975), p. 68.

26 Ellis, *Original Letters,* p. 43; *RHL Henry IV,* vol. 2, pp. 76–9, *Welsh Records,* pp. 52, 96; *Glendower,* pp. 101, 119; *Revolt,* pp. 163–4, 220.

27 Gabriel, 'Wales and the Avignon Papacy', pp. 70–86; *Welsh Records,* pp. 75, 81, 85, 110, 123–5; Griffiths, 'The Eyes of an Englishman', pp. 151–68; *Glendower,* pp. 31, 35, 83, 91, 98, 93–4, 109–25, 140, 143; *Revolt,* pp. 57–62, 116, 159, 164, 186–8, 212–14, 222.

28 *POPCE,* vol. 1, p. 304; *Glendower,* p. 98.

29 *Welsh Records,* pp. 75, 110, 127–8; *Glendower,* pp. 31–5, 40–1, 53, 64–7, 76, 131, 140–2; *Revolt,* pp. 29, 58, 138–47, 192, 199–207, 230–2, 310–13; R. A. Griffiths and R. Thomas, *The Making of the Tudor Dynasty* (Stroud, 1997, orig. 1993), p. 19; *OGC,* p. 35.

30 *Welsh Records,* p. 110; *Glendower,* pp. 23–7, 31, 34–5, 53, 58–9, 92, 137, 140, 143 n. 5; *Revolt,* pp. 137–43, 146–7, 174–96, 244, 293, 326.

31 Ellis, *Original Letters,* p. 43; *RHL Henry IV,* vol. 2, pp. 76–9; *Glendower,* pp. 82, 101, 119 n.1; *Revolt,* pp. 164, 220.

32 *POPCE,* vol. 1, p. 236; Watt, *Scotichronicon,* vol. 8, p. 103; *Glendower,* pp. 76, 86.

5: The Ambitions of the French Courtly Factions

1   B.-A. Pocquet du Haut-Jussé, *La France gouvernée par Jean Sans Peur, Les Dépenses du Receveur Général du Royaume* (Paris, 1959), p. 42 (author's translation).

2   M. Creighton, *A History of the Papacy from the Great Schism to the Sack of Rome* (London, 1907), vol. 1, pp. 61–101, 111–14, 136–226; R. Vaughan, *Philip the Bold* (London, 1962), pp. 43, 45–6, 55–6; G. Mollat, trans. J. Love, *The Popes at Avignon, 1305–1378* (London, 1963, orig. 1949), pp. 249–56, 262–8; Y. Renouard, trans. D. Bethell, *The Avignon Papacy, 1305–1403* (London, 1970), pp. 56–79; Crowder, *Unity, Heresy and Reform*, pp. 1–40; G. Barraclough, *The Medieval Papacy* (London, 1992), pp. 164–85.

3   T. Johnes, trans., *The Chronicles of Enguerrand de Monstrelet* (London, 1810), all entries are from vol. 1, pp. 42–4, 157–60, 188; L. Douët-d'Arcq, *La Chronique d'Enguerran de Monstrelet* (Paris, 1857), all entries are from tome 1, pp. 87–90; Vaughan, *Philip the Bold*, pp. 43, 45–6, 55–6; J. B. Morrall, *Gerson and the Great Schism* (Manchester, 1960), p. 6; Joliffe, *Froissart*, pp. 337–40; M. G. A. Vale, *Charles VII* (London, 1974), pp. 12–18; J. H. Shennan, *The Parlement of Paris* (Stroud, 1998), pp. 161–4.

4   Johnes, *Monstrelet*, pp. 42–4, 136–56, 163, 191–211; Vaughan, *Philip the Bold*, pp. 43, 45–6, 55–6; Vaughan, *John the Fearless*, pp. 29–48; Morrall, *Gerson*, p. 6; Vale, *Charles VII*, pp. 12–44; Shennan, *Parlement of Paris*, pp. 161–4; B. Schnerb, *Les Armagnacs et Les Bourguignons, la Maudite Guerre* (Paris, 2009), pp. 56–87.

5   d'Avout, *La Querelle* (Paris, 1943); Schnerb, *Les Armagnacs et Les Bourguignons*.

6   *Saint-Denys*, vol. 5, pp. 163–5; E. Jarry, *La Vie Politique de Louis de France, Duc d'Orleans, 1372–1407* (Paris, 1889), p. 102; F. D. S. Darwin, *Louis d'Orléans (1372–1407): A Necessary Prologue to the Tragedy of La Pucelle d'Orléans* (London, 1936), p. 19; Vaughan, *Philip the Bold*, p. 42; R. Knecht, *The Valois: Kings of France 1328–1589* (London, 2008, orig. 2004), pp. 41–6; Schnerb, *Armagnacs et Bourguignons*, pp. 20–1, 23–33.

7   A. de la Borderie, *Chronique de Bretagne de Jean de Saint-Paul, Chambellan du duc Francois II* (Nantes, 1881), pp. 52, 127; Darwin, *Louis d'Orléans*, pp. 19, 59–67; Salmon, *Society in Crisis*, p. 20; d'Avout, *La Querelle*, pp. 13–14; Vaughan, *Philip the Bold*, pp. 39–45; R. Vaughan, *Valois Burgundy* (London, 1975), p. 78 (Philippe was regent of Brittany, Savoy and Luxembourg at one stage); Knecht, *Valois*, pp. 41–2; Schnerb, *Armagnacs et Bourguignons*, pp. 20, 27–9.

8   *Saint-Denys*, vol. 3, pp. 738–45; Darwin, *Louis d'Orléans*, pp. 132–3, 139–41; Jarry, *La Vie Politique*, p. 102; d'Avout, *La Querelle*, pp. 26–8; Vaughan, *Philip the Bold*, p. 44; Schnerb, *Armagnacs et Bourguignons*, pp. 26–33.

9   Des Ursins, *Histoire de Charles VI*, p. 407; L. Douët-d'Arcq, *Choix de Pièces*

Notes 259

Inédites Relatives au Règne de Charles VI, 2 vols (Paris, 1863), vol. 1, pp. 157–60; Jarry, *La Vie Politique*, pp. 107–14, 134–63, 228, 295–9, 301–3, 438–9; Mirot, *La Politique Française*, pp. 42–5; Darwin, *Louis d'Orléans*, pp. 21–2; d'Avout, *La Querelle*, pp. 32–42, 54, 74; Pillement, *Pedro de Luna*, pp. 76–7, 108, 111, 125–6, 131–2; R. Blumenfeld-Kosinski and K. Brownlee, *The Selected Writings of Christine de Pizan* (New York, 1996), p. 20; Schnerb, *Armagnacs et Bourguignons*, pp. 32–5, 49–50, 56.

10 Jarry, *La Vie Politique*, pp. 97, 257–68; Darwin, *Louis d'Orléans*, pp. 59–67; d'Avout, *La Querelle*, pp. 14–15, 25, 56–83; *La France gouvernée*, p. 7; Vaughan, *Philip the Bold*, pp. 24–45; Knecht, *Valois*, pp. 44–8; Schnerb, *Armagnacs et Bourguignons*, pp. 20–1, 23, 27–30.

11 Darwin, *Louis d'Orléans*, pp. 27, 60; d'Avout, *La Querelle*, pp. 48, 52; Vaughan, *Philip the Bold*, pp. 24–31, 103–4; Vaughan, *John the Fearless*, pp. 43–4; Vaughan, *Valois Burgundy*, pp. 16, 71, 138–41, 150; Knecht, *Valois*, pp. 41–3.

12 *La France gouvernée*, pp. 53, 111, 124, 237, 271.

13 A. Tuetey, ed., *Journal d'un Bourgeois de Paris, 1405–1449* (Paris, 1881), pp. 1–3; A. Tuetey, ed., *Journal de Nicolas de Baye, greffier du Parlement de Paris, 1400–1417* (Paris, 1885), vol. 1, pp. 138–9; Jarry, *La Vie Politique*, pp. 184–97, 324–33; Darwin, *Louis d'Orléans*, pp. 74–90; d'Avout, *La Querelle*, pp. 77–81, 122; Vaughan, *Philip the Bold*, p. 66 (here Jacques is described as not of John's company); Knecht, *The Valois*, pp. 51–8; J. D. le Roulx, *La France en Orient au XIVᵉ Siècle, Expéditions du Maréchal Boucicaut* (Boston, 2006, orig. Paris, 1886), pp. 235, 284.

14 *La France gouvernée*, pp. 18, 23, 43, 53, 237; d'Avout, *La Querelle*, p. 152; Vaughan, *Valois Burgundy*, p. 62; R. Vaughan, *Philip the Good* (London, 1970), p. 4; Knecht, *Valois*, pp. 53–62.

15 C. Lannette-Claverie, *Collection Joursanvault, Sous-Série 6 J* (Orléans, 1976) (this work demonstrates the court of Orleans at work, their ranks and departments are listed as are their transactions, for example, pp. 222–3, 249–50, 321–7 et al.). Richard Vaughan's works on Valois Burgundy (especially *Valois Burgundy* pp. 48–50, 95–122, 162–93) and *La France gouvernée* do the same for Burgundian administration.

16 Tuetey, *Nicolas de Baye*, vol. 1, pp. 264, 306; d'Avout, *La Querelle*, pp. 122, 138, 150; Knecht, *Valois*, pp. 53–62.

17 Tuetey, *Nicolas de Baye*, vol. 2, pp. 206–8; Darwin, *Louis d'Orléans*, pp. 111–26; d'Avout, *La Querelle*, p. 83; Lannette-Claverie, *Collection Joursanvault* (evidence of the court of Orleans paying leaders of other factions), pp. 31–2 (sending golden cloth to Charles de Hangest, 1392), p. 45 (Jehan le Maingre, 'Boucicaut', 1393), pp. 47, 60 (Charles de Savoisy, 1397–8), 59 (Charles de Labret, 1397), 64 (Jehan de Bourbon, 'fils aîné du duc de Bourbon',

1398), 66 (Jehan, 'fils aîné de Bourgogne, comte de Nevers', 1398); Schnerb, *Armagnacs et Bourguignons*, pp. 91–101.

18 *La France gouvernée*, p. 7, 9, 15; G. Pillement, *Pedro de Luna, le Dernier Pape d'Avignon* (Paris, 1955), p. 140; Vaughan, *John the Fearless*, pp. 99–100, 193, 202, 204, 210; Shennan, *Parlement of Paris*, pp. 153, 166–87; Schnerb, *Armagnacs et Bourguignons*, pp. 168–73.

19 Jarry, *La Vie Politique*, p. 97; Darwin, *Louis d'Orléans*, p. 19; d'Avout, *La Querelle*, pp. 14–15; Vaughan, *Philip the Bold*, pp. 42–3; Knecht, *Valois*, pp. 44–8; Schnerb, *Armagnacs et Bourguignons*, pp. 20–1, 27, 57–61.

20 Darwin, *Louis d'Orléans*, pp. 19–21, 23–4, 30–1; d'Avout, *La Querelle*, pp. 32–43; D. M. Bueno de Mesquita, *Giangaleazzo Visconti, Duke of Milan (1351–1402)* (Cambridge, 1941), pp. 12, 31–6, 63–7, 203–4, 267; Vaughan, *Philip the Bold*, pp. 44, 54–6, 91, 109; Morrall, *Gerson*, pp. 6–11; E. R. Chamberlin, *The Count of Virtue: Giangaleazzo Visconti, Duke of Milan* (London, 1965), pp. 70–83, 89–93, 109–13, 175–80; Vaughan, *John the Fearless*, pp. 30–1; Schnerb, *Armagnacs et Bourguignons*, p. 56.

21 Riley, *Ypodigma Neustriæ*, pp. 336–7; Creighton, *History of the Papacy*, vol. 1, pp. 85, 88–9, 127–8, 162); Vaughan, *Philip the Bold*, pp. 28–30, 48; Vaughan, *Valois Burgundy*, p. 151; Bennett, 'Richard II and the Wider Realm', pp. 196–7; R. G. Davies, *Henry Despenser, d. 1406* (ODNB); Ainsworth and Diller, *Chroniques*, pp. 945–69; Preest, *Chronica Maiora*, pp. 180–2, 187–94.

22 Creighton, *History of the Papacy*, vol. 1, pp. 77–105, 111, 133–6, 160–5, 173–5; Chamberlin, *Count of Virtue*, pp. 70–1; Vaughan, *Philip the Bold*, pp. 40, 45–6, 55; Barraclough, *Medieval Papacy*, p. 166; Renouard, trans. Bethell, *Avignon Papacy*, pp. 72–3; Ainsworth and Diller, *Chroniques*, pp. 838–42, 985–6, 993–4, 999; Preest, *Chronica Maiora*, p. 183.

23 Creighton, *History of the Papacy*, vol. 1, pp. 74–85, 161–2; Chamberlin, *Count of Virtue*, pp. 150, 177; Vaughan, *Philip the Bold*, pp. 55–6; Morrall, *Gerson*, p. 7; Barraclough, *Medieval Papacy*, pp. 164–6, 173–5; Renouard, trans. Bethell, *Avignon Papacy*, pp. 72–5; Crowder, *Unity, Heresy and Reform*, pp. 3, 6–8, 10, 31; Donaldson, *Auld Alliance*, pp. 4–5, 24; Laidlaw, *The Auld Alliance* (the entire work); Macdougall, *An Antidote to the English*, pp. 18–20; Villalon and Kagay, *The Hundred Years' War: A Wider Focus*, pp. 3–175; Villalon and Kagay, eds, *The Hundred Years War (Part II): Different Vistas*, pp. 153–210.

24 Creighton, *History of the Papacy*, vol. 1, pp. 172–3; Mirot, *La Politique Française*, pp. 35, 42; Bueno de Mesquita, *Giangaleazzo Visconti*, pp. 12, 63, 66–7, 125, 155–8; Chamberlin, *Count of Virtue*, pp. 89–93, 109–13; Vaughan, *Philip the Bold*, pp. 43–4, 55–6; Morrall, *Gerson*, pp. 6–7, 10; Renouard, trans. Bethell, *Avignon Papacy*, pp. 72–5.

25 Jarry, *La Vie Politique*, pp. 107–14; Mirot, *La Politique Française*, pp. 5–41;

Darwin, *Louis d'Orléans*, pp. 18–40; Bueno de Mesquita, *Giangaleazzo Visconti*, pp. 155–8, 203–4, 267, 324; Chamberlin, *Count of Virtue*, pp. 152–5.

26 d'Avout, *La Querelle*, pp. 12, 19–21, 28, 32–43; Darwin, *Louis d'Orléans*, pp. 19–24; Bueno de Mesquita, *Giangaleazzo Visconti*, pp. 203–23, 267, 322–5; Chamberlin, *Count of Virtue*, pp. 175–88; Vaughan, *Philip the Bold*, pp. 44, 55–6, 109; Morrall, *Gerson*, pp. 6–11; Vaughan, *John the Fearless*, pp. 30–1.

27 Des Ursins, *Histoire de Charles VI*, pp. 409, 412; Douët-d'Arcq, *Choix de Pièces Inédites*, vol. 1, pp. 140–1; Jarry, *La Vie Politique*, pp. 203–4, 235–77, 295–9, 312–14, 318–19, 333–7; Darwin, *Louis d'Orléans*, pp. 19–21, 24–8, 30–3, 35–9, 47–9; d'Avout, *La Querelle*, pp. 48–52, 68–70, 74, 83; Pillement, *Pedro de Luna*, pp. 89, 112–13, 124–6, 131–6; Courteault, *Le Héraut Berry*, pp. 13–14, 17; Schnerb, *Armagnacs et Bourguignons*, pp. 55–73.

28 Des Ursins, *Histoire de Charles VI*, p. 421; Brown, *Black Douglases*, p. 214; J. Ross, 'Seditious Activities: The Conspiracy of Maud de Vere, Countess of Oxford, 1403–4', in Clark, *Authority and Subversion*, pp. 25–41; Schnerb, *Armagnacs et Bourguignons*, pp. 51–4.

29 Vaughan, *Philip the Bold*, pp. 40–5, 52–78, 107–9, 184–7, 201, 239–40; Morrall, *Gerson*, pp. 5–11; Vaughan, *John the Fearless*, pp. 4, 120; Renouard, trans. Bethell, *Avignon Papacy*, pp. 77–8; Vaughan, *Valois Burgundy*, pp. 78, 157–9; Barraclough, *Medieval Papacy*, pp. 174–5; Lalande, *Jean II le Meingre*, pp. 57–9; Magee, 'Le temps de la croisade bouguignonne: l'expedition de Nicopolis', in Paviot and Chauney-Bouillot, *Nicopolis, 1396–1996*, pp. 49–58; le Roulx, *La France en Orient*, pp. 166–200; Schnerb, *Armagnacs et Bourguignons*, pp. 23–8.

30 Mirot, *La Politique Française*, pp. 23–41; d'Avout, *La Querelle*, pp. 23–4, 30–1; Bueno de Mesquita, *Giangaleazzo Visconti*, pp. 203–4, 212, 215, 267; Vaughan, *Philip the Bold*, pp. 44, 55–6, 109; Morrall, *Gerson*, pp. 6–11; Lalande, *Le Livre Des Fais*, p. 116; Lalande, *Jean II le Meingre*, pp. 68, 97 n.3, 98–101; B. Schnerb, 'le contingent franco-bourguinon à la croisade de Nicopolis', in J. Paviot and M. Chauney-Bouillot, eds, *Nicopolis, 1396–1996, Actes du Colloque International* (Dijon, 1997), p. 67; Ainsworth and Diller, *Chroniques*, pp. 994–5; J. Black, *Absolutism in Renaissance Milan: Plenitude of Power under the Visconti and the Sforza 1329–1535* (Oxford, 2009), p. 2.

31 Riley, *Ypodigma Neustriæ*, pp. 341–7, 395; des Ursins, *Histoire de Charles VI*, p. 412; Mirot, *La Politique Française*, pp. 5–21; Vaughan, *Philip the Bold*, pp. 48–50; J. Campbell, 'England, Scotland and the Hundred Years War in the Fourteenth Century', in J. R. Hale, J. R. L. Highfield and B. Smalley, eds, *Europe in the Late Middle Ages* (London, 1965), pp. 184–216; Bean, 'Henry IV and The Percies', pp. 212–27; Donaldson, *Auld Alliance*, pp. 8–9; Brown, *Black Douglases*, pp. 212–4; F. Autrand, 'Aux origines de l'Europe moderne: l'alliance Franco-Ecosse au XIVe siècle', pp. 35–40; Joliffe, *Froissart's Chronicles*, pp. 263–77; Barrell, *Medieval Scotland*, pp. 149, 207–8;

Preest, *Chronica Maiora*, pp. 323–4; Macdougall, *An Antidote to the English*, pp. 49–50; Ainsworth and Diller, *Chroniques*, pp. 978–9, 988–90, 997.

32 *Fœdera*, vol. 8, pp. 368–9, 371–2; Riley, *Ypodigma Neustriœ*, p. 413; Bean, 'Henry IV and The Percies', pp. 212–27; Barrell, *Medieval Scotland*, pp. 150–3; Preest, *Chronica Maiora*, pp. 323–4, 341.

33 *POPCE*, vol. 1, p. 153; *RHL Henry IV*, vol. 2, pp. 61–3; W. Rees, ed., *Calendar of Ancient Petitions Relating to Wales* (Cardiff, 1975), p. 457.

34 Darwin, *Louis d'Orléans*, p. 24; Vaughan, *Philip the Bold*, pp. 16–38; Saul, *Richard II*, pp. 54, 155–86; W. M. Ormrod, 'Finance and Trade under Richard II', in Goodman and Gillespie, eds, *Richard II: The Art of Kingship*, pp. 155–86; Schnerb, *Armagnacs et Bourguignons*, p. 27.

35 Jarry, *La Vie Politique*, pp. 243–56, 272–7; Darwin, *Louis d'Orléans*, pp. 24–8, 30–3, 37–9, 48–9; d'Avout, *La Querelle*, pp. 48–53; Vaughan, *Philip the Bold*, pp. 54–6; Chamberlin, *Count of Virtue*, pp. 160–75; Vaughan, *Valois Burgundy*, p. 56; Schnerb, *Armagnacs et Bourguignons*, pp. 55–61.

6: The Alliance of 1404

1 *Welsh Records*, pp. 25, 28, 75, 76, 78.

2 Creighton, *History of the Papacy*, vol. 1, pp. 161–2; Vaughan, *Philip the Bold*, p. 55; Barraclough, *Medieval Papacy*, pp. 168, 174–7; Renouard, trans. Bethell, *Avignon Papacy*, pp. 55–8, 70–5; Morrall, *Gerson*, pp. 2, 10–16, 30–4; Crowder, *Unity, Heresy and Reform*, pp. 3, 6–8, 10, 31; Fryde, 'King John and the Empire', p. 336.

3 Creighton, *History of the Papacy*, vol. 1, pp. 108–11, 140–9, 151–7, 175–81; L. Mirot, *La Politique Française en Italie de 1380 à 1422* (Paris, 1934), pp. 28, 35; Darwin, *Louis d'Orléans*, p. 50; Bueno de Mesquita, *Giangaleazzo Visconti*, pp. 155–8; Morrall, *Gerson*, pp. 6–75; Chamberlin, *Count of Virtue*, p. 150; Barraclough, *Medieval Papacy*, pp. 168, 173–7; Renouard, trans. Bethell, *Avignon Papacy*, pp. 72–9; Crowder, *Unity, Heresy and Reform*, p. 3.

4 Darwin, *Louis d'Orléans*, p. 24; d'Avout, *La Querelle*, pp. 50–1, 54–5; E. M. Carus-Wilson, 'Trends in the Export of English Woollens in the Fourteenth Century', *The Economic History Review*, 3:2 (1950), pp. 162–79; Morrall, *Gerson*, pp. 7–11; Vaughan, *Philip the Bold*, pp. 16, 38, 47–58, 168–87; Barraclough, *Medieval Papacy*, p. 174.

5 Riley, *Ypodigma Neustriœ* pp. 359–73; *Saint-Denys*, vol. 1, pp. 606–7, vol. 2, pp. 75–81, et al.; Creighton, *History of the Papacy*, vol. 1, p. 162; A. Tuck, *Richard II and the English Nobility* (London, 1973), pp. 156–8, 178–9; Cuttino, *English Medieval Diplomacy*, pp. 96–7; Saul, *Richard II*, pp. 205–34; Bennett, *Richard II and the Revolution of 1399*, pp. 24–7, 49–53, 69–71, 80–3.

6 Bellaguet, *Saint-Denys*, vol. 2, 95–100, 131–83, 599–644, 654–7; Creighton, *History of the Papacy*, vol. 1, pp. 108–11, 140–57, 226–7; d'Avout, *La Querelle*, p. 66; Pillement, *Pedro de Luna*, pp. 82–111; Vaughan, *Philip the Bold*, pp. 45–7; Morrall, *Gerson*, pp. 10–11, 31–44, 65–6; Barraclough, *Medieval Papacy*, pp. 168–73; Renouard, trans. Bethell, *Avignon Papacy*, pp. 70–8; Vaughan, *Valois Burgundy*, p. 20; Ainsworth and Diller, *Chroniques*, pp. 737–42.

7 *Saint-Denys*, vol. 2, pp. 654–7; Jarry, *La Vie Politique*, p. 221; Creighton, *History of the Papacy*, vol. 1, pp. 157–9, 176; d'Avout, *La Querelle*, p. 66; Pillement, *Pedro de Luna*, pp. 94–113; Vaughan, *Philip the Bold*, p. 47; Renouard, trans. Bethell, *Avignon Papacy*, pp. 76–8.

8 Johnes, *Monstrelet*, pp. 55–86; *Saint-Denys*, vol. 3, pp. 25–31, 55–61; J.-A.-C. Buchon, ed., *Choix de Chroniques et Mémoires sur l'histoire de France*, J.-J. des Ursins, *Histoire de Charles VI* (Paris, 1838), p. 411; Douët-d'Arcq, *Monstrelet*, pp. 43–69; Creighton, *History of the Papacy*, vol. 1, p. 159; Morrall, *Gerson*, pp. 11, 55–7; Vaughan, *Philip the Bold*, pp. 44, 47, 51–2, 55–6, 183; Vaughan, *John the Fearless*, pp. 30–1; Shennan, *Parlement of Paris*, pp. 161–2; Knecht, *Valois*, p. 51; Schnerb, *Armagnacs et Bourguignons*, pp. 55–73.

9 *Saint-Denys*, vol. 3, pp. 71–6; Jarry, *La Vie Politique*, pp. 221, 282; Creighton, *History of the Papacy*, vol. 1, pp. 159, 175–7; Pillement, *Pedro de Luna*, pp. 114–26; Vaughan, *Philip the Bold*, p. 47; Morrall, *Gerson*, pp. 63–4.

10 Creighton, *History of the Papacy*, vol. 1, 159, 177–9; Pillement, *Pedro de Luna*, 112–13; Vaughan, *Philip the Bold*, 47; Morrall, *Gerson*, pp. 63–4; Grèvy-Pons, Ornato and Ouy, eds, *Jean de Montreuil, Opera*, vol. 1, pp. 79–82, 86–8, 93–102; Renouard, trans. Bethell, *Avignon Papacy*, p. 78.

11 Strachey, *Rotuli Parliamentorum*, vol. 3, p. 605; des Ursins, *Histoire de Charles VI*, pp. 418, 435; Ellis, *Original Letters*, pp. 24–6; Webb, 'Creton', pp. 1–442; Ross, 'Seditious Activities: The Conspiracy of Maud de Vere, Countess of Oxford, 1403–4', in Clark, *Authority and Subversion*, pp. 25–41.

12 Bean, 'Henry IV and The Percies', pp. 212–27; Kirby, *Henry IV*, pp. 152–8; A. King, '"They have the Hertes of the People by North": Northumberland, the Percies and Henry IV, 1399–1408', in Dodds and Biggs, *Henry IV: The Establishment of the Regime*, pp. 139–59; Dunn, 'Henry IV and the Politics of Resistance in Early Lancastrian England, 1399–1413', in L. Clark, ed., *The Fifteenth Century, Authority and Subversion* (Woodbridge, 2003), pp. 5–23; Preest, *Chronica Maiora*, pp. 315–17, 321, 326–9, 332, 336–9.

13 *Fœdera*, vol. 8, pp. 356–8; *Saint-Denys*, vol. 3, pp. 14–15, 200–9, 274–9; *RHL*, vol. 1, pp. 160–2; *POPCE*, vol. 1, pp. 221, vol. 2, pp. 83–4; *CPR, 1401–5*, pp. 22, 319; *Welsh Records*, pp. 105–6, 113–14; *Glendower*, pp. 76–82; Jones, *Gwydir Family*, p. 118; Davies, *Revolt*, pp. 192, 274–5; Given-Wilson, *CAU*, pp. 148–9 n. 2.

14 *Saint-Denys*, vol. 3, p. 167; Ellis, *Original Letters*, vol. 2, pp. 30–1; *Glendower*,
    p. 80; *Revolt*, p. 193; Nye, 'Public Diplomacy and Soft Power', pp. 94–5.
15 *Welsh Records*, pp. 23–39, 75–82; Fowler, *Hundred Years War*, pp. 186–7;
    Cuttino, *English Medieval Diplomacy*, pp. 8–10, 18, 94; D. Waley, *The Italian
    City Republics* (London, 1988), pp. 93–7.
16 *Saint-Denys*, vol. 3, pp. 164–5; A. Thierry, *Histoire de la Conquête de l'Angleterre
    par les Normands* (Paris, 1851), vol. 4, Appendix no. 7, pp. 299–300; Riley,
    Ypodigma Neustriæ, p. 406; Owen, 'Owain Lawgoch – Yeuain de Galles', pp.
    61–2; *Welsh Records*, pp. 23–4, 79–80, 103–6, 111–14; *Glendower*, pp. 16–18,
    123–5; J. Le Patourel, 'The Origins of the War', pp. 28–46, and J. Palmer,
    'The War Aims of the Protagonists', pp. 47–58, in Fowler, *Hundred Years
    War*; Cuttino, *English Medieval Diplomacy*, pp. 84–9, 94–6, 115; *Revolt*, pp.
    211–14; Shennan, *Parlement of Paris*, pp. 154–6; J. H. Shennan, *The Bourbons:
    The History of a Dynasty* (London, 2007), pp. 1–9; Bartlett, 'Heartland and
    Border: The Mental and Physical Geography of Medieval Europe', in *PIMA*,
    pp. 35–6.
17 Tuetey, *Bourgeois de Paris*, p. 6; Tuetey, *Nicolas de Baye*, vol. 1, pp. 65–7,
    290–3; Mirot, *La Politique Française* pp. 2, 17 n.35; Jarry, *La Vie Politique*, pp.
    50, 308–9; Vaughan, *Philip the Bold*, pp. 37, 71, 139–41, 143, 185, 199, 213,
    223; Grèvy-Pons, Ornato and Ouy, *Jean de Montreuil, Opera*, vol. 1, p. 206;
    Courteault, *Le Héraut Berry*, pp. 40–1; *Welsh Records*, pp. 25, 28, 31, 75, 78,
    81; Vaughan, *Valois Burgundy*, pp. 16, 83; Fowler, *Hundred Years War*, p. 187;
    Pugh, *Henry V and the Southampton Plot*, p. 40; Knecht, *Valois*, pp. 44, 54–5.
18 *Saint-Denys*, vol. 3, pp. 16–19; *Welsh Records*, pp. 30–1, 81; *Glendower*, p. 85 n
    5; Jarry, *La Vie Politique*, p. 282; d'Avout, *La Querelle*, p. 159; Vaughan, *Philip
    the Bold*, p. 56; J. D. le Roulx, *La France en Orient au XIVe siècle: Expéditions du
    Maréchal Boucicaut*, (Paris, 2005, orig. 1886), pp. 360, 362; H. Courteault,
    ed., *Les Chroniques Du Roi Charles VII Par Gilles Le Bouvier, Dit Le Héraut Berry*
    (Paris, 1979), p. 36 n.4; Schnerb, *L'Etat Bourguignon*, p. 153.
19 *Saint-Denys*, vol. 3, pp. 70–1; Tuetey, *Nicolas de Baye*, vol. 1, pp. 65–7, vol. 2,
    p. 30; Creighton, *History of the Papacy*, vol. 1, p. 177; Jarry, *La Vie Politique*,
    p. 405; Mirot, *La Politique Française*, p. 5; Renouard, trans. Bethell, *Avignon
    Papacy*, p. 78; d'Avout, *La Querelle*, p. 66; Vaughan, *Philip the Bold*, p. 57;
    Courteault, *Le Héraut Berry*, p. 5 n.4; le Roulx, *La France en Orient au XIVe
    siècle*, p. 362; Lannette-Claverie, *Collection Joursanvault*, pp. 9, 13, 35, 66,
    213–14.
20 Tuetey, *Nicolas de Baye*, pp. 264, 306; Jarry, *La Vie Politique*, pp. 226–34,
    308–9, 318–19; Darwin, *Louis d'Orléans*, pp. 58–9; d'Avout, *La Querelle*,
    pp. 54–5, 74, 76, 138; Vaughan, *Philip the Bold*, pp. 66, 68; Vaughan, *John
    the Fearless*, pp. 33–4; Lannette-Claverie, *Collection Joursanvault*, pp. 311–12;
    Courteault, *Le Héraut Berry*, p. 48; Schnerb, *L'Etat Bourguignon*, p. 153.

21 Lannette-Claverie, *Collection Joursanvault*, p. 77 (1404): 'Mandement de Louis, duc d'Orléans, à son conseiller Jehan Le Flament de faire payer par son trésorier général Jehan Poulain à Jehan de Rouvroy, son échanson, et à George de Helencourt, son panetier, la somme totale de 100 Francs pour les aider à s'équiper en vue du voyage que fait en Galles le comte de La Marche.'

22 Fowler, *Hundred Years War*, pp. 186–7; *Welsh Records*, pp. 27–8, 78.

23 *Welsh Records*, pp. 25, 28, 75, 76, 78.

24 Johnes, *Monstrelet*, pp. 55–86; *Saint-Denys*, vol. 3, pp. 55–61, 116–21; Douët-d'Arcq, *Monstrelet*, pp. 43–69; Cuttino, *English Medieval Diplomacy*, pp. 13–18; Given-Wilson, 'The Quarrels of Old Women', pp. 28–47.

25 *Saint-Denys*, vol. 2, pp. 675–7, 701–3; Douët-d'Arcq, *Choix de Pièces Inédites* vol. 1, pp. 157–60; *Welsh Records*, pp. 26, 76.

26 Riley, *Ypodigma Neustriæ*, p. 359; Cuttino, *English Medieval Diplomacy*, p. 84; Preest, *Chronica Maiora*, p. 291.

27 *Welsh Records*, pp. 26, 76–7.

28 *Fœdera*, vol. 8, p. 374; *RHL Henry IV*, vol. 1, pp. 281–2, 329–34, 367–70, 376–80, 384–5.

29 *Welsh Records*, pp. 26–7, 77.

30 *Fœdera*, vol. 8, p. 358; *Saint-Denys*, vol. 2, pp. 675–7, 701–3, vol. 3, 171–81; Douët-d'Arcq, *Choix de Pièces Inédite*, vol. 1, pp. 157–60; *History of the Royal Navy*, vol. 2, pp. 351–4, 355–8, 361–6; M. Jones, *Ducal Brittany, 1364–1399* (Oxford, 1970), pp. 103–71, 195; Tuck, *Richard II*, pp. 169, 196, 371; Cassard, 'Anglais et Bretons dans le duché sous Jean IV', pp. 21–42.

31 Riley, *Ypodigma Neustriæ*, p. 397; Bouchart, *Grandes Chroniques de Bretaigne*, pp. 172; Jarry, *La Vie Politique*, p. 278; Darwin, *Louis d'Orléans*, pp. 60–1; Vaughan, *Philip the Bold*, pp. 52–3, Preest, *Chronica Maiora*, p. 325.

32 *Fœdera*, vol. 8, p. 358; *Saint-Denys*, vol. 3, pp. 171–81; Nicolas, *History of the Royal Navy*, vol. 2, pp. 351–4, 355–8, 361–6; Courteault, *Le Héraut Berry*, p. 12.

33 *Welsh Records*, pp. 107, 115.

34 *Welsh Records*, pp. 107, 115.

35 *Fœdera*, vol. 8, pp. 356–8; *Saint-Denys*, vol. 3, pp. 158–61, 170–81; Johnes, *Monstrelet*, p. 102; Jarry, *La Vie Politique*, p. 285; d'Avout, *La Querelle*, pp. 54–5; Evans, *The Unconquered Knight*, pp. 100–34, 141–2, 148–52; Carriazo, *El Victorial*, pp. 139–40, 195–6, 186–215, 223.

36 Johnes, *Monstrelet*, pp. 88–9; *Saint-Denys*, vol. 3, pp. 1648, 198–201, 222–7; Douët-d'Arcq, *Monstrelet*, pp. 69–70; *POPCE*, vol. 1, pp. 264–6; *RHL Henry IV*, vol. 1, pp. 329–30, 331–5, 338–40, 367–70, 376–80, 384–5, 392. Note: The Saint-Denys Chronicler described a far smaller force of 800 men-at-arms and many crossbowmen in a fleet of sixty-two sailing ships (*OGC*, pp. 152–5).

37 *Saint-Denys*, vol. 3, pp. 222–7 (author's translation).

38 *Saint-Denys*, vol. 3, p. 167 (author's translation).

39 Carriazo, *El Victorial*, pp. 211–12 (author's translation, with thanks to Edgar Miranda and Valerie Brown).

40 This is incorrect: Owain and Richard were not related. However, this borrows from an idea that the Welsh rose in support of Richard: see Webb, 'Creton', pp. 1–433; Given-Wilson, *Chronicles*, pp. 137–52.

41 There is evidence that Glyn Dŵr operated an effective cavalry force, see Thomas, 'Oswestry 1400', pp. 117–26. Also, this implies that the Welsh were knights, or horsemen at least, therefore chivalrous and worthy of assistance.

42 This appears to refer to the 1405 Tripartite Indenture which sought to remove Henry and divide England and Wales into three parts. Whoever took the throne would be Owain's ally. It is well known that Charles VI sent Owain an army which included Jean de Hangest, Grand Master of Crossbows, and his troops, as well as wine on at least one occasion, see *Glendower*, pp. 78, 93–5, 102 and *Revolt*, pp. 166–9, 193.

43 Pero Niño's compatriot and adversary, Martin Ruiz, was given twenty galleys for the mission in 1404. He combined forces with Jacques de Bourbon and accomplished very little, despite the size and power of the French–Spanish fleet. In 1405 the French sent an army on campaign with Owain, possibly to enact the Tripartite Indenture, which could explain 'before and since' reference in the penultimate line. See *Revolt*, pp. 115–21, 193–5 and Evans, *Unconquered Knight*, pp. 100–1, 105, 131.

7: An Orleanist Coup?

1 *Saint-Denys*, vol. 3, pp. 322–3 (author's translation).

2 *POPCE*, vol. 1, pp. 236, 246, vol. 2, pp. 68–9; *Glendower*, pp. 86–90; *Revolt*, pp. 15–16, 118, 242, 246–8; *OGC*, pp. 88–91, 100–3.

3 *Ypodigma Neustriæ*, p. 412; *POPCE*, vol. 2, pp. 104–6; *Welsh Records*, pp. 30–9, 75–82; Kirby, *Henry IV*, pp. 182–3; P. McNiven, *Heresy and Politics in the Reign of Henry IV: The Burning of John Badby* (Woodbridge, 1987), pp. 122–3; Dunn, 'Henry IV and the Politics of Resistance', pp. 9, 17; S. Walker, 'The Yorkshire Risings of 1405: Texts and Contexts', in Dodd and Biggs, *Henry IV: The Establishment of the Regime, 1399–1406*, pp. 182–3; Preest, *Chronica Maiora*, pp. 336, 342.

4 *Welsh Records*, pp. 108–10, 116–17; *OGC*, pp. 112–15, 341–2 (author's arrangement and adaptation).

5 *Welsh Records*, pp. 108–10, 116–17; *Glendower*, pp. 92–5; *Revolt*, pp. 166–9; *OGC*, pp. 489–95.

6 *Ypodigma Neustriæ*, p. 399; Preest, *Chronica Maiora*, p. 327.

7 *RHL Henry IV*, vol. 1, pp. 138–40, 141–3, 144–5, 146–8, 149–51, 152–4, 155–9, 160–2.

8 *POPCE*, vol. 1, p. 248; *Glendower*, pp. 95–6; *Revolt*, pp. 118–19, 231; *OGC*, pp. 116–17, 342–4.

9 *Glendower*, pp. 96–8; Watt, *Scotichronicon*, vol. 8, pp. 100–9; *Revolt*, pp. 118–19, 212, 226; *CAU*, pp. 212–13.

10 Jarry, *La Vie Politique*, pp. 337–41; d'Avout, *La Querelle*, p. 47; Pillement, *Pedro de Luna*, pp. 124–6, 131–6; Morrall, *Gerson*, p. 68; Courteault, *Le Héraut Berry*, pp. 13–14; Lalande, *Jean II le Meingre*, pp. 130–1.

11 Des Ursins, *Histoire de Charles VI*, p. 420 (author's translation).

12 *Saint-Denys*, vol. 3, pp. 322–3 (author's translation).

13 *Saint-Denys*, vol. 3, pp. 302–3 (author's translation).

14 *CAU*, pp. xxix–xxxiii; Walker, 'The Yorkshire Risings of 1405: Texts and Contexts', p. 165.

15 *Ypodigma Neustriæ*, pp. 413–15; *POPCE*, vol. 1, pp. 264–6, 275–6; C. L. Kingsford, *English Historical Literature in the Fifteenth Century* (Oxford, 1913), pp. 282–3 (The Northern Chronicle); Kirby, *Henry IV*, pp. 185–8; P. McNiven, 'The Betrayal of Archbishop Scrope', *BJRL*, 54 (1971): 173–213; McNiven, *The Burning of John Badby*, pp. 72, 76–7, 123; Walker, 'The Yorkshire Risings of 1405: Texts and Contexts', pp. 161–84; Preest, *Chronica Maiora*, pp. 336–8; D. Biggs, 'Archbishop Scrope's *Manifesto* of 1405: "naïve nonsense" or reflections of political reality?', *Journal of Medieval History* 33 (2007): 358–71.

16 *Rotuli Parliamentorum*, vol. 3, pp. 604–7; *Ypodigma Neustriæ*, pp. 413–15; J. Raine, ed., *The Historians of the Church of York and its Archbishops* (London, 1894), vol. 2, pp. 309–19; M. H. Keen, 'Treason Trials under the Law of Arms', *Transactions of the Royal Historical Society* 12 (1962): 85–103; Kirby, *Henry IV*, pp. 1868; McNiven, 'The Betrayal of Archbishop Scrope', pp. 190–2, 206–7; *CAU*, pp. 202–3, 214–15; Dunn, 'Henry IV and the Politics of Resistance', pp. 9, 14–21; Walker, 'The Yorkshire Risings of 1405: Texts and Contexts', pp. 164–6, 179–82; Preest, *Chronica Maiora*, pp. 336–8.

17 *Rotuli Parliamentorum*, vol. 3, pp. 606–7; Kirby, *Henry IV*, p. 58; Tuck, *Richard II and the English Nobility*, p. 219; Saul, *Richard II*, pp. 413–16; *CAU*, pp. 58–9; Preest, *Chronica Maiora*, pp. 307–9.

18 *Saint-Denys*, vol. 3, pp. 428, 430, 429, 431; Williams, *Chronicque de la Traïson et Mort*, pp. 299–302 (author's translation); *RHL Henry IV*, vol. 2, pp. 61–3. (A letter from Prince John, later duke of Bedford, compellingly connecting the Scots to Bardolf's investment of Berwick, thus connecting the French to the Welsh, the Scots to Northumberland, and Northumberland to the Welsh. This is supported by Brown, *Black Douglases*, pp. 106–7.)

19 *Ypodigma Neustriæ*, pp. 413–15; Raine, *Historians of the Church of York*, vol. 2, pp. 292–304, 308–9; McNiven, 'The Betrayal of Archbishop Scrope', pp. 173–213; Kirby, *Henry IV*, p. 187; *CAU*, pp. 202–3; Preest, *Chronica Maiora*, pp. 336–8; Walker, 'The Yorkshire Risings of 1405: Texts and Contexts', pp. 172–5.

20 *Ypodigma Neustriæ*, pp. 359, 361, 363, 366, 370–3, 381, 398–402; Raine, *Historians of the Church of York*, pp. 298–304; McNiven, 'The Betrayal of Archbishop Scrope', pp. 200–1; Kirby, *Henry IV*, pp. 46–51, 86–91, 156–9; Tuck, *Richard II and the English Nobility*, pp. 156–8, 178–9; Saul, *Richard II*, pp. 204–34, 312, 439; *CAU*, pp. 48–51; Dunn, 'Henry IV and the Politics of Resistance', pp. 6–7, 13; Preest, *Chronica Maiora*, pp. 291, 296–7, 303, 315–17, 321–2, 326–9.

21 *Glendower*, p. 101; *Revolt*, pp. 117–18, 163–5.

22 *RHL Henry IV*, vol. 2, 76–9.

23 Tuetey, *Nicolas de Baye*, vol. 1, pp. 138–9; Darwin, *Louis d'Orléans*, pp. 74–84; d'Avout, *La Querelle*, 77–82; Vaughan, *John the Fearless*, pp. 33–7; Courteault, *Le Héraut Berry*, pp. 15–20; Schnerb, *Armagnacs et Bourguignons*, pp. 75–83.

24 *Saint-Denys*, vol. 3, pp. 262–7, 290–7; Jarry, *La Vie Politique*, pp. 337–41; Creighton, *History of the Papacy*, vol. 1, pp. 188–95; d'Avout, *La Querelle*, pp. 47, 77–82; Pillement, *Pedro de Luna*, pp. 124–6, 131–6 (Note: Pillement says Benedict withdrew in August, Creighton says October, p. 195; the latter seems the more reliable); Morrall, *Gerson*, p. 68; Lalande, *Jean II le Meingre*, pp. 130–9.

8: The Two French Invasions of 1405

1 *Saint-Denys*, vol. 3, pp. 322, 324.

2 Johnes, *Monstrelet*, pp. 28–9; *OGC*, pp. 202–5, 388–9 (author's translation).

3 J. H. Parry, ed., *Registrum Roberti Mascall: The Register of Robert Mascall, Bishop of Hereford (A.D. 1404–1416)* (Hereford, 1916), p. 6.

4 *Revolt*, pp. 193–4; Preest, *Chronica Maiora*, pp. 1, 7, 10–22, 339–41.

5 *Saint-Denys*, vol. 1, p. i; Johnes, *Monstrelet*, pp. xiv–xxv, 103–6; Douët-d'Arcq, *Monstrelet*, pp. i–xxiii, 81–4; K. Green et al., eds, *The Book of Peace* (Pennsylvania, 2008), p. 8.

6 Des Ursins, *Histoire de Charles VI, Roi de France*, p. 429; C. de Robillard de Beaurepaire, *Chronique normande de Pierre Cochon, notaire apostolique à Rouen* (Rouen, 1870), p. 211.

7 *Saint-Denys*, vol. 1, p. iv; Johnes, *Monstrelet*, pp. xiv–xxv; Douët-d'Arcq, *Monstrelet*, pp. i–xxiii.

8   *Saint-Denys*, vol. 3, pp. 322, 324, 326, 328 (author's translation).
9   *Saint-Denys*, vol. 4, p. 571; Douët-d'Arcq, *Choix de Pièces Inédites*, vol. 1, p. 164; Tuetey, *Nicolas de Baye*, vol. 1, pp. 153, 188–9, 209, vol. 2, pp. 10, 88–9, 209; Robillard de Beaurepaire, *Chronique normande*, p. 211 nn.4, 5; d'Avout, *La Querelle*, pp. 150–3; le Roulx, *La France en Orient*, pp. 171, 286; Courteault, *le Heraut Berry*, pp. 22 n. 2, 46–9; Lannette-Claverie, *Collection Joursanvault*, pp. 41, 82; C. Allmand, *The HundredYearsWar* (Cambridge, 1988), pp. 76–82; Archives Départementales de l'Hérault, A 1, folios 279 v° à 283 r°. Auteur de la transcription: Jean-Claude Toureille, available online: http://www. fordham.edu/halsall/french/bousico.htm [accessed 25/03/10].
10 Jarry, *LaVie Politique*, pp. 450–1; d'Avout, *La Querelle*, p. 76;Vaughan, *John the Fearless*, p. 30; J. Campbell, 'England, Scotland and the Hundred Years War in the Fourteenth Century', in J. R. Hale, J. R. L. Highfield and B. Smalley, eds, *Europe in the Late Middle Ages* (London, 1965), pp. 209–10; Cassard, *Le Trémazan des Du Chastel*, pp. 83–104.
11 Douët-d'Arcq, *Choix de Pièces Inédites*, vol. 1, p. 164; Kirby, *Henry IV*, p. 188; *Revolt*, p. 194; Preest, *Chronica Maiora*, pp. 339–41.
12 *Saint-Denys*, vol. 3, pp. 328–9, 'sexaginta leucas': 60 leagues is roughly 164 miles or 265 kilometres, but the route described in this account seems to cover roughly 70 miles or just over 110 kilometres.
13 Watt, *Scotichronicon*, vol. 8, p. 99.
14 Tuetey, *Nicolas de Baye*, vol. 2, p. 218; Bouchart, *Les Grandes Chroniques de Bretaigne*, p. 183; *La France gouvernée*, p. 111.
15 Douët-d'Arcq, *Choix de Pièces Inédites*, vol. 1, p. 164; Jarry, *La vie politique*, pp. 414–15; Evans, *Unconquered Knight*, p. 149; Carriazo, *El Victorial*, pp. 222, 246.
16 Douët-d'Arcq, *Choix de Pièces Inédites*, vol. 1, p. 164; Jarry, *La vie politique*, p. 97; d'Avout, *La Querelle*, pp. 14–15; Knecht, *Valois*, p. 48; Grèvy-Pons et al., *Jean de Montreuil, Opera*, vol. 2, pp. 111, 113.
17 Tuetey, *Nicolas de Baye*, vol. 1, pp. 181–2, 209; Jarry, *La vie politique*, pp. 50, 59, 97, 417–19; Courteault, *Le Héraut Berry*, p. 7 n.4; Lannette-Claverie, *Collection Joursanvault*, pp. 250, 252; C. A. G. Paz, 'The Role of Mercenary Troops in Spain in the Fourteenth Century: The Civil War', in France, ed., *Mercenaries and Paid Men*, pp. 331–42.
18 Johnes, *Monstrelet*, pp. 28–9; *OGC*, pp. 202–5, 388–9 (author's translation).
19 Johnes, *Monstrelet*, p. 105 n.; *Saint-Denys*, vol. 1, pp. 385–91, vol. 3, pp. 322–5; des Ursins, *Histoire de Charles VI*, p. 430; Lannette-Claverie, *Collection Joursanvault*, pp. 9–12, 24–7, 35, 87, 105, 178–9; Evans, *Unconquered Knight*, pp. 134–9; Carriazo, *ElVictorial*, pp. 219–22; Brown, *Black Douglases*, pp. 212–13; Laidlaw, *Auld Alliance*, pp. 41–2; Macdougall, *An Antidote to the English*, pp. 49–50; Joliffe, *Froissart's Chronicles*, pp. 263–77.

20 Johnes, *Monstrelet*, pp. 28–9; *Saint-Denys*, vol. 3, pp. 322–3; Douët-d'Arcq, *Monstrelet*, pp. 82–3; Parry, *Register of Robert Mascall*, p. 6; Preest, *Chronica Maiora*, pp. 339–41.

21 Johnes, *Monstrelet*, pp. 28–9; Douët-d'Arcq, *Monstrelet*, pp. 82–3; Douët-d'Arcq, *Choix de Pièces Inédites*, vol. 1, p. 164; Blanchard, *Lettres et Mandements*, vol. 4, pp. 31–2; *Glendower*, pp. 104 n. 1, 106.

22 *Saint-Denys*, vol. 3, pp. 166–7; Robillard de Beaurepaire, *Chronique normande* p. 211.

23 Williams, *Chronicque de la Traïson et Mort*, p. 168; Wylie, *History of England under Henry the Fourth*, vol. 1, p. 121; *CPR, 1396–9*, p. 40; *CPR, 1399–1401*, pp. 140, 249, 265, 426, 526; *RHL Henry IV*, vol. 1, pp. 384–5.

9: Invasion and Truce?

1 *RHL Henry IV*, vol. 2, pp. 76–9; *OGC*, pp. 116–19 (author's translation).

2 M. Postan, 'The Costs of the Hundred Years' War', *Past and Present* 27 (1964): 34–6; J. Sherborne, 'The Hundred Years' War: The English Navy: Shipping and manpower 1369–1389', *Past and Present* 37 (1967): 170–1, 174.

3 *CCR, 1385–89*, p. 208; Sherborne, 'The English Navy', pp. 167–74; I. Friel, *The Good Ship: Ships, Shipbuilding and Technology in England 1200–1520* (London, 1995), p. 149; C. Lambert, *Shipping the Medieval Military: English Maritime Logistics in the Fourteenth Century* (Woodbridge, 2011), pp. 108, 113, 125–6, 128–9, 154, 199–206.

4 *Revolt*, pp. 217, 231; Preest, *Chronica Maiora*, p. 339.

5 *Glendower*, p. 103 n.1; *Revolt*, p. 194.

6 *Glendower*, p. 104 n.2; G. Hodges, *Owain Glyn Dŵr and the War of Independence in the Welsh Border* (Little Logaston, 1995), pp. 134–8.

7 J. L. Kirby, ed., *Calendar of Signet Letters of Henry IV and Henry V (1399–1422)* (London, 1978), pp. 100–1, 105; H. Watt, '"On account of the frequent attacks and invasions of the Welsh": The Effect of the Glyn Dŵr Rebellion on Tax Collection in England', in Dodd and Biggs, *The Reign of Henry IV, Rebellion and Survival, 1403–1413*, pp. 48–81; Griffiths, 'Owain Glyn Dŵr's Invasion', pp. 111–22.

8 *RHL Henry IV*, vol. 1, pp. 155–9; *POPCE*, vol. 1, pp. 223–4, 229—30; Parry, *Register of Robert Mascall*, pp. v–vi, 16, 18–22, 35–6, 42, 49, 104–5, 116–24; Watt, 'On account of the frequent attacks and invasions of the Welsh', pp. 55–79.

9 Johnes, *Monstrelet*, p. 105; Douët-d'Arcq, *Monstrelet*, p. 83; Parry, *Register of Robert Mascall*, pp. v–vi, 16, 18–19, 20–2, 35–6, 49, 104–5, 116–24; Watt, 'On Account of the Frequent Attacks and Invasions of the Welsh', p. 57.

10 *POPCE*, vol. 2, pp. 77–8; *OGC*, pp. 80–1, 321–2.
11 *ANLP*, pp. 399–400.
12 *Revolt*, pp. 119–21.
13 *CCR, 1402–5*, pp. 460, 468–9.
14 *CCR, 1402–5*, pp. 527–8.
15 *CPR, 1405–8*, p. 61.
16 *CPR, 1405–8*, pp. 45, 48.
17 *CCR, 1402–5*, p. 469; *CPR, 1405–8*, pp. 43, 44.
18 *CPR, 1405–8*, p. 64; *CCR, 1402–5*, pp. 460, 529.
19 Johnes, *Monstrelet*, pp. 28–9; Douët-d'Arcq, *Monstrelet*, p. 83; *CPR, 1405–8*, pp. 37, 42, 47; *CCR, 1402–5*, p. 529.
20 *CCR, 1402–5*, p. 460.
21 *CFR, 1399–1405*, pp. 317–18.
22 Parry, *The Register of Robert Mascall*, p. 6.
23 *CPR, 1405–8*, pp. 35, 36, 41, 49, 57; *CCR, 1402–5*, p. 525.
24 *Glendower*, pp. 105–6. Lloyd suggests Henry was denied by rain, but does not say where this evidence comes from, and offers no explanation for the lack of such difficult conditions in either French chronicle.
25 *CPR, 1405–8*, pp. 55, 80; *CCR, 1405–9*, p. 1; *CFR 1405–13*, p. 4.
26 *Glendower*, pp. 106, 126; *Revolt*, p. 195.
27 Dunn, 'Henry IV and the Politics of Resistance', pp. 17, 22–3.
28 *RHL Henry IV*, vol. 1, pp. 155–9; *POPCE*, vol. 1, pp. 236, 278–9; *Glendower*, pp. 106–7 n.1; R. Turvey, 'The Marcher Shire of Pembroke and the Glyndŵr Rebellion', *Welsh Historical Review* 15:2 (1990): 16–35; *Revolt*, pp. 117, 188–9, 194–5, 234–6, 297–8; Griffiths, 'Prince Henry's War', pp. 170–3; *OGC*, pp. 80–1, 88–91, 102–3.
29 *CPR, 1399–1401*, pp. 117, 145; *CPR, 1405–8*, pp. 80, 181; *CCR, 1405–9*, p. 20; *Glendower*, 107; Turvey, 'The Marcher Shire of Pembroke and the Glyndŵr Rebellion', pp. 163–4; *Revolt*, p. 234.
30 *CPR, 1405–8*, p. 42.
31 *CCR, 1405–9*, p. 20.
32 *CPR, 1405–8*, p. 181.
33 *RHL Henry IV*, vol. 2, pp. 76–9; *Revolt*, pp. 117–18.
34 *CPR, 1401–5*, p. 475; *CPR, 1405–8*, p. 163; *CCR, 1402–5*, pp. 478–9; *Revolt*, p. 246. (Note:This also shows that the inland castles were supplied via the nearest coastal port, not across the land, in the case of Coity by a crayer at Ogmore.)
35 *POPCE*, vol. 1, pp. 278–9; *CPR, 1405–9*, pp. 80, 84, 147, 148, 149; *Glendower*, pp. 89, 105–6; *Revolt*, pp. 39, 43.
36 *POPCE*, vol. 2, pp. 77–8; *CPR, 1405–9*, pp. 80, 84, 149.
37 *Rotuli Parliamentorum*, vol. 3, pp. 569, 574–6; Griffiths, 'Prince Henry, Wales, and the Royal Exchequer, 1400–1413', p. 214; *Revolt*, pp. 122.

38 *Glendower*, pp. 99, 128; *Revolt*, pp. 122, 188–9, 254; *CAU*, p. 215.

39 *Glendower*, pp. 96–8; *Revolt*, p. 311. (Note: There is some confusion over who was held; Lloyd discussed the possibility of Gruffydd Yonge's capture and release that year [*Glendower*, p. 98 n.3], but dismissed it inconclusively. There might be a confusion with the English cleric and diplomat Richard Young who was taken by the Welsh around this time, perhaps slightly earlier [see Gabriel, 'Wales and the Avignon Papacy', p. 76].)

40 J. Smith, 'Cydfodau o'r Bumthegfed Ganrif', *BBCS* 21 (1966): 309–24, particularly pp. 313–15 (I am grateful to Dr Alun Williams of Cardiff University for his assistance with this article).

41 Smith, 'Cydfodau o'r Bumthegfed Ganrif', pp. 313–15 ('agreement meetings' seems a reasonable translation of 'cydfodau').

42 *Saint-Denys*, vol. 3, pp. 316–23 (it is noteworthy that de Savoisy is said to have spared the Genoese they found in England on the grounds that they were subjects of the French king, pp. 320–1); Evans, *Unconquered Knight*, pp. 107–32; Carriazo, *El Victorial*, pp. 186–215.

43 *Saint-Denys*, vol. 3, pp. 428–31; Williams, *Chronicque de la Traïson et Mort*, pp. 299–302 (author's translation); *RHL Henry IV*, vol. 2, pp. 61–3. (A letter from Prince John, later duke of Bedford, compellingly connecting the Scots to Bardolf's investment of Berwick, thus connecting the French to the Welsh, the Scots to Northumberland, and Northumberland to the Welsh. This is supported by Brown, *The Black Douglases*, pp. 106–7.)

44 *Saint-Denys*, vol. 3, pp. 428–31; Williams, *Chronicque de la Traïson et Mort*, pp. 299–302 (author's translation).

45 *Saint-Denys*, vol. 3, pp. 262–7, 290–7; Jarry, *La Vie Politique*, pp. 337–41; Creighton, *History of the Papacy*, vol. 1, pp. 188–95; d'Avout, *La Querelle*, 47; Pillement, *Pedro de Luna*, pp. 124–6, 131–6 (Pillement says Benedict withdrew in August, Creighton says October, p. 195; the latter seems the more reliable); Morrall, *Gerson*, p. 68; Lalande, *Jean II le Meingre*, pp. 130–9.

10: The Pennal Declaration

1 *Welsh Records*, pp. 54, 98.

2 *Welsh Records*, pp. 40–1, 83–4, 42–54 (52), 85–99 (96); *Glendower*, pp. 118–25; *Revolt*, pp. 169–73.

3 *Saint-Denys*, vol. 3, pp. 266–75, 284–9; Blumenfeld-Kosinski and Brownlee, *Selected Writings of Christine de Pizan*, pp. 201–16; Schnerb, *Armagnacs et Bourguignons*, pp. 75–83.

4 E. L. Du Pin, trans. anon., *A New Ecclesiastical History* (London, 1694),

vol. 13, p. 78; *Welsh Records*, pp. 42, 85; Griffiths, *Conquerors and Conquered*, pp. 123–38; *Revolt*, pp. 187–8; *OGC*, p. 35.

5 *Saint-Denys*, vol. 3, pp. 328–9; *Welsh Records*, pp. 23–39, 42, 75–82, 85–6; *Glendower*, pp. 82–6, 126; *Revolt*, pp. 116, 121, 192–5.

6 *Welsh Records*, pp. 40–1, 83–4; Grèvy-Pons et al., *Jean de Montreuil*, vol. 2, p. 96; Chamberlin, *Count of Virtue*, p. 71; Watt, ed., *Scotichronicon*, vol. 8, pp. 106–9; *CAU*, pp. 147, 151, 199–210; Marchant, *Chronicles*, pp. 164–71.

7 *Welsh Records*, pp. 40, 83.

8 *Glendower*, pp. 82, 101, 118–21; *Revolt*, pp. 116–17, 163–4, 169–70.

9 Ellis, *Original Letters*, p. 43; *RHL Henry IV*, vol. 2, pp. 76–9; *Welsh Records*, pp. 52, 96; *Glendower*, pp. 101, 119; *Revolt*, pp. 164, 220.

10 *Welsh Records*, pp. 43–51, 86–95.

11 *Welsh Records*, pp. 51–2, 95–6; *OGC*, pp. 347–50.

12 *Glendower*, pp. 118–21; *Revolt*, pp. 121, 162, 169–73.

13 *Welsh Records*, pp. 51, 54, 95–6, 98.

14 Grèvy-Pons et al., *Jean de Montreuil, Opera*, vol. 2, pp. 113, 159–218, esp. 201–2.

15 *Welsh Records*, pp. 53, 54, 96–8.

16 Gabriel, 'Wales and the Avignon Papacy', pp. 70–86; *Glendower*, pp. 118–21; Williams, *Welsh Church from Conquest to Reformation*, pp. 222–5; *Revolt*, pp. 169–73.

17 *Welsh Records*, pp. 52, 97.

18 *Welsh Records*, pp. 52, 97.

19 *Welsh Records*, pp. 52–3, 97.

20 *Welsh Records*, pp. 53, 97–8; *OGC*, pp. 347–50.

21 *Revolt*, p. 172.

22 *Glendower*, pp. 93–5, 100, 120; *Revolt*, pp. 166–9. See Charles VI's Letter to the English Nation, 1406, *Saint-Denys*, vol. 3, pp. 428–31, also in Williams, *Chronicque de la Traïson et Mort*, pp. 299–302, as well as N. Grèvy(-Pons), E. Ornato and G. Ouy, *Jean de Montreuil, Opera*, vol. 1, *Epistolario*, pp. 280–2.

23 *Welsh Records*, pp. 53, 98.

24 *Glendower*, p. 120; *Revolt*, p. 170.

25 W. H. Bliss, ed., *Calendar of Entries in the Papal Registers Relating to Great Britain and Ireland, Petitions to the Pope: Papal Register, A. D. 1342–1419*, (London: Eyre and Spottiswoode, 1896), pp. 48 (1344), 367 (1361), 516, 519 (both 1366); Vaughan, *Valois Burgundy*, pp. 112–13; Galliou and Jones, *The Bretons*, p. 278; Abse, *Letters From Wales* (1201), p. 14.

26 *Welsh Records*, pp. 53, 98.

27 *Welsh Records*, pp. 53–4, 98.

28 *Welsh Records*, pp. 54, 98.

29 R. N. Swanson, *Universities, Academics and The Great Schism* (Cambridge, 1979), pp. 216–17; *Revolt*, p. 171.

30 Matthews, *Welsh Records*, 54, 98.

31 *Ypodigma Neustriæ*, pp. 389–90, 398–402; Kirby, *Henry IV*, pp. 88, 93–4, 157–8, 187; Grèvy-Pons et al., *Jean de Montreuil, Opera*, vol. 2, pp. 196–7 (Traité Contre Les Anglais, étape 1); T. John, *Sir Thomas Erpingham, 1357–1428* (Dereham, 1999), p. 5; Dunn, 'Henry IV and the Politics of Resistance', pp. 5–23.

32 Dunn, 'Henry IV and the Politics of Resistance', p. 13.

33 *Ypodigma Neustriæ*, pp. 393–4, 413–15; Kirby, *Henry IV*, p. 187; Dunn, 'Henry IV and the Politics of Resistance', pp. 5–23; Williams, *Chronicque de la Traïson et Mort*, pp. 299–302.

34 *Welsh Records*, pp. 54, 98–9.

35 *Glendower*, p. 121; *Revolt*, p. 170.

36 *Welsh Records*, pp. 103–5, 111–13; *CAU*, pp. 148–53.

37 Creighton, *History of the Papacy*, vol. 1, pp. 85, 88–9, 127–8; Chamberlin, *Count of Virtue*, pp. 56–63; Vaughan, *Philip the Bold*, pp. 28–30, 48; R. G. Davies, *Henry Despenser, d. 1406* (ODNB, 2001); Ainsworth and Diller, eds, *Chroniques*, pp. 945–69.

38 Gabriel, 'Wales and the Avignon Papacy', p. 73; repeated in *Revolt*, p. 173. (This claim has not yet been substantiated in primary sources.)

39 N. Housley, *The Avignon Papacy and the Crusades, 1305–1378* (Oxford, 1986), pp. 9–81.

40 Morrall, *Gerson*, p. 59.

41 *Welsh Records*, pp. 50, 94; Pillement, *Pedro de Luna*, pp. 131–6; d'Avout, *La Querelle*, p. 47.

42 C. Eubel, ed., *Hierarchia Catholica Medii Aevi* (Rome, 1898), vol. 1, pp. 112, Joannes Trevor, p. 127, ludovicus (Lewis Byford) 14 August 1404, Boniface IX, Griffinus 14 February 1407, n.3, Decr. Doctor. Ben XIII (Av. T. 49 f. 57) 1407 April 25 (1418 hic Giffinusa Mart. V ad eccl. Rossen. in Scotia translates est.) 292 n.8, 26 April 1407 Benedict XIII appointed Adam Usk bishop of Llandaff, 336 n.10, A 23 maii 1408 ei a Gre XII data est facultas absolvendi scismaticos et rebelles in partibus Walliae ad unionem Ecclesiae redituros, all listed as 'suffr. Cantuarien' (Note: this is a collation of all of the traceable appointments made to Glyn Dŵr's clergy during the period of his reign); Gabriel, 'Wales and the Avignon Papacy', pp. 73, 78. 80; Williams, *Welsh Church From Conquest to Reformation*, p. 224; *CAU*, pp. xxxix, xxxv. (Note: other references cited by Gabriel were untraceable.)

43 Eubel, *Hierarchia Catholica Medii Aevi*, vol. 1, pp. 127, Griffinus 14 February 1407, n.3, Decr. Doctor. Ben XIII (Av. T. 49 f. 57) 1407 April 25 ei dedit facultatem absolvendi Owinum principem Walliae et alias personas eccl.

Et relig. Ac etiam laicas eidem principi subjectas, redeuntes ad obedientam suam, atque mandavit, et se informaret et referret de exaltanda eccl. Meneven, in metropolitanam. The mention of 'Meneven, in metropolitanam' suggests that Benedict was aware of the Welsh desire written in the Pennal Declaration for St David's to be the metropolitan church.

44 W. H. Bliss, ed., *Calendar of Entries in the Papal Registers Relating to Great Britain and Ireland: Petitions to the Pope, Vol. 1, A.D. 1342–1419* (London, 1896), pp. 623–4, 633.

45 *Welsh Records*, pp. 42–3, 85–6.

46 *Saint-Denys*, vol. 3, pp. 266–91; Creighton, *History of the Papacy*, pp. 195–6; Pillement, *Pedro de Luna*, p. 139; Vaughan, *John the Fearless*, p. 37; Schnerb, *Armagnacs et Bourguignons*, pp. 75–83.

47 *Saint-Denys*, vol. 3, pp. 432–9; Johnes, *Monstrelet*, pp. 167–74; des Ursins, *Histoire de Charles VI*, pp. 431–2; Robillard de Beaurepaire, *Chronique normande*, p. 218; Darwin, *Louis d'Orléans*, pp. 87–90; Vaughan, *John the Fearless*, pp. 38–9; Courteault, *Le Héraut Berry*, pp. 20–1; B. Schnerb, *L'Etat Bourguignon, 1363–1477*, (Paris, 2005), pp. 146–7; Schnerb, *Armagnacs et Bourguignons*, p. 85.

48 *Lettres et Mandements*, vol. 4, pp. 109–10, 117–18; Jarry, *La Vie Politique*, pp. 345–7; Darwin, *Louis d'Orléans*, p. 87.

49 Johnes, *Monstrelet*, pp. 174–6; *Saint-Denys*, vol. 3, pp. 374–91, 464–89; des Ursins, *Histoire de Charles VI*, pp. 432–7; Jarry, *La Vie Politique*, pp. 341–4; Creighton, *History of the Papacy*, vol. 1, pp. 195–6, 201–2; Pillement, *Pedro de Luna*, pp. 137–41; Morrall, *Gerson*, pp. 69–75; Shennan, *Parlement of Paris*, pp. 162–3, 169–70, 183–4.

50 Johnes, *Monstrelet*, pp. 169–74; *Saint-Denys*, vol. 3, pp. 426–39, 448–63; des Ursins, *Histoire de Charles VI*, pp. 435–6; Robillard de Beaurepaire, *Chronique normande*, p. 218; Vaughan, *John the Fearless*, pp. 38–9; *Glendower*, p. 133; Vaughan, *John the Fearless*, pp. 39–41; Preest, *Chronica Maiora*, p. 348; Schnerb, *L'Etat Bourguignon*, p. 147; Schnerb, *Armagnacs et Bourguignons*, pp. 85–7.

51 *Saint-Denys*, vol. 3, pp. 428–31; Williams, *Chronicque de la Traïson et Mort*, pp. 299–302; N. Grèvy(-Pons), E. Ornato and G. Ouy, *Jean de Montreuil, Opera*, vol. 1, *Epistolario*, pp. 280–2.

52 *Ypodigma Neustriæ*, pp. 423–4; Gabriel, 'Wales and the Avignon Papacy', p. 78; Kirby, *Henry IV*, pp. 218–19; *Revolt*, p. 186.

53 Jarry, *La Vie Politique*, p. 348; Darwin, *Louis d'Orléans*, p. 49; Schnerb, *Armagnacs et Bourguignons*, p. 90.

11: English Diplomatic Manoeuvring

1 Blanchard, *Lettres et Mandements*, vol. 5, p. 75.

2 Dunn, 'Henry IV and the Politics of Resistance', pp. 5–23.

3 *Saint-Denys*, vol. 3, pp. 200–9, 274–9.

4 Griffiths, 'The Eyes of an Englishman', pp. 151–68; A. Macdonald, Unpublished PhD Thesis: 'Crossing the Border: A Study of the Scottish Military Offensives against England c.1369–c.1403', University of Aberdeen, 1995, pp. 119–63.

5 Haydon, *Eulogium Historarium*, vol. 3, p. 388; *POPCE*, vol. 1, p. 134; *Glendower*, p. 28; *Revolt*, p. 263.

6 *Glendower*, pp. 39, 48–52, 66–7, 81, 150–2; *Revolt*, pp. 107, 112, 116–17, 194, 266.

7 *Glendower*, pp. 96–7, 152; *Revolt*, pp. 233, 326.

8 Griffiths, 'The Eyes of an Englishman', pp. 151–68; *Revolt*, p. 306.

9 Vaughan, *Valois Burgundy*, p. 130.

10 *RHL Henry IV*, vol. 1, pp. 345–7, 348–9, 356–60, *passim*.

11 Fowler, *Hundred Years War*, pp. 186–7; Cuttino, *English Medieval Diplomacy*, pp. 8–10, 18, 94.

12 *RHL Henry IV*, vol. 1, pp. 170–4, 214–25, 269, 318–29, 345, *passim*; vol. 2, 107–9, 167–70, 187–92, *passim*; Preest, *Chronica Maiora*, p. 340 n.1.

13 *RHL Henry IV*, vol. 1, pp. 171–4.

14 *RHL Henry IV*, vol. 1, pp. 177–85, 186–8, 188–90, 194–7, 197–9, 202–5, 230–1.

15 *RHL Henry IV*, vol. 1, pp. 177–85, 188–90, 242–4, 249–50, 253–5, 256–7, *passim*; vol. 2, pp. 61–3, 354–62.

16 Johnes, *Monstrelet*, p. 103; Douët-d'Arcq, *Monstrelet*, p. 81; *Saint-Denys*, vol. 3, pp. 322–3; *RHL Henry IV*, vol. 1, pp. 215–25; *Welsh Records*, pp. 28, 31, 78, 81.

17 *RHL Henry IV*, vol. 1, pp. 222–4.

18 *RHL Henry IV*, vol. 1, pp. 229–38, 245–8, 249–50, 256–7, 266–9, 294–9, 335–7, 345–7, 348–9, 356–60, 381; Vaughan, *John the Fearless*, pp. 21–2; Vaughan, *Valois Burgundy*, p. 41.

19 *RHL Henry IV*, vol. 1, pp. 329–35, 338–40, 367–70, 384–5, 392. 'XV millium armatorum ac equitum … ad occupandum et reædificandum castra in Wallia destructa et ad omnia mala ac damna possibilia nobis inferenda.'

20 *RHL Henry IV*, vol. 1, pp. 376–80, 385–92, 395–9, 402–4, 404–5.

21 *RHL Henry IV*, vol. 2, pp. 15–17, 25–7, 27–8, 40–3 (Richard Young, Rome's bishop of Bangor, and Thomas Pykworth joined Aston and Ryssheton), 43–4, 46–7, 48–9.

22 *RHL Henry IV*, vol. 2, pp. 59–61, 61–6, 72, 73–6, 83–114.

23 Johnes, *Monstrelet*, pp. 126–35; *Saint-Denys*, vol. 3, pp. 258–63; Douët-d'Arcq, *Monstrelet*, pp. 100–8; *RHL Henry IV*, vol. 2, pp. 53, 55–9, 67–71.

24 *RHL Henry IV*, vol. 2, pp. 107–9, 115–16, 120–2, 122–35.

25 Blanchard, *Lettres et Mandements*, vol. 4, pp. 1–2; Darwin, *Louis d'Orléans*, pp. 60–1; d'Avout, *La Querelle*, p. 71; Vaughan, *Philip the Bold*, p. 53; Kirby, *Henry IV*, pp. 135, 149–51.

26 Des Ursins, *Histoire de Charles VI*, p. 413; Bouchart, *Les Grandes Chroniques de Bretaigne*, p. 172; Darwin, *Louis d'Orléans*, pp. 60–1; Courteault, *Le Héraut Berry*, p. 12.

27 Blanchard, *Lettres et Mandements*, vol. 4, pp. 59, 61, 63, 69–71, 76, 77, 78, 82, 87, 99, 109–10, 117–18; Jarry, *La Vie Politique*, pp. 344–7; Darwin, *Louis d'Orléans*, p. 87; *RHL Henry IV*, vol. 2, pp. 115–16.

28 *Foedera*, vol. 8, pp. 483–4; Blanchard, *Lettres et Mandements*, vol. 5, pp. 12, 16, 17. 44, 45, 47, 63, 69; Preest, *Chronica Maiora*, pp. 340–1.

29 *Foedera*, vol. 8, p. 490; Blanchard, *Lettres et Mandements*, vol. 5, p. 75.

30 *RHL Henry IV*, vol. 2, pp. 167–9, 171–8.

31 *RHL Henry IV*, vol. 2, pp. 187–92, 193–9; Cuttino, *English Medieval Diplomacy*, pp. 19, 99; Nye, 'Public Diplomacy and Soft Power', p. 94.

12: Ailing France, Rising England

1 *POPCE*, vol. 1, p. 302.

2 *Saint-Denys*, vol. 3, pp. 266–91, 465–72; Creighton, *History of the Papacy*, pp. 195–6; Pillement, *Pedro de Luna*, pp. 137–41; Schnerb, *Armagnacs et Bourguignons*, pp. 75–83.

3 Johnes, *Monstrelet*, pp. 174–6; *Saint-Denys*, vol. 3, pp. 374–91, 464–89; des Ursins, *Histoire de Charles VI*, pp. 432–7; Jarry, *La Vie Politique*, pp. 341–4; Creighton, *History of the Papacy*, vol. 1, pp. 195–6, 201–2; Pillement, *Pedro de Luna*, pp. 137–41; Morrall, *Gerson*, pp. 69–75; Shennan, *Parlement of Paris*, pp. 162–3, 169–70, 183–4.

4 *Saint-Denys*, vol. 3, pp. 473–88; Creighton, *History of the Papacy*, pp. 195–6; Pillement, *Pedro de Luna*, pp. 140–1; Morrall, *Gerson*, p. 69.

5 Creighton, *History of the Papacy*, p. 199; Pillement, *Pedro de Luna*, pp. 136, 139; Morrall, *Gerson*, p. 72.

6 Creighton, *History of the Papacy*, pp. 204–5; Morrall, *Gerson*, pp. 69–75.

7 *Saint-Denys*, vol. 3, pp. 511–20, 583–625; Creighton, *History of the Papacy*, pp. 201–7; Pillement, *Pedro de Luna*, pp. 145–8; Morrall, *Gerson*, pp. 68–9.

8 Creighton, *History of the Papacy*, pp. 204–5; Pillement, *Pedro de Luna*, pp. 143–4, 150–1; Morrall, *Gerson*, pp. 73–4.

9 Creighton, *History of the Papacy*, pp. 208–9; Pillement, *Pedro de Luna*, p. 152.

10 Bliss, *Petitions to the Pope,Vol. 1*, pp. 623–4, *passim*.

11 Bellaguet, *Saint-Denys*, vol. 3, pp. 647–72; Creighton, *History of the Papacy*, pp. 209–14; Pillement, *Pedro de Luna*, pp. 148–52.

12 *Fœdera*, vol. 8, pp. 368–9, 371–2, 418, 430, 452; *Ypodigma Neustriæ*, p. 413; *RHL Henry IV*, vol. 2, pp. 162–5, 232–5; *CPR, 1405–8*, p. 168; Bean, 'Henry IV and The Percies', pp. 212–27; Preest, *Chronica Maiora*, pp. 323–4, 341, 341; Laidlaw, *Auld Alliance*, p. 49; Macdougall, *Antidote to the English*, p. 58; Brown, *The Black Douglases*, p. 105–9.

13 *Glendower*, pp. 149–54; Henken, *National Redeemer*, pp. 13, 64–5; *Revolt*, pp. 122–4.

14 *Glendower*, pp. 99, 129–30; *Revolt*, pp. 122–4, 188–9.

15 *CPR, 1405–8*, pp. 361–2; *Revolt*, p. 293.

16 *CPR, 1405–8*, p. 362.

17 *Glendower*, p. 131; Griffiths, 'Prince Henry, Wales, and the Royal Exchequer', p. 211; *Revolt*, pp. 124, 252–3.

18 *Rot. Parl.*, vol. 3, pp. 611–12; *Glendower*, p. 131; *Revolt*, pp. 124–5, 252–3.

19 *CPR, 1405–8*, p. 359; *Glendower*, p. 132; *Revolt*, p. 253; Preest, *Chronica Maiora*, pp. 356–8. (This also appears in *Fœdera*, vol. 8, p. 419, incorrectly dated.)

20 *Glendower*, pp. 131–3, 136–7, 153; *Revolt*, pp. 124–5, 151, 253, 293; Preest, *Chronica Maiora*, p. 358.

21 Jarry, *La Vie Politique*, pp. 97, 257–68; Darwin, *Louis d'Orléans*, pp. 19, 51–3, 59–67; d'Avout, *La Querelle*, pp. 14–15, 25, 56–83; *La France gouvernée*, p. 7; Vaughan, *Philip the Bold*, pp. 24–45, 52, 56–8; Vaughan, *John the Fearless*, pp. 41–3; Knecht, *Valois*, pp. 41–8; Schnerb, *Armagnacs et Bourguignons*, pp. 20–1, 23, 27–30, 64.

22 Darwin, *Louis d'Orléans*, pp. 12, 19–21, 23–4, 30–1, 47; d'Avout, *La Querelle*, pp. 32–43; Bueno de Mesquita, *Giangaleazzo Visconti*, pp. 12, 63, 66–7, 203–4, 267; Vaughan, *Philip the Bold*, pp. 44, 55–6, 109; Morrall, *Gerson*, pp. 6–11; Chamberlin, *Count of Virtue*, pp. 89–93, 109–13, 175–80; Lalande, *Le Livre Des Fais*, p. 116; Lalande, *Jean II le Meingre*, pp. 68, 97 n.3, 98–101; B. Schnerb, 'le contingent franco-bourguinon à la croisade de Nicopolis', in J. Paviot and M. Chauney-Bouillot, eds, *Nicopolis, 1396–1996, Actes du Colloque International* (Dijon: Société des Annales de Bourgogne, 1997), p. 67.

23 Jarry, *La Vie Politique*, pp. 203–4, 272–5; Darwin, *Louis d'Orléans*, pp. 21–4, 28, 35–6, 47–8; d'Avout, *La Querelle*, pp. 48–53; Courteault, *Le Héraut Berry*, pp. 13–14; Schnerb, *Armagnacs et Bourguignons*, p. 57.

24 Tuetey, *Nicolas de Baye*, vol. 1, pp. 138–9; Jarry, *La Vie Politique*, p. 353; Darwin, *Louis d'Orléans*, pp. 24–8, 37–9, 48–9, 64, 74–90; d'Avout, *La Querelle*, pp. 77–82; Vaughan, *John the Fearless*, pp. 30–7; Courteault, *Le Héraut Berry*, pp. 15–20; Schnerb, *Armagnacs et Bourguignons*, pp. 75–83.

25 Jarry, *La Vie Politique*, pp. 333–7, 353–4; Darwin, *Louis d'Orléans*, pp. 28, 35–6, 39–40, 49, 78–90; d'Avout, *La Querelle*, p. 82; Schnerb, *Armagnacs et Bourguignons*, p. 82.

26 Jarry, *La Vie Politique*, pp. 354–5; Darwin, *Louis d'Orléans*, pp. 111–26; d'Avout, *La Querelle*, p. 83; Morrall, *Gerson*, p. 13; Vaughan, *John the Fearless*, pp. 44–8; Courteault, *Le Héraut Berry*, pp. 21–2; Preest, *Chronica Maiora*, p. 361; Schnerb, *Armagnacs et Bourguignons*, pp. 91–101.

27 *POPCE*, vol. 1, pp. 302–3.

28 *POPCE*, vol. 1, p. 302, 'sans ce q le dit Oweyn soit compris en icelles', 'le dit Oweyn nest pas nomez'.

29 *POPCE*, vol. 1, p. 302, 'doit estre soubgiz de la C[ouronne]'.

30 *Fœdera*, vol. 8, pp. 484–5, 504–6.

31 *Fœdera*, vol. 8, pp. 506–7, 507–8, 508–9, 508–13.

32 Blumenfeld-Kosinski and Brownlee, *The Selected Writings of Christine de Pizan*, pp. 224–9.

33 *Welsh Records*, pp. 26, 76–7.

34 Darwin, *Louis d'Orléans*, pp. 155–72; d'Avout, *La Querelle*, pp. 98–9; Morrall, *Gerson*, pp. 13, 74; Chamberlin, *Count of Virtue*, pp. 81–2, 178; Schnerb, *Armagnacs et Bourguignons*, pp. 103–15.

35 Creighton, *History of the Papacy*, pp. 208–9, 214–20; Pillement, *Pedro de Luna*, p. 152; Lalande, *le Livre des Faits*, pp. 370–8; Lalande, *Jean II le Meingre*, pp. 146–8.

36 *Fœdera*, vol. 8, pp. 490, 511–12, 514–15, 521–5; *Saint-Denys*, vol. 3, pp. 511–20, 583–625; Creighton, *History of the Papacy*, pp. 201–7, 220; Pillement, *Pedro de Luna*, pp. 145–8, 153–4; Morrall, *Gerson*, pp. 68–9.

37 *Saint-Denys*, vol. 4, pp. 19–28; Creighton, *History of the Papacy*, pp. 220–4; Pillement, *Pedro de Luna*, pp. 140, 154–5, 162–4.

38 Gabriel, 'Wales and the Avignon Papacy', pp. 82–3n.; *Glendower*, p. 143; Davies, *Revolt*, p. 190.

39 Douët-d'Arcq, *Choix de Pièces Inédites*, p. 309; Douët-d'Arcq, *Monstrelet*, p. 259; Preest, *Chronica Maiora*, p. 341. Note: *Glendower*, p. 136 n.5 cautiously disagrees with Monstrelet.

40 Williams, *Chronique de la traison et mort*, pp. 299–302; *RHL Henry IV*, vol. 2, pp. 61–3; *Saint-Denys*, vol. 3, p. 431.

41 Creighton, *History of the Papacy*, pp. 224–7; Pillement, *Pedro de Luna*, pp. 156–72.

42 *Saint-Denys*, vol. 3, pp. 745–9; *CPR, 1408–13*, p. 82; Kingsford, *English Historical Literature in the Fifteenth Century*, p. 283; *Glendower*, pp. 130–7; Vaughan, *John the Fearless*, p. 69; Kirby, *Henry IV*, pp. 218–21; Griffiths, 'Prince Henry, Wales, and the Royal Exchequer, 1400–1413', p. 211; *Revolt*, pp. 125, 186, 253, 293; Preest, *Chronica Maiora*, pp. 359–60.

43 F. Devon, ed., *Issues of the Exchequer* (London: Record Commission, 1837),

pp. 321, 326–7; *Glendower*, pp. 136–7; Kirby, *Henry IV*, pp. 220–1; Griffiths, 'Prince Henry, Wales, and the Royal Exchequer', p. 211; Hodges, *The War of Independence in the Welsh Border*, p. 150; *Revolt*, p. 253, 293, 326.

44 Douët-d'Arcq, *Monstrelet*, pp. 256, 259; G. Burnett, ed., *Exchequer Rolls of Scotland*, (1880), vol. 4 (Edinburgh, 1880), p. 71; *CCR, 1409–1413*, pp. 10–11; *Glendower*, pp. 126, 128 n1, 140–2; J. B. Smith, 'The Last Phase of the Glyndŵr Rebellion', *BBCS* 22 (1966–8): 250–60, esp. 253 n1; Friel, *The Good Ship*, p. 159; *Revolt*, pp. 214, 234–6, 297–8, 300–1, 310–11; Preest, *Chronica Maiora*, p. 341.

45 Creighton, *History of the Papacy*, pp. 234–52; Morrall, *Gerson*, pp. 13, 93; Kirby, *Henry IV*, pp. 221–2; Crowder, *Unity, Heresy and Reform*, pp. 41–64.

46 Darwin, *Louis d'Orléans*, pp. 184–7; *RHL Henry IV*, vol. 2, pp. 247–53, 254–6; Courteault, *Le Héraut Berry*, pp. 26–30; Vaughan, *John the Fearless*, pp. 49–66; Schnerb, *Armagnacs et Bourguignons*, pp. 115–23.

47 Blanchard, *Lettres et Mandements*, vol. 5, pp. 103, 105, 107–8, 136–7; d'Avout, *La Querelle*, pp. 105–28; Morrall, *Gerson*, pp. 13–15; Vaughan, *John the Fearless*, pp. 75–87; Courteault, *Le Héraut Berry*, pp. 40–5; Vaughan, *John the Fearless*, p. 82; Knecht, *Valois*, pp. 44, 54–5; Green et al., *The Book of Peace*, pp. 14–15; Schnerb, *Armagnacs et Bourguignons*, pp. 136–42.

48 *RHL Henry IV*, vol. 2, pp. 278–83, 287–94. (Note: the King of Castile's mother was Henry IV's sister.)

49 Dickinson et al., *A Source Book Of Scottish History*, pp. 168–71.

50 *Saint-Denys*, vol. 4, pp. 475–9; d'Avout, *La Querelle*, pp. 134, 142–5; Vaughan, *John the Fearless*, pp. 91–2; Courteault, *Le Héraut Berry*, pp. 45–6; Schnerb, *Armagnacs et Bourguignons*, p. 153.

51 *Saint-Denys*, vol. 4, pp. 509–13, 523–9 (includes a noteworthy anti-English rant by the chronicler); Tuetey, *Nicolas de Baye*, vol. 2, p. 30; d'Avout, *La Querelle*, pp. 146–52; Vaughan, *John the Fearless*, pp. 92–3; Courteault, *Le Héraut Berry*, pp. 46–7; Schnerb, *Armagnacs et Bourguignons*, pp. 152–6.

52 Blanchard, *Lettres et Mandements de Jean V, duc de Bretagne*, vol. 5, pp. 155, 166–7.

53 Bellaguet, *Saint-Denys*, vol. 4, pp. 569–79; Vaughan, *John the Fearless*, pp. 139–41; Courteault, *Le Héraut Berry*, pp. 48–9; Lannette-Claverie, *Collection Joursanvault* (1410–12), p. 209, *passim*.

54 *Glendower*, pp. 142, 154; *Revolt*, pp. 227, 302; Preest, *Chronica Maiora*, p. 383.

55 Courteault, *Le Héraut Berry*, p. 49; Knecht, *Valois*, p. 56; Schnerb, *Armagnacs et Bourguignons*, pp. 156–8. Note: A defamatory passage describes the desperation with which the Armagnacs sought English support, in which it was claimed that the dukes of Berry, Orleans and Bourbon, as well as the count d'Alençon, agreed to go in person with Henry against the duke of Burgundy, but also against the Welsh and the Irish. While it demonstrates their feeble

desperation as well as their treachery to their Welsh allies, it is certainly a
Burgundian invention to tarnish the names of their rivals. This appears in
Johnes, *Monstrelet*, vol. 2, pp. 240–1; repeated in Jean de Wavrin, trans. W.
Hardy and E. Hardy, *Chronique* (London: HMSO, 1887), vol. 4, book 6, Ch.
26, pp. 147–8 and presented as fact by Wylie, *History of England under Henry
the Fourth*, vol. 4, p. 67.

56 Darwin, *Louis d'Orléans*, p. 223; d'Avout, *La Querelle*, pp. 134, 154–5, 159;
Vaughan, *John the Fearless*, pp. 91–2, 97; Vaughan, *Valois Burgundy*, pp. 153–4;
Courteault, *Le Héraut Berry*, p. 49; Knecht, *Valois*, p. 56; Schnerb, *Armagnacs
et Bourguignons*, pp. 156–8, 161.

57 *Saint-Denys*, vol. 4, pp. 691–702; d'Avout, *La Querelle*, 156; Courteault, *Le
Héraut Berry*, pp. 49–51; Vaughan, *John the Fearless*, p. 97; Schnerb, *Armagnacs
et Bourguignons*, pp. 159–61.

58 *Saint-Denys*, vol. 4, pp. 705–23; Douët-d'Arcq, *Choix de Pièces Inédites*,
pp. 352, 359; *RHL Henry IV*, vol. 2, pp. 322–5, 328–32; d'Avout, *La Querelle*,
p. 159; Vaughan, *John the Fearless*, p. 97; Courteault *Le Héraut Berry*, p. 51;
Blumenfeld-Kosinski and Brownlee, *The Selected Writings of Christine de Pizan*,
pp. 229–48; Green et al., *The Book of Peace*, pp. 28; Schnerb, *Armagnacs et
Bourguignons*, pp. 160–1.

13: Constance – A Last Stand for Wales?

1 Crowder, *Unity, Heresy and Reform*, p. 117.

2 Creighton, *History of The Papacy*, vol. 2, pp. 3–50; Pillement, *Pedro de Luna*,
pp. 228–34; Vaughan, *John the Fearless*, pp. 210–12; Leff, *Heresy in the Later
Middle Ages*, vol. 2, pp. 606–708; Peters, *Heresy and Authority*, pp. 277–97;
Lambert, *Medieval Heresy*, pp. 306–82; H. Kaminsky, *A History of the Hussite
Revolution* (Los Angeles, 1967), pp. 141–3; Crowder, *Unity, Heresy and Reform*,
pp. 92–103.

3 H. Hutchison, *Henry V* (London, 1967), p. 131; Vaughan, *John the Fearless*, pp.
99–101, 193–210; Allmand, *Lancastrian Normandy*, pp. 2–8, 11–12; E. Jacob,
Henry V and the Invasion of France (Westport, 1984), pp. 90, 106; Galliou and
Jones, *The Bretons*, p. 237; Knecht, *Valois*, pp. 56–8; Green et al., *The Book of
Peace*, pp. 16–21; Schnerb, *Armagnacs et Bourguignons*, pp. 163–208, 211–14,
217, 224–31.

4 Hutchison, *Henry V*, pp. 104–9; T. Pugh, *Henry V and the Southampton Plot*
(Stroud, 1998).

5 Hutchison, *Henry V*, pp. 110–17; Jacob, *Henry*, pp. 90–1; A. Curry, *The Hundred
Years War* (Basingstoke: Macmillan, 1993), pp. 97–8; Allmand, *Hundred Years
War*, pp. 28–9.

6   Hutchison, *Henry V*, pp. 119–26; Jacob, *Henry V*, pp. 95–106; Curry, *Hundred Years War*, pp. 94–102.

7   H. T. Evans, *Wales and the Wars of the Roses* (Stroud, 1998), pp. 23, 27–8, 35; *Revolt*, p. 311; A. Curry, *The Battle of Agincourt: Sources and Interpretations* (Woodbridge, 2009), pp. 118, 163–4.

8   Jacob, *Henry V*, p. 106; Lalande, *Boucicaut*, pp. 169–74; M.-J. Arn, 'Charles, Duke of Orléans (1394–1465)', *ODNB* [accessed 13/08/10].

9   Vaughan, *John the Fearless*, pp. 209, 213; M. G. A. Vale, *Charles VII*, (London, 1974), p. 21; Knecht, *Valois*, pp. 58–9; Schnerb, *Armagnacs et Bourguignons*, p. 226.

10 Hutchison, *Henry V*, p. 126; Jacob, *Henry V*, p. 95.

11 P. Contamine, *Guerre, Etat et Société à la Fin du Moyen Age* (Paris, 1972), pp. 208–373; P. Ordioni, *Le Pouvoir Militaire en France, de Charles VII a Charles de Gaulle* (Paris, 1981), pp. 31–5, 51–66, 67–72.

12 *Fœdera*, vol. 9, pp. 377–82; Creighton, *History of The Papacy*, vol. 2, pp. 65–6; Loomis, 'Nationality at the Council of Constance', p. 521; Cuttino, *English Medieval Diplomacy* (August 1416), p. 99; A. R. Myers, *English Historical Documents, Vol. 4, 1327–1485* (London, 1969), p. 218; F. Taylor and J. S. Roskell, trans. and ed., *Gesta Henrici Quinti: The Deeds of Henry the Fifth* (Oxford, 1975), pp. 127–37, 157, 173–9; G. L. Harriss, *Henry V: The Practice of Kingship* (Oxford, 1985), pp. 22, 24, 188.

13 Creighton, *History of The Papacy*, vol. 2, pp. 76–81; Gabriel, 'Wales and the Avignon Papacy', pp. 70–86; Loomis, 'Nationality at the Council of Constance', pp. 508–27; Gwynn, 'Ireland and the English Nation at the Council of Constance', pp. 183–233; Jarman, 'Wales and the Council of Constance', pp. 220–2; Vaughan, *John the Fearless*, pp. 210–12; Crowder, *Unity, Heresy and Reform*, pp. 24–8, 109–26.

14 Crowder, *Unity, Heresy and Reform*, pp. 113–26. See also Griffiths, 'Crossing the Frontiers of the English Realm in the Fifteenth Century', in *PIMA*, pp. 211–25.

15 Crowder, *Unity, Heresy and Reform*, pp. 116–19.

16 Crowder, *Unity, Heresy and Reform*, p. 117.

17 Crowder, *Unity, Heresy and Reform*, p. 121.

14: Owain's Last Days?

1   *Glendower*, pp. 154.

2   *CCRs, 1409–1413*, pp. 10–11; Sayles, *Select Cases*, pp. 113–15; Friel, *Good Ship*, p. 159; Smith, 'The Last Phase of the Glyndŵr Rebellion', p. 256; *Revolt*, pp. 299–304.

3 *CCR, 1409–13*, p. 15; J. E. Messham, 'The County of Flint and the Rebellion of Owen Glyndŵr in the Records of the Earldom of Chester', *Flintshire Historical Society Publications* (1967–8), vol. 23, pp. 1–33; Turvey, 'The Marcher Shire of Pembroke and the Glyndŵr Rebellion', pp. 151–68; Griffiths, 'The Eyes of an Englishman', p. 124; Smith, 'The Last Phase of the Glyndŵr Rebellion', pp. 252–5; *Revolt*, p. 299.

4 Ellis, *Original Letters*, vol. 1, pp. 1–8; *RHL Henry IV*, vol. 1, pp. 35–8; Smith, 'The Last Phase of the Glyndŵr Rebellion', pp. 250–60; Griffiths and Thomas, *Making of the Tudor Dynasty*, pp. 23–4; *Revolt*, p. 293–4, 299–304, 310.

5 Bowen, *Statutes of Wales*, pp. 37–9; Smith, 'The Last Phase of the Glyndŵr Rebellion', pp. 252–5; Myers, *English Historical Documents, Vol. 4*, pp. 862–3; Taylor and Roskell, *Gesta Henrici Quinti*, pp. 3–11, 183–5; Harriss, *Henry V, The Practice of Kingship*, pp. 34, 61–2, 97, 100–2, 106, 111–13; P. Corbin and D. Sedge, *The Oldcastle Controversy* (Manchester, 1991), pp. 1–8; *Revolt*, pp. 1–2, 300–1, 308.

6 *CPR, 1413–16*, pp. 137, 195, 342, 404; *Glendower*, p. 154; Griffiths, 'The Eyes of an Englishman', pp. 124, 132 (some of these fines were commuted); Smith, 'The Last Phase of the Glyndŵr Rebellion', pp. 253–5; *Revolt*, pp. 244, 301.

7 Smith, 'The Last Phase of the Glyndŵr Rebellion', pp. 253–5, 259; Myers, *English Historical Documents, Vol. 4*, pp. 863–4; Taylor and Roskell, *Gesta Henrici Quinti*, pp. 183–5; Harriss, *Henry V*, pp. 12, 90, 156; Corbin and Sedge, *The Oldcastle Controversy*, pp. 1–8; John, *Sir Thomas Erpingham*, p. 11.

8 Smith, 'The Last Phase of the Glyndŵr Rebellion', 'Text D', p. 259.

9 *CPR, 1416–22*, p. 89; Smith, 'The Last Phase of the Glyndŵr Rebellion', p. 255; Davies, *Revolt*, pp. 244, 326.

10 *POPCE*, vol. 2, pp. 231–2; Smith, 'The Last Phase of the Glyndŵr Rebellion', pp. 253–5; *Revolt*, pp. 307–8.

11 Vaughan, *John the Fearless*, pp. 55, 58 n., 87, 141, 260; Brown, *Black Douglases*, pp. 214–15.

12 Eubel, ed., *Hierarchia Catholica*, vol. 1, p. 292; Gabriel, 'Wales and the Avignon Papacy', pp. 82–3 n.; A. Gwynn, 'Ireland and the English Nation at the Council of Constance', *Proceedings of the Royal Irish Academy* (1939), vol. 45, p. 202; Jarman, 'Wales and the Council of Constance', pp. 220–1.

13 *La France gouvernée*, pp. 48–50, 102, 104, 141, 142, 145, 238.

14 Vale, *Charles VII*, p. 33; Brown, *Black Douglases*, pp. 216–17; Chevalier, Les Alliés écossais au service du roi de France au XVe siècle, in Laidlaw, *Auld Alliance*, pp. 48–53; Macdougall, *An Antidote to the English*, p. 62.

15 *Revolt*, pp. 297–304.

16 Bouchart, *Les Grandes Chroniques de Bretaigne*, p. 175; *La France gouvernée*,

pp. 8–9; Vaughan, *John the Fearless*, pp. 215–27, 263–86; Vale, *Charles VII*, pp. 25, 28–31; Morrall, *Gerson*, p. 15; Allmand, *Lancastrian Normandy*, pp. 8–19; Knecht, *Valois*, pp. 59–62; Schnerb, *Armagnacs et Bourguignons*, pp. 233–58, 265–71.

17 E. Cosneau, *Les Grands Traités de la Guerre de Cent Ans* (Paris, 1889), pp. 100–15; Bouchart, *Les Grandes Chroniques de Bretaigne*, p. 182; Vale, *Charles VII*, pp. 31–2; Vaughan, *Philip the Good*, p. 4; Allmand, *Lancastrian Normandy*, pp. 18–24; Knecht, *Valois*, pp. 62–3; Schnerb, *Armagnacs et Bourguignons*, pp. 275–88, 295–301.

18 *CPR, 1416–22*, pp. 254, 294; Smith, 'The Last Phase of the Glyndŵr Rebellion', p. 255; Courteault, *Le Héraut Berry*, pp. 305–6; Allmand, *Lancastrian Normandy*, pp. 63, 80 n., 197–8, 281, *passim*; H. T. Evans, *Wales and the Wars of the Roses* (Stroud, 1998), pp. 27–40.

19 Smith, 'Cydfodau o'r Bumthegfed Ganrif', pp. 309–24; Smith, 'The Last Phase of the Glyndŵr Rebellion', p. 256.

20 *CPR, 1416–22*, p. 335 (Note: 'reasons' should read 'treasons'); Smith, 'The Last Phase of the Glyndŵr Rebellion', pp. 255–6; *Revolt*, pp. 2, 293, 310.

21 G. A. Williams, 'The Later Welsh Poetry Referencing Owain', *OGC*, pp. 522–3.

22 Bowen, *Statutes of Wales*, pp. 40–1.

23 Hodges, *Owain Glyn Dŵr*, pp. 156–66; *Revolt*, p. 327; *CAU*, p. 263.

24 *OGC*, pp. 503–4, 497–517.

25 E. Henken, *National Redeemer, Owain Glyndŵr in Welsh Tradition* (Cardiff, 1996), pp. 51–88; E. Rees, *A Life of Guto'r Glyn* (Talybont, 2008), pp. 19–32, 48–51, 69–73; *OGC*, pp. 519–50.

26 *OGC*, p. 547.

27 T. Jones, ed., *Brut y Tywysogion* (Cardiff, 1952), pp. 79–80, 84, 88, 93.

28 *OGC*, pp. 126–35, 354–7.

29 Rees, *Guto'r Glyn*, pp. 48–51; *OGC*, pp. 519–20, 533.

Conclusions

1 http://www.historyofparliamentonline.org/volume/1386-1421/member/greyndore-sir-john-1356-1416; C. L. Kingsford, 'Grey, Richard, fourth Baron Grey of Codnor (*c*.1371–1418)', rev. R. A. Griffiths, *ODNB*, online edn, January 2008. Available online: http://www.oxforddnb.com/view/article/11556 [accessed 07/12/15].

2 *Revolt*, pp. 229–342; D. Kilcullen, *Counterinsurgency* (London, 2010), pp. 29–49, 192–212; *OGC*, pp. 497–550.

Selecteð Bibliography

Primary Sources

Unpublished Sources

Archives Départementales de l'Hérault, A 1, folios 279 v° à 283 r° (Letter from King Charles VI to Jehan (II) le Maingre, 'Boucicaut', in 1412). Accessed and downloaded from: http://www.fordham.edu/halsall/french/bousico.htm

All of the following are held in the Bibliothèque Nationale de France (BNF), Paris:

J392. 27 (The commission to Owain's envoys, 10 May 1404)

J516B.40 (Pennal Declaration preamble, 31 March 1406)

J516.29 (Pennal Declaration, 31 March 1406)

J623. 96 (Owain's ratification of the Treaty of Alliance, signed 12 January 1405)

J623. 96 bis (The Treaty of Alliance between Charles VI and Owain Glyn Dŵr, 14 June and 14 July, 1404)

Printed Sources

Ainsworth, F. and Diller, G. T., eds, *Jean Froissart, Chroniques: Livre I et Livre II* (Paris: Librairie Générale Française, 2001)

Baud, P. le, Charles de la Lande de Calan, ed., *Cronicques et Ystoires des Bretons* (Nantes: Société des Bibliophiles Bretons et de l'Histoire de Bretagne, 1907)

Beaucourt, G. du Fresne de, *Histoire de Charles VII* (Paris: Picard, 6 vols, 1881–91)

Bellaguet, L. ed., *Chronique du Religieux de Saint-Denys, le Regne de Charles VI, de 1380 à 1422* (Paris: Crapelet, 6 vols, 1840)

Blanchard, R., *Lettres et Mandements de Jean V, duc de Bretagne, de 1402 a 1406* (Nantes: Société de Bibliophiles Bretons et de l'Histoire de Bretagne, 5 vols, 1889–95)

Blanchard, R. and Twemlow, J. A., eds, *Calendar of Entries in the Papal Registers Relating to Great Britain and Ireland, AD 1404–1415* (London: HMSO, 14 vols, 1893–1960)

Bliss, W. H. ed., *Calendar of Papal Letters, 1198–1304* (London: Eyre and Spottiswoode, 1893)

Borderie, A. de la, *Chronique de Bretagne de Jean de Saint-Paul, Chambellan du duc Francois II* (Nantes: Societe des Bibliophiles Bretons, 1881)

Bouchart, A., *Les Grandes Chroniques de Bretaigne, composées en l'an 1514* (Nantes: Société De Bibliophiles Bretons, 1886)

Bourchier, J., *The Chronicle of Froissart* (London: David Nutt, 6 vols, 1901–3)

Bowen, I., ed., *Statutes of Wales* (London: Unwin, 1908)

Bower, Walter, Watt, D., ed., *Scotichronicon* (Aberdeen: Aberdeen University Press, 9 vols, 1987–98)

Brereton, G., ed. and trans., *Froissart Chronicles* (Harmondsworth: Penguin, 1968)

Bromwich, R., *Dafydd ap Gwilym: A Selection of Poems* (Llandysul: Gomer Press, 1982)

Buchon, J-A-C., ed., *Choix de Chroniques et Mémoires sur l'histoire de France, J.-J.des Ursins, Histoire de Charles VI* (Paris: Auguste Desprez, 1838)

Burnett, G., ed., *Exchequer Rolls of Scotland* (Edinburgh: H. M. General Register House, 23 vols, 1880)

Capes, W. W., ed., *Register of John Trefnant, Bishop of Hereford (A.D. 1389–1404)* (Hereford: Wilson and Phillips, 1914)

Carriazo, J. de Mata, ed., *El Victorial: crónica de don Pedro Niño, conde de Buelna, por su alférez Gutierre Díez de Games* (Madrid: Espasa-Calpe, 1940)

Chaplais, P., *English Royal Documents: King John – Henry VI, 1199–1461* (Oxford: Clarendon, 1971)

——*English Medieval Diplomatic Practice* (London: HMSO, 1975–82)

——*Essays in Medieval Diplomacy and Administration* (London: Hambledon, 1981)

Charrière, E., ed., *Chronique de Bertrand du Guesclin par Cuvelier* (Paris: Firmin Didot, 2 vols, 1836–9)

Clancy, J. P., trans., *Medieval Welsh Lyrics* (London: Macmillan, 1965)

——*Medieval Welsh Poems* (Portland: Four Courts Press, 2003)

Clarke, M. V. and Galbraith, V. H., eds, 'The Deposition of Richard II: Chronicle of Dieulacres Abbey, 1381–1403', *BJRL*, 14 (1930)

Cosneau, E., *Les Grands Traités de la Guerre de Cent Ans* (Paris: Picard, 1889)

Courteault, H., ed., *Les Chroniques Du Roi Charles VII Par Gilles Le Bouvier, Dit Le Héraut Berry* (Paris: Centre National de la Recherche Scientifique, 1979)

Davies, J. S., *An English Chronicle of the Reigns of Richard II, Henry IV, Henry V, and Henry VI written before the year 1471* (London: Printed for the Camden Society, 1856)

Delachanel, R., *Chronique des Règnes de Jean II et Charles V* (Paris: Renouard, 4 vols, 1909–20)

——*Histoire de Charles V* (Paris: Auguste Picard, 1928)

Deslisle, L., *Chronique des Quatre Premiers Valois, 1327–1393* (Paris: Renouard, 1862)

Deslisle, L. and Berger, E., eds, *Receuil des Actes de Henri II, roi d'Angleterre et duc de Normandie* (Paris: Imprimerie Nationale, 4 vols, 1909–27)

Devon, F., ed., *Issues of the Exchequer* (London: Record Commission, 1837)

Dickinson, W. C., Donaldson, G. D. and Milne, I. A., eds, *A Source Book of Scottish History, From Earliest Times to 1424* (Edinburgh: Thomas Nelson, 3 vols, 1952–4)

Douët-d'Arcq, L., *La Chronique d'Enguerran de Monstrelet* (Paris: Renouard, 1857)

——*Choix de Pièces Inédites Relatives au Règne de Charles VI* (Paris: Renouard, 2 vols, 1863–4)

Douglas, D. C., gen. ed., Rothwell, H. and Myers, A. R., eds, *English Historical Documents* (London: Eyre and Spottiswoode, 12 vols, 1968–77)

Edwards, J. G., ed., *Calendar of Ancient Correspondence Concerning Wales* (Cardiff: University Press Board, 1935)

Ellis, H., ed., *Original Letters Illustrative of English History* (London: Harding and Lepard, 2 vols, 1827)

Eubel, C., ed., *Hierarchia Catholica Medii Aevi* (Rome: N.p., 1898)

Evans, J., trans., *The Unconquered Knight: A Chronicle of the Deeds of Don Pero Niño, Count of Buelna, by his Standard-bearer Gutierre Diaz de Gamez (1431–1449)* (Woodbridge: The Boydell Press, 2004, orig. 1928)

Finke, H., ed., *Acta Concilii Constanciensis* (Munster, 4 vols, 1896–1928)

Given-Wilson, C., ed. and trans., *Chronicles of the Revolution 1397–1400: The Reign of Richard II* (Manchester: Manchester University Press, 1993)

——ed. and trans., *The Chronicle of Adam Usk, 1377–1421* (Oxford: Oxford University Press, 1997)

Given-Wilson, C., Phillips, S., Ormrod, M. and Martin, G., eds, *The Parliament Rolls of Medieval England, 1275–1504, Vol. 8, Henry IV, 1399–1413* (London: Boydell, 16 vols, 2005)

Grèvy-Pons, N., Ornato, E. and Ouy, G., eds, *Jean de Montreuil, Opera* (Paris and Turin: Cemi and Giappichelli, 4 vols, 1964–86)

Hardy, T. D., ed., *Rotuli Litterarum Patentium,* (London: Record Commission, 1835)

Hardy, W. and Hardy, E., trans., *Jean de Wavrin, Chronique* (London: HMSO, 1887)

Hingeston, F. C., *Royal and Historical Letters during the reign of Henry IV* (London: Longman, 2 vols, 1860–4)

Johnes, T., trans., *The Chronicles of Enguerrand de Monstrelet* (London: Longman, 1810)

——trans., *The Chronicles of Enguerrand de Monstrelet* (London: W. Smith, 2 vols, 1840)

Joliffe, J., ed. and trans., *Froissart's Chronicles* (London: Penguin, 2001, orig. 1967)

Kingsford, C. L., *English Historical Literature in the Fifteenth Century* (Oxford: Clarendon, 1913)

Kirby, J. L., ed., *Calendar of Signet Letters of Henry IV and Henry V (1399–1422)* (London: HMSO, 1978)

Lalande, D., ed., *Le Livre Des Fais Du Bon Messire Jehan Le Maingre, Dit Boucicaut, Mareschal De France et Gouverneur De Jennes* (Geneva: Droz, 1985)

Lannette-Claverie, C., *Collection Joursanvault, Sous-Série 6 J* (Orléans: Archives Départementales du Loiret, 1976)

Legge, M. D. ed., *Anglo–Norman Letters and Petitions from All Souls MS. 182* (Oxford: B. Blackwell for the Anglo–Norman Text Society, 1941)

Livingston, M. and Bollard, J. K., eds, *Owain Glyndŵr: A Casebook* (Liverpool: Liverpool University Press, 2013)

Loomis, R. and Johnston, D., trans., *Medieval Welsh Poems: An Anthology* (Binghamton, NY: Medieval & Renaissance Texts & Studies, Pegasus, 1992)

Lucas, P. J., ed., *John Capgrave, Abbreuiacion of Cronicles* (Oxford: Oxford University Press, 1983)

Luce, S., ed., *Chronique de J. Froissart* (Paris: Renouard, 1888)

Macaulay, G. C., ed., Bourchier, J., trans., *Chronicles of Froissart* (London: Macmillan, 1913)

Marx, W., ed., *English Chronicle, 1377–1461: Edited from Aberystwyth, National Library of Wales MS 21068 and Oxford, Bodleian Library MS Lyell 34* (Woodbridge: Boydell, 2007)

Matthews, T., ed. and trans., *Welsh Records in Paris* (Carmarthen: Spurrell, 1910)

Maxwell-Lyte, H. E., ed., *Calendar of the Patent Rolls Preserved in the Public Record Office: Edward III* (London: HMSO, 16 vols, 1891–1916), *Richard II* (London: HMSO, 6 vols, 1895–1909) *Henry IV* (London: HMSO, 4 vols, 1903–9) *Henry V* (London: HMSO, 2 vols, 1910–11)

—ed., *Calendar of the Close Rolls Preserved in the Public Record Office: Edward III* (London: HMSO, 14 vols, 1892–1913)

—ed., *Calendar of the Fine Rolls Preserved in the Public Record Office: Edward III* (London: HMSO, 5 vols, 1913–24), *Richard II* (London: HMSO, 3 vols, 1926–9)

Michaud, J. F., ed., *Anciens mémoires du XIV siècle de la vie du fameux Bertrand du Guesclin* (Paris: Didier, 1854)

Nicolas, N. H., ed., *Proceedings and Ordinances of the Privy Council of England* (London: Record Commission, 7 vols, 1834–7)

Parry, J. H., ed., *Registrum Roberti Mascall. The Register of Robert Mascall, Bishop of Hereford (A.D. 1404–1416)* (Hereford: Cantilupe Society, 1916)

Pocquet du Haut-Jussé, B-A., *La France gouvernée par Jean Sans Peur, Les Dépenses du Receveur Général du Royaume* (Paris: Presses Universitaires de France, 1959)

Preest, D., trans., *The Chronica Maiora of Thomas Walsingham* (Woodbridge: Boydell, 2005)

Raine, J., ed., *The Historians of the Church of York and its Archbishops* (London: Longman & Co., 3 vols, 1879–94)

Rees, D. and Jones, J. G., eds, *Thomas Matthews's Welsh Records in Paris* (Cardiff: University of Wales Press, 2010)

Reynaud, G., ed., *Chronique de J. Froissart* (Paris: Renouard, 9 vols, 1894)

Riley, H. T., ed., *Ypodigma Neustriæ A Thoma Walsingham* (London: Longman et al., 1876)

Robillard de Beaurepaire, C. de, ed., *La Chronique Normande de Pierre Cochon* (Rouen: A. Le Brument, 1870)

Rymer, T., ed., *Fœdera, conventiones, literae, et cujuscunque generis acta publica, inter reges Angliae, et alios quosvis imperatores, reges, pontifices, principes, vel communitates, ab ineunte saecula duodecimo, viz. ab anno 1101, ad nostra usque tempora, habita aut tractata; ex autographis, infra tempora, habita aut tractata; ex autographis, infra secretiores Archivorum regiorum thesaurarias, per multa saecula reconditis, fideliter exscripta* (London: HMSO, 20 vols, 1704–35)

Sayles, G. A., ed., *Select Cases in the Court of the King's Bench under Richard II, Henry IV and Henry V – Coram Rege Roll, no. 560 (Easter 1401), m. 18 (crown)* (London: Selden Society, 1971)

Stamp, A. E., ed., *Calendar of the Close Rolls Preserved in the Public Record Office: Richard II* (London: HMSO, 6 vols, 1914–27), *Henry IV* (London: HMSO, 5 vols, 1927–38), *Henry V* (London: HMSO, 2 vols, 1929–32)

—ed., *Calendar of the Fine Rolls Preserved in the Public Record Office: Henry IV* (London: HMSO, 2 vols, 1931–3), *Henry V* (London: HMSO, 1934)

Stones, E. L. G., ed., *Anglo–Scottish Relations, 1174–1328* (Oxford: Clarendon, 1970)

Strachey, J., ed., *Rotuli Parliamentorum ut et Petitiones, et placita in Parliamento tempore Edwardi R. III* (London: No discernible publisher, 6 vols, 1776–7)

Taylor, F. and Roskell, J. S., trans. and ed., *Gesta Henrici Quinti: The Deeds of Henry the Fifth* (Oxford: Clarendon, 1975)

Thorpe, L., trans., *Gerald of Wales: The Journey Through Wales / The Description of Wales* (Harmondsworth: Penguin, 1978)

Tuetey, A., ed., *Journal d'un Bourgeois de Paris, 1405–1449* (Paris: Champion, 1881)

—ed., *Journal de Nicolas de Baye, greffier du Parlement de Paris, 1400–1417* (Paris: Renouard, 2 vols, 1885–8)

Webb, J., ed. and trans., 'A Translation of a French Metrical History of the deposition of King Richard the Second by Jehan Creton', *Archaelogia*, 20 (1823)

Williams, B., *Chronicque de la Traïson et Mort de Richart Deux roy Dengleterre* (London: Bentley, 1846)

Secondary Sources

Abse, J., ed., *Letters From Wales* (Bridgend: Seren, 2000)

Allmand, C., *Henry V* (London: Historical Association, 1968)

——*Lancastrian Normandy 1415–1450: The History of a Medieval Occupation* (Oxford: Clarendon, 1983)

——ed., *Society at War: The Experience of England and France during the Hundred Years War* (Edinburgh: Oliver and Boyd, 1983)

——*The Hundred Years War, England and France at War c. 1300–c. 1450* (Cambridge: Cambridge University Press, 1988)

Anderson, B., *Imagined Communities: Reflections on the Origin and Spread of Nationalism* (London: Verso, 2006)

Anderson, G. and W., eds, *The Chronicles of Jean Froissart* (London: Centaur, 1963)

Arn, M.-J., 'Charles, Duke of Orléans (1394–1465)', *ODNB*, 2008 edn

d'Avout, J., *La Querelle des Armagnacs et des Bourguignons, Histoire d'une crise d'Autorité* (Paris: Gallimard, 1943)

Ayton, A. C., *Knights and Warhorses, Military Service and the English Aristocracy under Edward III* (Woodbridge: Boydell, 1999, orig. 1994)

Baker, D. N., ed., *Inscribing the Hundred Years' War in French and English Cultures* (Albany, NY: State University of New York Press, 2000)

Barber, C., *In Search of Owain Glyndŵr* (Abergavenny: Blorenge, 1998)

Barker, J. W., *Manuel II Palaeologus (1391–1425): A Study in Late Byzantine Statesmanship* (New Brunswick, NJ: Rutgers University Press, 1969)

Barraclough, G., *The Medieval Papacy* (London: Thames and Hudson, 1992, orig. 1969)

Barrell, A. D. M., *Medieval Scotland* (Cambridge: Cambridge University Press, 2000)

Barrow, G. W. S., *Feudal Britain* (London: Edward Arnold, 1956)

——*The Anglo-Norman Era in Scottish History* (Oxford: Clarendon, 1980)

——*Kingship and Unity: Scotland 1000–1306* (Edinburgh: Edinburgh University Press, 1989)

——*Scotland and its Neighbours in the Middle Ages* (London and Rio Grande: Hambledon Press, 1992)

Barthes, R., trans. Lavers, A., *Mythologies* (London: Vintage, 2000, orig. Paris 1957)

Bean, J. M. W., 'Henry IV and The Percies', *History* 44:152 (October 1959): 212–27

Bennett, M. J., *Richard II and the Revolution of 1399* (Stroud: Sutton, 1999)

Bent, J. T., *Genoa: How the Republic Rose and Fell* (London: C. Kegan Paul, 1881)

Biggs, D., 'Archbishop Scrope's *Manifesto* of 1405: "Naïve Nonsense" or Reflections of Political Reality?', *Journal of Medieval History* 33:4 (2007): 358–71

Bisson, T. N., *The Crisis of the Twelfth Century: Power, Lordship and the Origins of European Government* (Princeton and Oxford; Princeton University Press, 2009)

Black, J., *Absolutism in Renaissance Milan: Plenitude of Power under the Visconti and the Sforza 1329–1535* (Oxford: Oxford University Press, 2009)

Blumenfeld-Kosinski, R., ed. and trans., *The Selected Writings of Christine de Pizan*, trans. Brownlee, K. (New York and London: Norton, 1996)

Boardman, S. I., 'Robert III (d.1406), King of Scots', *ODNB*, 2008, orig. 2004.

Boardman, S. I., 'Stewart, Robert', *ODNB*, 2008, orig. 2004.

Bradley, A. G., *Owen Glyndwr and the Last Struggle for Welsh Independence, with a Brief Sketch of Welsh History* (London: Putnams, 1901)

Brough, G., 'Owain's Revolt? Glyn Dŵr's role in the Outbreak of the Rebellion', *Studies In History, Archaeology, Religion And Conservation* 2:1 (2015): 1–30

Brown, A. L., 'Percy, Thomas, Earl of Worcester (c.1343–1403)', (2008); *ODNB*, 2004; online edn, Jan 2008 and 2010

Brown, A. L. and Summerson, H., 'Henry IV (1367–1413)', (2010), all entries in *ODNB*, 2010 edn

Brown, M., *The Black Douglases: War and Lordship in Late Medieval Scotland, 1300–1455* (East Linton: Tuckwell Press, 1998)

——*The Wars of Scotland, 1214–1371* (Edinburgh: Edinburgh University Press, 2004)

Brown, M. H., 'Stewart, Murdoch', *ODNB*, 1994

Bueno de Mesquita, D. M., *Giangaleazzo Visconti, Duke of Milan (1351–1402)* (Cambridge: Cambridge University Press, 1941)

Carr, A. D., 'The Barons of Edeyrnion, 1282–1485', *Merioneth Historical and Record Society Journal* 4 (1961–4): 231–43

——'The Gentry of Dinmael and their Lineage', *Denbighshire Historical Transactions*, vol. 13 (1964): 9–21

——'Welshmen and the Hundred Years' War', *WHR* 4 (1968): 21–46

——'A Welsh Knight in the Hundred Years' War', *Transactions of the Honourable Society of Cymmrodorion* (1977): 40–53

——*Owen of Wales: The End of the House of Gwynedd* (Cardiff: University of Wales Press, 1991)

——*Medieval Wales* (Basingstoke: Macmillan, 1995)

Carus-Wilson, E. M., 'Trends in the Export Woollens in the Fourteenth Century', *The Economic History Review*, 3:2 (1950), pp. 162–79

Chamberlin, E. R., *The Count of Virtue: Giangaleazzo Visconti, Duke of Milan* (London: Eyre and Spottiswoode, 1965)

Chapman, A., *Welsh Soldiers in the Later Middle Ages, 1282–1422* (Woodbridge: Boydell and Brewer, 2015)

Chapman, G., *Catechism of the Catholic Church* (London: Cassell, 1994)

Cheney, C. R., *The Papacy and England, 12th–14th Centuries* (London: Variorum, 1982)

Chotzen, T. M., 'Yvain de Galles in Alsace-Lorraine and Switzerland', *BBCS* 4 (1928): 231–40

Clancy, J. P., *Medieval Welsh Poems* (Portland: Four Courts Press, 2003)

Clark, L., ed., *The Fifteenth Century: Authority and Subversion* (Woodbridge: Boydell, 2003)

Coativy, Y., ed., *Le Trémazan des Du Chastel: du château fort à la ruine* (Brest-Landunvez: Centre de Recherche Breton et Celtique, 2006)

Contamine, P., *Guerre, État et Société à la Fin du Moyen Âge: Études sur les Armées des Rois de France, 1337–1494* (Paris: Mouton, 1972)

Corbin, P. and Sedge, D., *The Oldcastle Controversy* (Manchester: Manchester University Press, 1991)

Creighton, M., *History of the Papacy from the Great Schism to the Sack of Rome* (London: Longmans, Green, and Co., 6 vols, 1907–11)

Crowder, C. M. D., *Unity, Heresy and Reform, 1378–1460: The Conciliar Response to the Great Schism* (London: Edward Arnold, 1977)

Curry, A., *Hundred Years War* (London: Macmillan, 1993)

——ed., *Agincourt, 1415: Henry V, Sir Thomas Erpingham and the Triumph of the English Archers* (Stroud: Tempus, 2000)

——ed., *The Battle of Agincourt: Sources and Interpretations* (Woodbridge: Boydell, 2009, orig. 2000)

Cushway, G. R., *Edward III and the War at Sea: The English Navy, 1327–1377* (Woodbridge: Boydell, 2011)

Cuttino, G. P., *English Medieval Diplomacy* (Bloomington: Indiana University Press, 1985)

Darcy-Bertuletti, Y., 'Tableau Des Mesures Les Plus Courantes En Usage Dans Le Pays Beaunois', published online: http://www.beaune.fr/IMG/pdf/Metrologie.pdf, 1–9

Darwin, F. D. S., *Louis d'Orléans (1372–1407): A Necessary Prologue to the Tragedy of La Pucelle d'Orleans* (London: John Murray, 1936)

Davies, J., *A History of Wales* (Harmondsworth: Penguin, 1994, orig. *Hanes Cymru*, London: Allen Lane, 1990)

Davies, N., *Vanished Kingdoms: The History of Half-Forgotten Europe* (London: Allen Lane, 2011)

Davies, R. G., 'Henry Despenser, d. 1406', *ODNB*, 2008 edn

Davies, R. R., *The Age of Conquest: Wales 1063–1415* (Oxford: Oxford University Press, 1991, originally *Conquest, Coexistence, and Change: Wales 1063–1415* (Oxford: Oxford University Press, 1987)

——*The Revolt of Owain Glyn Dŵr* (Oxford: Oxford University Press, 1997, orig. 1995)

——'Mortimer, Roger (V), First Earl of March (1287–1330)', *ONDB*, 2008 edn

Davies, S., *Welsh Military Institutions, 633–1283* (Cardiff: University of Wales Press, 2003)

Davis, R. H. C., *History of Medieval Europe* (Harlow: Longman, 2006)

Denieul-Cormier, A., *The Renaissance in France, 1488–1559* (London: Allen and Unwin, 1969)

Dodd, G. and Biggs, D., *Henry IV: The Establishment of the Regime, 1399–1406* (Woodbridge: York Medieval Press in association with Boydell Press, 2003)

—*The Reign of Henry IV: Rebellion and Survival, 1403–1413* (York: York University Press, 2008)

Donaldson, G., *The Auld Alliance: The Franco-Scottish Connection* (Edinburgh: Saltire Society – Institut Français d'Ecosse, 1985)

Du Pin, E. L., trans. anonymously, *A New Ecclesiastical History* (London: Childe, 13 vols, 1694, originally in French, 58 vols, 1686–1704)

Duby, G., trans., Vale, J., *France in the Middle Ages, 987–1460* (Oxford: Blackwell, 1991, orig. 1987)

Duncan, A., *Scotland: The Making of the Kingdom* (Edinburgh: Oliver & Boyd, 1975)

Epstein, S. A., *Genoa and the Genoese, 958–1528* (Chapel Hill and London: University of North Carolina Press, 1996)

Evans, B., 'Owain Glyn Dŵr's Raid on Ruthin (1400)', *Denbighshire Historical Society Transactions* 49 (2000): 23–5

Evans, D. H., 'An incident on the Dee during the Glyn Dŵr rebellion', *Denbighshire Historical Society Transactions* 37 (1988): 5–40

Evans, E. J., 'The Authorship of the Deposition and Death of Richard II Attributed to Créton', *Speculum* 15 (1940): 460–77

Evans, H. T., *Wales and the Wars of the Roses* (Stroud: Sutton, 1998, orig. 1915)

Favier, J., *La Guerre de Cent ans* (Paris: Editions Fayard, 1980)

Febvre, L., ed. and trans. Rothstein, M., *Life in Renaissance France* (Cambridge, MA and London: Harvard University Press, 1977)

Fenwick, H., *The Auld Alliance* (Kineton: The Roundwood Press, 1971)

Fleming, I., *Glyndŵr's First Victory: The Battle of Hyddgen, 1401* (Talybont: Y Lolfa, 2001)

Foucault, M., 'The Subject and Power', *Critical Inquiry* 8:4 (Summer 1982): 777–95

Fowler, K., *The Age of Plantagenet and Valois: The Struggle for Supremacy 1328–1498* (London: Elek, 1967)

—ed., *The Hundred Years War* (London: Macmillan, 1971)

France, J., *Crusades and the Expansion of Catholic Christendom, 1000–1714* (London and New York: Routledge, 2005)

—ed., *Mercenaries and Paid Men: The Mercenary Identity in the Middle Ages* (Leiden: Brill, 2008)

Friel, I., *The Good Ship: Ships, Shipbuilding and Technology in England 1200–1520* (London: British Museum Press, 1995)

Fulton, H., *Dafydd ap Gwilym and the European Context* (Cardiff: University of Wales Press, 1989)

—*Selections from the Dafydd ap Gwilym Apocrypha* (Llandysul: Gomer, 1996)

—'Owain Glyn Dŵr and the Use of Prophecies', *Studia Celtica* 39 (2005): 105–21

Fychan, C., *Pwy Oedd Rhys Gethin?* (Aberystwyth: Cymdeithas Lyfrau Ceredigion, 2007)

Gabriel, J. R., 'Wales and the Avignon Papacy', *Archaeologia Cambrensis* vol. 78 (1923): 70–86

Gallarotti, G. M., 'Soft Power: what it is, why it's important, and the conditions for its effective use', *Journal of Political Power* 4:1 (2011): 25–47

Galliou, P. and Jones, M., *The Bretons* (Oxford and Cambridge, MA: Blackwell Press, 1991)

Geary, P. J., *Myth of Nations: The Medieval Origins of Europe* (Woodstock: Princeton University Press, 2003)

Genet, J-P., 'English Nationalism: Thomas Polton at the Council of Constance', *Nottingham Medieval Studies* 38 (1984): 60–78

Giles, L., *Sun Tzu on the Art of War, the Oldest Military Treatise in the World* (London: Luzac, 1910)

Goldberg, P. J. P., *Medieval England: A Social History 1250–1550* (London: Arnold, 2004)

Goldsmith, Dr and Morrell, Mr, *The History of England, from the Earliest Times to the Reign of George II* (London: Brightly and Kinnersley, 2 vols, 1807)

Goodman, A. and Gillespie, J., eds, *Richard II: The Art of Kingship* (Oxford: Clarendon, 1999)

Goodman, A. E., 'Owain Glyndŵr before 1400', *WHR* 5 (1970–1): 67–70

Green, D., *Edward the Black Prince: Power in Medieval Europe* (Harlow: Pearson, 2007)

Green, K. et al., eds, *The Book of Peace by Christine de Pizan* (Pennsylvania: Pennsylvania State University Press, 2008)

Griffith Davies, J. D., *Owen Glyn Dŵr* (London: Scholartis, 1934)

Griffiths, R. A., 'Some Secret Supporters of Owain Glyn Dŵr?', *BBCS* 20 (1962–4): 77–100

—'Some Partisans of Owain Glyn Dŵr at Oxford', *BBCS* 20 (1962–4): 282–92

—'The Glyndwr Rebellion in North Wales Through the Eyes of an Englishman', *BBCS* 22 (1966–8): 151–68

—*King and Country: England and Wales in the Fifteenth Century* (London: Hambledon, 1991)

—*Conquerors and Conquered in Medieval Wales* (Stroud: Alan Sutton, 1994)

—ed., *The Fourteenth and Fifteenth Centuries* (Oxford: Oxford University Press, 2003)

—'Owain Glyn Dŵr's Invasion of the Central March of Wales in 1402: the Evidence of Clerical Taxation', *Studia Celtica* 46 (2012): 111–22

—'Prince Henry, Wales, and the Royal Exchequer, 1400–1413', *BBCS* 32 (1985): 202–15

—'Prince Henry's War: Armies, Garrisons and Supplies during the Glyndŵr Rising', *BBCS* 34 (1987): 165–74

Griffiths, R. A. and Thomas, R., *The Making of the Tudor Dynasty* (Stroud: Sutton, 1997, orig. 1993)

Griffiths, S. B., ed. and trans., *Sun Tzu: The Art of War* (London: Oxford University Press, 1963)

Guenée, B. and Lehoux, F., *Les Entrées royales françaises de 1328 à 1515* (Paris: Editions du Centre national de la recherche scientifique, 1968)

Gwynn, A., 'Ireland and the English Nation at the Council of Constance', *Proceedings of the Royal Irish Academy* 45 (1939): 183–233

Hale, J. R., Highfield, J. R. L. and Smalley, B., eds, *Europe in the Late Middle Ages* (London: Faber and Faber, 1965)

Hallam, E. M. and Everard, J., *Capetian France, 987–1328* (London: Longman, 2001)

Harriss, G. L., *Henry V: The Practice of Kingship* (Oxford: Oxford University Press, 1985)

Hearder, H. and Loyn, H. R., eds, *British Government and Administration: Studies Presented to S B Chrimes* (Cardiff: University of Wales Press, 1974)

Henken, E. R., *National Redeemer: Owain Glyndŵr in Welsh Tradition* (Cardiff: University of Wales Press, 1996)

Hewitt, H. J., *The Organization of War under Edward III* (Barnsley: Pen and Sword, 2004)

Hodges, G., *Owain Glyn Dŵr and the War of Independence in the Welsh Borders* (Logaston: Logaston, 1995)

Housley, N., *The Avignon Papacy and the Crusades, 1305–1378* (Oxford: Clarendon, 1986)

—*Crusaders* (Stroud: Tempus, 2002)

Hunt, R. W., Pantin, W. A. and Southern, R. W., eds, *Studies In Medieval History Presented To Frederick Maurice Powicke* (Oxford: Clarendon, 1948)

Hutchinson, H. F., *Henry V* (London: Eyre and Spottiswoode, 1967)

Hyland, A., *Warhorse, 1250–1600* (Stroud: Sutton, 1998)

Jack, R. I., 'Owain Glyn Dŵr and the Lordship of Ruthin', *WHR* 2 (1964–5): 303–22

—'Grey, Reynold', *ODNB*, 2008, orig. 2004.

Jacob, E. F., *Henry V and the Invasion of France* (Westport: Greenwood, 1984, orig. 1947)

Jarman, A., 'Wales and the Council of Constance', *BBCS* 14 (1951): 220–2

Jarman, J. A. O. and Hughes, G. R., eds, *Guide to Welsh Literature* (Swansea: Davies, 1976)

Jarry, E., *La Vie Politique de Louis de France, Duc d'Orleans, 1372–1407* (Paris: Picard, 1889)

John, T., *Sir Thomas Erpingham, 1357–1428* (Dereham: Larks, 1999)

Johnston, D., trans., *Iolo Goch: Poems* (Llandysul: Gomer, 1993)

Jones, E. J., *Authorship of the Deposition and Death of Richard II Attributed to Créton* (Cambridge, MA: Medieval Academy of America, 1940)

Jones, J. G., ed., *Sir John Wynn: History of the Gwydir family, and Memoirs* (Llandysul: Gomer Press, 1990)

——*Wynn family of Gwydir: Origins, Growth and Development c.1490–1674* (Aberystwyth: Centre for Educational Studies, 1995)

Jones, M., *Ducal Brittany, 1364–1399: Relations with England and France during the Reign of Duke John IV* (London: Oxford University Press, 1970)

Jones, R., 'Re-thinking the Origins of the "Irish" Hobelar', *Cardiff Historical Papers* 1, (2008), 4–24

——*Bloodied Banners: The Forms and Functions of Martial Display on the Medieval Battlefield* (Woodbridge: Boydell and Brewer, 2010)

——*Knight: Warrior and World of Chivalry* (Oxford: Osprey, 2011)

Jordan, W. C., *Ideology and Royal Power in Medieval France: Kingship, Crusades and the Jews* (Aldershot: Ashgate, 2001)

Kagay, D. J., 'Disposable Alliances: Aragon and Castile during the War of the Two Pedros and Beyond', *Albany State University Papers* (2010)

Kaminsky, H., *A History of the Hussite Revolution* (Los Angeles: University of California Press, 1967)

Keen, M., 'Treason Trials under the Law of Arms', *Transactions of the Royal Historical Society* 12 (1962): 85–103

——*Pelican History of Medieval Europe* (Harmondsworth: Penguin, 1969)

Kilcullen, D., *Counterinsurgency* (London: Hurst and Co., 2010)

Kirby, J. L., *Henry IV of England* (London: Constable, 1970)

Knecht, R., *The Valois: Kings of France 1328–1589* (London: Hambledon, 2008, orig. 2004)

Laidlaw, J., ed., *The Auld Alliance: France and Scotland over 700 Years* (Edinburgh: The University of Edinburgh, 1999)

Lalande, D., *Jean II le Meingre, Dit Boucicaut (1366–1421), Étude d'une Biographie Héroïque* (Geneva: Droz, 1988)

Lambert, B. and Ormrod, W. M., 'Friendly Foreigners; International Warfare, Resident Aliens and the Early History of Denization in England, c. 1250–c. 1400', *English Historical Review* 130, no. 542 (2015): 1–24

Lambert, C. L., *Shipping the Medieval Military: English Maritime Logistics in the Fourteenth Century* (Woodbridge: Boydell, 2011)

Lambert, M., *Medieval Heresy: Popular Movements from the Gregorian Reform to the Reformation* (Oxford: Blackwell, 2002, 3rd edn, orig 1977)

Lang, S. J. 'Bradmore, John (d. 1412)', *ODNB*, 2010 edn

Leff, G., *Heresy in the Later Middle Ages: The Relation of Heterodoxy to Dissent c. 1250 c. 1450* (Manchester: Manchester University Press, 2 vols, 1967)

Lehoux, F., *Jean de France, Duc de Berry. Sa vie, son action politique (1340–1416)* (Paris: Picard, 1966–8)

Lewis, P. S., ed., Martin, G. F., trans., *The Recovery of France in the Fifteenth Century* (London: MacMillan, 1971)

Livingston, M., 'Owain Glyndŵr's Grand Design: *The Tripartite Indenture* and the Vision of a New Wales', *Proceedings of the Harvard Celtic Colloquium*, 33 (2013): 145–68

——'The Battle of Hyddgen, 1401: Owain Glyndwr's Victory Reconsidered', *Journal of Medieval Military History* 13 (2015): 167–78

Lloyd, J. E., *History of Wales from the Earliest Times to the Edwardian Conquest* (London: Longmans, Green, 1948, orig. 2 vols, 1911–12)

Lloyd, J. E., Jenkins, R. T., Davies, W. Ll. and Davies, M. B., eds, *Dictionary of Welsh Biography* (London: Blackwell, 1959)

——*Owen Glendower (Owain Glyndwr)* (Felinfach: Llanerch, 1992, orig. 1931)

Lodge, E. C., *Gascony Under English Rule* (London: Methuen and Co., 1926)

Loomis, L. R., 'Nationality at the Council of Constance. An Anglo–French Dispute', *American Historical Review* 44:3 (1939): 508–27

Macdonald, A., 'Crossing the Border: A Study of the Scottish Military Offensives against England c.1369–c.1403', Unpublished PhD Thesis, University of Aberdeen, 1995

Macdougall, N., *An Antidote to the English: The Auld Alliance, 1295–1560* (East Linton: Tuckwell Press, 2001)

Marchant, A., *The Revolt of Owain Glyndŵr in Medieval English Chronicles* (Woodbridge: Boydell & Brewer, 2014)

Maund, K., *The Welsh Kings. Warriors, Warlords and Princes* (Tempus: Stroud, 2006, orig. 2000)

McNiven, P., 'The Cheshire Rising of 1400', *BJRL* 52 (1970): 375–96

——'The Betrayal of Archbishop Scrope', *BJRL* 54 (1971): 173–213

——*Heresy and Politics in the Reign of Henry IV: The Burning of John Badby* (Woodbridge: Boydell, 1987)

Messham, J. E., 'The County of Flint and the Rebellion of Owen Glyndŵr in the Records of the Earldom of Chester', *Flintshire Historical Society Publications* 23 (1967–8): 1–33

Mirot, L., *La Politique Française en Italie de 1380 à 1422* (Paris: Picard, 1934)

Mollat, G., trans. Love, J., *Popes at Avignon, 1305–1378* (London: Nelson, 1963, orig. 1949)

Moore, D., *The Welsh Wars of Independence* (Stroud: Tempus, 2005)

Morrall, J. B., *Gerson and the Great Schism* (Manchester: Manchester University Press, 1960)

Neillands, R., *Hundred Years War* (London and New York: Routledge, 2001)

Newhall, R. A., 'The War Finances of Henry V and the Duke of Bedford', *English Historical Review* 36 (1921): 172–98

Nicolas, N. H., *History of the Royal Navy* (London: Bentley, 1847)

Nye, J. S. Jr, 'Soft Power', *Foreign Policy* 80 (Fall 1990): 153–71

—'Public Diplomacy and Soft Power', *The Annals of the American Academy of Political and Social Science* 616 (March 2008): 94–109

Ordioni, P., *Le Pouvoir Militaire en France, de Charles VII a Charles de Gaulle* (Paris: Albatros, 1981)

Ormrod, W. M., 'Finance and Trade under Richard II' in A. Goodman and J. Gillespie, eds, *Richard II: The Art of Kingship* (Oxford: Clarendon, 1999)

Owen, E., 'Owain Lawgoch – Yeuain de Galles: Some Facts and Suggestions', *The Transactions of the Honourable Society of the Cymmrodorion* (1899–1900): 6–105

—'Owain Lawgoch – A Rejoinder', *The Transactions of the Honourable Society of the Cymmrodorion* (1900–1): 98–113

Palmer, J. J. N., *England, France and Christendom, 1377–99* (London: Routledge and Paul, 1972)

Paviot, J. and Chauney-Bouillot, M., eds, *Nicopolis, 1396–1996, Actes du Colloque International* (Dijon: Société des Annales de Bourgogne, 1997)

Perroy, E., trans., Wells, W. B., *Hundred Years War* (London: Eyre & Spottiswoode, 1965, orig. 1951)

Peters, E., *Heresy and Authority in Medieval Europe* (London: Scholar, 1980)

Phillips, J. R. S., 'When Did Owain Glyn Dŵr Die?', *BBCS* 24 (1970–2): 59–77

Pillement, G., *Pedro de Luna, le Dernier Pape d'Avignon* (Paris: Hachette, 1955)

Postan, M. M., 'The Costs of the Hundred Years' War', *Past and Present* 27 (1964): 34–53

Pratt, D., 'Wrexham Militia in the Fourteenth Century', *Denbighshire Historical Transactions* 12 (1962–4): 26–40

Pryce, H. and Watts, J., eds, *Power and Identity in the Middle Ages: Essays in Memory of Rees Davies* (Oxford: Oxford University Press, 2007)

—*J. E. Lloyd and the Creation of Welsh History: Renewing a Nation's Past* (Cardiff: University of Wales Press, 2011)

Pugh, T. B., *Henry V and the Southampton Plot* (Stroud: Sutton, 1998)

Raine, J., ed., *The Historians of the Church of York and its Archbishops* (London: Longman and Co., 1879–94)

Razi, Z. and Smith, R., *Medieval Society and the Manor Court* (Oxford: Clarendon Press, 1996)

Rees, E. A., *Welsh Outlaws and Bandits: Political Rebellion and Lawlessness in Wales, 1400–1603* (Birmingham: Caterwen Press, 2001)

—*A Life of Guto'r Glyn* (Talybont:Y Lolfa, 2008)

Rees,W., ed., *Calendar of Ancient Petitions relating to Wales* (Cardiff: University of Wales Press, 1975)

Renouard, Y., trans., Bethell, D., *Avignon Papacy, 1305–1403* (London: Faber, 1970)

Roberts, G., *Aspects of Welsh History: Selected Papers* (Cardiff: University of Wales Press, 1969)

Roderick, A. J., *Wales through the Ages* (Aberystwyth: Davies, 2 vols, 1959–60)

Rodger, N. A. M., *The Safeguard of the Sea: A Naval History of Britain* (London: HarperCollins, vol. 1, 1997)

Rogers, C., *War Cruel and Sharp: English Strategy Under Edward III, 1327–1360* (Woodbridge: Boydell, 2000)

Roncière, C. de la, *Histoire de la marine Francaise, II: La guerre de cent ans: révolution maritime* (Paris: Plon-Nourrit, 1914)

Rose, S., ed., *The Navy of the Lancastrian Kings: Accounts and Inventories of William Soper, Keeper of the King's Ships, 1422–1427* (London: Allen and Unwin, 1982)

Roulx, J. D. le, *La France en Orient au XIVe siècle: Expéditions du Maréchal Boucicaut*, (Paris: Elibron, 2005, orig. 1886)

Runyan, T. J., 'Ships and Mariners in Later Medieval England', *The Journal of British Studies* 16:2 (Spring 1977): 1–17

Salmon, J. H. M., *Society in Crisis: France in the Sixteenth Century* (London: Ernest Benn, 1975)

Saul, N., ed., 'The Despensers and the Downfall of Edward II', *English Historical Review* 99 (1984): 1–33

—*England in Europe, 1066–1453* (London: Collins and Brown, 1994)

—*Richard II* (New Haven:Yale, 1997)

Schnerb, B., *L'Etat Bourguignon, 1363–1477* (Paris: Perrin, 2005)

—*Armagnacs et Bourguignons, La maudite guerre, 1407–1435* (Paris: Perrin, 2009, orig. 1998)

Setton, K. M., *Papacy and the Levant* (Philadelphia: American Philosophical Society, 2 vols, 1976–8)

Shennan, J. H., *The Parlement of Paris* (Stroud: Sutton, 1998)

—*The Bourbons:The History of a Dynasty* (London: Continuum, 2007)

Sherborne, J. W., 'The Hundred Years' War: The English Navy: Shipping and Manpower 1369–1389', *Past and Present* 37 (1967): 163–75

—'Richard II's Return To Wales, July 1399', *WHR* 7 (1974–5): 389–402

Shibing,Y., *Sun Tzu:The Art of War* (Ware:Wordsworth, 1993)

Siddons, M., 'Welshmen in the Service of France', *BBCS* 36 (1989): 160–84

Smith, D. M., *Guide to Bishops' Registers of England and Wales: A Survey from the Middle Ages to the Abolition of Episcopacy in 1646* (London: Offices of the Royal Historical Society, 1981)

Smith, J. B., 'Cydfodau o'r Bumthegfed Ganrif', *BBCS* 21 (1966): 309–24

——'The Last Phase of the Glyndŵr Rebellion', *BBCS* 22 (1966–8): 250–60

——'Gruffudd Llwyd, Sir (d. 1335)', *ODNB*, 2008 edn

Smith, Ll., 'Glyn Dŵr, Owain (c.1359–c.1416)' *ODNB*, 2008 edn

Spufford, P., *Handbook of Medieval Exchange* (London: Offices of the Royal Historical Society, 1986)

Steel, A., *Richard II* (London: Cambridge University Press, 1941)

Storey, R. L., *Thomas Langley and the Bishopric of Durham, 1406–1437* (London: S. P. C. K., 1961)

Swanson, R. N., *Universities, Academics and The Great Schism* (Cambridge: Cambridge University Press, 1979)

Thierry, *Histoire de la Conquête de l'Angleterre par les Normands* (Paris: Panthéon, 1851), vol. 4

Thomas, G. C. G., 'Oswestry 1400: Glyndwr's Supporters on Trial', *Studia Celtica* 40 (2006): 117–26

Tuck, A., *Richard II and the English Nobility* (London: Edward Arnold, 1973)

——'Richard II (1367–1400)', *ODNB*, 2004 edn

Turvey, R., 'The Marcher Shire of Pembroke and the Glyndŵr Rebellion', *WHR* 15:2 (1990): 151–68

Vale, M. G. A., *Charles VII* (London: Eyre Methuen, 1974)

Vaughan, R., *The Valois Dukes of Burgundy: Sources of Information* (Hull: University of Hull publications, 1965)

——*John the Fearless* (London: Longmans, 1966)

——*Philip the Good: the Apogee of Burgundy* (London: Longmans, 1970)

——*Charles the Bold: The Last Valois Duke of Burgundy* (London: Longman, 1973)

——*Valois Burgundy* (London: Allen Lane, 1975)

Villalon, A. J. and Kagay, D., eds, *The Hundred Years War: A Wider Focus* (Leiden: Brill Publishing, 2005)

——*The Hundred Years War (Part II): Different Vistas* (Leiden: Brill, 2008)

Waley, D., *The Italian City Republics* (London: Longman, 1988)

Walker, D., *Medieval Wales* (Cambridge: Cambridge University Press, 1990)

Walker, S., 'Percy, Sir Henry (1364–1403)', *ODNB*, 2010 edn

Wheeler, B. and Wood, C. T., eds, *Fresh Verdicts on Joan of Arc* (New York and London: Garland, 1996)

Williams, A. H., *Introduction to the History of Wales* (Cardiff: University of Wales Press, 1948)

Williams, G., *Welsh Church from Conquest to Reformation* (Cardiff: University of Wales Press, 1962)

—*Owain Glyndŵr* (Cardiff: University of Wales Press, 1993)

—*Introduction to Welsh Poetry: From the Beginnings to the Sixteenth Century* (London: Faber and Faber, 1953)

Williams, G. A., *When Was Wales?* (Harmondsworth: Penguin, 1985)

Williams, W. Ll., 'Owain Lawgoch', *Transactions of the Honourable Society of the Cymmrodorion* (1900–1): 87–97

Wylie, J. H., *History of England under Henry the Fourth* (London: Longmans, Green, 4 vols, 1884–98)

Internet-based Resources

http://www.fordham.edu/halsall/french/bousico.htm [accessed 25/03/10]

http://www.historyofparliamentonline.org [all entries accessed between April and August 2015]

http://www.reddit.com/r/ArtefactPorn/comments/2zwxjr/golden_helmet_of_the_french_king_charles_vi_found/

Oxford Dictionary of National Biography, online edn, January 2008 and subsequently updated, http://www.oxforddnb.com [all entries accessed between March 2008 and December 2015]

Index